PHILOSOPHY OF MENTAL REPRESENTATION

PHILOSOPHY OF MENTAL REPRESENTATION

Edited by

Hugh Clapin

CLARENDON PRESS · OXFORD

OXFORD
UNIVERSITY PRESS

Great Clarendon Street, Oxford OX2 6DP

Oxford University Press is a department of the University of Oxford.
It furthers the University's objective of excellence in research, scholarship,
and education by publishing worldwide in

Oxford New York

Auckland Bangkok Buenos Aires Cape Town Chennai
Dar es Salaam Delhi Hong Kong Istanbul Karachi Kolkata
Kuala Lumpur Madrid Melbourne Mexico City Mumbai Nairobi
São Paulo Shanghai Singapore Taipei Tokyo Toronto

and an associated company in Berlin

Published in the United States
by Oxford University Press Inc., New York

First published 2002

British Library Cataloguing in Publication Data

Data available

Library of Congress Cataloging in Publication Data

Philosophy of mental representation / edited by Hugh Clapin.
p. cm.
Papers presented at a meeting.
Includes bibliographical references and index.
1. Philosophy of mind—Congresses. 2. Mental representation—Congresses. I. Clapin, Hugh.
BD418.3 .P447 2002 128.2—dc21 2001055472

ISBN 0–19–825051–7
ISBN 0–19–825052–5 (pbk.)

10 9 8 7 6 5 4 3 2 1

Typeset in Adobe Sabon
by Kolam Information Services Pvt. Ltd., Pondicherry, India

Printed in Great Britain
by Biddles Ltd., Guildford & Kings Lynn

ACKNOWLEDGEMENTS

This collection arises from the University of Sydney Peak Research Meeting on Mental Representation held in August 1999 at Peter Brown's Three Field Farm in Blue Hill, Maine. The participants were: Hugh Clapin (convenor), Andy Clark, Rob Cummins, Daniel Dennett, John Haugeland, and Brian Cantwell Smith. Ruth Millikan was invited but, unfortunately, was unable to attend. Joan Wellman and Josefa Toribio also attended sessions of the workshop.

The Meeting was part of the 'New Theories of Mental Representation' U2000 Research Project of the Department of Philosophy at the University of Sydney. Additional support was provided by the Center for Cognitive Studies, Tufts University, the Research Institute for Humanities and Social Sciences at the University of Sydney, and from a University of Sydney Research Grant for 1999.

My thanks go to Teresa Salvato for recording the meeting, and for the fantastic job she did in transcribing the discussion; to Jim Schatz of the Blue Hill Farm Inn who looked after us very well; to Dan and Susan Dennett for their fine hospitality, and to Dan Dennett's family—the Dennetts and Wardells—who finished off the week by preparing a magnificent clam bake and lobster picnic.

In preparing the collection for publication I have had excellent help from my Research Assistant Sarah Stewart, and very helpful feedback from Stephen Gaukroger, Brian Keeley, Ruth Millikan, Phillip Staines, John Sutton, and two anonymous readers for OUP.

My partner Belinda has provided me with limitless emotional and practical support for which I thank her deeply. Together with our daughter Anna, she fills my days with joy.

H.C.

Contents

LIST OF FIGURES

CONTRIBUTORS

HUGH CLAPIN is a U2000 Postdoctoral Research Fellow in Philosophy at the University of Sydney. He holds B.Sc. and Ph.D. degrees from the University of New South Wales, and has taught at the Australian National University and the University of Sydney. His publications include 'Connectionism Isn't Magic' (*Minds and Machines*, 1991) and 'Problems with Principle P' (*Pacific Philosophical Quarterly*, 1997), and he is the editor (with Peter Slezak and Phillip Staines) of the collection *New Theories of Mental Representation* (forthcoming).

ANDY CLARK is Professor of Philosophy and Cognitive Science in the School of Cognitive and Computing Sciences, University of Sussex. Educated at the University of Stirling, Andy pursued undergraduate studies in Philosophy and took a Ph.D. addressing issues in Philosophy and Evolutionary Biology. He taught briefly at the University of Glasgow before accepting a 'new blood' appointment at the University of Sussex in 1985 where he later became Reader and then Professor in Philosophy and Cognitive Sciences. He has taught at Washington University in St Louis, where he was Professor and Director of the Philosophy-Neuroscience-Psychology Program. He is the author of four books: *Microcognition* (1989), *Associative Engines* (1993), *Being There: Putting Brain, Body and World Together Again* (1997) and *Mindware: An Introduction To The Philosophy of Cognitive Science* (2001).

ROBERT CUMMINS is Professor of Philosophy at the University of California, Davis. Rob's BA is from Carleton College, and his Ph.D. in Philosophy is from the University of Michigan, 1970. He has taught at Johns Hopkins (Philosophy), the University of Wisconsin at Milwaukee (Philosophy), the University of Illinois at Chicago, the University of Colorado (Philosophy and Cognitive Science). His books include *The Nature of Psychological Explanation* (1983), *Meaning and Mental Representation* (1989), and *Representations, Targets and Attitudes* (1996). He specializes in mental representation, and in the foundations of psychology, AI, and Cognitive Neuroscience. His edited volumes include *The History of Modern Phil-*

osophy (with David Owen), *Modern Moral and Political Philosophy* (with Tom Christiano), *Philosophy and AI* (with John Pollock), and *Minds, Brains and Computers* (with Denise Dellarosa Cummins).

DANIEL DENNETT is University Professor and Director of the Center for Cognitive Studies at Tufts University. Dan received his BA in philosophy from Harvard in 1963, and his D.Phil. in philosophy from Oxford in 1965. He taught at the University of California at Irvine from 1965 to 1971, when he moved to Tufts, where he has taught ever since, aside from periods visiting at Harvard, Pittsburgh, Oxford, and the École Normal Supérieure in Paris. His first book, *Content and Consciousness*, appeared in 1969, followed by *Brainstorms* (1978), *Elbow Room* (1984), *The Intentional Stance* (1987), *Consciousness Explained* (1991), *Darwin's Dangerous Idea* (1995), and *Kinds of Minds* (1996). He co-edited *The Mind's I* with Douglas Hofstadter in 1981. He is the author of over 100 scholarly articles on various aspects on the mind, published in journals ranging from *Artificial Intelligence* and *Behavioral and Brain Sciences* to *Poetics Today* and the *Journal of Aesthetics and Art Criticism*. His most recent book is *Brainchildren: A Collection of Essays 1984–1996* (1998).

JOHN HAUGELAND is Professor of Philosophy at the University of Chicago. He received his Ph.D. from the University of California at Berkeley in 1976, and works and teaches principally in philosophy of mind, philosophy of science, metaphysics, Kant, and early Heidegger. He is the editor of *Mind Design II* (1997), and the author of *Having Thought* (1998), *Artificial Intelligence: The Very Idea* (1985), 'Truth and Finitude: Heidegger's Transcendental Existentialism' (in Mark Wrathall and Jeff Malpas (eds.), *Heidegger, Authenticity, and Modernity: Essays in Honor of Hubert L. Dreyfus* (2000)), and *Syntax, Semantics, Physics* (in a forthcoming volume edited by John Preston).

BRIAN CANTWELL SMITH is University Professor at Duke University. He previously taught cognitive science, computer science, and philosophy at Indiana University, was principal scientist at the Xerox Palo Alto Research Center (PARC), and Adjunct Professor of Philosophy at Stanford University. He was a founder of the Center for the Study of Language and Information at Stanford University (CSLI), a founder and first President of Computer Professionals for Social Responsibility (CPSR), and President (1998–9) of the Society for Philosophy and Psychology (SPP). After studying at Oberlin College, he received his BS, MS, and Ph.D. degrees from the Massachusetts Institute of Technology (1974, 1978, 1982). His research focuses on the conceptual foundations of computing (including the use of computational metaphors in such fields as philosophy, psychology, cognitive science, physics, logic, and art), philosophy of mind, consciousness, and metaphysics and epistemology. He is the author of *On the Origin of Objects* (1996), a proposal for a unified metaphysics of ontology and epistemology.

EDITOR'S NOTE

In this collection the reader will find close and testing analyses of the views of five eminent philosophers of mind: Andy Clark, Robert Cummins, Daniel Dennett, John Haugeland, and Brian Cantwell Smith. This is a record of an extraordinary philosophical meeting that took place over six days at Three Field Farm and the Blue Hill Farm Inn, Blue Hill, Maine, in August 1999: the University of Sydney Peak Research Meeting on Mental Representation.

At this meeting each of the five was asked to comment on specific aspects of the contribution of one of the others. The subject of the commentary then replied. Given the small size of the audience—these five, the convenor (Hugh Clapin), Joan Wellman, and Josefa Toribio—participants were free to interrupt, challenge, and seek clarification from the speakers during, and at the end of, each presentation. Collected here are the commentaries, replies, and edited excerpts from the discussion.

Commentators were directed to particular writings of their subjects (chosen by the convenor in consultation with the subject), and asked to address the questions: How does, and ought, cognitive science specify, identify, and make use of mental representations? How does representational content depend on the representations themselves? What is the metaphysics of mental representations?

The result of this testing intellectual exchange is a rich tapestry of problems and proposed solutions. While the participants share a close engagement with the empirical and theoretical results of cognitive science, and dissatisfaction with traditional ('classical') approaches, their treatment of mental representation and its metaphysics differ profoundly.

While it is best to allow the contributors to speak for themselves, some readers may benefit from the brief introduction to the relevant aspects of the contributors' work which begins each Part. In the Introduction I have offered a sketch of the background debates and problems that frame the contributions in this volume.

During the meeting I presented a paper that offered one way to draw these five philosophical positions together on the questions of content, representational vehicles, and ontology. That paper, 'Tacit Representation in Functional Architecture', along with some of the associated discussion, appears in Part 6.

Readers may wish to take one of two approaches to the discussion sections. Much excellent discussion arose from interruptions to the original papers, and may be read at the appropriate place in the paper (in the familiar manner of endnotes). The discussion relating to each Part is collected together in one place at the end of the Part, however, and may also be read as a single entity separate from (but related to) the papers. I have endeavoured to facilitate both approaches.

The discussants make occasional reference to authors, ideas, and examples which may not be familiar to all readers. As a consequence, I have added a small number of explanatory footnotes which I hope aid this collection's accessibility. Similarly, discussants make occasional reference to papers or discussion which appear elsewhere in this volume. Where reference is made to another Part of this collection, I have added cross-references in footnotes.

(The order of the Parts has been rearranged a little, to take advantage of the particular strengths of each Part in the context of publication. For example, Haugeland's précis history of cognitive science in Part 1 provides an excellent introduction to all the papers. Chronologically, the papers were presented, and may be read, in the following order: Part 6 (Clapin), Part 3 ('On Haugeland'), Part 2 ('On Dennett'), Part 4 ('On Cummins'), Part 5 ('On Smith'), and Part 1 ('On Clark').)

Square brackets, [ ], indicate an editorial addition or amendment, except where they appear within a quotation, in which case they indicate an addition provided by the author of the chapter in which the quote appears. Footnotes to the discussion are attributed to the editor, or to the participant who elected to add the footnote (as appropriate).

A word about referring in print to the discussion sections: this material was all said in off-the-cuff discussion. It would not be fair to hold the speakers to every detail—we can look to the papers here, and their other published material for careful argument and nuanced consideration. The value of the discussion is in seeing what sorts of moves these fine philosophers make when asked for clarification; what kinds of considerations give them pause; what corners they allow themselves to be pushed into, and how they extract themselves from such difficulties; and in following the expert speculations of five of the best philosophers of mental representation you could find. In particular, if you are inclined to quote or otherwise refer to any of the discussion, please ensure it is acknowledged as *discus-*

sion, as opposed to ordinary published writing. For example 'In discussion, Clapin has acknowledged that pigs might fly. See *Philosophy of Mental Representation*, p. xv.'

The week in Blue Hill was philosophically enormously rich, and immensely enjoyable. I hope readers will take with them a sense of the committed engagement, and the sheer love of ideas, demonstrated by the participants.

H.C.

The University of Sydney
February 2001

Introduction

Two mysteries continue to frame debate in contemporary philosophy of mind. The first is the nature of consciousness. In particular, how can our conscious experience fit into the growing body of scientific knowledge about the mind and the brain? The second mystery is intentionality. How can our thoughts be *about* other things?

For some time intentionality has appeared the easier of these two problems, and it seems that significant progress has been made. The invention of automatic computing devices in the middle of the century, following important theoretical work by Alan Turing, showed that a machine could manipulate and make use of internal representational states, thus providing an example of how the mind's internal representations might operate. Throughout the 1980s and 1990s much work has been done on the questions of how material states of mind could bear content.

The most popular kind of solution revolves around the causal relationships between content and representation: the kind of mental state that is typically caused by being in the presence of cows thereby represents cows.

There has also been constructive debate about the possible nature of the representational vehicles that carry mental content. Is the inner code language-like, or pictorial, or holographic? The popular solution here is that thought is, to a large extent, linguistic.

The papers and discussion in this volume are firmly focused on making some progress in understanding the enduring problem of intentionality. Serious questions are raised about the apparent successes in this area, and radical solutions are offered.

Intentionality and Mental Content

Consider the relationship between a mind and the world it inhabits. Minds not only exist in the world, they think *about* the world. In considering what I shall eat for dinner this evening, I think *about* different kinds of meals, how difficult or enjoyable they are to prepare, what ingredients are in my kitchen, how much it would cost me to dine out, and whether I can afford that cost, and so on. I can think about things that are in front of my eyes, things that exist but are not present (such as the eggs in my fridge at home), things that do not yet exist (such as the dinner I will cook), and even things that have never and will never exist (such as a truly perfect soufflé cooked by me). Minds are often directed towards the world, and this directedness or 'aboutness' is often termed *intentionality*.[1] More specifically, these examples illustrate that the mind is able to *represent* the world. The basic problem of mental representation is that of better understanding this relationship between mind and world.

It is not only minds and their thoughts that have these special intentional properties. Words, numerals, road signs, artificial symbol systems, and artworks are also *about* things other than themselves. These familiar kinds of representation also pose an explanatory problem: By virtue of what do they represent?

Toward the end of the nineteenth century, Franz Brentano (1874/1973) made use of this observation in distinguishing the mental from the physical. Since mental phenomena have the property of intentionality, and physical phenomena clearly do not, the mental could not be identical to the physical.

Late twentieth-century philosophers of mind generally do not share Brentano's conviction that the mental is irreducible to the physical. They tend to agree, however, that intentionality is a 'mark of the mental'—something that sets the mental apart from the (non-mental) physical world and that is in sore need of explanation in a materialist theory of mind.

The problem of representation is very closely related to the problem of intentionality. While whole minds can have the property of being intentional, and whole minds can represent the world as being some way or another, such intentional minds need not be populated with inner states deserving of the name 'representation'. The idea that the intentionality of whole minds is explained by way of an inner economy of internal representational states is one popular proto-theory—but it is not universally accepted.

It has been about fifty years since the cognitive revolution in the scientific study of the mind (marked by the rise of artificial intelligence and

---

[1] See Searle (1983), Barwise and Perry (1983), and Crane (2001) for good discussions of intentionality.

cognitive psychology), and the (re)turn to materialism and naturalism in the philosophy of mind, as marked by Smart's (1959) and Place's (1956) statements of mind–brain identity theory. Over that time much excellent work has been done on the issues of mental representation and intentionality. Despite the enormous scientific advances in the cognitive sciences, it is not clear that materialist philosophy of mind has come to a consensus even about how to approach the problem of mental representation, let alone what to say about it.

Intentionality is closely related to folk psychology. Ordinary people ('the folk') talk about human minds as if they contain beliefs, desires, hopes, fears, and so on. The folk use these mental objects in explaining behaviour: Why did I go to the fridge? Because I was hungry (I *desired* food) and I *believed* there was food in the fridge. This sort of very ordinary psychological explanation is the basis of what has become known as folk psychology. Beliefs, desires, and so on are known as 'propositional attitudes'— believing there is food in the fridge is taking the attitude of belief toward the proposition, 'There is food in the fridge'. I could take a different attitude to the same proposition, for example if I *feared* there was food in the fridge, or the same attitude to a different proposition, for example if I *believed* that swans are white.

Propositional attitudes are intentional states: the mental state driving me to the fridge is *about* the fridge, and so an explanation of how it is humans have and use propositional attitudes would go a long way toward explaining intentionality.

Daniel Dennett (1971; 1981; 1991*b*) is well known for an account of intentionality that divorces a mind's intentionality from the representational properties of its inner workings. According to Dennett, we ascribe propositional attitudes according to how well such an ascription predicts the behaviour of the thing in question. Adopting the intentional stance towards people is typically the quickest, easiest, and most accurate way of understanding what people will do under various circumstances; for example, how they will behave when they are hungry and food is nearby, or when they have made a promise and intend to keep the promise.

Adopting the intentional stance is not always a great help, however, even where people are concerned. If a person is comatose and falling from an airplane, ascribing beliefs and desires to them will not be the best way to predict what will happen. In that case we are better off using the laws of physics (or 'adopting the physical stance', as Dennett would say). According to Dennett, intentionality is constituted more by a certain

pattern of behaviour than it is by an economy of inner mental representations. This is not to deny, however, that inner representational states may
play a vital role in explaining that pattern of behaviour.

Compare Dennett's explanation of intentionality with that due to Jerry
Fodor (1975; 1981; 1987; 1994). According to Fodor, the intentional
features of human minds are explained by the processing of a set of
language-like inner representations—the so-called 'language of thought'.
On Fodor's theory, propositional attitudes are not only attitudes to propositions: they are attitudes to *sentences*. My belief that there is food in the
fridge, according to Fodor, is explained by my taking the attitude of belief
toward the inner mentalese sentence, 'There is food in the fridge'. Of
course there is no explanation of intentionality without an explanation
of how the 'words' of the language of thought carry content, and Fodor
subscribes to a version of the causal/informational theory of content
(Fodor's particular version (1990) is dubbed 'asymmetric dependence').
(The language of thought account is compatible with other theories of
content, however.)

Fodor's popular theory amply demonstrates the importance of computing to contemporary debates in the philosophy of mind. The idea of the
automatic processing of inner representational states has been strongly
influenced by the practice of computing. Secondly, many computational
representations have, or appear to have, fundamental linguistic properties
such as productivity and systematicity. The former is the ability of a representational scheme to generate an indefinite number of valid complex
representations from a finite set of atomic representations. The latter is
that feature of systems of representation whereby a system that can understand a given complex sentence can also understand systematic variants of
that sentence. A simple example is the suggestion that anyone who can have
the thought 'John loves Mary' can have the thought 'Mary loves John'. One
explanation for the systematicity and productivity of thought is that there is
a language of thought, and languages are systematic and productive.[2]

(Fodor's approach to cognitive science is an excellent example of what
has become known as 'classical' cognitive science (Fodor and Pylyshyn
1988). The classical approach is impressed by the abilities of computers,
and constructs models of the mind that make use of structured internal
symbolic states akin to those found in computers. The term 'classical' was
introduced to help define what it is that connectionist research rejects.)

---

[2] See the appendix to Fodor (1987); Fodor and Pylyshyn (1988); and Cummins (1996*b*).

A more radical response to explaining folk psychology is to eliminate it. Paul Churchland (1981) has argued that folk psychology ought be understood as a scientific paradigm which is in the process of being replaced by modern science. In the course of this replacement (largely by neuroscience in Churchland's view) the folk psychological ontology of beliefs, desires, wishes, and fears will be eliminated. That is, the propositional attitudes will be found to be as fictional and imaginary as were the Ptolemaic universe and phlogiston.

The classical approach to cognitive science has been challenged by connectionist models of mind.[3] Connectionist models make use of large arrays of interconnected 'units' that are based on a simplified model of neural architecture. There are a number of different forms of representation identifiable in various kinds of connectionist networks. Networks are capable of 'local' representation, typically in schemes where each unit has a single semantic interpretation. The second form of representation in such networks is that found in the activation of the network's units. This activity is typically presented as a vector whose elements are the activity level for each unit in a certain location in the network. A third kind of representation is found in the connectivity of the units: which units are connected to which, and with what weights. This connectivity can be described by a matrix that assigns weights to each possible unit-to-unit connection, and is sometimes referred to as the network's 'weight matrix'.

This can be contrasted with computational and linguistic representational schemes where discrete units of representation correspond to discrete items of information. Thus in a computational representation of the play Hamlet there is a discrete component of the computer's memory that represents Hamlet's anguished question 'To be, or not to be?' Most of the computer's memory could be damaged and many other lines from the play lost, but as long as certain pieces were left behind, this line would still be represented. But if damage were done to the connectivity of many connectionist networks, damage would be done to all the information in the network—nothing would be left unscathed. At the same time, however, some aspect of all the information would be retained; albeit in a degraded form. This 'holographic' or 'distributed' nature of some connectionist representation appears to offer quite different representation and computational abilities to that familiar from artificial intelligence.

[3] See e.g. Bechtel and Abrahamsen (1991), Clark (1989; 1993), Dennett (1983) (and the 'Reflections' following the reprint in Dennett 1987), Clapin (1991) and van Gelder (1991).

One well-known example of connectionist cognitive modeling is the NETtalk network due to Sejnowski and Rosenberg (1987a, b). NETtalk is a processing device that learns to produce speech (phonemes) in response to written words: it is a machine that reads aloud. Like many connectionist networks, NETtalk has a number of layers of units: the input layer, the output layer, and in between a set of 'hidden' units. The connectivity of the network is initially random, and so at first it produces gibberish. It receives feedback on its successes or failures which it uses to readjust the weights between its units until it comes to speak with remarkable proficiency. (An excellent philosophical introduction to connectionism in general, and NETtalk in particular, may be found in Clark's *Associative Engines*, 1993.)

Representational Content

If there are inner representational states, we need an account of how those inner states are able to carry content or meaning. At first blush, it seems clear that it is something extrinsic to the physical make-up of a token representation that explains its representational properties. The word 'cow', for example, only has the meaning it does because of how we speakers of English treat and use it. For the same reason 'wco' has no meaning in English.

Driven by the idea of inner representational states—perhaps constituting a language-like system—the mental content debate has concentrated on what sort of relation between a token representation and its content might fit the needs of intentionality.[4] The standard candidates include similarity, causal connection (or 'natural information'), evolutionary history, and conceptual role (these are not always mutually exclusive options).

While similarity is a superficially plausible explanation of how pictures, photographs, scale models, and sculpture represent, it is not a popular solution to the problem of *mental* representation because of the obvious dissimilarity between neurological states and most of the things they are meant to represent: clumps of neural tissue have little in common with cows. Sophisticated accounts, however, make use of a more abstract notion of similarity: isomorphism or structure-sharing. The central notion

---

[4] See Cummins' *Meaning and Mental Representation* (1989) for an excellent overview of the mental content debate.

is that a mental representation of a cow will share abstract structural features of the cow in the same way that a graph of a cow's milk production shares its structure with the quantity of milk produced over time.

Similarity accounts face further difficulties. It seems that pictures and scale models do not tend to compose into grammatical sentences the way that arbitrary words can, nor do structural representations look to be good candidates for representing propositional knowledge. None the less, there have been, and still are, defenders of some form of imagery, similarity, or isomorphism as a basis of mental representation, including psychologists Shepard and Cooper (1982) and Kosslyn (1980), and philosophers McGinn (1989) and Cummins (1996a and Part 4 of this volume).[5]

The most thoroughly investigated option involves the causal connections between the world and the mental states that represent the world. This idea is given particular weight by the idea that there is a strict, non-intentional notion of information satisfied by such causal connections. Fred Dretske (1981) provided a major contribution by arguing that there is a robust, objective (and thus for present purposes non-intentional) 'information' relation between a cow and a mental token 'cow', in the case where the presence of cows reliably causes the presence of mentals tokens 'cow's. This idea that reliable (usually causal) connection—'indication'—could be the basis of mental content sparked an important and widespread debate about the details of this promising suggestion. Despite its very attractive features, this approach has difficulty dealing with two absolutely central aspects of intentionality: error and non-existence.

Intentionality denotes the 'aboutness' of mental states (and some non-mental things such as words whose intentionality may derive from that of mental states). But thoughts need not be *about* existing things, or things with which we have had any causal connection. I can think about Plato and Kant, about angels and demons, about fictional characters and future people. There is absolutely no direct causal connection between tokens of 'Plato' in my mind and the presence of Plato before me.

Even trickier than the problem of non-present content is the issue of error. It is characteristic of my thinking that I can sometimes be wrong. If the thing I'm seeing is a long way away, and the sun has set, and I'm not looking very closely, I might think to myself 'Lo, there is a cow' when in fact I am actually looking at a horse. The problem here is that even though

---

[5] A richer discussion of the issues surrounding similarity-based representation may be found in Goodman (1976), Haugeland (1991), Block (1981), McGinn (1989), and Tye (1991).

I used my mental term 'cow' erroneously, it (on this occasion at least) was caused by the presence of a horse, and on Dretske's basic theory, this suggests that my mental token 'cow' means *cow or horse on a dark night far away*. But of course my mental token 'cow' in fact just means *cow*. Because error gives rise to disjunctive correlations, this problem is known interchangeably as the 'error' problem and the 'disjunction' problem.

There are a number of approaches to this problem. All revolve around keeping correlation as the core of the basis of meaning, and adding fiction, non-existence, and error as special cases. Dretske's (early) solution was to distinguish between a learning period in which the actual correlation stands, and a post-learning period of use in which applications of 'cow' to non-cows can be said to be erroneous (Dretske 1981). Fodor's (1990) solution is to argue that whatever the mechanism, mental states are 'asymmetrically dependent' on their contents. This means, roughly, that horse-caused 'cow' tokens depend on cow-caused 'cow' tokens but not the other way around.[6]

The important feature of evolutionary accounts of content, for example that of Ruth Millikan (1984; 1993), is that the content of a mental token is fixed in part by its evolutionary function. In the same way that hearts have the evolutionary function to pump blood because they were selected for pumping blood, the evolutionary purpose of a given token of 'cow' may be derived (by a somewhat more convoluted route), and this purpose is to accurately represent the thing in front of me, presently a cow. Thus while my erroneous thought about a cow was caused by a horse, the mechanism in my brain which produced the thought has, in the current context, the evolutionary function of representing a cow.

Evolutionary accounts ('teleosemantics') may also make use of natural information or similarity in their account of representation, but are relieved of the error problem through the device of evolutionary function. They are attractive in part because they provide the promise of a naturalistic explanation of normative properties, such as intentionality, that is thoroughly integrated with the evolutionary commitments of the rest of biological science.

Teleosemantic theories of content have their fair share of problems, too. For example, it seems to many that representational content is a

---

[6] This simplifies a complex position—the asymmetric dependence is in fact between the law that cows cause 'cow's and the law that horses cause 'cow's. See Fodor (1990), especially ch. 4 'A Theory of Content II: The Theory'.

synchronic, rather than a diachronic, property of mental states. If I suddenly popped into existence a moment ago, with no evolutionary history, I would still have all the same material mental states as I do now, and behave just as I do now, but (according to teleosemantics) I would not have a true mind because nothing I think would mean anything—I would lack intentionality.

Conceptual role (or sometimes 'functional role') semantics is well described by Quine's image of the 'web of belief'.[7] The basic idea is that the meaning of an individual representation is drawn from its place in the web of representations and inferences using those representations. Words appear to be chosen more or less arbitrarily to represent their contents, however, once chosen, the way a given word interacts with other words explains its content. It seems that one cannot claim to know what 'cow' means if one knows nothing of milk, udders, grass, calves, bulls, farms, etc. Meanings, it is claimed, are essentially intricately interrelated (Block 1986 and Harman 1987).

The practice of computer programming also lends some plausibility to conceptual role semantics (in artificial intelligence 'procedural semantics' is a variety of conceptual role semantics). Arbitrary and strange patterns of electrical activity or magnetic distribution, with little or no causal contact or similarity with external objects, none the less seem to get the representational job done.

Conceptual role theories are criticized on the grounds that they provide no principled basis for meaning identity or even meaning similarity. My web of concepts is likely to be different from yours, probably in large degree. Given that my tokens of 'cow' get their meaning from my web of concepts, and your tokens of 'cow' get their meaning from your web, we must mean different things by 'cow'. What is worse is that it isn't even clear that we can discuss the *similarity* of our meanings. Once two webs differ at all, there is arguably no objective measure of similarity. This problem reappears in considering translation between languages and in considering radical theory change in science.[8]

Hilary Putnam's important paper 'The Meaning of "Meaning"' (1975) (along with Kripke, 1972 and Burge, 1979) has given rise to a new terminology about meaning. Putnam is concerned to distinguish mental

---

[7] See Quine (1951) and Quine and Ullian (1978). Conceptual role semantics is defended by Block (1986), Devitt (1981), and Lycan (1984). See also ch. 9 ('Functional Roles') of Cummins (1989).

[8] See Fodor and LePore (1992) for a detailed critical discussion.

states that could be fully described by reference only to the brain states of the person concerned, from those states that could be fully described only by reference to objects and states of affairs outside the person concerned. The first kind of states—those that supervene on brain states—are now typically called 'narrow' states, while the second sort—those that super- vene on a combination of brain states and how things are in the rest of the world—are called 'wide' (or 'broad') states.

Due in part to the distinction made by Frege (1892/1960) between the sense and the reference of a term, it has been common to think that some aspects of the meaning of a mental representation may be determined purely by factors 'inside the head'. So while the referent of 'cow' is typically external to the mind, the sense of 'cow' may be discovered simply by investigating the mind itself. For example, the sense might be given by its conceptual role, which looks to be a narrow property. An important part of Putnam's conclusion was that meaning is not a narrow psycho- logical state. In arguing for this conclusion, Putnam refers to his inability to distinguish beech trees from elms, and notes his beech concept is identical to his elm concept; none the less his use of the terms 'beech' and 'elm' refer to quite different sorts of trees. So concepts, which are internal states, could not by themselves determine reference.

After considering a range of examples, including the now well-known 'Twin-Earth' cases, Putnam concludes that anything that could fit the requirement of determining reference must be a wide state, and, on the assumption that meaning determines reference, meaning must therefore be wide. This generally accepted conclusion has the important consequence for theories of meaning that they must investigate the mind's interaction with the world in order to fully understand semantic phenomena.

Representation and Cognitive Science

Despite lengthy, detailed, and sometimes brilliant contributions to the debate surrounding representational content, there remain many out- standing questions and problems. What follows is a brief overview of the set of concerns that lies behind much of the discussion in this volume. The philosophers appearing here share a deep interest in the contribution of the cognitive sciences to the problems and issues that constitute the philoso- phy of mind, and so these concerns derive in equal measure from the philosophical and cognitive scientific literatures.

Language

Too often, a discussion of mental representation becomes a discussion of language. This is understandable to the extent that language is a conspicuously human kind of representation, and seems strongly implicated in the uniquely human mental capacities. It enables our rich expressive abilities on topics as diverse as immediate perceptual experience and abstract concepts; on the cow in front of me and quantum mechanics. Through disciplines such as linguistics and psycholinguistics, language has been the topic of rigorous and successful scientific study. Language is the model on which the familiar artificial languages of formal logic are based, and philosophers have long studied its inferential features. Additionally, language has been an important inspiration in the development of programmable computers, and in artificial intelligence (AI). Computer codes are called 'languages', and much research has been done on computer production and understanding of natural languages.

But, as is sometimes pointed out by both philosophers and scientists (such as McGinn 1989; Clark 1993; Smith 1997), there is more to representation than language (and more to language than representation). Pictures which paint a thousand words demonstrate the poverty, in some contexts, of sentential expression. Scale models facilitate reasoning and explanation obscured by formulae and description. Much of what constitutes computer representation—lists, trees, hash tables and so on—defies description as linguistic. More pointedly, cognitive science is increasingly looking away from propositional models of representation toward quite different alternatives. For example, the distributed representations offered by connectionist networks seem to be quite different in kind from either words or pictures (van Gelder 1991; Haugeland 1991; Clapin and O'Brien 1998). AI researchers (such as Brooks 1991) are looking to replace complex lists of rules with simpler guidance systems for their robots. Dynamical systems theory suggests that we think of internal mental processing in dynamic numerical terms instead of static representational ones (Port and van Gelder 1995).

Given that there is more to representation than language—and these other options are being actively and fruitfully followed by cognitive scientists—there is a profound danger in concentrating too much on the example of natural language. For a start, our linguistic abilities are one of the key *explananda* of human cognition (Dennett 1977). Fodor's proposal that we explain human linguistic capacity by the actions of an inner linguistic capacity (and specifically, that we explain language understanding by saying that natural language is translated into a language of thought) is too quick a move. While fans of the language of thought are quick to point out tactics for blocking an explanatory regress, the move to an *internal* language remains worrying because we do not fully understand what an internal automatic system of linguistic representation would really be like. It could not be much like natural language (it is used internally for reasoning and belief storage, not externally for communicating, for a start), nor is it likely to be much like the cumbersome, hand-crafted computer machine codes or programming languages.

Secondly, there is the risk of assuming that features peculiar to linguistic representation are also essential to mental representation. Thoughts, presumably, need not be restricted to the single dimension of expression allowed to writing (left to right along the page, in the case of English) and speaking (in time). Thirdly, it is not at all clear that we fully understand what makes languages different from pictures and holograms (Haugeland 1991; Clark 1993). Is it the arbitrariness of words that is essential to language, or compositional semantics? What marks the difference between a hieroglyphic language and a system of pictorial representation? In short, when looking inside a brain, how would we know whether we are looking at a language or not?

Fourthly, there may be a crucial difference between written and spoken language. It seems clear that the invention of writing was a very important cultural innovation that allowed the accurate preservation and retrieval of information. It is at least arguable that writing permits different kinds of thoughts and reasoning processes from talking, and that oral cultures differ in important ways from those dependent on writing. Fifthly, the power of language (productivity, meta-representation, abstractness) is presumably not available to creatures that have no language, but that plausibly have mental processes. Does language, including the language of thought, come all at once with all these powerful abilities, or can it be acquired gradually, bit by bit, over evolutionary time-scales?[9]

Computation

The central place of mental representation in cognitive science is due in part to the theoretical and practical innovations that eventuated in modern 'von Neumann architecture' computers. Mathematician and logician Alan

---

[9] See e.g. Patricia Churchland's (1986: 388–9) discussion of the 'infralinguistic catastrophe'.

Turing developed the idea of an abstractly described 'machine' that could implement clear algorithms (the 'Turing machine'). For any finitely specified algorithm, there exists a Turing machine that can implement that algorithm. This means that any task that can be fully decomposed into a finite number of discrete steps can be automated by such a machine: it can be 'effectively computed'. More excitingly, Turing showed that some Turing machines—*universal* Turing machines—could act like any other Turing machine, and thus could carry out any finite algorithm whatsoever. This result is the foundation of modern computing.

Turing machines consist of indefinitely long tapes divided up into squares, and a 'head' that can 'read' the tape. The squares may be blank, or may contain symbols from a specified alphabet. The head reads the tape by being able to determine, for any square on the tape, which symbol, if any, the square contains. The 'state' of the head determines how it responds to a given symbol, and symbols in turn may change the head's state. A universal Turing machine uses some of the symbols on the tape to describe a specific Turing machine, and as a consequence it acts as if it were that specific Turing machine. The universal Turing machine is the forerunner of the modern computer, where a computer program stored in the computer's memory describes a particular algorithm, which is implemented by the computer.[10]

In considering the nature of representation, it is important to recognize that at its very heart, the theory of effective computation relies on symbolic representations. The symbols stored on the Turing machine's tape are representations, and they both explain and cause the behaviour of the Turing machine, and do so according to their semantic interpretation. The genius of Turing, von Neumann, and the other pioneers of computing was to show that machines could be built whose behaviour was flexible because they 'read', 'understood', and 'followed' their internal representations.

The cognitive revolution overcame behaviourist concerns about inner representational states in large part by pointing to computers. Computers operate autonomously on the basis of inner representation states, without falling into an explanatory regress, so why not people? The computational trick was to construct representational vehicles whose physical, syntactic, and semantic properties converged. Thus machine languages

---

[10] See Haugeland's *Artificial Intelligence: The Very Idea* (1985) for an excellent introduction to Turing machines.

are constituted by strings of binary digits whose physical properties (a pattern of electrical activity of a certain sort) in the context of the central processing unit correspond with certain grammatical or syntactic properties (111100100100010, where the first seven digits name the instruction and the remaining digits denote the numbers to be added) and thereby justify their semantic properties ('add 2 and 2'). In short, syntax mirrors semantics, and syntax (cleverly implemented) has the appropriate physical effect.

Artificial intelligence is that branch of cognitive science that takes seriously the possibility of intelligent computers. John Haugeland has coined the useful term 'Good Old Fashioned AI' (GOFAI) to describe the core elements of this approach. GOFAI is committed to an explanation of intelligence that appeals to inner mental representations that constitute an automated formal system. In practice, GOFAI is the research program that aims to implement intelligence by writing the right program for a von Neumann architecture computer. GOFAI assumes that (explicit) rules and representations, in computational code, will be sufficient to implement human-style intelligence. (GOFAI is classical cognitive science applied to the particular domain of AI.)

The question remains, however: do computational representations *really* have semantic properties? It has certainly not been demonstrated that they have any of the properties ascribed by the popular philosophical theories of content—causal, teleosemantic, similarity, or conceptual role (though procedural semantics was an attempt to attribute meaning to computational representations along conceptual role lines).[11] Given the centrality of the computational model to cognitive science, careful consideration of that model is warranted.

John Searle's (1980) Chinese Room argument is a well-known attack on the more ambitious goals of artificial intelligence. Searle imagines replacing a computer's central processing unit with an English-speaking person inside a room; the person has to process Chinese characters according to instructions in English. Searle's argument, in short, is that just as the English speaker has no understanding of the Chinese she is processing, so the computer has no understanding of the symbols it is processing. As a consequence, no such computer may be said to have the understanding or intentionality of a person.

---

[11] Fodor's critique of procedural semantics is in 'Tom Swift and His Procedural Grandmother' (1978).

Searle's argument is unconvincing to many (see, for example, the many commentaries following the article), however it highlights an important question: 'By virtue of *what* could a computer be said to understand the symbols it contains?'

On close inspection, we find little in computer programming or AI representations that is familiar. Computer languages, while often loosely based on English, are composed almost entirely of commands, and their grammar is a strictly enforced impoverished subset of English grammar. But high-level computer code does no work until it is compiled (or interpreted) and then actually running. And the processing of computer instructions has little in common with the understanding of natural languages. Perhaps more importantly, the data structures used to store knowledge, belief, and goals in computers—matrices, lists, hash tables, binary trees, and other abstract structures—are even further removed from familiar kinds of representation such as pictures and sentences (Cummins 1986; Clark 1993; and Smith 1997). Searle's Chinese Room demonstrates the gap between two natural languages (English and Chinese); the gap between computational data structures and natural languages is perhaps even greater. This raises the question of whether the representations of which computers make use, and that they might be said to 'understand', are really the right kinds of thing to underwrite cognitive science's faith in internal representation.

Explicit and Tacit

Knowledge comes in explicit and tacit forms. Psychologists say my knowledge of how to ride a bicycle is tacit knowledge because it is available neither to consciousness nor inference. When I memorize my shopping list, my knowledge of it is explicit. I can recall it at will ('Do I need eggs?'), scroll through it in my mind, and make inferences about it ('Why is buttermilk on the list? I must have been planning pancakes'). Typically we think of individual representations or systems of representation as explicit forms of content, however there is also room to consider what information is stored, and perhaps even used, in a tacit rather than explicit form. Outside psychology, explicitness is no longer tied to consciousness: explicit but unconscious representations are recognized by many theories of cognition.

The question of how to draw the tacit/explicit distinction has arisen a number of times in the history of cognitive science. In *The Concept of Mind* (1949) Gilbert Ryle used the distinction between 'know-how' and 'knowledge-that' to argue that the ability to entertain explicit propositional content (knowledge-that) was a kind of skill that must rest on tacit know-how, and so 'intellectualist' appeals to propositional knowledge to explain tacit knowledge (e.g. riding a bike or tying one's shoes) was doomed to failure, since that propositional knowledge would itself need to be explained by further know-how.

Fodor's (1968) paper 'The Appeal to Tacit Knowledge in Psychological Explanations' defended cognitive ('intellectualist') explanation of exactly this sort against Ryle's behaviourist attack by noting that some systems (e.g. computers) are simply wired in such a way as to follow explicit instructions. As Dennett notes in his paper 'Styles of Mental Representation' (1983), appeals to computational representation of this sort do not do away with tacit content and know-how. Saying that the computer is just hardwired to follow the machine code instructions is just another way of saying that it has the know-how to do this.

The language of thought hypothesis tends to place a strong emphasis on explicit representation in cognitive explanation, and pays little attention to tacit content. The interplay between tacit and explicit content has continued to intrigue cognitive scientists, however. In AI, attention has been given to the inexplicit knowledge a computer program has—its 'procedural knowledge'—noting that there is a trade-off between tacit and explicit content. Tacit procedural content incurs no storage costs; however, it is inflexible (Fodor 1978; Cummins 1986).

A significant part of the connectionist challenge to the language of thought and traditional cognitive psychology rests on the fact that connectionist networks appear not to make use of explicit representation in either information storage *or* inference. In fact, it appears that the computation takes place over the tacit representation rather than over explicit symbols as is the case in GOFAI systems.[12] This new and exciting way of explaining representation and cognition demands further consideration of the tacit/explicit distinction.

Vehicle and Content

A useful distinction to make when considering representation in general, and mental representation in particular, is that between the representational vehicle and the content carried by that vehicle. Just as a backpack is a vehicle for carrying contents such as books and lunch, a representational

---

[12] See O'Brien and Opie (1999) and Clapin (1999*b*) for a discussion of this issue.

vehicle is a (typically) physical object that carries meaning. The pattern of ink created by the word 'good' is a physical object that need have no intentional properties. It communicates content (goodness) and that content is distinct from the pattern of ink.

Computers, following the lead of formal logic, lend themselves easily to this image. The vehicle of content is the pattern of electrical activity (or magnetic fields on disks)—an unproblematically physical state—while the content is whatever we ascribe. (Of course it is the central power of computers that the content we ascribe can align with the physical and syntactic powers of the symbol.)

Distinguishing between vehicle and content is often critical to thinking clearly about representation. For example, in considering the difference between a picture of a castle and a written description of a castle, there is at least some sense in saying that the content is the same in both cases (the castle), but the vehicles are clearly different in kind. It is an unresolved question whether different kinds of vehicles are associated with different kinds of content—though see Haugeland's 'Representation Genera' (1991) for a defence of the view that pictures carry different kinds of contents from sentences.

Reduction and the Social

Generally speaking, cognitive science has assumed a hierarchically reductionist picture of mental explanation. Social properties are composed of, and explained by, persons with minds; minds are composed of, and explained by, neurons, and so on down to physics.[13]

There are alternatives to this explanatory hierarchy, however. One popular alternative is to suggest that (at least some) mental properties are derived from social properties, not vice versa. Wittgenstein, for example, suggests that it is being a part of a speech community that gives meaning to our words and thoughts.[14] More generally, humans are social beings, and much of our thinking and mental activity is directed towards others. Critics of the reductionist tendencies of materialist philosophy of mind, such as Dreyfus and Haugeland (both influenced by Heidegger)[15] are inclined to

---

[13] See e.g. Dennett's (1971; 1981) discussion of the relation between the intentional, design, and physical stances; and Newell's (1980; 1982) discussion of levels of explanation.

[14] I have in mind the 'Private Language Argument' and associated discussion in Wittgenstein (1958).

[15] See Dreyfus (1979) and Haugeland this volume, Parts 1 and 3. See also Winograd and Flores (1986).

concentrate on the richness of the human experience of *understanding* another person or their utterance, and of the way in which people and things *matter* to us. Understanding and mattering are undoubtedly intentional, and placing them at the root of the explanatory tree presents a radically different view of mental representation and cognitive science.

There is also a strong interest in moving beyond the hierarchy of social-mental-biological-physical. Dennett's (1971; 1981; 1991*b*) intentional stance explanation of intentionality doesn't reduce the property of intentionality to biological components; rather, it describes intentionality as a pattern of behaviour visible to certain kinds of rational observers. Such an explanation makes use of social concepts such as explanation and physical and biological concepts such as behaviour.

Metaphysics

Intentionality, and thus representational cognitive science, raises important metaphysical questions. Intentionality—aboutness—describes the relation between the mind and the objects in the world the mind considers. The way the world is understood by the mind is mediated by intentionality, and so a deeper understanding of intentionality brings with it a deeper understanding of our relationship to the objects of the world.

According to much cognitive science, representations mediate mind and world. A natural approach is to proceed on the basis of a relatively straightforward realism: the world is composed of things that exist independently of our minds, and the scientist's job is to discover what those things are and how they interact. The radical alternative is to suggest that our conceptual schemes, beliefs, and desires somehow think the world into existence, and that talk of a mind-independent world is a naïve fantasy.

Both positions are uncomfortable and unattractive. It is clear that sometimes there are choices available in how we see the world (do I attend to the beauty of the sunset or to an atmospheric chemist's explanation of the color?), and those choices are associated with representational media (thinking of the sunset pictorially as composed of color and shape, or in atmospheric and physical terms as a form of light diffraction). To the extent that these choices are inconsistent, a problem arises regarding which (if any) is *correct*; which actually corresponds with the world.

The German Enlightenment philosopher Immanuel Kant argued in his *Critique of Pure Reason* (1781/1929) for a middle road between realism and idealism, wherein the structure of reasoning (and thus of rational minds) is acknowledged as a contributor to the structure and character of the world as we understand it. This contribution is absolutely necessary and thus universal, argued Kant, and so it cannot be 'factored out' or otherwise overcome.[16]

Contemporary cognitive science places much explanatory burden for the structure of rational minds on the shoulders of mental representation. But it offers a plethora of possible kinds of mental representation. If, as has been argued, some kinds of content are only available to some kinds of representation (Haugeland 1991), then some aspects of the world may be unavailable to those who don't use the appropriate form of mental representation to think. Different options in how the mind represents the world could demand different ways of understanding the world and the objects it contains.

Intentionality, according to Brentano (1874/1973) marks a *metaphysical* boundary between mind and world. The contemporary mood favours coalescing the mind into the world. What is not always recognized is that this is a major ontological *project* that is not achieved simply by stating one's materialist assumptions.

For example, in his book *On the Origin of Objects* (1996), Brian Cantwell Smith argues that the traditional approach to computational theory (assumed as bedrock by the cognitive sciences) has left us with a thoroughly misleading picture of computational representation. Far from being abstract systems of arbitrary symbols, computational representations cannot be considered apart from their material circumstances: understanding them requires understanding both the nature of the tokens, and more importantly, the fundamental ontological nature of the world they represent.

Conclusion

If I were to draw a single conclusion from this collection, it would be this: cognitive science—the *representational* science of mind—has nothing like a clear and universal concept of representation and this fact is holding it back. This isn't merely a point about linguistic usage, of course. The problem is that we don't fully understand what external representation

---

[16] See sections 6.1.6 and 6.1.7 'Logic: Ontological Assumptions' and 'Perception' of this volume, and my 'Kantian Metaphysics and Cognitive Science' (1999c).

is, we can't agree on what intentionality is, and we have little idea of what inner states deserve to be called representational.

This isn't as negative a conclusion as it may appear. The right questions are being asked in order that replacement precisifications might be developed. The contributors offer a range of promising approaches to providing us with a deeper and more fruitful understanding of this critical aspect of cognitive explanation.

PART I
On Clark

Texts

'Where Brain, Body and World Collide' (1998*a*).
'The Dynamical Challenge' (1997*a*).
'The Presence of a Symbol' (ch. 6 of *Associative Engines*, 1993).
'Being, Computing, Representing' (ch. 8 of *Being There*, 1997*b*).

Andy Clark's important contributions to recent philosophy of cognitive science are marked by persistent attempts to bring together the key insights of traditional cognitivists with those of more radical theories, including Connectionism, Non-Linear Dynamical Systems Theory, anti-representationalism of various sorts, and embodiment-focused accounts of cognition. Clark's picture of human cognition emphasizes the continuity between human and animal cognition, on the grounds of evolutionary continuity.

This perspective provides significant food for thought. Many animals have systems of communication and signalling, and some apes have been taught rudimentary sign-languages, all of which makes human language appear less singular. It is well known that the fundamental anatomy and functioning of human brains shares much with that of primates, and other mammals generally. Our perceptual abilities, too, have many similarities.

Cognitive ethology has been highly successful as an approach to animal cognition. It emphasizes the importance of understanding animal minds as embedded in their natural environments.[1] Non-Linear Dynamical Systems

---

[1] See e.g. Allen and Bekoff (1997).

Theory has emphasized the value in treating cognitive systems as complex dynamical systems that 'couple' with their environments.[2] This approach is largely non-representational, but none the less offers new ways to explain subtly context-sensitive behaviour.

Clark has closely considered these (and many other) recent advances in cognitive science and found that they offer a profound challenge to the classical picture. While humans have distinctive capacities that are significantly removed from those of even our nearest animal neighbours, these differences may be explained in a minimalist way that preserves the overwhelming similarities between humans and animals. Put simply, Clark argues that the key difference is the environment we have created for ourselves, particularly the linguistic environment. It is a tool that makes possible a range of thinking that is otherwise unavailable, and opens up new domains; for example, the financial and political.

In the specific case of mental representation Clark argues that much of what might look to be propositionally encoded knowledge might in fact be stored tacitly, or non-propositionally, in connectionist weight vectors and in the environment in which the creature is embedded.

Clark has made a significant contribution to our understanding of the explicitness of representation, arguing that information is stored explicitly in a system to the extent that it is readily available to, and multiply deployable in that system. Thus the explicitness of storage is a system-relative notion. This move is the first step in demystifying the importance of explicit symbolic structures in mental architectures. Language and other symbol-systems are the epitome of explicit representation, but appear to be profoundly unbiological and human-specific. By understanding explicitness to encompass all sorts of structures that are multiply deployable to a specific system, Clark opens the way for an important compromise: explicit symbols may have a vital role in explaining animal cognition, but they are unlikely to be anything like human languages.

In his commentary, Haugeland is concerned that Clark's emphasis on our continuity with animals disguises a fundamental divide marked by our essential use of norms such as truth and goodness. Humans display a deep 'norm-hungriness'; deep in the sense that the desire is almost insatiable, and in the sense that the norms are unique in their richness and complexity. Haugeland is particularly concerned that we recognize the importance of sophisticated norms in making language possible. He agrees that the

---

[2] See e.g. Port and van Gelder (1995).

advent of human language itself raised new problems and opened up new cognitive domains; however, he wants to draw our attention to the group coordination problem presented by linguistic conventions.

Andy Clark on Cognition and Representation

JOHN HAUGELAND

Cognitive science—as contrasted with its predecessors, behavioral science and cybernetics—emerged in the mid-1950s, with the seminal works of Miller, Gelanter, and Pribram (1960), Newell and Simon (1958), and Chomsky (1968), among others. It was called 'cognitive science' because it took as its central topic of investigation cognition—that is, knowledge, or, more generally, thought. Moreover, it took as its primary concern human thought (though, in so far as animals could be deemed to think, they would be included too). In the seminal works just mentioned, the new science had a paradigm in the proper Kuhnian sense: a body of concrete scientific achievement that was 'sufficiently unprecedented to attract an enduring group of adherents away from competing modes of scientific activity' and 'sufficiently open-ended to leave all sorts of problems for the redefined group of practitioners to resolve' (Kuhn 1962: 10).

The basic assumptions of the resulting research tradition were most explicit and visible in the exciting subtradition that John McCarthy dubbed 'artificial intelligence': the design and implementation (in digital computer programs) of what are now often called 'classical' or 'GOFAI' systems. In such systems, 'thinking' ('reasoning', 'problem solving') takes the form of rule-governed manipulations of broadly sentence-like internal tokens. Their sentence-likeness consists in this: (1) they are composites of atomic units (drawn from a prespecified finite list of atoms) and formed according to finitely many prespecified recursive formation rules; (2) each well-formed token has a semantic interpretation that is fully (and recursively) determined by its form and the atoms of which it is composed; and (3) the manipulation rules, though sensitive only to the forms of the manipulated tokens, are designed so as to preserve, on the whole, various semantic desiderata (such as truth, probability, and/or conduciveness to goal achievement). The inspiring idea was that human thought itself must have essentially this same structure.

That tradition, still flourishing in many quarters, reigned almost unchallenged for more than a quarter of a century—an astonishing tenure, given the rapid pace of change in the fifteen years since. I say *almost* unchallenged, of course, because, starting already in the 1960s, Hubert Dreyfus (1972/1979/1992) had carefully identified, characterized, and documented most of the now well-known and widely conceded limitations of GOFAI systems—an extended critique that has been, I suspect, more influential than is usually acknowledged. More than that, Dreyfus also undertook to say systematically what would have to be done instead in order to implement genuinely human-like intelligence and being-in-the-world—including a remarkable number of the characteristics more recently touted (perhaps sometimes over-touted) as fundamental advantages of the various newer approaches. What Dreyfus has never done, however—and this, surely, is why he is so under-credited—is to say how to implement what he could clearly see is needed. He is purely a philosopher, not at all a scientist.

Andy Clark, too, is first and foremost a philosopher; but he will accept no such limitations. His concrete criticisms—and they are many and incisive—are always accompanied by a vision of how to remedy the identified shortcomings, a remedy well grounded, moreover, in a broad, up-to-date knowledge of current research. Few philosophers if any could claim to have been, over the years, as close to the cutting edge as Clark. The penalty for this (there's seldom a free lunch) may be that he's been less ahead of the curve than Dreyfus; but the compensating reward is the possibility of making positive progress.

Another notable merit of Clark's vision—and a mark of the true philosopher—is that he consistently maintains a broad perspective. Never in his elaboration and exploitation of the latest ideas and findings does he lose sight of what else is at stake in the larger picture, of how things have ultimately to be integrated, of why different and older ideas had also seemed so attractive. Thus I much admire a chapter-opening observation like the following—the kind of issue to which others, in their enthusiasm, are sometimes blind:

It is natural to wonder, however, just how much leverage (if any) this approach [biological reason: a rag-bag of 'quick and dirty' on-line stratagems] offers for understanding the most advanced and distinctive aspects of human cognition— not walking, reaching, wall following, and visual search, but voting, consumer choice, planning a two-week vacation, running a country, and so on.

(Clark 1997b: 179, hereafter: BT)

While it is true that Clark goes on to argue that 'biological reason' may offer more leverage here than one might expect, and while it is also true that his list of 'the most advanced and distinctive aspects of human cogni- tion' (voting, consumer choice, etc.) is somewhat tailored to fit the line he's about to take, it is emphatically not true that he is trying to hide real problems under some shiny new rug, or maintain that all aspects of cognition can be made to sleep in the same size bed.

It is all too easy to look back dismissively at Newell and Simon's 1957 prediction that, by 1967, a GOFAI system would have: (1) become the world's chess champion (unless the rules barred it from competition); (2) discovered and proven an important new mathematical theorem; and (3) written music accepted by critics as having considerable aesthetic value (Newell and Simon 1958). Their list too, of course, was highly tailored to what they thought they already knew how to do; and their closest call was off by a factor of four. But these predictions were made a scant eighteen months after the completion of the very first AI program (their own Logic Theorist); and that success was already more than anyone would have dared to dream even a generation before.

My point, like Clark's, is not to remember the shortfalls of GOFAI—after all, one-quarter out of three ain't bad in this business, and they're not done yet—but to remember the aspirations. Chess, theorem proving, and mu- sical composition may or may not be the most advanced aspects of human cognition, but they certainly are distinctive; and on none of them is any connectionist or dynamical artefact anywhere near the proficiency of GOFAI systems, even as of 1967. Rumelhart and McClelland's (1986) past-tense network is tantalizing in its error profiles; Sejnowski and Rosen- berg's (1987*a, b*) NETtalk does a remarkable job of mapping spelling to phonemes; Chalmers's (1990) passivization RAAM is at least as impressive as a dog on its hind legs. Yet, at century's end, no non-classical AI system can hold a candle to Winograd's 1972 SHRDLU as an interlocutor.

Needless (I trust) to say, I have not suddenly become a GOFAI evangelist. But giving credit as due is a salutary aid to modesty—and, in these instances, also a reminder of what it is we're really after (or, at least, an important part of it). To be sure, with each new beginning, we should target our early efforts wisely; and there is genuine wisdom in looking first where the light is best—or seems best at the moment. But let us never forget that the real topic of cognitive science is human cognition—including whatever that may turn out to encompass (body, world, language, history, dasein, ?). Dennett once asked: 'Why not the whole iguana?' The point, however, was to start with the whole, not to settle for the iguana.

Clark is, of course, very aware of the conspicuous differences between human cognitive capacities and those of even our nearest evolutionary cousins; and he is by no means a diehard foe of internal representations. But his deep appreciation of biological and other scientific results leads him to frame his thinking in a way that might be summed up with these three principles: (1) since we evolved from anthropoids not so long ago, our native endowments ('wetware') can't be all that different from theirs; (2) the fundamental macro capacities of vertebrate wetware are tunable dynamical couplings and rapid pattern-completion; and (3) the basic point of all cognition is the advantageous adjustment of behavior to environmental circumstances. Much of his writing—including but not limited to what he recommended we read for this workshop—amounts to a brilliant and often original exposition of just how powerful this framework can be. A great deal of that discussion, whether grounded in biological/physiological observations or laboratory simulations, naturally applies equally to people and (other) animals. After all, one of the guiding principles is that much of what is true of us, even as cognitive agents, is true of us because it is true of all vertebrates—or, at any rate, all primates. Moreover, whatever it is that is distinctive of us alone must be such that it could have been built on that common foundation with only rather modest physiological changes.

Thus, when Clark turns (in the chapters of *Being There* following the one to which he directed our attention—ch. 8), to the question of what differentiates us from other animals, he begins by reiterating the similarities, and only then locating what he sees as the essential difference.

In the remaining chapters, I shall tentatively suggest that there is no need to posit such a great divide [between detached human reason and the cognitive profiles of other animals], that the basic form of individual reason (fast pattern completion in multiple neural systems) is common throughout nature, and that where we human beings really score is in our amazing capacities to create and maintain a variety of special external structures (symbolic and social-institutional).

(*BT*: 179)

And, on the next page:

> Human brains...are not so different from the fragmented, special-purpose,
> action-oriented organs of other animals and autonomous robots. But we excel
> in one crucial respect: we are masters at structuring our physical and social
> worlds so as to press complex coherent behaviors from these unruly resources.
> ...Or, to look at it another way, it is the human brain plus these chunks of
> external scaffolding that finally constitutes the smart, rational inference engine
> that we call mind.   (*BT*: 180)

Now, I have a lot of sympathy with this—especially the last formulation.
But I would like to start with some not-so-sympathetic questions that
might motivate at least a different rhetorical emphasis. In the first place,
how do we tell a 'great divide' from a case in which things are 'not so
different'? Is there a great divide between a hunk of uranium a little under
critical mass and one a little over? How about between a universal Turing
machine and one that just moves any finite string six spaces to the left?
Obviously, it depends on which properties you attend to. So, which properties of brains should we attend to? Human babies, and no others, can
learn natural languages—primarily because of differences in their brains.
This strikes me as an enormous difference.

But is this more like the uranium case or the Turing machine case? That
is, is it just a threshold crossed by a quantitative increment in the same old
stuff, or is it a more basic structural difference? Clark seems committed to
the former. But why? I think the answer can be gleaned via a historical
parallel. How could Newell and Simon make their 1957 predictions with
such confidence and fanfare, and on the basis of so little evidence? I think
the reason is this. They knew that their systems could already do unprecedented things; it was clear they had barely scratched the surface of what
could be done by similar means; and they couldn't imagine anything else
(physically implementable) that could do anything cognitive at all. Likewise, the leading lights of today—including Clark—already know that
pattern-completion networks can do unprecedented things; it's clear that
they have barely scratched the surface of what such networks can do; and
they can't imagine anything else (neurally implementable) that could do
anything cognitive at all. (I trust it's obvious that this parallel is far from
unflattering.) It's equally obvious, however, that the parallel is meant to
give pause. I (like Dreyfus—another comparison that no one should find
unflattering) have no idea at all about what other mechanisms might be
implementable in neural wetware, let alone how to do it. But I think we

should pay serious heed to the above-scouted limitations of network models of linguistic competencies—*vis-à-vis* even SHRDLU (never mind the Turing test)—as seriously, indeed, as we note the limitations of SHRDLU itself and its successors.

Still, the capacity to learn and use natural languages is surely implementable somehow in human brains (or brains-cum-bodies, or brains-cum-bodies and words); and this is all that Clark's main point really depends on. For he wants to argue that language itself, and many other cultural artefacts (tangible and otherwise), are integral to human cognition and intelligence. That is, they are not merely products of our intelligence, and available to be employed by it, but are literally constitutive components of it, without which it could not exist as it does at all. It is important to emphasize the radicalness of this thesis. It's not just that our minds, residing somehow within our skulls, must, in order to reach their full potentials as minds, be shaped and informed by external, culturally preserved influences. Rather, our mentality itself is substantially external to our skulls, and even our bodies, both because it resides in part in communal practices, and because it resides in part in material objects (mostly artefacts) outside anybody's skull or body. (Of course, manual and other corporeal skills, which may reside in part within our bodies but outside our skulls, belong to the total picture as well.)

This is the thesis with which I am largely sympathetic. And—contrary to what some readers of my recent work might expect—I think that public language is its centerpiece. All the same, it seems to me that Clark's approach to these phenomena is oddly impoverished; and I think I know why. It derives from the fact that he comes to them from the direction of animal studies, brain research, and computer modeling. The trouble with animals, brains, and models is that none of them is actually a member of anything like a human community—nor, therefore, does any of them have a history (in the proper sense) or belong to a tradition. At the first order of description, the essence of each of these lies in public norms.

Now, before I take another breath, perhaps I had better stop a moment to stay the hounds at my flanks. Once, when I was discussing the distinctive importance of human communal norms, Franz de Waals said he'd be pleased to introduce me into one of his chimp communities, where, he assured me, I'd find myself 'normalized' real fast. No doubt, lacking other resources (and going along with the gag), I'd soon enough learn to take my turn with the food, and steer appropriately clear of the females. But comparing these and their ilk to the norms that structure a human society is like comparing an abacus to a computer, a kite to an airplane, or alarm calls to a language. To be sure, there are identifiable similarities, and maybe even ancestral relations; and these certainly bear reflection. But, I want to say, letting such thin and primitive analogies blind one to the far larger and more important differences is an even graver failing than overlooking the parallels altogether.

Clark's blindness, however, is in the other eye. To judge from what he says, he doesn't see the relevance of social normativity at all. Yet surely this, more than anything, is what distinguishes people from all the other animals—even if it is, in some sense, only a matter of (vast) degree, slowly accrued over the eons.   *Discussion point 1.1*

Consider how he structures his examples. Postponing language till the final chapter, he begins by pointing out certain respects in which business firms and other large organizations are actually more rational than individual people. For instance, they're better at maximizing profits, maximizing votes in an election, and so on, than individuals are at getting the most for the least in a supermarket. But note first that this sort of 'rationality'—quantitative cost-benefit maximizing—is just the sort of thing that trees, beehives, and suitably interpreted servo-mechanisms also excel at. And, as Clark would be the first to agree, they come to be good at it for the same reason: the poorer ones are selected out. But this is not at all what Aristotle meant when he called us rational animals, or Descartes when he said 'thinking things'.

Clark makes another observation about human social organizations, however: 'Where the external scaffolding of policies, infrastructure, and customs is strong and (importantly) is a result of competitive selection, the individual members are, in effect, interchangeable cogs in a larger machine' (*BT*: 182).

Not unlike bees in a hive, one initially supposes. But bees can only serve as cogs in one very specific larger 'machine', whereas people—and only people—can be members of a huge variety of different institutions and organizations, including quite a few at the same time. Now, why is that? The answer—incontestable, I think, once you attend to it—is that human beings can learn to abide by norms, mostly from their elders and peers. Indeed, to a large extent, they can't help it, not, mainly, because compliance is imposed upon them (though there's some of that), but because they are (as Clark might put it) norm-hungry. It is precisely by virtue of being 'normalized'—which is to say, standardized in highly specific ways—that people can reliably function as the institutional 'cogs' that Clark calls

them. Such normalizing is a pervasive and basic feature of humankind—
with only the faintest antecedents in any other surviving species—and it
has enormous survival value. (I suspect these last two facts are related:
once any population got sufficiently on board the normative bandwagon,
the competitive advantage of whoever had the most and best norms
was always sufficient to wipe out their nearest competitors.) *Discussion
point 1.2*

Now, there are various things to say about norms and evolution. First, of
course, the native wetware endowment of homo sapiens has to have
evolved so as to support our norm-susceptibility and norm-hungriness.
Accordingly, I should think that a prime topic for investigations of how
human intelligence is grounded in our distinctive brains would be the
neural implementation of our capacity for social normativity. Yet Clark
never mentions such a thing; nor, so far as I know, does anybody else. It's
just not on their biological—and simulation-oriented—radar screens.

A second important connection between social norms and evolution—
and one of which Dennett, at least, has long been aware—is that communal bodies of norms are themselves a powerful new medium of selective
evolution. Though its implementation is entirely different from that of
genetic evolution, the form of the mechanism is essentially the same. The
current generation of a community passes on to the next its own genetic
heritage, along with whatever minor alterations might have occurred
along the way. So, the space of possible 'normotypes' is slowly explored,
with less competitive variations (communal phenotypes) eventually
weeded out in the familiar way.

Now, this social-normetic medium of evolution is more complicated
than its genetic understorey, and in some ways better. It's more complicated because not only is there competition between communities (expressing the full phenotype), but there is also competition among
individuals within the communities (each expressing part of the phenotype). But it is often better because it is intrinsically faster: norms are just
more plastic than genes. Hence, for one thing, it is relatively easy for
advantageous normetic material to migrate from one communal organism
to another—thereby propagating without having to wait for the outcome
of phenotypic competition. And, for another, the greatly enhanced intelligence which normative structures in part enable (I'll get to that in a
moment) can itself be directed upon those very norms in ways that lead
to deliberate improvements in the normotype—which are then propagated, passed on, and preserved as usual.

Last April (at the New Orleans APA), Dennett (1999) pointed out that memes too can function as a medium of selective evolution, and, moreover, one that is plausibly more primitive than norms. Memes differ from norms in that they propagate and are passed on by imitation only, whereas with norms there is also the further mechanism of social pressure in favor of conformity. Thus, an individual may imitate or not, as the spirit moves her; but if she defies her community's norms, steps will typically be taken to bring her back into line. *Discussion point 1.3*

Surely Dennett is right that memes are more primitive than norms (and also older) inasmuch as they require qualitatively less by way of neural implementation. But I think they are also qualitatively less powerful as a medium of evolution—basically because they are too plastic. A signal advantage of conformism-enforced norms is that the structures of a community can rely on the fact that almost all its members will abide by almost all its norms (situationally parameterized, of course) almost all the time. This makes it feasible to have communal norms that are collectively advantageous only because various others are reliably in place. It wouldn't do for me to mimic you in accepting shells for my sheep if I couldn't count on the next guy to accept those shells in turn for his chickens—not to mention, count on everybody else to acknowledge that those chickens then belonged to me. So norms, unlike memes, can sustain an elaborate, interdependent social structure, with all the obvious advantages that that makes possible.

Before proceeding, I want to point out another subtle feature of social norms that I believe may have been highly consequential for the human race. Unlike memes (or habits or proclivities), norms have a kind of 'normative gravity'. To see what I mean, notice first that what become 'normalized' in a community are not so much behaviors as dispositions to behave. Conformist interventions (scolding or shunning, for instance) cannot alter a deviant act already done; but they can reduce that agent's tendency to deviate again. But normal behaviors (according to the same norm) are, of course, never exactly alike; rather, they are sufficiently alike to be, so to speak, within the same orbit. And, when an individual's dispositions stray from producing behavior within these orbits (that is, types), they are 'pulled back in'. That's what I mean by normative gravity.

Gravity, as any skyward glance reveals, abhors a uniform distribution, promoting instead tight clumps of matter, separated by large empty gaps. Tight clumping, however, with the complementary gaps, is one of the essential prerequisites of digitalness. Digitalness, as we all know, is a

great boon to certain kinds of computational and representational efficiency—in particular, the kinds we often call 'quasi-linguistic' or 'logical'.
But language is—by most lights, including Clark's—the crowning achievement of human evolution. It is, of course, a contemporary commonplace
that language is a norm-governed social institution. What I have been
suggesting in these two paragraphs is that social norms may have laid
the groundwork for language in a more basic way as well, by enabling the
digitalization of behavioral types.

What, then, does Clark say about language—what he calls 'the ultimate
artefact'? Everybody agrees, of course, that public language is extraordinarily valuable as a medium of communication—and, if written, also
recording—not only of facts, but also of requests, attitudes, instructions,
predictions, and so on. No doubt this is the primary explanation of its
original evolutionary advantage. But what Clark maintains—and I think
it's both a very good point and also convincingly argued—is that language
brings with it many other powerful advantages. For instance, if one has the
benefit of language, then one can 'talk oneself through' (perhaps by rehearsing prior instructions) the various steps of some complicated activity.
Indeed, the very description of the activity in words may be essential to the
process of breaking it down into a series of steps.

(We should not lose sight, of course, of Dreyfus's point that breaking an
activity down into a series of steps is sometimes a counter-productive
distortion; but neither should we lose sight of the fact that, in other cases,
it can be a tremendous asset.)

In the course of his discussion, Clark gingerly quarrels with a thesis of
Dennett's to the effect that the acquisition of language actually transforms
the character of the brain as a cognitive/computational engine. In particular, it converts (at least part of) the brain into a kind of serial processor
that, among other things, makes possible our specific sort of consciousness
and sense of self. Clark suggests on the contrary that, rather than effecting
a reorganization of the brain itself, language functions as a complementary
external tool that dramatically augments its native capacities. Or, to put it
another way that reflects a passage I quoted earlier, external language and
internal brain might better be thought of as together forming a single
larger cognitive engine with qualitatively new cognitive capacities.

I don't really want to take sides here, but it seems to me that much turns
on whether 'acquisition of language' is understood phylogenetically or
ontogenetically. It goes with my earlier complaint about the sorry state
of connectionist language systems that I am sympathetic to the suggestion

that the evolution of linguistic capability went hand-in-hand with important innovations in brain structure—including, perhaps, a certain kind of serialization. But an individual's learning of a language could, at most, complete the final stages of this process in some way tuned to its particular environment. All of this remains compatible, I hasten to add, with Clark's basic idea that the mind itself is 'implemented' in structures that extend well beyond the individual brain, including especially those such as language that are provided by society and culture.

Given all that I have agreed with, and the few further observations that I have tentatively proposed, I can't forbear in closing a short trot on my own current hobby-horse—the question of truth. Surely the emergence of language, and, in particular, of assertion, made the issue of truthfulness both possible and urgent in a new way. (I will simply leave aside here the delicate matter of truth outside linguistic contexts.) Obviously, no sooner is there the possibility of telling the truth than there is the possibility of lying. And no sooner is the latter possible than it will be actual—there's just too much to be gained by deceiving and getting away with for it not to be tried. And, therefore, right from the start, declarative discourse brings with it the issue of whom to believe and when. But I want to focus on another question of truth that I suspect didn't come into view until much later—perhaps not even until historical times. This is the question that hinges on the distinction between appearance and reality. Thus, it's one thing to suppose that someone (a speaker or reporter) is deceiving you—or has got things wrong. But it's quite another to suppose that the thing itself (right before your eyes) is deceiving you—or is somehow wrong. Of course, the two cases are easily confounded.

For instance, in ruses, traps, and disguises, things may not be as they appear; but the deception is still attributable to some agent's ill intent; and the invocation of spirits or demons can extend the same account to hallucinations and even dreams. Accordingly, I think, a simple culture can get along quite well without any appearance/reality distinction that goes beyond deliberate machinations.

Science, however, cannot, and for two related reasons. On the one hand, science looks for explanatory items and properties that operate, so to speak, 'behind the scenes', not detectable without special instruments. And, on the other, if you can't see or feel, even roughly, what your instrument is measuring, how do you know that it's measuring anything at all, not to mention measuring it correctly? Thus, it takes a far greater conceptual leap from the ordinary to say that everything consists of atoms in the void, or that a voltmeter measures something called 'potential difference', than to say that God created it all in six days, or reveals His plans in tea leaves and entrails.

So my question is about the conception of truth that science needs, not the one grounded in the trustworthiness of agents (though, of course, I don't mean that the former is relevant only to science). I call this newer conception objective truth. And the question is: How is it possible, and what does it depend on? And I think the first step of the answer is a variation on familiar triangulation arguments—not, however, from the perspectives of two perceivers, but rather from the results of two measurements or experiments, especially ones performed in two quite different ways. If we can measure potential difference with a voltmeter based on the magnetic field produced by a current through a known resistor, and also with one based on electrostatic repulsion, or stellar distances via annual parallax and also via spectral red shift, and if we consistently get the same answers both ways, then we know we're onto something.

But this answer depends on something else: we have to have a reason to believe that the disparate techniques ought to produce the same results, a reason, moreover, based on our understanding of what it is that we're measuring. That is, we need a theory. Life being what it is, however, scientists aren't always going to get consistent results; indeed, consistency in experimental results is actually hard to achieve. Instruments are hard to design and calibrate; experimental conditions are hard to control; errors in technique are hard to detect; and on and on. So, on what grounds do scientists persist in the face of empirical recalcitrance? To put it more pointedly, on what grounds do they reject what, on the face of it, is contrary evidence, claiming it to be 'bad data'? I think the answer is a kind of faith—or, to use a less loaded word, a kind of commitment to the overall theory they currently hold. Only on the basis of this theory can they actually 'triangulate' on their objects via distinct and disparate experiments. And only on the basis of multiple such triangulations can they reasonably identify some putative measurements as 'outliers', and thus plausibly unreliable. But that's just to make the distinction, among scientific results, between appearance and reality. Hence, the appearance/reality distinction—in regard to the new objective conception of truth—depends essentially on the kind of faith or commitment that investigators have in their (current) theories.

And this is the route back to cognitive science. I suggest that we can't really have understood the human mind—and, in particular, with regard to its very distinctive capacity (perhaps only a few thousand years old) to seek objective truth—until we have understood its capacity for faithful commitment. But this is quite different from anything like a belief or a desire, let alone competent negotiation of the immediate environment. This essential topic for cognitive science has, I think, not yet even made it to the scientific horizon. *Discussion point 1.4*

The Roots of 'Norm-Hungriness'

ANDY CLARK

I really loved Haugeland's comments, not least because they raised—clearly and precisely—a bunch of issues that I haven't got much (if any) idea how to resolve. Yet they are issues that are deeply relevant to this workshop and to the broader project of understanding mind and cognition.

I want to pick up on just two of the issues Haugeland raises, namely: Is there a 'great divide' between human cognition and simple animal cognition? And, Why do I have so little to say about the issues of norms and normativity—am I really 'norm-blind', and if I am, is that a problem?

Before proceeding to all this, however, let me just state that Haugeland captures my general orientation very well indeed. The three claims that he ascribes to me are indeed ones that I endorse, and that shape much of my work. I do indeed hold that (1) our native wetware cannot be that deeply different from that of other primates, (2) that what that wetware best supports are fluent perceptuo-motor couplings of organism and environment and (3) that cognition itself is, as a result, profoundly action-oriented. In seeking to understand and explain what is most distinctive about *human* cognition, I thus lay great emphasis on the wider web of supporting technologies (including the ur-technology of public language) in which our biological brains go about their business. The obvious caricature, that humans are just chimps with filofaxes, is thus not too far off the mark.

On the face of it, this is just crazy. You can give a chimp a filofax, but you can't make it plan a vacation or run a country. And many of Haugeland's worries, it seems to me, are rooted in just that kind of discomfort. I am thinking here of his probing concerning the size and location of the 'cognitive divide' and his positive suggestions concerning biological innovation and 'norm-hungriness'.

Concerning the great divide (presence or absence thereof), Haugeland offers two nice cases for comparison. The first involves a hunk of uranium that is just under critical mass, and the second hunk that is just over. Here we seem to confront a genuine threshold that is nevertheless crossed courtesy of a simple increment in amount of the same old stuff. The second case involves a special purpose Turing machine that performs a single function: it takes any finite string and moves it six spaces (cells) to the left, as compared to a Universal Turing Machine capable of implementing any computable function. The difference here is, it seems, more basic and structural. The second is a deeply different machine, not just a larger version of the first one.

The human infant, Haugeland asserts, has the only (kind of) brain on the planet that can really learn a full-blooded, human-style language. If we lay this brain against the brain of, say, a chimpanzee, is the difference more like that displayed in the first (uranium) or second (Turing Machine) case? Haugeland's worry is that (he thinks) I depict it as more like the first case: the same old resources, but targeted on a new class of entities (words). Haugeland's own view, by contrast, is that there must be a major structural difference at work, something more akin to the deep architectural differences displayed in the second case.

Haugeland thus questions a thesis I have lately called 'Cognitive Incrementalism'. This is the idea that you get genuine, human-style cognition by simply adding an incremental sequence of bells and whistles to a computational architecture dedicated to pattern-recognition and perceptuo-motor control. But here's the catch: I don't count myself as a dyed-in-the-wool adherent to cognitive incrementalism; I don't think that we can understand what makes us who and what we are by taking simple cases of coupled organism-environment unfolding and adding a few tweaks and nudges. And this for the very reason Haugeland notes, namely, the need to get to grips with the distinctive phenomena that (in part) motivated the development of the original ideas of Good Old Fashioned Artificial Intelligence in the first place—phenomena such as the ability to track the non-existent (unicorns), the distal (the Eiffel Tower), and the abstract (acts of charity). Understanding these key capacities requires us to understand a genuinely different form of cognitive architecture, a different machine, in roughly the sense of the Turing Machine case mentioned above.

But (and here's where I think Haugeland's example cases mislead us) why suppose that the differences that *make* it a different machine lie largely in the head? The underlying assumption, which I think we must reject, is that the cognitive machine just *is* the machine in the individual head. My suspicion is thus that there *is* a deep structural divide at work, but that it is one that becomes visible only once we attend not just to the brain but to the larger brain-cognitive environment coalition itself, paying special attention to the role of language and other representational tools.

One major challenge, if you are tempted by this kind of story, is (as Haugeland points out) to account for the pivotal human capacity to acquire and use public language, and to develop other cognitive props and scaffolding, *without* first positing a major structural change inside the head. There are, obviously, a number of popular bootstrapping stories that might help hereabouts. Maybe some relatively minor neurological change allows a simple combinational language to get a foothold in human understanding, and the resultant minimally extended machine provides the niche for a slightly more advanced understanding, and so on. (Dennett's image of cranes building bigger and bigger cranes is an especially apt one for such a process.) But there is an additional, potentially very powerful, but much less widely noticed process that may also be contributing to all this, and which I'd like to at least gesture at here. It is the process, convincingly described by Terry Deacon (1997) in his book, *The Symbolic Species*, of what might be termed 'reverse fitting'. More specifically, it is the idea that public language may be easily learned because it (the language) has adapted to the biases and proclivities of human users (rather than the typical story in which our brains are adapted for language). To clarify this, think of a language as itself a replicating and mutating entity that evolves by processes of variation and differential selection and where easy acquisition by a human 'host' is a prime fitness parameter. *Discussion point 1.5*

Deacon's idea, then, seems to be that there is a small but crucial biological change that allowed multi-item, combinational languages to be initially learnable by us, and that once this foothold was secure, the other process (of reverse fitting) ushered in potent additional means of change and refinement.

Now Haugeland's suggestion, I think, is quite different: it is much more highly brain-oriented. The idea seems to be that the chimp (for example) lacks a kind of rampant 'norm-hungriness' and that this difference is rooted in a neural innovation for normivorousness. As a result of that innovation we and we alone are nature's voracious normivores. ***Discussion point 1.6***

Haugeland's idea is that our rampant norm-generation and norm-sensitivity is the crucial difference that marks the great divide, and that the neural innovation for norm-hungriness is something that brain science itself ought to (but doesn't) target. He thus worries, graciously but firmly, that I (along with the bulk of my cognitive science colleagues) am blind to the very thing that is most distinctive about human reason. 'To judge from what he [Clark] says, he doesn't see the relevance of social normativity at all. Yet surely this, more than anything, is what distinguishes people from all the other animals' (Haugeland, this volume, p. 30).

I'm thus blind, Haugeland fears, to the very arena in which language makes its most distinctive and empowering contribution: as a tool for the creation, refinement, and development of communal norms. ***Discussion point 1.7***

I plead guilty, but without remorse. For the view I have come to hold depicts norm-sensitivity and norm-hunger as *secondary* effects of our linguistically enhanced capacity to target biologically basic processing resources on increasingly abstract and higher-order domains. Now this needs a *lot* of unpacking and illustrating. But I'll have to make do with a bare-bones summary (plus example) here.

The first move is to show that all known learning algorithms (both classical and connectionist) flounder in the face of a certain kind of complexity in the training data (see Clark and Thornton 1997). Roughly speaking, they pick up on simple (rather than highly complex or relational) statistical regularities. The second move is to suggest that the main trick for learning about higher-order regularities is to recode the training data so that complex hidden regularities emerge as simple surface regularities. ***Discussion point 1.8***

Here's an example, which I borrow from Chris Thornton. Imagine a system with feature detectors for Ace, King, Queen, and so on looking for regularities in poker hands. It will find AAA and so on. But what about the more complex relational regularities, for example, that Q J 10 9 8 and A K Q J 10 (mixed suits) are both instances of 'straights'? Or again, compare learning about the number of *sets* in a hand. The trick to learning about the more complex regularities is first to objectify the simpler ones, that is to label certain sequences as 'straights', 'sets', and so on. At that point, the complex higher-order problems (of counting sets etc.) become reduced to simple first-order problems relative to a new domain of objects. Complex feature detectors are thus just simple feature detectors whose domains include other feature detectors. (All this should put you in mind of Elman's lovely work on incremental learning in the 'Starting Small' paper, 1991). So of course you need the basic feature detection first.

The third move is to display public language itself as a kind of 'found encoding'—a class of 'found items' (as Dennett might say) that serve to render such complex regularities as simpler objects for further thoughts. That's why I don't see the cognitive benefits of language use as purely, or even mainly, communicative (see my 1998b). The deep benefit is the provision of this new and potent class of cognitive objects able to fold in complex regularities. *Discussion point 1.9*

Here's an example. Thompson, Oden, and Boyson (1997) is a study of problem-solving in chimps (*Pan troglodytes*). What Thompson *et al.* show is that chimps trained to use an arbitrary plastic marker (a yellow triangle, say) to designate pairs of identical objects (such as two identical cups), and to use a different marker (a red circle, say) to designate pairs of different objects (such as a shoe and a cup), are then able to learn to solve a new class of abstract problems. This is the class of problems—intractable to chimps not provided with the symbolic training—involving recognition of *higher-order* relations of sameness and difference. Thus presented with two (different) pairs of identical items (two shoes and two cups, say) the higher-order task is to judge the pairs as exhibiting the *same* relation, that is to judge that you have two instances of *sameness*. Some examples of such higher-order judgments (which even human subjects can find hard to master at first) are:

Cup/Cup   Shoe/Shoe
= 2 instances of first-order sameness
= an instance of higher-order sameness

Cup/Shoe   Cup/Shoe
= 2 instances of first-order difference
= an instance of higher-order sameness

Cup/Shoe   Cup/Cup
= 1 instance of first-order difference and 1 of first-order sameness
= an instance of higher-order difference

The token-trained chimps' success at this difficult task, it is conjectured, is explained by their prior experience with external tokens. For such experience may enable the chimp, on confronting, for example, the pair of identical cups, to retrieve a mental representation of the *sameness* token (as it happens, a yellow triangle). Exposure to the two identical shoes will likewise cause retrieval of that token. At that point, the higher-order task is effectively reduced to the simple, lower-order task of identifying (internal representations of) the two yellow plastic *tokens* as 'the same'.

Experience with external tags and labels thus enables the brain itself, by *representing* those tags and labels, to solve problems whose level of complexity and abstraction would otherwise leave us baffled—an intuitive result whose widespread applicability to human reason is increasingly evident. Learning a set of tags and labels (which we all do when we learn a language) is, we may thus speculate, rather closely akin to acquiring a new perceptual modality. For like a perceptual modality, it renders certain features of our world concrete and salient, and allows us to target our thoughts (and learning algorithms) on a new domain of basic objects. This new domain compresses what were previously complex and unruly sensory patterns into simple objects. These simple objects can then be attended to in ways that quickly reveal further (otherwise hidden) patterns, as in the case of relations-between-relations. And of course the whole process is deeply iterative—we coin new words and labels to concretize regularities that we could only originally conceptualize thanks to a backdrop of other words and labels. The most powerful and familiar incarnation of this iterative strategy is, perhaps, the edifice of human science itself.   *Discussion point 1.10*

The thing that I really care about, then, is this process of objectification in which a set of simple tokens stands in for complex features and relations and makes available new, quasi-perceptual, spaces for reasoning.   *Discussion point 1.11*

The final move, the one I am least confident of, is to then depict the much-vaunted space of norms and reasons as a space that is, if you like, artificially constructed using such tokens and stand-ins: a space populated by tokens for complex and otherwise invisible features, relations, and commonalities. Reason-giving discourse is, paradigmatically, a matter of negotiating good trajectories through this space. The more higher-order the space is, the more peculiar to us the kinds of norms involved will seem to be. Thus consider as a partial parallel humanity's ongoing exploration of *financial space*. The first move is (let's say) the creation of stocks and shares. But with these new objects in hand, we conceive and create the notion of futures, and options, and then options on futures, and so on (see Arthur 1994). We thus confront a cascade of activity that at once creates and explores a financial space. Moral space, I suggest, is similarly constructed. We may see moral (and, generally, norm-involving) discourse and activity as emergent from

(1) a biologically basic capacity for simple pattern recognition and what Dennett (1996) calls ABC learning and (2) the opportunity, largely provided by the found resources of public language, to target those capacities on a new ('locally effective' as Smith might say) 'virtual' realm populated by 'entities' such as rights, duties, and obligations (for a nice account, see Wellman 1999). *Discussion point 1.12*

So I think that you create and explore these spaces at the same time. I think in some way that's true of all the spaces of reason. I hope that that doesn't make me some kind of woolly relativist or non-realist, because I also think that the spaces we create are constrained by the way the world is. *Discussion point 1.13*

Now recall (at last!) Haugeland's suggestion that cognitive science should be investigating the neural basis of norm-hungriness ('a prime topic for investigations...would be the neural implementation of our capacity for social normativity. Yet Clark never mentions such a thing...' Haugeland, p. 31).

I don't treat this as a neuroscientific target because I just don't believe there needs to be any *neural* innovation which makes us more norm-hungry than other animals. Instead, I locate the difference (which leads to the explosion of norms and which *does* stand in need of cognitive scientific explanation) in the availability of more and more complex 'virtual worlds' in which to move, act, and think. So the difference, for me, is that the social, legal, and political landscapes visible to human thought and reason are (partly due to the pattern-objectifying effects of words, labels, and language) much more numerous, abstract, and multi-layered than those visible to non-linguistically empowered thought and reason. Operating in these rarified landscapes, our biologically basic capacities for pattern-recognition and social navigation come to look like a mysterious engagement with a *sui generis* 'space of reasons'. In fact, we're not so much norm-hungry as unusually norm-bombarded.

Haugeland ends with some fascinating and wonderfully original comments on trust, objective reality, and faithful commitment. I wonder, in passing, whether there might be a dimension of faithful commitment closely akin to a kind of cognitive blindness—an inability to see alternatives, leading to inertia. But of course the *other* thing that Haugeland is highlighting here is not simple resistance but the ability to treat a commitment *as* a commitment: to see oneself as bound in some way. This process, it seemed to me, might involve yet another kind of objectification. *Final discussion*

Discussion

1.1
p. 30 CLARK What would be nice examples of that, social normativity, just so that I get a context?

HAUGELAND Oh, rituals, customs, clothing, linguistic conventions.

CLARK And in the chimp case, what sorts of things did Franz de Waals have in mind as chimp norms?

HAUGELAND Oh, well there are things about whom you can groom and when, and where you're allowed to go, when, and which females you can cavort or consort with, and food patterns, and there are special places, places to poop and places to sleep, and stuff like that that are communally established.

CLARK But you think both that the chimps obey norms, and that we do?

HAUGELAND I would much prefer not to admit that chimps have norms. But I think actually that I don't get to do that.

CLARK That was one of the things that I didn't get quite clearly, whether you were sort of saying, OK, we're very different to the chimps in respect of having norms, or, we're not very different in respect of having norms, we've just got more of them.

HAUGELAND We're very different in just how much of our lives is norm-governed. How much of our lives and behavior—

SMITH And also the character of the norms.

HAUGELAND Well, there are structural interdependencies and perhaps compounding and things like that which make qualitative differences.

1.2
p. 31 DENNETT Wait a minute. Is that a group selection point you're making?

HAUGELAND Yeah, group or species.

DENNETT You've got a big limit on your credit card. That's a very expensive assumption you're making there, when you take on a group selection hypothesis of a very strong sort—

HAUGELAND Well, OK, I want to hear about that, but among the better norms will be a tradition of making better tools, for instance.

CLARK So is that what makes a norm better? What makes a norm better is that it makes people that have the norm do better?

HAUGELAND Well, as we all know 'better' can mean lots of things, but that's one sense of it, it's the same way as one talks about better organization in animals, it's just transposed.

CLARK It's just because often when I'm talking with people that seem impressed by norms, what they're impressed by is the fact that you can't unpack norms in terms of any notion of better that I can normally get to grips with.

HAUGELAND Well, you certainly cannot explain normativeness in terms of betterness, but that doesn't mean you can't evaluate bodies of norms as better or worse on any of a variety of scales.

DENNETT Why can't you do the former?

HAUGELAND Because there's a completely different etiology of the norms. And the norms are grounded in imitation and censoriousness and a dominant tradition. They could be very counter-productive, and sometimes they are.

SMITH But you're not ever going to allow evolution to be the bedrock here?

HAUGELAND Well, it's the bedrock. It's like carbon is the bedrock too. It's a bedrock of some of the stuff. It isn't going to be the measure of truth. The point about commitment is that it allows you to leave behind governance by the norm. It allows you take responsibility. You can't leave behind being governed by norms, but you can leave behind norms as the only governance.

CLARK Then there are cases when memes and norms kind of phase together. You know, where someone is being introduced to an academic discipline or something. The student is pretty well required to take on board some of the memes that are passing around to get going. That seems like a case where it's just both, to me. 1.3 p. 32

HAUGELAND Well, a meme is just a superset.

CUMMINS Andy's case is just a case where they happen to have norms about memes. But here's one big difference. You combine two genes, you don't get a new gene. You combine two memes, you often do get a new meme. And so the combinatorics of it are really very different. There is a kind of directedness to memes that introduces variability in memes into the scheme in ways that are very non-random.

DENNETT Very non-random, yes, but, even there, don't overstress the differences. Gene combination is now realized to be a much more ubiquitous phenomenon than it used to be thought. But the directedness is still really important. Genetic engineering is a special case of natural selection, where the selecting environment consists of genetic engineers in their laboratories and all the rest. And you get directed mutation, in effect. Memetic engineering has been around for a long time. But, before there was memetic engineering there was still memetic transmission by essentially clueless...

HAUGELAND Carriers.

DENNETT Carriers; our ancestors who were engaging in sort of folkloric transmission and clueless revision. But now we're deeply into memetic engineering, and we have been for a long time. But that, we should recognize, is a new phenomenon in our species, in the same way that genetic engineering is a very recent addition to genetic trajectories. It is a rather striking point. We've had genetic evolution going on on this planet for close on 4 billion years, and you've only had, for twenty years or so, a particular subspecies of that, which is genetic engineering. But now, it just changes the rules of what's possible. There are now plants that glow in the dark because they have firefly genes spliced into them, and that could not have arisen by the old transmission route. The same thing is true in memetic recombination. But it wasn't always true. And in the early days of memetic transmission, it was much more, as it were, classically Darwinian. At least that's what I would argue.

HAUGELAND That sounds pretty plausible.

1.4   CLAPIN I couldn't understand the second of the two cases being con-
p. 36   founded.

HAUGELAND I'm talking about the—as one might say—the conceptual development of the species. The possibility of deliberately fudged reports, false reports, is simultaneously there, and therefore the problem of judging, not just what happened, but the report, is this trustworthy—trustworthiness is actually an older notion than truth.

SMITH Suppose that Rob and I are paddling down the river and I say, 'Hey there's John,' and Rob says, 'You stupid goon, that's a piece of driftwood.' Surely that's pretty easy, isn't it?

HAUGELAND Yes, that's a misperception.

CUMMINS He's talking about cases like the straw in the water, where they look bent and even when you figure it out, they keep on looking bent, but you know it isn't right.

HAUGELAND The moon still looks bigger on the horizon even when you know better.

SMITH Sure, I understand that, but I don't think that you need that in order to have truth.

CUMMINS Well, you have to have norms of objectivity in place that make it intelligible to say that the illusion persists. That is, it's not changing shape as I pull it out of the water, and stuff like that.

HAUGELAND Another way to judge the truth of a proposition than just going and checking again. There's got to be another consideration; in effect, triangulating on whether it's true or not. If you don't have that other consideration there's nothing to do but check again.

SMITH I don't think this is so different from misperception. If I think it's John, and Rob says it's driftwood, I don't just say I'm going to go back exactly to where I was, and look from exactly the same angle. I'd sort of look around or something, or go closer.

CUMMINS Yeah, but think about what that amounts to. Let me just play John advocate for a minute here. I don't believe it, but, just think about it. You gotta think that you're looking at the same thing but from different angles—

HAUGELAND You've got to know that it couldn't have been driftwood and suddenly have become John.

CUMMINS That's right. You gotta have enough normativity in place so that going back and looking again is an intelligible thing to do in this situation.

SMITH Right. That's exactly my point. That's exactly why I don't think misperception is so mild.

CUMMINS No, but the point is that you can, that it's the reaction to misperception that's the issue here.

SMITH Well, what I'm trying to say is I would have thought that we actually use pretty sophisticated strategies for resolving misperception, including at least inchoate forms of real norms, real objectivity, and so on and so forth. I'm agreeing with you, I actually think it's tremendously impressive what one does to correct misperception like that. And I would have thought that that would be conceptually simpler than dealing with deceit.

CUMMINS But the case with the straw in the water is interesting, because going back and looking again just doesn't help, just isn't relevant.

CLARK So the really sophisticated achievement is to be able to say, that despite all appearances, something isn't as it seems.

HAUGELAND That's an illustration of it, that's a way into the topic of why objectivity is another question than deciding which or who are the most reliable reporters, and whom to believe, and if we all agree then its settled. It's a different question from that.

DENNETT I have a dog, let's say, and, if I'm like Ulysses, I've been away for a long time. And I come back, and I play a trick on old Argos.[3] I have a wax copy of my head, I have clothes that have my scent on it, and so forth. And I arrange to plant this out in the field where the dog will see it. And the dog sees it and comes running out wagging its tail and barking and then it freaks out. And it checks and it checks and it sniffs and it sniffs and it looks and it looks and growls, and it does a whole lot of stuff. Now, if I understand you right here, you're saying that—and I think that I agree with you—absolutely nothing Argos can do counts as what we can do, which is, deciding that—no, appearances to the contrary, this just isn't Ulysses.

HAUGELAND Well, surely Argos is going to get tired, dejected, and go away. So, I can't pretend that that won't happen. And that is going to be, among other things, a loss of his long-lost master.

CUMMINS But you know what, the thing is, the chance is that he's going to do the very same thing tomorrow, and the next day.

HAUGELAND But not forever though.

CUMMINS This is where I'm going to get off this train. But, the idea of the illusion that persists in spite of all of these things... you've got a whole British empiricist philosophy based on the idea that a persistent illusion is the real thing. It's good enough until the real thing comes along.

CLAPIN But, why does language help you get on top of that?

CUMMINS Well, it's not language so much. It's norms that help you get on top of that, and language just helps you with norms. I think that's the line.

HAUGELAND Well, language helps you with articulation. I want to say a little bit more about Argos. I don't think Argos can go out enthusiastic-

---

[3] [See also Dennett on Smith, this volume, section 5.1.4, and Dennett, *Kinds of Minds* (1996: 113–16)—ed.]

ally to greet Ulysses as he sees it, and do anything that does the job of saying, I was wrong, I was fooled. All that can happen is, he can be, well, driven back into another state, and lose the happiness.

DENNETT Now, I think this case is actually nicely pivotal, because it helps me see a burden which I think you've set and I don't know how you'd meet it. It would be nice now to know what the cash value is of the difference of the state the dog can go into—the disillusioned state—and the state that a person can go into, which isn't just that the person can talk about it and can articulate it in words, because that's for free, we've got that. The dog can't say it, he can't say it to himself, he can't say it to anybody else. Now, that's not enough. What I want to see is, what it is that, in virtue of being able to say it, if that's the way the story goes, what further competence does the state have? What's the difference between the state a person can go into, from the state that the dog can go into . . . ?

HAUGELAND OK, well, first, let's see what it is that the person can do that the dog can't, setting aside why it's a good thing to be able to do that. And I do not accept the burden of having to explain what this would be without making use of the fact that people have language.

DENNETT Fine, but you have to go beyond the fact that you can't talk about it.

HAUGELAND Well, I have to say, what they can say, for which there could be no counterpart unless you can say it. And what they can say is, 'I thought it was Ulysses, but it wasn't' or 'It looks like Ulysses, but it isn't.' 'So-and-so thinks it's Ulysses, but it isn't. She's wrong. I was wrong. I would be wrong if I fell for what it looks like now.'

CLARK So does that whole class of things fall into this category, that, roughly, you can say the dog can make a new judgment, but it can't judge it's own judgments?

HAUGELAND Each of the examples I gave had that form.

DENNETT Meta.

HAUGELAND Yeah. I'm leery of making it be the possibility of going meta. Maybe that's right. Or maybe it presupposes it and there's more.

CUMMINS I think the answer to Dan's question is, not only can you say all of those things, but you can make it stick. Words are cheap, right? The point is: what has to be in place for it to be possible to make it stick when you say that?

HAUGELAND That's right. I can undertake to show that, although it looks like Ulysses it isn't, or I can undertake to show that, although you think

it's Ulysses, you're wrong. And I can do that with actions or I can do
that by articulating reasons. And here's a way I can convince you it's
not Ulysses: by going up and knocking on it and it sounds hollow; that
might convince you it's not Ulysses. I can also convince you it's not
Ulysses by reminding you that we left Ulysses in chains, not twenty
minutes ago, ten miles from here.

DENNETT And it's impossible blah blah blah; yeah.

CLARK Is this where we cross the great divide?

HAUGELAND A big difference between us and the animals? Yes. What I'm
trying to talk about now is, I believe something quite different from
that, that doesn't automatically come with language but is made possible by language, later.

DENNETT A little digression, see if anybody agrees with me, but this
reminds me of something that has been tantalizing me for years.
Somewhere David Lewis contrasts *in sensu composito* and *in sensu
diviso* generalizations.[4] And here's how the contrast goes. Claim (not
Lewis's): animals are only capable of believing general propositions *in
sensu composito*. That is, consider that case of learning that all orange
mushrooms are toxic. What the dog can learn, perhaps learning from
training from its mother, is the disposition, whenever you see an orange
mushroom, to shun it. That is, the disposition to acquire a particular
'this is toxic' belief, whenever encountering a particular orange mushroom.

SMITH 'Any' instead of 'all'.

DENNETT There's no way that it can get in a state of believing all orange
mushrooms are toxic, which is a different state, and the Ulysses case
had a similar flavor to it. Argos has lots of, as it were, the right
dispositions, *vis-à-vis* this dummy in the field that smells right and so
forth, but there's a thing it can't get its head around, which we can get
our heads around. The difference between having an unbounded disposition to believe particulars of a certain ilk, and believing the universal quantification, is that you can treat the belief in the second case as
an object in its own right, and can build with it, and can even use it as a
step in inference. That is, it's detachable in a way that your disposi-
tional state is not. The point is, if you've simply got the disposition,
then you don't have a representation. You've just got the disposition to

---

[4] [In *Convention* (Lewis 1969: 64–8 and 183–4). Lewis credits Abelard with the distinction—
ed.]

make representations under particular circumstances. And in the other case you've got a representation which you can then—

CUMMINS I don't like this at all. This sounds like a meta point to me.

DENNETT I think it is.

SMITH Let me try to put my finger on Dan's intuition. Meta is cheap. It may be that what's expensive is not going meta; what's expensive is having an object-level object to go meta on.

DENNETT That's exactly my point.

CUMMINS All right. It just seems much clearer to me in the bent straw case, for some reason.

SMITH So it's the objectification of the belief, it's not the meta-representation.

CLARK I think that's right.

DENNETT Yes, exactly.

HAUGELAND I can't imagine what that could mean.   1.5

CLARK I only know of a few concrete exemplars of stuff like that, one is   P. 39
just a little simulation. It was by Hare and Elman [1995] and you have a connectionist network that is trained on Old English and it has to learn the verb forms, I think. The system is trained, although not quite to perfection. So it goes through a period of training, and then you stop it. You then use its current performance to train the next generation of connectionist network, and you then use that performance to train the next one. What Hare and Elman found is that over time, they actually saw the kinds of transitions towards new verb structures that were found in the transition between old English and new English, most of which were simplifications, and one or two of which were actually irregularizations, since it's actually beneficial to certain kinds of connectionist learning to have little spots of grouped irregulars—

CUMMINS If I remember this, in particular you start to get rid of inflection.

CLARK Yes, inflection seems to go down. It's a very small case but it is a case where it looks very much as if what you end up with is a cultural tool that is going to be learned by connectionist networks, such that the tool itself is clearly evolving so as to be more easily acquirable by networks like that over time. So OK, there are no unbiased learning machines. Human brains are highly biased. But if you can get the product to fit the pre-existing biases, then it can look like Chomsky was right, although he wasn't. Instead of an innate language acquisition device you've just got innate biases to which the language itself is very neatly tailored.

HAUGELAND Well, it's not hard to believe that language is such that it's learnable and usable by us. I mean it must be that. And it's not much harder to believe that there are directions in language trajectories that are sort of consistent. It's very hard to believe that you can talk about language separate from us, as if it came along and found us and needed us and so adapted to us. That doesn't seem to make much sense.

DENNETT Language can get up and going at a time when infection of new human brains with language was a much dicier thing. It could still get up and going, and then language could evolve to become easier and easier so that it could infect brains much more swiftly, and more brains. That's just the crudest way of putting this.

CLARK I think you do have to be a bit less crude than that, because you need also to see constant pressure for complexification, as simple languages make possible more complex life forms that will reward the presence of more complex language. There's pressure to complexification, then the acquirability thing in turn pressures for simplification.

CUMMINS And there's the usual sources of variation, English being a wonderful case where you've got a lot of recombination messing everything up again.

DENNETT John, just take some of the simplest and most peripheral features of language, such as whether or not pitch is going to play a marked role, and think that whether or not pitch plays a marked role really depends on how good brains are at distinguishing pitch and keeping pitch separate. And how well pitch information is transmitted over long distances, when you're shouting, when you're speaking *sotto voce*, and so forth. And then you begin to realize that a language might start off using pitch to play a very important role, and then that role could become problematic and be simply replaced without anybody's conscious decision by some other more salient, more reliably distinct or discriminated feature, and it can take thousands of years for the sort of R&D to optimize the set of physical features, especially since the selection pressure is, of course, an actuarial phenomenon. It's probabilistic, and it's going on in many different places all over the world. It should be obvious, I think, that language is a much more labile and volatile thing than a brain is. You only make a new brain every fifteen or twenty years, but language can change on a week-to-week basis if there's pressure for it.

CLARK Yes, once you think of language as a kind of largely external technological tool as you were earlier saying, then you would expect changes of the kind that we see in other external technological tools, like video recorders. The early ones were a bit horrible to use, and they're getting easier to use, and that's because the ones that proliferate are the ones that are easier to use. It's just that.

HAUGELAND I don't have any problem with all of that. I don't have any problem with English being a richer and more powerful language now than it was a thousand years ago, partly because of imports and partly because of new things to talk about, and partly because of the ubiquity of writing, and a whole bunch of things. It's hard for me to believe, though, that a pressure towards the easiness of acquiring a natural language,

CUMMINS And use.

HAUGELAND acquiring and using it—but where the easiness is a function of the neural structure, and so not environmental factors—hasn't made essentially all of the essential decisions long before a thousand years ago.

CLARK Don't be overwhelmed by that Old English to New English example; that's just to show the possibility of evolution in cultural objects, as driven by the existing biases in a learning device. In some way I'm deeply interested in biased learning. All learning devices have to be biased and somehow that's the key to successful learning. Getting the biases right would be the key to really successful learning but since we're not God, we don't know what all the biases should be. So instead we come to learn the kinds of things that we have the right biases for. It's a rather pessimistic view of the bits of the universe that are going to be visible to human reason, but that's OK.

SMITH There are also some funny things, like 'input': it's the only 'np' in English, because in fact 'np' morphs to 'mp', but someone just put 'in' and 'put' together and we haven't had time to . . . it'll be 'imput' in 100 years. So recombinance could keep throwing up stuff that just needs, as it were, mashing down into the simplification. That seems to me to be ongoing.

HAUGELAND I agree with that, that seems plausible. And there are long-term trends in vowel changes and in consonant changes, over Indo-European and other languages as far back as they can track them. And it'll go through this to this to this to this. And you can locate—you find a text, you can locate it using this, you can reconstruct the etymologies of current words by running the changes back and you say, oh, that's what it came from back there.

DENNETT And now, with that factual premise out, I have to grind my memes axe one time here. There is a lamentable tendency among those who face this fact—the fact that pronunciation shifts such as those predicted by Grimm's Law occur—to ask themselves: How do these shifts benefit people? Why are these changes adaptive to people? where they're thinking about the purposes of people and their aims, and so forth. Here's the fundamental memetic point. It might be the wrong question. The right question might be, How does it benefit the language? That is, as a replicating device, it may not make it easier for us to communicate, it may not help us to communicate faster or better or more efficiently. All it may do is make that habit a more robust replicator. It may be a bad habit. It may be a positively bad habit, like putting 'fuckin'' in between every other word. It may not be useful, but it may just replicate because it exploits a bias in the hardware that it needs to replicate. And it may just replicate the way a virus does.

HAUGELAND This is the point I made about norms and goodness.

DENNETT Exactly, that's why I say you're a memeticist without realizing it. Bad norms can flourish just fine especially in a domain of censoriousness.

1.6 HAUGELAND I'll buy that.
p. 40

1.7 HAUGELAND Oh, other way around, actually. Norms are what really
p. 40   make language possible.

CLARK OK, I know you think that. Now I'm going to argue it's the other way around. So I want to suggest that this may be to put the cart before the horse.

CUMMINS Why can't it just be both? I mean clearly some norms could make language possible, and language could make some norms possible, but this isn't an either/or—

CLARK You need to be as norm-hungry as a chimp in order for language to get going. But I don't think that the difference that makes humans special is a wetware difference in norm-hungriness. I think norm-hungriness is a secondary effect of getting language going. And I think that that's diametrically opposed to John's position.

HAUGELAND Yes.

1.8 CUMMINS Now, you know, it depends on what you mean by recoding.
p. 40   I mean another trick is to speed it up or slow it down. For example, a good trick for teaching music students about the structures of certain

kinds of classical pieces that they can't hear, is to speed it up. And it just pops out, anyone can hear it then, right?

CLARK To speed it up amounts to recoding relative to the biases of that device.

DENNETT In the same way that changing the medium does that, making it visual or making it auditory, those are recodings, too.

CLAPIN But it's not much more than zooming out, right? It's just you're seeing some structure because its more salient when you zoom in or zoom out.

SMITH But rendering the relational local is one of the things that I have long felt is in the bag of tricks of programming. I think there are enormous amounts of that. It's interesting because I thought about that at lunch after you [Cummins] had said 'What else could there be other than isomorphism?' Right. Rendering relational things local, right, so that the consistency of a database, which is a relational fact, you turn in into a predicate letter C, and boom—you have an effect you can't get relations to drive.

CUMMINS Well, that's what I think too, but I think it started out as a communicative thing, and it got exapted for these purposes. 1.9 p. 41

CLARK It did. No doubt about that.

DENNETT It's used as labels.

CLAPIN So what's the difference between the third move and the poker hand—calling a poker hand a straight?

CLARK Nothing, really, it's just that here I'm talking about public language in particular, and saying look, it does the same kind of thing. It reduces complex regularities to objects, on which you can then train the same old pattern-completing, pattern-detecting devices to detect more regularities, then you can create more objects, and once you've objectified them you can do the trick again—that's the story.

CLAPIN So applying the second move to language, is the third move?

CLARK Yes, right.

SMITH I would agree with you, but I would suggest that rendering locally effective an abstractional relation is actually a better way to describe it than recoding. Because the problem is, I can come up with a zillion recodings that will fail. 1.10 p. 42

CUMMINS And that will include things like my speeding up the tape, or all kinds of different sorts of—

SMITH It could, yeah it could.

DENNETT That's right, it could include those as subspecies of that, interestingly different from labeling.

CUMMINS I just think those are interesting ones because they're particularly mechanical and witless to do, and don't require much training. I mean you just need, as it were, to have in your box of tricks, try doing it faster, try doing it slower, you don't need a lot of direction.

CLARK And if sometimes that gives you the recoding you need, that's great.

1.11
p. 42 SMITH Just to comment on the isomorphism of language, one of the things that's true, which fits with this point about ordinary languages, is that you objectify the one word, so like, $R(a, b)$: the objects are a and b and the relation is R. And you go to the language, a and b remain objects but the relation R turns into an object, namely the predicate letter 'R'. You can get a trinary relation up here where you get a binary relation down here. So that kind of standard linguistic encoding does one layer of objectification differently. If you go higher you'd get a second one. So it actually fits—in spite of the fact that you can set the isomorphisms up because you'd say this relation goes with this relation or something like that. The fact that it's isomorphic hides the fact that the standard linguistic encoding does one order of objectification. But I think you're right. Objectification is often what matters, because once you get objectifications you can get tokens of the objectification and then you can get causal effect, where you can't get relations that do work.

CLARK So I think there is a deep relation between that and any coherent notion of internal representation. That internal representations are in some sense the product of some process of objectification like that.

CLAPIN The strength of 'objectifies' there, it's not sort of John's notion? [See Part 3—ed.]

CLARK No, in fact it's literally 'makes an object'.

SMITH I don't think 'object' is even the right word. I think being *locally effective* is actually what's mattering, not being an *object* in the sense of objective. It's just that we tend to think, we as theorists tend to objectify that which is local and effective. So locality and effectiveness are—this is my own view—they're what's doing the work. I think that is actually the real insight in computing. So oddly enough I think this [Clark's account] is a better computational theory of the mind than Fodor ever articulated in a very curious way.

1.12
p. 43

CUMMINS I'm kind of attracted to this idea on occasion though I still am kind of on the fence about this, but when you think about the case of, as it were, language evolving to be more learnable, why wouldn't you think the same thing of these virtual worlds?

CLARK Oh sure, that it's in their fitness interest to insinuate themselves into our cognitive horizons.

CUMMINS Well, the thing that makes it hard for people like John and me to understand the language case, is because, it isn't, sort of, there. But you know there's this kind of set of practices and the practices evolve and so on. And we can kind of think about that. But if you think about it that way then of course the same process ought to be operating here.

DENNETT Well, fine, and then, why not suppose that those are habits?

CLARK I think so.

DENNETT Plus, for instance, the virtual worlds used to be populated with such entities as tribal honor, group sakes, and things like that and group sakes and tribal honor fall by the wayside and you get left with pale shadows of them like rights and duties.

HAUGELAND Can I ask you—with regard to the last sentence, is the word 'moral' doing any work in it? I mean isn't it just a claim about reason?

CLARK It's a claim about reason in general. I simply think moral reason is one place you can apply it. The other place I thought of was mathematical reason, any kind of reason.

HAUGELAND So any kind of, as one might say, abstract reasoning.

CLARK Abstract reasoning. One could say that that is the notion of reason, that many people have in mind when they try to distinguish the space of reasons from the other spaces that we human beings negotiate.

SMITH But one of the things about moral reason is that it has to do with morality, right?

CLARK That's OK, that's fine. Mathematical reasoning has to do with mathematics.

HAUGELAND And surveying reasoning has to do with surveying.

CUMMINS The reason I asked the former question is once again, this has a kind of funny anti-realist feel to it, in the following sense, that rather than, as it were, seeing norms as things which are kind of recalcitrant, things against which our performances are measured, what happens is, in this view, the virtual world populated by the norms themselves just evolves to make us more easily amused. There's this old worry in science when you find some problem that you can't explain, and one thing you can say is, well, gee that's just the best we can do here.

Physicists like to say this kind of thing, this is the best we can do here, and you just have the wrong standards of explanation. That's always a suspicious move, because the idea is that you trade in a failure of explanation for just becoming more easily amused. Now this looks like a mechanism for doing that on a cosmic scale.

CLARK Okay, is that bad?

DENNETT Well, I see what you're saying, but I think the answer is, yes, and? You're wondering what the counter-mechanism is that keeps family values intact.

CLARK You want us to discover moral facts, not create them.

CUMMINS That's right. The fact that—or I don't care about moral facts necessarily but it looks like the same thing's going to happen with physics and everything else on this story—

CLARK Well I think that discovery and creation are . . . you're working in a mid-space here. You're discovering genuine higher-order properties, but ones that you would never have had a hope in hell of discovering were it not for the fact that you were looking through the special lenses provided by objectified relations.

CUMMINS Why isn't the virtual world discovering your soft points?

CLARK Yes, it is. That would be a very Dan way of putting it. Some of the virtual worlds out there are discovering our cognitive soft spots.

SMITH I think that the word 'virtual' is misleading. I guess I think the bottom line is that what one has to do is recruit the vanishingly small fraction of the properties in the world that are effective in order to stand in an intentional relationship (or something like that) toward the sum total of everything there is, most of which is not effective, like the average height of us. There's nothing virtual about the average height of all these people—

CLARK OK, yeah, I'm not wedded to the word 'virtual'. I just mean that there's a sense in which—

SMITH But see, a new virtual world, it seems to me that's what's triggering Rob's queasiness. And here I'm actually with him, because I don't think there's anything new or virtual about this stuff. These things are actual, real—

DENNETT We play chess, we don't play schness, or chess prime [i.e. chess']. There are uncountably many variants on chess. They are onto-logically . . . in a certain sense they're all the same. It is a brute fact that one of them is actual on this planet, namely chess, that's the one we play. But the discoveries that you can make about chess, whether or not there is a mating net in a certain predicament—you can also make discoveries of that same sort about schness, which nobody plays, and never will, but it's perfectly definable, and you can learn things about that abstract object, even though nobody ever plays it. And so that's the sense in which they're virtual.

HAUGELAND Well, that's a sense in which *they're* virtual, but not a sense in which what Andy was talking about is virtual.

DENNETT But, chess, for all its concrete reality, can be thought about independently of that concrete reality, as if it were just like schness.

SMITH Right, but responsibility, and, reliability, and things like that it seems to me are actually crucially different from chess in not sharing what chess and schness have in common, which is that . . . roughly their ontological existence doesn't hinge on our representing them.

DENNETT It doesn't? I'm surprised to hear that from you—

SMITH So am I. (*Laughter*) 'Isn't so massively dependent on the representation of them as chess is' . . . something like that.

CUMMINS That's not what bothers me. What bothers me is what Dan said before about the fact that really bad norms can get perpetuated, right? What's important is . . . you know, it's not the goodness or the badness of a norm, but the way it couples in with the replicating mechanism. And so, basically, what this is saying here is that the world you're going to end up negotiating, through which these trajectories occur, is the world that's done the best job at replicating itself.

CLARK I think I buy that.

DENNETT Yes, right.

CUMMINS That's what you think? Right. Well, OK.

SMITH That scares the hell out of me.

CUMMINS I think . . . I in my crude realism and John in his other way, were looking for something a little more resilient and a little more recalcitrant than that. Something that would push back more than this.

HAUGELAND Well that is indeed what the constitutive standards and the resolute commitment are for. The idea, after all, is to find a way for the world to push back on all the fancy theory and invention of concepts and terms.

CLAPIN There is another place you can get a bit of anti-realism here, which is that when you're doing recoding, maybe even of the simple sort, of the compression sort, but certainly more robust recoding, you might get fixed on features of the code, not features of the distal thing—so you're 1.13
p. 43

definitely going to come up against the worry that the recoding or the abstraction can move you away from the world.

CLARK Yeah, in fact it had better in some sense. It needs to move you away from the brute world in a way that still keeps you in touch with things that matter.

CUMMINS No, but what will matter are the features of the recoding that lead to its replication.

DENNETT No, but these problems sort themselves out. We've already seen the example. [See the Final discussion of Part 2, p. 109—ed.] Should the stalemate rule of chess be changed? Or, to take an even more dramatic case, I love Bobby Fischer's recent suggestion: that the way to make chess a better game and live up to its . . .

HAUGELAND Become itself again.

DENNETT Become itself again is to have the randomization of the positions of the pieces in the back row before every game, which destroys the role of rote learning of book openings.

Final discussion
p. 43

HAUGELAND You said that we're not norm-hungry but norm-bombarded. And that we are not really different from the chimps, or not much, with regard to our susceptibility to normalization.

CLARK With regard to the susceptibility of our brains to normalization.

CUMMINS Our brains aren't that different.

CLARK Take the bigger (culturally extended) machine in which there is a genuine structural divide between us and the chimps and then, yes.

HAUGELAND Well, OK. First, I gladly accept as useful and interesting the characterization of one of the merits of language that it allows you to abstract from complexities in current situations such that second-order complexities can become salient and so on, and second-order relations, etc. And that clearly is a model for a whole lot of stuff like that that can happen. And that language in particular, one of its great values is to enable that so that we can understand our world by categorizing things, and then categorizing the categories and relations among them and so forth. Cool. That that could be proposed as what we have instead of neurally based—or neurally enabled—social norm-hungriness seems to me impossible because the structures that language has and that therefore it enables—ways in which language is used, word by word, and then compositionally, and then further compositions, and so on—those have to be socially shared, and propagated, right? Not much of this can be invented by any one person. What we have is the heritage of these digestions and so on that make the world negotiable in a much better way and so you need an account of how it is that there can be such a complex structure that is heritable, that is passed on from generation to generation and remains relatively stable, doesn't just go all woolly like slang. And my proposal is that norm-hungriness at the sort of organism level, built into the infant as it comes onto the scene is a way of accounting for the propagability and thus the possibility of the very kind of structure that you so rightly point to the importance of.

CLARK That is absolutely the divide between us. You think that multiple norm-sensitivity is a prerequisite of getting language going, whereas I think it's an upshot of getting language going.

HAUGELAND But I certainly agree that there come to be lots of other norms that wouldn't be possible without language.

CLARK In the evolutionary picture I would have to try and tell some sort of story where, to learn the early languages, you didn't need to be multiply norm-sensitive, you just needed to be norm-sensitive enough to get a little simple language sort of grooved into you. And then that in turn makes possible a larger amount of norm-sensitivity that opens up a space for different kinds of language to then parasitize you, ones that need sensitivity to more and more norms.

HAUGELAND But how can language parasitize you, or a community, if not because of the linguistic norms? Unless the language can be passed from one generation to the next, in a way that the next generation can hold it and save it for the following.

DENNETT Perfect place to answer your earlier question, your evolutionary question about the relationship between the evolution of the brain and the evolution of language. The way you've put the question makes it look as if the problem for language is that people are going to be sloppy. People are going to be all over the map, things are going to drift apart unless there are lots of norms to hold people in check. That's one possibility, that's as it were one end of the spectrum. At the other end of the spectrum is, for the moment just say, by magic, people just aren't sloppy. They're just really built all just the same, in some regard, so they don't need norms. They just automatically do the same thing, without any correction needed at all. So you think, well that's magic. What you need to get some of that magic, is the evolution of language to fit the brain, if language will evolve to find those regularities that need minimal norm-correction to sustain. If there is anything which is really uniform across brains, then you don't need a norm for that. Language will simply run piggyback on that static regularity, and that is enough to get it up and running. Once it's up and running then we can cycle norms back in, and then we can get norm-bound as hell.

CUMMINS But even more, once it gets up and running, because it confers an advantage on its users, it will help select for the very guys that you're talking about, and there will be even more uniformity.

DENNETT That's right. People whose brains don't have those uniformities in them are not going to have as many kids. You get the Baldwin effect, too.

PART 2

On Dennett

Texts

'Styles of Mental Representation' (1983).
'Things about Things' (forthcoming).
'Making Tools for Thinking' (2000).
'Making Things to Think With' and 'Talking to Ourselves' in *Kinds of Minds*
(1996: 134–52).

Dennett is undoubtedly one of the giants in contemporary philosophy of
mind. He has consistently urged a deflationary and scientifically grounded
account of key mental capacities such as intentionality and consciousness.
He argues forcefully that evolutionary explanation (properly understood)
has enormous explanatory power which undercuts over-complicated, intellectualist accounts of mind (Dennett 1995a). Dennett's most significant
contribution to the field of mental representation is his account of intentionality wherein a system is properly called intentional when and only
when its behaviour is best explained and predicted by taking the intentional stance; that is, by assuming it is a rational agent with goals and
beliefs. Dennett claims that intentional states such as the propositional
attitudes are to be understood as patterns of behaviour rather than datable
states of an agent's nervous system.

None the less Dennett does not deny that internal content-bearing states
are critical to the explanations posed by cognitive scientists, and he has
recently returned to the topic of how best to understand these 'things about
things'. In an important earlier paper, 'Styles of Mental Representation',

Dennett (1983) argued that whatever explicit representations there are to be found in the mind of cognitive agents, it must be understood that they derive their representational abilities from what he terms 'tacit' representation. Tacit representation describes content that is embodied by a system or organism. One kind of tacit knowledge is the know-how of a digital computer. It tacitly knows how to follow certain rules, namely, machine instructions. Dennett understands one sort of tacitly represented information as the information that a system has that allows it to use and manipulate explicit representations, but which is not itself encoded explicitly.

Dennett has extended this way of thinking about internal representation in his recent writings on the topic. Here we find two main themes. First, that the 'aboutness' in the phrase 'things about things' may be cashed out in a large range of ways, from the propositional content of the phrase 'that apple is edible' to a behavioural directedness with respect to the apple that constitutes the apple's being treated as edible by the system. The phenomena captured by the term 'mental content' are immensely varied and admit of radically different explanatory strategies. Dennett's second theme is that cognitive agents are composed of various sorts of 'tools for thinking', and that mental representations (of various sorts) are simply a particular kind of tool for thinking.

This focus on tools is another example of Dennett's deflationary approach to cognitive explanation. Tools may be more or less complex, and require more or less sophistication of their users. Methodologically, looking for tools permits various strategies of decomposition. 'Tools' is a general term without the philosophical baggage of 'content,' 'representation', or 'mind.'

While Dennett's well-known theory of stance-dependent intentionality downplays the importance of inner linguistic items, he does provide a central role for language in understanding human cognition. Having beliefs is a relatively cheap and widespread ability, however a certain sophisticated kind of thinking is peculiar to humans and rests on explicit linguistic representations.

In 'Making Tools for Thinking' (Dennett 2000) Dennett talks of the importance of what he calls 'florid representing'—a certain kind of sophisticated self-conscious capacity that involves thinking *about* one's representations in order to think about the world. Natural language—a complex system of symbols, grammar, and meaning capable of easy meta-representation—clearly makes a big contribution to florid representing.

So is Dennett in fact a closet language-of-thoughter? Well, no; but Clark's commentary presses Dennett on the importance of language to cognition. In particular, Clark asks whether there is a stable picture to be wrought from the combination of Dennett's claims that cognitive agents are 'bags of mind tools' and that inner representations and external language are both just particular sorts of tools. Given Dennett's emphasis on tacit, skill-based content, Clark worries that the distinction between the representational and the non-representational is easily lost, and the supposed distinctiveness of florid representing becomes difficult to capture.

Minds, Brains, and Tools

ANDY CLARK

2.1.1 Reading Dennett

The selected texts for this discussion were two recent pieces by Dennett ('Things about Things' (forthcoming), and 'Making Tools for Thinking' (2000), henceforth TAT and MTT respectively) and one oldie-but-goodie ('Styles of Mental Representation' (1983), henceforth SMR). What was most striking, to me, was the way these three small texts seemed to fit together and, collectively, help to illuminate the shape of Dennett's whole corpus, from the work on stances all the way to the work on consciousness and personhood. I found this exhilarating, and I hope my enthusiasm—tempered though it is by a few doubts and worries—shows through.

Here's how I plan to proceed. I'll start by presenting what I take to be Dennett's position. I will do this, however, in the most blatant, outrageous, and caveat-free way possible, as I want to home in fast on some key issues (I am also keen to see if Dennett can endorse these deliberately provocative formulations). I then raise an initially obscure question, but one that is, I think, ultimately important and revealing: the question is, 'Could it really be (mind)tools *all the way down*?' Dennett's provocative answer, I suggest, is an emphatic 'Yes'. I then turn to the issues concerning aboutness and internal representations, and explore the relations between Dennett's heavy emphasis on skills and tools and his rejection of certain core ideas about contents and vehicles. In the final section I offer a tentative illustration of the big picture, using recent work on numerical cognition as a concrete case study. There is a brief conclusion rehearsing some outstanding questions for the tool-based vision of mind.

2.1.2 What Minds are Made Of

One way to say what I think Dennett (TAT, MTT, SMR) is up to is by a simple triplet of questions and answers. Showing what these questions and answers *mean* is the real goal of this section.

Q. What are minds made of?
A. Tools for thinking.
Q. Who or what *uses* the tools to *do* the thinking?
A. No one, nothing. The tools-R-us.
Q. Intentionality, aboutness, content, and consciousness: can all these really be brought into being by grab-bags of userless tools?
A. Yes.

The first point to notice, given the topic of the present workshop, is the constant emphasis on tools rather than on internal representations. Traditional ('intellectualist'—see SMR) cognitive science had it that minds were made of internal representations. Dennett, as far as I can see, simply denies this outright. The things in there (in the head) or out there (in the world) worth calling representations are not, according to Dennett (SMR) fundamental. What are fundamental are the skills bequeathed by the tools that build know-how tacitly into the system. Dennett, in SMR (and inspired by Ryle 1949 with perhaps a whiff of Wittgenstein), offers a neat little argument designed to show why this *must* be so.

First, Dennett distinguishes three ways in which information may be incarnate in a system. The information may be explicit, tokened as syntactically distinct, reliably interpretable symbols (SMR: 215). Second, it may be implicit: logically (actually, I suspect 'logically' may be unnecessarily strong here) implied by whatever *is* stored explicitly (SMR: 216). Third, it may be tacit: 'built into the system in some fashion that does not require it to be represented (explicitly) in the system' (SMR: 218). The pocket calculator, it is said (SMR: 221–2), represents numbers explicitly (on screen and in buffers). But arithmetical truths and axioms are nowhere tokened in the machine, nor are they logically implied by what *is* tokened (sequences of numbers). So such truths and axioms are at best tacitly 'represented'—the rules are incarnate in the hardware in much the way the laws of hydrodynamics are reflected in the bodily form of a fish.

Dennett next asks in virtue of what any explicit representations have the contents they do? Imagine a pattern of electrical activity, in the pocket calculator, which explicitly represents the number 7 in binary code (SMR:

221). Now keep the token of the number 7 intact, but rewire the hardware so that the device embodies no tacit knowledge of the rules of arithmetic. Does it still carry the content we previously identified? There is doubtless some room for maneuver here, especially once we import additional considerations concerning the history and design of a device. But the basic intuition to be pumped is the negative one. To quote Dennett, 'Explicit representations, by themselves [are] quite inert as information bearers...They *become* information bearers only when given roles in larger systems' (SMR: 217). And how do you get an appropriate role in a larger system? Only, it seems, if the system is set up so as actually to *do* things—to move and act in the world (in our case) or at the very least to go from one representation to another (as in the case of the pocket calculator). And what *this* requires, on pain of an infinite regress of rules and recipes, is to be part of a system that has some *tacit* knowledge (know-how) which can put the representations to work without requiring more layers of representation to do so (SMR: 218). Conclusion: tacit knowledge (non-represented skills and know-how) is *more fundamental than inner tokens and internal representations.*

But the need for some such underlying structure of tacit knowledge is, surely, accepted on all sides. Fodor, in his (1987) *Psychosemantics* concedes that 'a computer in which the principles of operation are *only* explicitly represented is just like a blackboard on which the principles are written down... when you turn the thing on, nothing happens' (Fodor 1987: 23). What is interesting and powerful about Dennett's treatment is not the insight itself—which is familiar enough—but the way Dennett puts it to work as the cornerstone of a different way of looking at intelligence and meaning. What we find in the two more recent treatments (TAT and MTT) is, precisely, a way of following through on the Rylean argument that reveals genuine points of disagreement with 'intellectualist' cognitive science and that paints a very different picture of what *matters* about minds and persons: a picture in which tools and skills take center stage and in which the primary 'vehicles' of content are the embodied capacities of whole agents embedded in a cultural and ecological niche. Dennett thus ends up rather startlingly close to a Heideggerian vision of the nature of cognition, though this is not a theme I am competent to explore.

The key to Dennett's alternative lies in the first of our opening question-and-answer pairs: 'What are minds made of?' 'Tools for thinking' ('minds are composed of tools for thinking', MTT: 4). This is a theme that is increasingly prominent in Dennett's work (see especially the closing chapters of Dennett (1996) and chs. 12 and 13 of Dennett (1995*a*). It is best unpacked, I want to suggest, in terms of three overlapping but independent sub-themes:

1. External tools augment and transform biological cognition.
2. External symbols somehow pave the way for 'florid representing'.
3. Florid representing is what distinguishes mere believers from genuine understanders.

I do think that Dennett, in MTT and elsewhere (Dennett 1996), is effectively arguing for (3). But although there are plenty of sentences in Dennett cognate with (1) and (2), there is nothing that embodies (3) quite so boldly and blatantly. Let's creep up on it, then, by way of the less provocative sub-themes.

The idea that external items can augment and scaffold both behavior and thought is pretty evidently true, and arguably of deep importance. The sailor armed with hooey and alidade[1] can achieve feats of navigation that would baffle the naked brain, as Hutchins (1995) exhaustively documents. And—perhaps more importantly for this discussion—the way such tools work is by affording the kinds of inner reasoning and physical manipulation that best *fit* our brains, bodies, and evolutionary heritage. Our visual acuity and pattern-matching skills, for example, far outweigh our capacities to perform sequences of complex arithmetical operations. The slide-rule is a tool that transforms the latter (intractable) kind of task into a more homely one of manual action and visual cognition. Tools can thus reduce humanly difficult classes of problems to ones that better suit our skills, both cognitive and physical.

A big question about tools, of course, is how did they get here? If tools are tricks for pressing increased functionality out of biologically basic strategies, what kinds of minds can make the tools that make new kinds of minds? This is an issue that Dennett touches on in MTT in his discussion of 'found objects'. The idea is to reveal certain kinds of tool-discovery procedure as falling entirely under the umbrella of blind trial and error learning. Köhler's chimps, in initially playing around with sticks and boxes, were not actively (MTT: 5–6) trying to solve the food acquisition problem. Instead they were just 'familiarizing themselves with objects in their environments'. In this process, affordances may well be spotted (perhaps the

---

[1] Hutchins (1995: ch. 3) describes these in detail. An alidade is a kind of telescopic sighting device; a hooey is a one-armed protractor used for marking lines on charts.

stick happens to touch a banana and so on). One of Dennett's major themes is thus that the initial path and successful tool use need not involve a process of conscious design in which thoughts about the tool/problem fit guide a search for good tools. Instead, recognition of tool/problem fit, if it comes at all, may well come *after* the event of successful use.

Indeed, we should go further and observe that not just the discovery of tools, but also their evolution, improvement, and refinement, can proceed with little or no deliberate design activity on our part. The trick here—as laid out by Dennett (1997) and by Deacon (1997: ch. 4)—is to recognize the tools as *themselves* a class of replicating entities whose 'success' (widespread replication) or 'failure' (extinction) depends on the extent to which we adopt them. Tools in general (and language in particular, more on which later) may thus be seen (ibid. 112) as rather like viruses— incapable of reproducing on their own, dependent on a host's metabolic and reproductive systems, yet susceptible to processes of variation and differential reproduction sculpted by their success or failure at invading host organisms. By seeing tools as entities with their own selective histor- ies, we make room for what Deacon calls 'a flurry of adaptation . . . going on outside the brain' (ibid. 109).

In focusing our attention on the evolution of external tools, Dennett is thus concerned to avoid what I call 'the paradox of active stupidity' (Clark 2001: ch. 8). This would be the idea that making the moves that sculpt the environment so as to allow *cheap* problem-solving itself requires *expen- sive*, advanced, design-oriented cogitation. The threat being that only *clever* brains could make their worlds smart so that they could be dumb in peace—a result that would deprive the tool-based scenario of its appealing role in both originating and partially constituting advanced, reflective thought and reason. The observations about found objects, trial and error manipulation, and tools as replicators, along with the clear potential for tool-based bootstrapping (using one tool to design another and so on), are meant as a response to this natural worry.

The most potent of these bootstrapping resources—the tool of tools—is surely language itself. And Dennett's long-term corpus is littered (that sounds bad—I mean 'liberally sprinkled') with suggestions and specula- tions about the way 'words do things with us' (Dennett 1991*a*: ch. 8). In the papers under discussion, what words are said to do for us is to open up the space of thinking about thinking, and to thus enable what Dennett (MTT) calls 'florid representing'. Representing is florid, we are told, when it is 'deliberate', 'knowing', 'self-conscious'—when you either do, or at any rate could, appreciate that you are manipulating objects that represent. This kind of florid representing is contrasted, by Dennett, with the sense in which a state of the visual system may 'represent' the presence (say) of a food item, and even with the sense in which a young child or chimpanzee may unreflectively use representational tools (symbols) as part of a 'cause-effect communication system' (Gauker 1990) to achieve a goal. It is, in short, one thing to learn that using the word 'ice cream' or touching a symbol for banana will help assuage hunger, and quite another to appreciate the word or symbol *as* having a representational role: as being an object that is about other objects, as being a 'thing about things' (TAT). Notice, finally, that according to Dennett an agent might even use meta-representations without genuinely appreciating the notion of a representational role. The chimp or child may represent the care-giver as believing that the food is in the red box (might 'have a theory of mind') yet not exhibit 'the *knowing* competence to *use representations*' (MTT: 5, original emphasis).

I was not quite sure how best to understand this last idea, which none the less looks quite central to the project of MTT, so let me pause to review the claim. What is at issue, it seems, is the florid or 'witting' (MTT: 5) use of representations. This is somehow tied to the notion of 'thinking about thinking'—a notion I make use of in some of the work Dennett cites. One idea hereabouts is that once a thought or argument is rendered as an external symbolic object (a string of typed words or repeatable sounds) it is itself suddenly available as an object for further thought or scrutiny (see Jackendoff 1996). Dennett's idea may thus be that external symbolic objects allow us *unwittingly* (at first) to treat a token of thought as an object for further thought. If we then realize that that is what we did, we have stumbled into the ranks of the *florid* representers—beings who have become aware of the practice of using things to represent things, and who can then self-consciously exploit this technique in cultural practices, in the delineations of explicit norms, and so on. At this point, one might say, the sky (hook) is the limit.

Dennett's suggestion, thus rendered, is that witting representational practice depends—contingently but crucially—on the prior unwitting use of external objects as representations, and that this, in turn, is just a special instance of the use of found objects (including, perhaps, involuntary cries or facial gestures—see Dennett 1991a: ch. 7) as tools.

Which brings us to the third and final sub-theme, and the motivation behind a lot of Dennett's recent work. Or so I want to claim. This is the

idea (which I admit Dennett does not state in quite so many words) that
florid representing distinguishes mere 'believers' from genuine thinkers
and understanders. This may come as a shock to any who think of Dennett
as a mad-dog instrumentalist who places Einstein, the lectern, and the
thermostat on a simple continuum of intentional-stance-worthiness. A
case could be made that such a depiction was always demonstrably mistaken, but I shan't pause for that. Instead, just savor a few remarks culled
from the more recent corpus:

I am tempted to say that even if they [chimpanzees] do have beliefs about beliefs,
they may well be incapable of *thinking about thinking*. They may, indeed, not
really be capable of thinking at all (in some florid but important sense of
'thinking'). (MTT: 4, original emphasis)

thinking—our kind of thinking—had to wait for talking to emerge.
                                                      (Dennett 1996: 130)

In order to be conscious—in order to be the sort of thing it is like something to
be—it is necessary to have a certain sort of informational organization . . . [one]
that is swiftly achieved in one species, ours, and in no other . . . My claim is not
that other species lack our kind of *self*-consciousness . . . I am claiming that what
must be added to mere responsivity, mere discrimination, to count as consciousness *at all* is an organization that is not ubiquitous among sentient organisms. (Dennett 1995*b*: 347)

our kind of consciousness is . . . in surprisingly large measure, an artifact of our
immersion in human culture. (ibid. 346)

Florid representing, consciousness, and thinking about thinking are thus
tied together, with the whole bundle depicted as historically dependent on
the emergence of a special kind of mind-tool linked to speech or other
forms of linguistic representation. What linguistic objects do is position us
to acquire the *idea* of representation, thus priming the cultural explosion
of mind-tools (notations, slide-rules, laws, norms, advice, education) that
sculpt plastic neural circuits and help constitute human intelligence. Such,
at any rate, is my gloss on suggestive, but occasionally cryptic, assertions
such as, 'It is because the lions can't talk to each other that they also can't
come to use tokens of other sorts to represent, non-linguistically. And it
is by that indirect route, I think, that we come to construct our minds'
(MTT: 7).

Whatever instrumentalist leanings Dennett has or may have had, it
seems clear that he *also* insists on genuine and important organizational
differences. Differences so important, indeed, as to render certain kinds of

adaptively potent organization (in the chimps and lions, for example) unable to support 'real thinking' (in the florid sense) or real consciousness. Since chimps and lions remain rather wonderful candidates for the intentional stance, this organizational dividing line must be drawn between grades of *believer*: some believers (the florid representers) are real thinkers while others are not.

It wasn't entirely clear to me, however, exactly why floridity seemed to matter so much here, at least as far as the individual cognizer was concerned. What puzzled me was this: couldn't a person be simply transformed (upgraded, cognitively reconfigured, etc.) by the full culturally available array of mind-tools (language, text, notations, etc.) without ever forming the clear understanding that the symbols are used to represent objects and states of affairs, that is, without ever achieving a florid understanding of symbol use? Certainly, the fact that *some* agents become self-conscious of the representational role of symbols might help explain the explosion of mind-tools over historical time. But couldn't some other individuals reap the benefits of this explosion without ever achieving the kind of witting understanding of symbol-use that Dennett stresses?

At this point I was led to wonder whether 'witting use' really had to imply (as it had seemed to) something like explicitly formulated reflective awareness, or whether the wittingness might *itself* take the form of a kind of tacit know-how. For example, knowing how to develop new representational schemes, being able quickly to learn new schemes developed by others, and so on. My guess, however, is that Dennett really *does* mean to insist on explicit, conscious, reflective awareness of the idea of representational role. But I fear this may be requiring too much if floridity is to be the mark of the typical human subject. *Discussion point 2.1*

A few more puzzles will serve to close this initial sketch. The first is about mind-tools in general, and the puzzle is: must new (culturally developed) mind-tools always involve either new *representational* systems (for example, arabic numerals) or new media for the storage and manipulation of such representations (pen, paper, smart cards)? Bluntly, are mind-tools always centered, one way or another, on *representations*?

Consider some candidate mind-tools: the abacus (numeric representations), the slide-rule (ditto), PC (loaded with representations and new representation-manipulating capacities). There are, of course, farmer's tools such as the rake (that Haugeland sometimes mentions).[2] But it is

---

[2] [See §16 of 'Mind Embodied and Embedded' (Haugeland 1995)—ed.]

not obvious that this is a *mind*-tool as such, though it certainly helps transform the agricultural problems that the mind confronts. ***Discussion point 2.2***

I am led to wonder, in fact, whether what *makes* something a mind-tool is not, precisely, that it figures centrally in some representation-involving process. This could make sense if, for example, the very idea of a *cognitive* process was tied up with the idea of a process that crucially involves the use and manipulation of representations—objects whose role is to stand in for other objects and state of affairs (for more on this, see Clark and Grush 1999).

I am not entirely satisfied with such a characterization, but I am equally unsure how else to distinguish the class of mind-tools from the more general class of tools. Even if we helped ourself to the notion of an 'intuitively cognitive process', it is not quite clear that all the props and aids that contribute to such a process should be considered mind-tools. A nice puzzle-case, suggested by my colleague Larry May, is the coffee I drink while working. The caffeine clearly aids cognitive processes, but is it a mind-tool? Is a morning run a mind-tool, too (it certainly alters neuro-transmitter balances and so on)? ***Discussion point 2.3*** I wonder just how and where to draw the line—or perhaps Dennett's claim is that there *is* no line, that mind and cognition are literally inseparable from everything else. The latter move may sound appealing, but it is hard to accommodate given Dennett's large scheme. I believe that Dennett (like me) wants the agent to be in part *constituted* by the weave of mind-tools. But neither of us, I think, wants the agent to be in part constituted by just everything that the biological body uses. That, however, seems to require finding some way to keep the mind-tools distinct from the rest. ***Discussion point 2.4***

Moreover, it may even be necessary to make distinctions within the (already problematic) class of mind-tools themselves. Perhaps not *all* mind-tools should be thought of as helping constitute the cognitive agent. A further puzzle would then be how to distinguish a tool that aids thought from a tool that actually *implements* part of the thinking. These are all deep and important issues, which will loom large in the next section.

2.1.3 Could it be Tools *All the Way Down?*

A good place to start is with the second opening question: Who or what uses the tools to do the thinking? The answer here, which I suspect is deeper and more difficult than it initially appears, is no one. No one *uses* the mind-tools. The mind *is* the collection of mind-tools (Mind-tools-R-us). It is at this point that the questions about tools also phase into Dennett's perennial concerns about persons and about consciousness. So there are lots of issues here, and I shan't attempt to get to grips with them all. But here's one which gets pretty quickly to the heart of things.

Consider language, Dennett's 'tool of tools'. One question that can be asked is this: If language is to be thought of as a tool, what becomes of the user? Specifically, is language a tool used *by* thought processes, or does the tool here *constitute* the thinking? Like Dennett, I am deeply committed to some kind of 'cognitive involvement' (Carruthers 1996) of public symbolic codes in thought—that is to say, I don't see the public codes as merely vehicles for the communication and external encoding of thought but as active contributors to the processes of thinking. But I think it is useful to distinguish some further possibilities concerning the *kind* of involvement at issue.

To focus this, take a simple case reported by Henser (2000). Japanese/English bilingual speakers will sometimes use a phrase such as: 'I just wanted to say that I feel really *moshiwakenai*[3] about it.' This is an instance of what Henser calls 'code-switching': suddenly jumping from one linguistic system to another. A more common example of code-switching is when counting. A speaker who is absolutely fluent in English may very well switch back to their native tongue for *sotto voce* calculation, and even bilinguals tend to have a preferred language for counting. Why switch codes? It is not that the ideas cannot be expressed in the other language. But it may well be that certain cognitive routines are easier to organize, or better practiced, using internal representations of specific public symbols. Henser thus introduces the notion of a 'lingpack'—a set of mental items (perhaps in mentalese) that hang together and are packaged via a public symbol as a manipulable item for use in propositional thought (ibid. 28). Different languages select different lingpacks, and a lingpack need not be 'unzipped' (exploded) to be used. 'Moshiwakenai' is a lingpack in Japanese, but not in English, hence the cognitive economy afforded by code-switching.

Henser's story is tempting, but it appears to remain uncommitted on an arguably crucial issue. It does not distinguish between:

---

[3] *Moshiwakenai*, according to Henser, means an apology made in the context of a relationship whose hierarchical structure renders the apologist unable to 'presume on the indulgence' of the other, so it typically occurs when the lower-ranking persons wants to apologize to the higher. See Henser (2000: 33).

1. The idea that we (sometimes) *think in* (say) English, and
2. The idea that we only *think* in some special inner code or codes (say 'mentalese') but that while we do so we also (sometimes) use inner representations of actual words in some specific language (e.g. *moshiwakenai*) to help organize, focus, and recall ideas and sequences of ideas.

On the face of it, this is a real and perhaps important distinction. Consider an analogy. I often use pen and paper to help me organize, focus, and recall ideas. But it does not seem to follow that I 'think in' pen and paper... though (on the third hand) it *is* true that the pen and paper form part of an extended cognitive and problem-solving system with my biological brain. This is the distinction between 'thinking in' and 'thinking with'. In the case of the code-switching examples, the evidence seems compatible with either option. What the results suggest is that the specific lingpacks available in different languages make some kinds of thinking easier or harder, and hence that code-switching can be indicated. But this could equally well be because the subjects, although doing all the *thinking* in mentalese, need internal representations of specific lingpacks to focus, hold, and organize the thoughts.

I myself have tended to favor this latter option (see e.g. Clark 1998*b*). It also fits nicely with results concerning the effects of having different number words on arithmetical performance. For example, one Chinese (Cantonese) dialect has very brief words for numbers and speakers show a random digit recall span of 10 as against our 'magic number 7'—for a lovely account see Dehaene (1997: 102–3). Code-switching would thus be indicated for that task for a bilingual Cantonese/English speaker, even if all that is involved is an internal representation of the phonetics of the words for the digits as a way of aiding recall.

I have begun to wonder, however, whether Dennett might perhaps be committed to *denying the distinction between 'thinking with' and 'thinking in'*. For suppose someone (like Dennett) holds that content and aboutness get into the picture in virtue of skilled engagement (or perhaps the potential for skilled engagement) between agent and world. It could then very well be the case that no *single* mind-tool can support the kinds of flexible, skilled engagement characteristic of what we call 'understanding', 'grasp of meaning', and so on. To the extent that thought and understanding thus depend on the activity of multiple *non-privileged* mind-tools, there is no *more* reason to treat internal representations of public language words as 'merely derivatively contentful' (as only a second-grade content-bearer) than there is to thus treat a symbol in mentalese, or a mental image, or any *other* aspect of any one of our myriad mind-tools. Instead, they are all on a par, and *none* of them have the kind of intrinsic 'aboutness' that is sometimes posited as a kind of cognitive scientific grail. Strings of words, we might be tempted to say, cannot in themselves constitute a thought. But neither, on this picture, can anything else. Thought is an intrinsically more holistic phenomenon, dependent always and everywhere on the action of multiple mind-tools, not all of which *can* (as we saw in section 2.1.2) consist in inner tokenings of anything worth calling a representation. Here, then, is a point to ponder: does Dennett's story imply the breakdown of the superficially sensible distinction between 'thinking *with* a tool (e.g. English)' and 'thinking *in* a code' (e.g. mentalese)?

Let's suppose for a moment that it does. One cost of any such breakdown looks likely to be the erosion of any clear distinction between the tools and the user. A user just is a bundle of tools, and no tool is *privileged*—no tool *constitutes* the user in a way other tools do not. Instead, a loose coalition of tools (or 'skill-supporting components') together support the range of flexible engagements and responses characteristic of intelligence and thought.

It is not surprising, from this perspective, to find Dennett unworried by the idea of the environmentally extended mind (see also Clark and Chalmers 1998)—witness the comments towards the end of MTT (pp. 8–9) concerning the way the distribution of tasks across biological brain and local environment makes 'our minds so much more powerful than all other animal minds'. The idea here seems to be that language uniquely positions us to create a cascade of new mind-tools that literally transform us into more powerful (but extended) cognitive engines—an idea also familiar from Dennettian accounts of the origin of consciousness. *Discussion point 2.5*

We thus tiptoe into some metaphysically challenging terrain recently explored by Beth Preston in her work on tool use and cognition. Preston (1998) defends a broad notion of tool use based on Heidegger's notion of equipment—a notion that avoids the (I think arbitrary—see Clark and Chalmers 1998) restriction of tools to items external to the biological organism, and opts for a function-based account in which bodily parts (e.g. hands) and biological cognitive elements (e.g. biological memory) end up on a par with external items such as rakes and shopping lists. Dennett's story, I believe, is similarly (and properly) liberal, and ultimately confronts the same problem—that:

The user has in some sense disappeared in a welter of equipment...if all the bodily parts of an organism, including its mental states...are equipment, you have a situation where you peel away layers of equipment as you would peel away the layers of an onion, ending up with nothing at all in the way of a central core. (Preston 1998: 545)

This strikes me as a perfectly acceptable place to end up, though intuitions clearly differ. It is, at any rate, hard to see how to *avoid* this without embracing some equally problematic story—for example, anointing some aspect of the inner goings-on as the 'real cognitive engine' with all the rest relegated to 'mere' support and data-storage (which leads to a kind of unwelcome cognitive *shrinkage*[4]), or simply *insisting* that the biological agent is the cognitive agent and factoring out the sources of behavioral complexity accordingly. **Discussion point 2.6**

None of this, however, forces us to give up on the morally and socially crucial notion of *persons* and of thinking *agents*. One potential reconstruction might begin with the phenomenological facts of first-person experience. A tool/user divide might then be motivated by facts about how things *seem* to an agent—the pen, the automobile, and the blind man's cane do not typically strike the agent as simply parts of the environment, but as integrated probes and equipment through which to think and act. New tools and ill-matched tools do not lend themselves to this knitting in. The user, on this view, is not any old bag of tools but whatever bag of tools functions, at a given moment, as transparent equipment for thought and action.

Another (more Dennettian) reconstruction might highlight the set of tools that support the so-called 'user-illusion' (Dennett 1991a: chs. 7, 10; 1995b). It is here that the issues about tools and users phase rapidly into the ones about consciousness and content, and it may be worth pausing to review the story. Human consciousness, according to Dennett, gets much of its character from the cultural imprinting of a kind of 'user-illusion'.

---

[4] Herbert Simon took this route. After observing the importance of environmental complexity in determining behavior, he adds, 'a human being can store away in memory a great furniture of information...I would like to view this information-packed memory less as part of the organism than of the environment to which it adapts' (Simon 1996: 53). The 'organism' for Simon thus shrinks to something uncomfortably small (not unlike the read/write head of a Turing machine or the CPU of a digital computer). But nothing *that* impoverished seems likely to equate with our intuitive idea of an agent, who surely has goals, plans, memories, and so on.

'*Our* kind of consciousness', Dennett claims (1995*b*: 346) 'is not anything we are born with, not part of our innate hardwiring, but in surprisingly large measure, an artifact of our immersion in human culture'. This extraordinary immersion in a sea of culture and language (itself, to be sure, made possible by *some* difference in innate hardware) creates, in the human brain, a new kind of cognitive organization—a new 'virtual machine'—that allows us to weave a kind of ongoing narrative (about who we are, and what we are doing, and why we are doing it) that artificially 'fixes' our cognitive contents. The content is, of course, not *really* fixed (see TAT), because underneath the personal-level narrative stream the more fundamental multiple processing streams (Dennett's 'multiple drafts') are still going like the clappers. But there is, courtesy of the new top-level virtual organization, a striking difference: we now *report* the presence of a specific stream of experiences, a stream, if you will, of *judgings* or *macro-takings*, in which there seems to be a clear fact of the matter concerning the nature of our current subjective state. It is the presence of this serial stream of apparently fixed contents that explains, on Dennett's account, our tendency to believe in *qualia*. But what these qualia really are now turns out to be nothing but the string of judgments made by the top-level, linguistically infected, narrative-spinning virtual machine: a machine installed not by nature, but by the almost incalculable effects, in reasonably plastic human brains, of our early immersion in a sea of words and culture, or more generally by our immersion in a sea of external symbolic items and self-reflective cultural practices.

The upshot is that *believing* is pervasive and fundamental. But human-style conscious awareness requires an extra layer of judgment rooted in a culturally inculcated capacity to spin a privileged report or narrative: 'the story you or I will tell if asked (to put a complicated matter crudely)' (Dennett 1995*b*: 348). Consciousness is *achieved*, not given. Notice then that much of the burden is thus shifted from the notion of consciousness to the notion of personhood. For it is personhood that now emerges (via the ongoing narrative) as the primary culture-driven achievement, and one again deeply linked to the activity of the linguistic mind-tools we appropriate from our symbol-rich environment.

Here then is another way in which the notions of *persons* and *agency* may be reconstructed despite the image of the user as *nothing but* a bag of (embodied, embedded) mind-tools. Even if no tool or tools are intrinsically privileged, only certain combinations of tools will yield the user-illusion

that, for Dennett, distills consciousness from the flux of adaptive response.[5]

2.1.4 Internal Representations, Vehicles, and Skills

Dennett's views on internal representation and vehicles of content are best
appreciated, I want to suggest, against this challenging backdrop of ideas
about mind-tools. In this section I want to sketch these ideas (drawing
heavily on TAT), fill in the connections (using the ideas developed in
sections 2.1.2 and 2.1.3), and raise a few questions.

In TAT, Dennett suggests setting aside two idealizing assumptions often
made in the study of intelligent systems. The first concerns 'how to capture
content' and the second 'how to isolate the vehicles of content from the
"outside" world' (TAT: 1). Concerning content capture, Dennett's main
point is that we should not assume that wherever there is a genuinely
contentful state, there is an accurate and exhaustive propositional description of the content of that state. Dennett gives the example of a 'piece of
cognitive machinery' whose operation does indeed give someone a 'thing'
about redheads, subtly adjusting their responses to all situations in which
redheads are suspected of playing a role. Yet this 'thing about redheads',
undeniably (?) contentful as it is, and despite its having a perfectly good
physical vehicle 'in the head', does not seem amenable to accurate and
exhaustive propositional specification.

Dennett's suspicion is, I think, that *most* of the inner mechanisms
supporting cognitive contents are like that: they are components and
circuitry that display *non-propositional aboutness*. One of the interesting
things about Rodney Brooks's recent work, according to Dennett, is thus

---

[5] In thus opting for a clear dividing line between species in terms of the cultural imprinting of
a user-illusion, Dennett may create a subtle background tension with his own deflationary
account of qualia. For in rebuffing the fans of qualia, Dennett sometimes accuses them of
'inflating differences in degree [of richness, control, etc.] into imaginary differences in kind'
(Dennett 1997: 419). But Dennett *also* wants to claim that humans really are *different*,
possessing (courtesy of language and cultural immersion) an informational organization that
makes us (and not the lions, etc.) genuinely conscious (recall e.g. Dennett 1995*b*: 347 quoted
earlier). I find it hard to reconcile this notion of an organizational dividing line *among species*
with Dennett's equally firm insistence (see Dennett 1997) that *within* the human species, various
phenomena of response and discrimination mark only differences in degree. For pretty clearly
some of those phenomena are rooted in phylogenetically old pathways that we share with other
animals, while others will hook directly into the kinds of new informational organization
created by our 'immersion in human culture' and responsible for 'our kind of consciousness'
(which now looks to be the real kind—the kind associated with florid representing).

that in the Cog project, it is 'pushing these profoundly non-propositional models of contentful structures into territory that is recognizable as human psychology' (TAT: 2). Dennett also suggests, intriguingly, that treating these non-propositional contents as something like *implicit* beliefs can be misleading, as it again invites us to propositionalize and 'linguify' contents fundamentally ill-suited to sentential capture (TAT: 2).

Dennett's emphasis on non-propositional kinds of content is a very natural accompaniment to his stress on skills (section 2.1.2 above) and on mind-tools (section 2.1.3). Skilled engagement between agent and world is, for Dennett, the root of all content, and this kind of skill-based content was said to be explanatorily prior to the kinds of content typically associated with explicit 'internal representations', and to be associated instead with a variety of other mind-tools: pieces of bodily, neural, or environmental structure tuned and selected so as to support certain kinds of skilled engagement with the world.[6] Propositional format representations (which may or may not exist inside the head as well as out in the world) are just one such mind-tool among many, and should not be privileged as the sole genuine bearers of content.

But just how does the emphasis on skilled engagement comport with the emphasis (in MTT and elsewhere) on florid representing as (roughly) the mark of 'real' understanding? At first sight, there seems to be a tension between these two claims. Seeing just how they fit together is crucial to understanding Dennett's big picture.

Florid representing occurs, recall, when there is a *knowing* use of *representations* (see MTT: 2), where representations are (at least) some kind of manipulanda: objects that bear contents and that can be somehow shuffled, reorganized, and recombined in ways sensitive to, and exploitative of, those contents (see MTT: 9). The claims then fit together like this.

---

[6] Much of what Dennett has to say here seems nicely compatible with the sort of skill-based approach associated with the work of Gareth Evans (1982) and various contemporary apostles of 'non-conceptual content'. Grush (1998), for example, follows Evans in suggesting that many aspects of experiential content are *constituted* by sensorimotor skills. To experience something as *pulsating*, for example, is to be able in principle (i.e. assuming no bio-mechanical breakdowns) to coordinate a number of motor actions (swinging a baton, tapping your fingers) with the sound. A being lacking *all* such skills could not, on this account, directly perceive a sound *as* pulsating (see Grush 1998: para. 21); though they might infer that it is. Moreover, the content of such skill-based states is never reducible to a set of propositions believed: instead, the sensorimotor skills are what creates the contents that can later, perhaps, figure in other (propositional) episodes of thought and reflection. Dennett's tendency to view skilled engagement as the root of all content (see SMR and Part 2) seems motivated in a somewhat similar way, though without the emphasis on experiential content.

The objects (the manipulanda) involved in florid representing bear the contents they do only in virtue of a bedrock of skills and capacities, rooted in multiple non-propositional mind-tools. But florid representing depends on making those skill-based contents into *objects* suitable for the exercise of *other* (non-propositional) skills—skills of combining, shuffling, and so on. And it is this 'objectification' of certain aspects of content that supports the highly versatile and open-ended range of thought characteristic of (and perhaps uniquely characteristic of) human understanding. Finally, relating all this to other themes in MTT, it is our experiences with public symbols that are said to teach us to make more manipulable objects of our thoughts and ideas. In a very real sense then—and returning briefly to the themes of section 2.1.3—neither type of vehicle of content (the mechanisms support-ing skilled response or the manipulable objects that behave more like classical *representations*) is privileged in supporting 'real understanding'. Instead, *real understanding emerges from the interactions between these various kinds of mind-tool.*

Dennett's take on internal representation is thus that talk of internal *representations* (rather than simply talk of internal content-supporting mechanisms) become increasingly appropriate as the inner items become more object-like and more manipulable. In earlier work, Dennett stressed the lack of any 'clear dividing line' between devices that really have internal representations and those that don't (see, for example, Dennett 1981: 32). But as the versatility and manipulability of inner (or outer) items diminishes, so too does the usefulness of treating them *as* internal representations (MTT: 9).

I was not entirely sure, from Dennett's most recent treatments, just how big a role he is now giving to the *knowing* capacity to manipulate repre-sentations. The notion of 'witting' and 'knowing' uses of representations looms large in the discussions of florid representing. Yet I know of no argument that would show 'witting usability' to be an essential aspect of anything worth calling an internal representation. In Clark and Grush (1999), for example, we argue that a robust notion of internal representa-tion requires the presence of *something like* Dennettian manipulanda, and suggest that the acid test for the presence of such manipulanda is whether the organism can use the items to guide appropriate behavior in the absence of the objects or states of affairs the items are 'about'. In developing this picture, we are concerned to make room for kinds of manipulanda that are *not* (or not necessarily) wittingly used, nor propositional in format, taking as our key example the reuse, off-line, of circuitry developed to smooth the on-line production of fluent motor action. Such circuitry then appears able to support mental imagery and the off-line rehearsal of motor routines. Genuinely non-propositional manipulanda such as these, we suggest, act as a kind of bridge between structures implicated in skilled motor engagements in the here and now and structures capable of 'standing in' for distal or non-existent states of affairs. And they may also lay some of the cognitive groundwork for similar operations using *internal models of linguistic symbols*.

Dennett, too, must confront the difficult question of how the human species ever became capable of the prodigious feats of real symbol manipulation in which we engage. Saying that we internalize capacities to manipulate external symbolic items is not (as Dennett well realizes) enough. We badly need to understand what special non-linguistic skills prime the human brain to thus benefit, so wonderfully, from the provision of external symbolic structure. This is a question to which no one yet has a compelling answer (but see Deacon 1997 for an interesting attempt).

The second assumption challenged in TAT concerns the 'isolability' of the vehicles of content from the outside world, including the biomechanics of the body. Once again, the story makes good sense in the skill- and tool-based context we have been exploring. Dennett questions the idea of a pure information processing device neatly bounded at each side by transducers and effectors (TAT: 2–3). Another way to put the point is perhaps this: that once you have a *skill-based* vision of content, you should no longer restrict the psychologically relevant system to the system that trades in internal representations. Instead, the primary unit of analysis (to borrow a term from Hutchins 1995) spreads to include items such as bodily form (see Dennett's comments on the bird's wing etc., TAT: 5) and local context (see the comments on distributed intelligence, MTT: 8). Here, then, is a further important consequence (and compare with the non-skill-based discussion of these issues at the end of section 2.1.2 above) of the emphasis on tools and skills: the notion of cognition itself, and hence of the true *targets* of psychological understanding, is subtly altered to encompass *all* the tools and tricks that promote adaptive success. The special subclass that involves internal representations (understood as manipulable content-bearing tokens) is again not privileged, and emerges as just another part of the mosaic. (This may be one way of reading Dennett's strictures (TAT: 4–5) against the image of the 'walking encyclopedia'.) ***Discussion point 2.7***

The attack on isolability has a second dimension also. The issues here concern the degree of insulation and fire-walling *between* cognitively important processes. Dennett's point here is that a certain kind of inter-process leakage can be a powerful source of effects which may then be co-opted into new, adaptively potent, strategies. Dennett here talks of features that are not random noise but whose usefulness emerges only when neighboring components learn to use them to create 'new functional structures' (TAT: 7). One concrete case that has some of the features Dennett describes, and which I will float for comments and reactions, involves recent work on what has become known as evolvable hardware.

Certain chips, called FPGAs (field programmable gate arrays) contain logic blocks that can be reorganized and reprogrammed *in situ*, thus falling somewhere between our old notions of software and hardware. Using a new, easy-to-reconfigure chip (a Xilinx XC6216), Thompson (Thompson *et al.* 1996; Thompson 1997) ran a process of simulated evolution (a modified genetic algorithm) to find a chip design capable of distinguishing two sounds (a 1 kHz and a 10 kHz tone). The evolutionary regime was, importantly, working with a real Xilinx chip, repeatedly reprogramming (in effect rewiring) and testing actual physical devices. After 5,000 generations, the chip was able to perform the task. What is interesting, from the present point of view, is how it worked. The successful chip used just 21 of the available 4,000 logic blocks, making it 'one or two orders of magnitude smaller than one would expect from conventional methods' (Thompson 1997: 389). And it bought this efficiency by exploiting low-level physical features and inter-component leakage in ways that pressed functionality from effects that a human engineer would have tried hard to suppress. Some logic blocks, in fact, seemed to be disconnected and idle, yet deleting them caused the circuit to fail. The explanation, according to Thompson, is that 'they must be interacting by some subtle property of semiconductor physics such as electromagnetic coupling or interacting through the power supply wiring' (ibid.).

Here, then, we have a concrete (albeit low-level) case in which inter-component 'leakage' and 'noise' provides the raw material for a new adaptive strategy, just as Dennett suggests. Moreover, and this is why I mention the example, there is a serious sense in which the exploitation of this kind of effect challenges the traditional pictures of computation and of software as an autonomous level in nature. Thompson and his colleagues prefer to view the chip as 'a dynamical system, not a computational one', since its success depends so heavily on the 'continuous-time . . . unfolding of the laws of semiconductor physics' (ibid.). The idea, I think, is that one cannot understand how this system works by thinking of it in terms of an

interconnected array of logic boxes, each one performing an isolated function or operation. *Discussion point 2.8*

Several themes here come satisfyingly together. Recall Dennett's comments (TAT: 2) about the distortive effects of restricting psychological
explanations to operations on propositional contents, instead of really
trying to understand how a component accomplishes a task, and his
skepticism (TAT: 4–5) about cognitive scientific 'boxology' and its imagined separation of software and hardware. The story of the evolved
FPGA chip confirms the force of these worries and shows how they also
bear on issues concerning computation and internal representation. Standard computational and representational approaches, we may well suspect,
are overly focused on one kind of content and one kind of mind-tool, and
insufficiently sensitive to the depth of the canvas upon which nature
sketches its strategies for adaptive success.

One can, of course, try to recast the notions of representation and
computation to embrace more and more of the territory Dennett and
others are exploring. My own tendency, indeed, has been to do just that
(see Clark 1997*b*). But what matters most is not, of course, what we call
these strategies. Only that we recognize the roles they play in enabling
intelligent behavior. In fact, things only get *really* radical when proponents
of alternative approaches attack the very idea that psychological explanation must plot relations between states identified, at least in part, in terms
of their *contents*. I do not *think* that Dennett, for all his worrying about
propositional modes of content capture, wants to do that. But we should at
least note the following question: In attacking the fixation with propositional modes of content specification and drawing attention to the complex roles of body, world, and physical hardware, does Dennett envision a
content-based but largely non-propositional science of the mind, or does
he envision a withering away of the role of content altogether? The answer
seems to be (see e.g. TAT: 2) that he still sees cognitive scientific explanation as essentially content-involving, but that we should be aware of the
inadequacy and inaccuracy of most (all?) of our specifications of content.
But this is a point that might reward further clarification.

2.1.5 Numerical Cognition: A Case Study

Here's a summary of what I take to be Dennett's big picture. Minds are
grab-bags of (userless) tools for thought. Propositional specifications fail
to capture the essence of most of the contents supported by the tools.

Content and aboutness is initially determined by the skilled engagements made possible by the tool-complexes. And talk of internal representations becomes increasingly appropriate as the skilled engagements become more flexible and open-ended courtesy of the creation of more manipulable content-bearing tokens: a process that probably originates in experiences of *external* symbol use.

This is a compelling but rather abstract and schematic story, so I'd like to end with a concrete case study that seems to illustrate many of the central ideas.

Dehaene *et al.* (1999) ask: 'does the human capacity for mathematical intuition depend on linguistic competence or on visuo-spatial representations?' (p. 970). The answer that emerges is 'both'—what makes us uniquely (as a species) competent in mathematics is the interplay between very different sets of mind-tools, with human embodiment and motor skills acting as a source of 'bridging manipulanda'. More precisely Dehaene (1997) and Dehaene *et al.* (1999) adduce a diverse body of evidence in support of a complex picture of human mathematical skill. The picture has three main components:

1. It depicts an innate, biological competence at low-grade approximate arithmetic: a simple number sense, shared by infants and other animals, and involving the rough appreciation of changes in quantity, of relative quantities, and of a couple of precise quantities such as oneness, twoness, and threeness.

2. It depicts a culturally acquired capacity to think about exact quantities (other than 1, 2, and 3) courtesy of verbal and language-specific representations of numbers.

3. It speculates that the cultural-evolutionary processes that allowed us to develop the symbol systems supporting exact mathematics crucially involved the use of body parts as stand-ins for numbers.

Preliminary evidence for the hypothesis of distinct systems supporting exact and approximate arithmetic comes from studies (Dehaene *et al.* 1999) of Russian/English bilinguals. Subjects were taught, in one of the two languages, a set of exact or approximate sums of two-digit numbers. They had to select the correct sum from two candidates. In one condition (the exact condition) they were told to select the answer from two numerically close candidates. In a second condition (the approximation condition) they were told to estimate the result and select the closest candidate. After training, performance in the approximation condition was shown to be unaffected by switching the language, whereas in the exact condition, language switching resulted in asymmetric performance, with subjects responding much faster if the test language corresponded to the training language. From this and several related studies, Dehaene *et al.* concluded that the knowledge used for the approximation tasks is stored in a non-linguistic format, whereas the knowledge used for exact arithmetic is stored in a genuinely language-specific format. Dehaene (1997: 102) also observes that different languages and number notations yield different typical numerical skills. English speakers asked to memorize 7 single-digit numbers have a 50 per cent chance of failure whereas Chinese speakers nearly always succeed. This is because Chinese number words are so brief. The typical numerical-list memory of speakers of a certain Cantonese dialect is a full 10 digits, revealing digit-span as a 'culture-and-training-specific value [that] cannot be taken to index a fixed biological memory size parameter' (Dehaene 1997: 103). (Speakers of any language can, however, improve their skills by the use of new mind-tools such as digit grouping and recoding.)

A second line of evidence draws on lesion studies in which (to take one example) a patient with severe left-hemisphere damage cannot determine whether 2 + 2 is 3 or 4, but reliably chooses 3 or 4 over 9, indicating a dissociation between the mind-tools supporting approximate and exact numerical reasoning.

Finally, and perhaps most dramatically, Dehaene *et al.* (1999) present neuroimaging data from subjects engaged in exact and approximate numerical tasks. The exact tasks show significant activity in the speech-related areas of the left frontal lobe, while the approximate tasks recruit bilateral areas of the parietal lobes implicated in visuo-spatial reasoning. These results are presented as a demonstration 'that exact calculation is language dependent, whereas approximation relies on nonverbal visuo-spatial cerebral networks' (p. 970) and that 'even within the small domain of elementary arithmetic, multiple mental representations are used for different tasks' (p. 973).

Dehaene (1997: 91) rounds off the story with some cultural-evolution-ary and developmental speculation. The cultural-evolutionary question is, of course, 'How did *homo sapiens* alone ever move beyond approxima-tion?' And the answer, in part, is of course 'the human ability to devise symbolic numeration systems' (ibid.): the ability to create external representations, that become internalized as language-dependent mind-tools. This process began, Dehaene suggests, with the use of body parts as stand-ins for numbers. Once you use one, two, and three fingers (say) as stand-ins for the biologically appreciable quantities of oneness, twoness, and threeness, it becomes possible to discover accidentally that an additional oneness can be tracked by associating the new quantity with a fourth finger. Historical and multicultural studies, reported in detail by Dehaene, show the body-part roots of many names for numbers. The developmental process is also discussed, and here Dehaene makes some nice points about the need somehow to establish links between the linguistic labels and our innate sense of simple quantities. At first, it seems, children learn language-based numerical facts *without* such appreciation. According to Dehaene, 'for a whole year, children realize that the word "three" is a number without knowing the precise value it refers to' (ibid. 107). But once the label gets attached to the simple innate number line, the door is open to understanding that all numbers refer to precise quantities, even when we lack an intuitive sense of what the quantity is (for example, my intuitive sense of fifty-threeness is not distinct from my intuitive sense of fifty-twoness). What all this amounts to, in Dennett's terms, is, of course, the gradual installation, via a route that passes through external symbolic notations, of a new and potent virtual machine in the head: a culturally incubated mind-tool for exact arithmetic. But this mind-tool, Dehaene insists, retains some of the character of the basic biological arithmetical device. Dehaene approvingly quotes von Neumann: 'When we talk about mathematics, we may be discussing a *secondary* language, built upon the primary language used by the central nervous system' (von Neumann 1958, quoted in Dehaene 1997: 236). This recalls some issues first raised way back in section 2.1.2. Are all mind-tools really on a par, or are some privileged—the *real* tools of understanding? What we may dimly glimpse in this example is a way in which each bald assertion contains an element of truth. Humans must, according to Dehaene, ultimately use an analog, and rather fuzzy, number-line to represent quantity: a conjecture that explains the so-called distance effect by which it takes us (unlike a digital computer) longer to compare two close numbers than two distant ones. Exact mathematical tasks do, however, require the use of internal representations of number symbols. But our claim to genuine numerical *understanding* seems to rest on the presence of *both* kinds of skill, and (crucially) the presence of certain bridges and links that put our exact calculations in contact with our biological sense of quantity and relative position in an array. Numerical understanding thus depends crucially on both systems, but it is in a real sense 'grounded' in the more biologically basic one. The image to avoid is the one of simple translation from a public to a biological code. For no such translation is possible or necessary. Instead, the two resources collaborate, and there are crucially important links and bridges between them. Seeing the deep difference between this picture and the Fodorian image of translation into a central code is, I think, crucial. *Discussion point 2.9*

So *is there* an internal representation of, let's say, '98'? I think the answer that now emerges is 'No'! What we have are genuine internal representations of the *word* 'ninety-eight' (or perhaps of the phonetics of the word) and of the *numeral* '98', and genuine internal representations of rough quantity and relative location in an array. Mathematical understanding then depends heavily on the interplay and links between skills dependent on the representations of number words and skills dependent on the biologically basic resource for approximate arithmetic. And in the latter case, at least, these skills are not rooted in familiar (digital, discrete token manipulating) kinds of computation but in the operation of a fundamentally analog device. *Discussion point 2.10*

2.1.6 Conclusions: The Big Lacuna(e)

I've tried to show just how radical and challenging Dennett's emphasis on skills and mind-tools can be, and how it subtly shifts the focus from simple notions of internal representation and computation to the complexities of interaction between different kinds of mind-tools. Along the way, I've tried to highlight and explore some themes that are less commonly discussed than (say) Dennett's view about consciousness and the intentional stance, but that seem to me to be the essential backdrop to all the rest. These include the image of mind-tools *all the way down*, and the idea that no mind-tool or class of mind-tools is essentially privileged in an explanation of thought and understanding.

The concrete tales concerning hardware evolution and numerical cognition were then meant to show both how (very) much Dennett has got right, and how (very) far there is still to go. The emphasis on skills, multiple mind-tools, and loops involving external symbol systems are nicely supported by the latter, while the former lends weight to the qualms about simple notions of content and computation, and about the isolability of inner vehicles. But there are, of course, trouble spots. It's not *really* clear, for example, what holds the bag of mind-tools together as an agent—can narrative really bring persons into being? It is not *really* clear in what sense the various mind-tools are on a par, since some are clearly much more biologically basic than others (though I suspect there is no deep problem here: they are on a par in one sense, in that no tool is intrinsically contentful in a way the others are not, but there may still be a sense in which some tools are built on the foundations laid by others). It is not clear exactly what florid representing amounts to, or why it is as important as Dennett seems to think. It's not *at all* clear how best to understand the crucial processes of interaction and coordination by which the various classes of mind-tool interact—especially the crucial case of the interactions between the mind-tools dependent on external symbol systems and their more biologically basic counterparts. And it is not *at all* clear what, in the biological evolution of our species, opened the door to the creation and use of such potent external symbol systems in the first place. With lacunae like those, who needs enemies?

Reply to Clark

DANIEL DENNETT

I pretty much agree with Clark's comments, and I just want to confirm some of his suspicions. I'm particularly glad he pointed to the places where I contrasted, say, having beliefs about beliefs with thinking about thinking, and started talking about florid representation as being a different sort of thing or a special sort of thing, because I think that's where this workshop is heading most interestingly and fruitfully.

I also want to draw attention to a point that came up this morning in our discussion of Haugeland's work. [See Part 3—ed.] It's a point that's also in my review of his book (Dennett 1999). Haugeland wants to resist the over-intellectualization of commitment. He does not want commitment to be explicable in terms of propositions deemed true or anything else that looks even a little bit Cartesian or intellectualist. I appreciate his motivation: anything that keeps Cartesianism at bay is a good thing, anything that keeps propositions and propositional attitudes impoverished and out in the street is a good thing, but I think he's overdone it a little bit.

The truth is almost embarrassingly obvious, that it is human natural language that sets us apart from the other species, because it gives us, and only us, for the first time, a genuinely open-ended compositional, manipulable, medium of representation suitable for any topic. It does this by a process which is fundamentally indirect. It's not, as Smith was fearing [See Discussion point 2.10], that mathematicians are thinking about numerals, or that people are thinking about the word 'Dan'. No, you can use the word 'Dan' to refer to Dan and you can think silently ('in your head') about Dans by thinking with 'Dan's, but in general the capacity to do that is parasitic on the more florid capacity to think about the words as representations. This is like the barefoot water-skier who has to learn to ski with skis before throwing them away. Once you've learned how to think about words—to have words themselves as perceptual objects, noticing two words that rhyme, noticing that this is a noun and that's a verb, and so forth—then, and probably only then, do you really get a human mind. Perhaps there are a lot of human beings who talk, but they don't know they're talking. They use words in all sorts of wonderful ways, hardly aware of what they're up to, but they don't yet have the sort of full human minds that Haugeland and Smith talk about.

There is a presumption that operates among philosophers, who really have thought about thinking about thinking about thinking, and thought about words about words—we've gone meta; it is in our blood: we tend to think that a lot of the insight that we have achieved by doing this is generally shared in the populace. But I don't think it is. I think that most people are pretty clueless about this as we all know from teaching introductory philosophy. 'What's your ontology?' 'I beg your pardon!' This is not a question that people take to naturally. ***Discussion point 2.11***

Clark raises a very good point about the distinction between, as he says, 'being savvy with the talk' and 'being savvy about the talk'. [See Discussion point 2.11—ed.] When I introduced the idea of florid representation, I didn't settle that issue, and I still haven't got it clear in my own head how to deal with that. How virtuosic could one be as a language user and still be essentially unreflective about this? I think that's an empirical question. I don't know the answer. ***Discussion point 2.12***

I think there can be, for instance, a lying virtuoso who is extremely good at deceiving others and yet still isn't really reflective about what it is to deceive or what it is to lie. Such unreflective know-how is possible in principle. Moreover, it's actual, and even normal: to wit, the linguistic competence of a 5-year-old. [See Discussion point 2.12—ed.] And yet it doesn't follow from this that we would do well to understand that competence from the bottom up. We would do better to think of language as if it was harder for us than in fact it is—as if we had to work at it; as if we had to remind ourselves of what words were for. Actually I think the historical truth is that it was a lot harder to use language in the 'olden days' than it is now. I think there has been a lot of Baldwin effect selection for linguistic competence, and that the first of our ancestors who used language found this a much more challenging and taxing activity than we do today.

I agree with Haugeland that there's a watershed between Sheila the dog's capacity to make mistakes, and the human being's capacity to make mistakes. [See Haugeland's reply in Part 3—ed.] I think that his way of trying to capture that watershed in terms of commitment errs on the side of thinking that commitment is more dissociable from language than in fact it is. I think it's coming to be able to have conversation and use language that (for example) enables one to play chess.

It's not that all thinking is talking to yourself. On the contrary, talking to yourself is often a substitute for thinking. My suggestion is that talking, and then learning to talk to yourself, is a biologically necessary preamble to developing the sort of virtual machines that make human thought possible, whether it's linguistic or not. Our acquisition of language works, crudely, by making us adept representation-appreciators of a certain sort. We get used to going back and forth between the representation and the represented. Whether it's a map and a city, or a name and the guy whose name it is, there is a trick we master of using a representation to refer to an object. This is not a natural act (Deacon 1997 has a good discussion of this). It is something that is hard to acquire, and we should expect to have to tell a convoluted story about how people come to get their heads in a sort of habit state where this becomes natural. Once it becomes natural, it looks as if it's just biological, part of being *Homo sapiens*. If we see our linguistic talents as simply wired in, we are on the path to a language of thought. But this is exactly what shouldn't be taken for granted. It's not that we don't have the link of reference, or that that link doesn't exist in lots of subhuman creatures or maybe even Smith's supersunflowers or something like it (Smith 1996: 202 ff.). What is distinctly human is the appreciation of that link as a matter of course. It's our becoming fluent in the use of those links that makes a human mind a human mind. *Final discussion*

Discussion

2.1
p. 73 CUMMINS Well, depending on how biological you think language is, if you're over toward Pinker [1994] on that side of things, then that strikes me as a really good candidate for exactly this sort of thing.

DENNETT What strikes you?

CUMMINS Spoken language as opposed to written language, on the grounds that the former is much more biological, as the latter is clearly cultural. And it was witting in its origins, at least, if not in its continued use, whereas the other, presumably, just evolved.

DENNETT I think this is very interesting. One of my favorite ways to stop people from thinking in a certain way, is I suggest to people, reformulate the language of thought hypothesis, where the language of thought is a spoken language only. It's not a written language, and so you can't help yourself to any of the features of language which are really only features of written language. And the whole project of course immediately just crashes—

CLAPIN Like what kind of properties?

HAUGELAND Perseverance of the tokens, for one thing.

CLAPIN But audiotape does that for spoken language.

HAUGELAND Well, audiotape was even more recent than writing.

CLAPIN Well, you can imagine storing sound in a way that can be used again.

DENNETT Well, I think that if you just try that exercise, you find it's really hard. You start saying, wait a minute, what can I do, what can the brain do with a merely spoken language? How does it store things? And you begin to realize that lots of things you've been taking for granted you just can't help yourself to any more.

CLAPIN I want to hear some stronger examples. First of all I thought OK, maybe inferences, you know, where you're thinking of form, but actually, you can present inferences verbally perfectly well, just in such a way that you hear the same pattern again and you see what's repeated.

CUMMINS And we're remarkably bad at it.

CLAPIN Oh yeah, but Dan's position seemed to be stronger than just good and bad. Some things just aren't possible, in spoken language that are in written language, and I'm not sure that's...

DENNETT Well, I'm not sure I want to make that point that strongly. I just want to get people sensitized to the likelihood that they're using vision, blackboards, words; stable tokens that sit somewhere. They're using those features of written language to anchor their imagination when they think about the language of thought. And if they do, they should know they're doing it. I remember one time Patty Churchland said— I thought it was a brilliant comment—people are always drawing attention to the fact that, as any new technology comes along, it becomes the metaphor for the mind. So we have the clockwork, the steam engine, the dynamo, the telephone exchange, the laser, and so forth, she said, but of course the granddaddy of all of this is writing. And the seductive analogy of what the brain is, is this great big writing machine.

SMITH There's also the idea that the content of uses of words is exhausted by the content the token can have. This is, I think, a very serious mistake, and it absolutely comes from writing.

DENNETT Let me just pause and say about the rake, to stop and think that what rakes are for is for sorting. They're a mechanized sorting algorithm. 2.2 p. 74

CLARK But does that make it a mind-tool? I mean that makes it sound like a mind-tool—

DENNETT Well, yes, yes exactly. My point is that a sieve or a rake, is, after all, for separating kinds.

CUMMINS It's clear with something like a can-opener, I think. I mean when you ask people, do you know how to open a can? Well, what they know is how to use a can-opener and all the rest of the knowledge is in the thing.

CLARK The can-opener, is that a mind-tool?

CUMMINS Well I know how to open a can because I've got a can-opener, and I know how to run the can-opener. And it knows how to open the can.

CLARK Okay, the presence of the tool makes a difference to the knowledge that you have.

CUMMINS Yeah, it expands my knowledge.

CLAPIN I thought mind-tools were not just about adding a bit of know-ledge—all sorts of things can add knowledge—but mind-tools actually are things that help you think better or differently. Now I'm not sure knowing how to open a can is important if you're interested in cognitive processes.

DENNETT Or they may instead help you by permitting you to do something without thinking, but before you had to think.

CUMMINS It looks troublesome to try and draw a principled distinction between say, compiling extensive knowledge and just offloading it into the can-opener.

2.3 DENNETT If you think about the organism facing an environment, and
p. 74 then having an option of improving the environment to make its life easier—digging a burrow, neatening things up, putting down scent trails: all of those are improvements. They are sort of capital improvements in your environment to make life easier for you. Now I don't see any reason to draw some particular line across that and say, 'and these are the mind-tools'. They are all changes in the world which are designed—wittingly or not—to improve the competence of an organism who may benefit in some sense.

CLAPIN So they're really life tools. That some of them have something to do with mental capacities isn't really part of the picture, is it?

HAUGELAND Then growing fur counts.

CLAPIN Yeah, exactly.

CUMMINS What the picture is, is that 'mind' just doesn't pick out a very interesting category.

DENNETT Well, it's a really interesting empirical question to which I do not know the answer, and as far as I know, nobody does, whether any non-human species, as it were, deliberately makes marks on the world in order to cut down its cognitive load. There's scent trails, but just the making of marks in the world in order to make a cognitive task easier.

CLAPIN Yes, but that's what I thought the category was. I can see why you might want to include can-openers there, but, not every tool that makes life easier reduces your cognitive load.

DENNETT Some of them make life easier by filling your belly.

CUMMINS All that shows is that there's a blurry boundary. The fact that 2.4
    there's no clean line between alive and dead doesn't mean there aren't p. 74
    some clearly dead things.

CLARK It's not really a matter of looking for a clear boundary. It's just that
    anything that I can think of that helps you in any way at all soon looks
    like it should fall clearly on the mind-tool side of the boundary if we
    understand things this way.

CLARK What I want to attribute to Dan, although I don't think he expli- 2.5
    citly says this, is that in the end, the distinction between something that p. 77
    implements part of the thinking and something that is a tool for thought
    is a distinction without a difference. That there is no distinction there.

DENNETT Show me why I shouldn't say that.

CLARK I actually think you should.

SMITH Can I get a clarification of what's being agreed to here? Is it that
    there simply is no distinction, or that there's no theoretically interesting
    sharp boundary to be drawn?

CLARK I don't think it's an issue about sharp lines. I hope it's not...
    I think it really is an issue about whether there's a distinction there at all.

SMITH So when I say, 'Where are you, mostly?', you can say, 'Over here in
    this chair.' See, that's a much stronger thesis than just not signing up for
    a sharp boundary.

CLARK Well, I think that's a thesis that I'd have to sign up for.

SMITH Well, this is very important. If I make a racist comment, and you
    say to me, 'Brian—you can't make a racist comment,' I don't get to say,
    'It wasn't me; it was the whole dinner-table.'

DENNETT Well, let me challenge even that. Part of being an ethically
    competent individual is preparing your environment to make it easier
    for you to be ethically competent. Tying strings around your finger as
    reminders, keeping substances that will lure you into addiction out of
    your house, and so forth.

CUMMINS Publicly declaring your promises.

DENNETT Exactly. All of these things offload into the world aspects of
    your responsibility, and the myth that there is this sort of responsible
    nugget, independent of the environment that it has prepared for itself,
    is, I think, wrong.

SMITH But you don't punish the string.

DENNETT I promised to give you the recipe for chocolate cake. I wrote the
    recipe for chocolate cake down and put that in a safe place to give to

you. Somebody else comes along and burns that recipe. Now, I can't keep my promise. It's not my fault. I mean, I did everything right. The environment has let me down.

SMITH Right, but the point is that you discharged your responsibility. It's not that you and the paper failed your collective responsibility.

CUMMINS Is that really right, or is it just that it's very hard to incarcerate situations?

HAUGELAND No, you can't even find them culpable.

CLARK I think the sense in which we think that the paper isn't in some way culpable is no different to the sense that we think that some little bit of neural tissue isn't culpable. Some tiny bit of neural tissue: clearly you want to say, well, that wasn't culpable, but still, it's part of the larger system that failed its duties.

DENNETT Right. I think this is where Locke is right. The notion of a person is a forensic notion, and that's just a brute fact about the notion of a person and the notion of responsibility. It's not a metaphysical fact about the nature of persons intrinsically in themselves. It's just that if you have moral responsibility, you have to have something which counts as a locus, and that's what we call a *person*. Not their proper parts and not their accoutrements and not their companions.

CLARK I think maybe when we think about these issues we're overly impressed by the idea that if you took the piece of paper away you still have a perfectly good agent. A kind of subtraction principle. And of course that's true of a little bit of neural tissue, too, you know. Take it away, and it's still a perfectly good agent.

CUMMINS There's clearly a slippery slope, here.

CLARK It's like saying, OK the tree wasn't part of the forest, because if you take it away you still have a forest. If you take away enough, sure. In the end you end up with nothing. But it could be that if you take away enough of the physical and cultural surroundings, you pretty well end up with nothing too.

DENNETT Well, an example that I use in *Kinds of Minds* [1996] is this: you have people, old people particularly, who are perfectly competent if you leave them in their own apartment, where they've got everything signposted and everything familiar. You put them in the hospital and they're unable to dress themselves, unable to feed themselves. They seem to be totally incompetent, because you've simply put them in an environment where they don't recognize anything. And you move them back into their well-prepared environment and they're just fine, they can handle themselves just great.

CUMMINS But do you want to be saying that it wasn't him that you put in the hospital?

CLARK In a certain sense that is what you have to say, yeah.

DENNETT You only put part of him in the hospital. If you put him all in the hospital, if you move the whole apartment to the hospital, he's a healthy person.

CLAPIN Andy, I'm now hearing that you are agreeing with Dan a lot on this extended mind stuff. So I've got a bit lost with the criticism about tools for use.

CLARK In a way it's not really a criticism. I was just trying to clarify to what extent Dan allows the notion of a mind-tool to be a notion of something that can actually extend the agent. Lacking any way of separating mind-tools off from just all the rest of the stuff that helps you get along, then you have a threat of unbounded extension, or extension that includes stuff that seems uncomfortable. And that was sort of my worry. I don't have a solution to that. It's a worry about my own view as much as it's a worry about Dan's view.

SMITH Why do you agree with the first part of the sentence?   2.6

CLARK 'The user has in some sense disappeared in a welter of equipment'—   p. 78
Well, the user is now constituted by the welter of equipment—that would be the way to put it. The user doesn't disappear. You now see the user for what they are. The user just is the welter of equipment.

HAUGELAND The user as distinct from the equipment, has disappeared, in favor of just the equipment.

CLARK Hence the lack of a distinction between a tool for thought and part of the thinking.

CLAPIN And so the equipment has no user.

CUMMINS You've got to be a little careful here. It's not that the equipment has no user. Any particular piece of equipment might be used by another piece of equipment. There can be consumers and producers and so on—

DENNETT This is key for your view because you've got to have all those intender mechanisms.

CUMMINS That's right. That's why I'm sensitive to this. It's just that there's no exempt user, if you like.

CLARK Right: there's no exempt user that constitutes the agent, in some sense. There can be lots of users in there in some way. Or lots of instances of use.

CUMMINS That's right.

2.7
p. 83

CLAPIN So, is that to suggest that representation is necessary, not sufficient?

CLARK Yes, if a process is going to be a cognitive process, then somewhere along the way it intersects with a representational process. I suspect that may be true, or at least the way we should use that word if we want to kind of keep in line with the way cognitive science seems to use that word.

DENNETT Well, but, at lunch we were talking about such things as the control of your gait when you're running. Now, the question is whether in any interesting sense at all that's a cognitive process. It's a control structure, it's in your nervous system, there are states in that nervous system that are content bearing, that are information bearing about the phasic properties of your legs and so forth. It's such that you can identify a source of misinformation, of misstep, and so forth. Now, it seems to me it's like Darwin saying thank goodness for extinction, we don't have all the intermediate cases to worry about. We could never identify a species, if it weren't for the fact that the isthmuses between the islands have all disappeared. If we could say that in this case then we'd say, look, here's cognition over here and it always involves representation. Then we have all this other stuff, and, even though we can't define the dividing line, we don't have to worry about it because there aren't all these intermediate cases. But that's just not true. And it seems to me that in the case of cognition, the isthmuses are still there. They're in things like control of locomotion and grasping, to use the case that Rob was talking about earlier. It does look as if we really do have something more like the continuum of cases all the way from the immune system and digestion, up to the fanciest schmanciest cognition. See that's what fuels some of my, sort of verificationism. We're not niggling about boundaries, here. We're saying, look, there really isn't any interesting . . . it's not like night and day.

CUMMINS Why isn't this kind of like what I said years ago about functions? [See Cummins 1975; 1983—ed.] It's just that, the more you get toward the florid case, the more kind of cognitive it looks, and the more you go the other way, it's less cognitive, but the fact of the matter is, there isn't any very principled distinction here. It's just that you kind of mark your distance from these poles in terms of how cognitive it looks to us. But to sort of think there must be somewhere between the way an ant controls locomotion and when I go jogging, that really kind of turns it into the real thing...

SMITH There just is this sweep, as Dan says, and in fact naming the sweep will end up being pretty boring—the way physicists don't use the word 'physical'—they don't care about what things are physical and what aren't. What they care about is energy, mass, charm, and so forth. So the question is, what are the fine-grained notions that we will end up using? We have a remarkable amount of agreement, such that in fact we may almost be ready to let go of that *R*-word, and actually make some progress. I don't know if we can make any progress this week, but I mean historically. But it strikes me as much harder to know what the theoretical types are that are an order of magnitude more fine-grained than the notion of representation.

CLARK This reminds me of Aaron Sloman's [1984] take on this stuff, which has always been that you confront a big design space, incorporating all sorts of important distinctions. But there's no distinction between the intelligent systems and the rest, or the truly computational systems and the rest.

CLARK It seems to me that stories like that suggest that we may just really underestimate the kind of canvas on which nature sketches its solutions. 2.8 p. 85

CUMMINS Or really overestimate multiple realizability.

CLARK Right. Or have a limited notion of what the vehicles of content might be like. Indeed of what computation might be like. Adrian Thompson says it isn't a computational solution if it's using properties like that. Other people just say this shows how large the space of possible computational solutions is.

HAUGELAND Well, that would be a solution that has and lacks various properties, that has the property of exploiting fewer of the gates than you would have otherwise thought possible. Off the top of my head, I'll bet it's much more susceptible to variations in temperature. And chip to chip variations, and...

CLARK One reason why we suppress those effects...

CUMMINS Well, John's point is interesting biologically, too, because it means a system like that is going to be difficult to replicate in a way that preserves functionality. Now, that's not quite true because if what you replicate is not, as it were, the chip, but as it were, the developmental recipe, then you don't replicate the chip, you just replicate a process which recapitulates their experiments every single time.

SMITH Well, there's another point, which is that software boundaries actually leak... all you need for replication is just that it be digital at some level, which can be in some sense be arbitrarily far down. And then above that you can have this kind of thing and it doesn't matter... I think digital *implementation* is the idea, not digitality *per se*. That's what's powerful about computing: digital implementation.

HAUGELAND And that's because you repeat it at that bottom level and all the bugs come with it.

2.9   CLARK As long as you don't think that relating has to take the form of
p. 89   precise translation, I think you can tell an interesting story in which our cognitive capacities are literally expanded by the presence of that cultural item, as opposed to insisting that the cultural item first gets turned into some version of mentalese before use.

SMITH Well there is an issue which also relates to Deacon [1997], whether if you accept that it's not translation, what the other possibilities are, if it's inside the skull.

CLARK Their coordination.

SMITH No, but the question is whether it requires implementation. It's not that you necessarily have programmable field arrays unused in your brain which you code up. One possibility is that you use more circuits that are like the old circuit in order to implement a new machine. So you're using one set of mental capacities directly, to do a certain kind of thinking. And then you use another set of mental capacities to implement some virtual machine on top of them which then does its own thing authentically. I guess what I'm saying is that there's a substantial question, when you extend internally, what the biological mechanism for that external extension is. Is it actually new neural wiring, or is it an implementation? I think implementation is such an extraordinarily powerful notion. And I think this ties in with things that Dan thinks.

CLARK All I wanted out of this really was the idea that coordination needn't involve translation. Coordination between the cultural resource and the biologically basic resource may be essential and it may be that coordination that actually constitutes the thought, or the content of the thought. The content of the thought might be constituted by coordination between these different resources. So if you then go into the head and look for the content bearer of that thought, you don't find it.

CLAPIN This sounds like what Rob calls a concept rather than an application. If you're looking for what you know about threeness or fiveness, you've got to look for something like that.

CUMMINS A particularly crude application of this would be the Fodor view about language understanding. My language understander not only has to be able to represent the symbols of the language, but it has to represent what the symbols of the language represent. And a much more modest idea is, no, what I need is the ability to represent the symbols of the language and then let them do their own thing.

CLARK That's exactly right. That's just where this should go.

SMITH Except it's not clear you want the word 'represent'. You want to be able to *something* the symbols in the language. And that word might be 'implement' as much as 'represent'. It's not obvious they can be represented.

CLARK So I think that there's actually something there that Fodor and Churchland share, that they both make the same mistake, thinking that external resources, if they're going to contribute to cognition, must do so by being translated into an internal scheme. Fodor has a particular version of that story, Churchland has another one, but neither of them are able to accept that coordination might be what counts, not representation.[7] 2.10 p. 89

SMITH It seems to me if you wanted to convince either Fodor or Churchland there is a question that's left open—and this is why implementation does matter—which is that, yes, let's say, you can coordinate the two. But if you're going to internalize the one in order that it be coordinatable with, you've got to get it in somehow.

CLARK That's why I think you don't really have to internalize it. Maybe that's the issue. I don't think you have to implement the external tool internally, if you like, in order to coordinate with it.

CUMMINS I think this is more like the can-opener case. You learn how to open a can by learning how to run the can-opener, and the whole point is, you don't want to internalize the can-opener, because if you do, it will be implemented differently, and you won't get the can open any more.

SMITH No. I understand that I don't want to internalize the can-opener.

CLARK But I guess the farmer doesn't exploit the rake by translating it into sort of muscle-ese. Muscles are involved in exploiting the rake, but it's

---

7 [See e.g. Fodor (1975: ch. 1) and Churchland (1995)—ed.]

very funny to think that it's some kind of translation of the rake that's involved.

SMITH Right, but it seems to me unlikely that our interaction with words and numerals is as external as rakes or can-openers. I do think that something goes on in our head, and I think it's interesting. Suppose in fact that at some level it is vector-field settling and turbulent attractors...

CLARK But sometimes the targets of those vector fields are words.

SMITH See, implementation and representation are very interestingly close notions. They bear lots of resemblance. But I think there are certain ways in which they are not the same. Normally if you turn on a representation, what is represented doesn't start doing anything. But if you turn on your brain and start doing arithmetic, you get the answer. You can actually run it; whatever relationship your brain state bears to the symbolic numerical code, you can actually get it to go. That makes me think it's more implementation-like than representation-like.

CLARK Implementation is? I think maybe I don't understand what you mean by implementation.

CLAPIN I think I agree with Brian. Think of a simple contained system like a formal logic, like predicate calculus or something. You can do some stuff with it, prove something interesting. Now, that's a tool. That's a really good tool for a certain kind of thinking. But it seems to me you've got to know an awful lot of stuff. It's back to know-how and tacit rules and stuff. And there's a sense in which you can recreate that tool at any time. You know so much about that system. You've got so much knowledge—if you're competent at it—that it doesn't need to exist in the world except when you bring it into existence. This is quite different from the rake or the can opener. There's no way you want to internalize the can opener. But it seems to me it's part of what it is to be able to manipulate predicate calculus that you actually internalize a lot of it.

CUMMINS Why think you internalize the predicate calculus rather than a recipe for reinstantiating it?

CLAPIN Because you don't need to reinstantiate it.

DENNETT An example I use in *Kinds of Minds* [1996] is, can you alphabetize the words in this sentence in your head? And the fact is you can, we can, but only because we've become so good at memory management and little mnemonic tricks and we had lots of practice with things like index cards years ago. So we recreate the process which is much easier if we've got index cards, or writing it down on a blackboard. It's a sort of stunt. We can do it in our heads if we have to, but the fact that we're doing it in our heads tells us very little about why this stuff works and what kind of a tool it is. The fact is it's much easier to do it out in the world. It's like barefoot water skiing. Yeah, it's possible, you really have to start with the skis on, then you can kick them off if you're really virtuosic, but the fact is, don't make the mistake of thinking that, as it were, the external implementa are somehow irrelevant to the capacity that you have. And I think in general with regard to words, it's words as mnemonic crutches, it's words as attention holders, reminders, they're like the string around the finger. It's the sound of the word, it's the fact that we have all these associations, and we have to learn how to manipulate those objects.

SMITH But Dan, it seems to me that what you're saying now is at odds with what I think of as the core of your idea, which I think I agree with: which is that we are assemblages of tools in a sense...

DENNETT It's not at odds with that, I don't think. Why do you think it is?

SMITH Because it seems to me if I'm thinking conceptually about something, some argument in philosophy or something, and you come and say, 'What are you thinking about, Brian?' And I say 'I'm thinking about whether in fact if these three things were to happen this other thing would happen which would block this outcome I want'; some sort of complicated logical structure, say, about whether the dam will break. It seems to me that you want to say that I'm thinking about whether the dam will break. You don't want to be forced to conclude that I'm thinking about the words 'the dam'.

CLARK I think part of what's going on is that you are precisely thinking about the word.

SMITH If you think that, then I think that Dan articulated that view right, but I think that's crazy. I believe this is exactly the difference between representation and implementation. What I teach my freshman is that you can tell whether x implements y or x represents y by doing the following: blow x up, and see if y got destroyed. If it did it was implementation; if not, it was representation. Implementation is essentially supervenience.

CUMMINS That's just what Dehaene did, that's exactly what he did. He blew up the language and then it was destroyed.

CLARK But it fits, blow up the representations of the words and you lose the ability to think about the exact number 98. If you can't represent the word to yourself, you can't have those thoughts.

HAUGELAND That's implementation. You don't blow up 98.

SMITH You don't blow up 98 because you represent 98, but if you're implementing the word and if you blow up your brain cells you blow up your representation, right?

DENNETT Now I'm lost.

SMITH Let's draw a picture. [See Fig. 2.1—ed.] Let's have [connectionist activation] vectors or something, and then the word 'dam', and here's an actual dam. And here are two relationships; between something in the brain—neurons—and a word (α), and another relationship between the word and the thing in the external world (β). And my proposal is that this (α) is approximately the head. This (α) is an implementation relationship, and this (β) is a representation relationship. (This ['dam'] is of course a use of the word, it's not a type.) The idea is if I blow this [the vectors] up, this [the word] goes away, why? Because, just like in a computer system, if this [the word] was a list, and this [the vectors] is the C++ that implements it, it's just the same system under a different level of description. And what's amazing about implementing a list in C++ is you just configure C++ in such a way that it is a device which, at a different level of description, is this [the word or list]. And that is an extraordinarily powerful technique. And I guess my feeling is that it differs rather a lot from this kind of relationship (β).

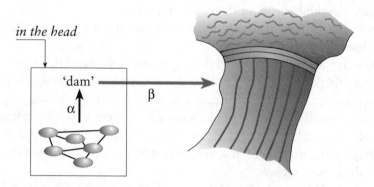

Fig. 2.1 Implementation and representation relationships

DENNETT Sure, of course.

CLARK Sure.

SMITH But then the question is, is this head thinking about the dam? And what I was saying to you, Dan, is I thought that what was core about your idea about tool use and us being assemblages, is that we manage to actually have this tool. We actually have it for real. We don't represent this tool, we actually have this tool. We make it, we actually construct it, and then we're thinking about dams. It seems that what Andy just said is: all we're doing is thinking about this tool.

CLARK No, you're thinking about the dam in virtue of thinking about that tool, and . . .

HAUGELAND In virtue of using the tool.

CLARK In virtue of using it.

CUMMINS There we go.

SMITH The point is, if you want to know how contents relate to representations, you have to figure out the level of description at which you're going to parse the brain. Because if you're actually implementing virtual machines in there, the physiology that Churchland gives you may actually be as irrelevant . . .

CLARK I'm going to put a thought on the table. I don't think you could think about moral issues unless you can think about words for moral issues, and I think the same is true for mathematics.

DENNETT Yep.

SMITH Unless you can think about the words, not just use the words?

CLARK Well, OK, I don't want to get too florid.

CLAPIN This is the difference.

HAUGELAND That's the trouble, that's a *philosophical* question. You can't think about moral issues *philosophically* unless you can think about the words.

CLAPIN You're happy with a large bulk of the population, particularly pre-twentieth century, not having human minds? 2.11
p. 92

DENNETT Well, of course not. In a way I'm not happy with it.

CLARK But in a way it all goes back to that issue about floridity, and know-how. Because couldn't someone be really savvy with the talk without being savvy about the talk, if you like?

DENNETT Right.

2.12 SMITH But what about 5-year-olds? Many of whom don't have the con-
p. 92   cept *word*.

DENNETT Well, exactly. They are in one sense language virtuosos. They're
very good. But they're not reflective about their use of language.

Final   CLARK But those are very different things again. The appreciation of the
discussion   link or being fluent in the use of it.
p. 93   DENNETT Yeah, exactly.

CLAPIN Clarification. You can still represent dams, for example? You can
still think about dams if you don't have language?

DENNETT Well you can behave *vis-à-vis* dams in all sorts of really adroit
ways. Because you've got something in your head which has information about dams. If you're a beaver for instance. They're like the
thing about redheads. They are a structure in the brain which becomes
active, does its thing when dams are an issue.

CLARK Think about something more advanced than the dam. Think
about justice, the concept of justice. Now it seems to me very likely
that the only way human beings can ever have a vector that in some
sense allows them to think about justice is by having a vector that puts
them in contact with the word 'justice'.

CUMMINS No, I don't believe that for a minute. I think I can have dams as
targets without words. I don't think I can have somehow discursive
dam thoughts without words.

CLARK What about other targets, targets like justice or charity?

CUMMINS Yeah, sure.

CLARK What is it to have your learning apparatus pointed at justice, as it
were?

CUMMINS Let's go back to John's case because it's sort of on the table.
[See Part 3—ed.] Chess versus schness. The idea is, you're the selection
agent. You've got a population down there and we assume that all the
relevant things are heritable and so forth. You're going to select for
success at chess. I'm going to select for success at schness. And we're
going to assume that in fact the distinction between chess and schness is
just beyond our populations altogether. Now, on, I think, everybody
else's view at this table, the consequence of that last condition is that
there isn't any difference between having knight forks and schnight
forks as targets. But on my view there is a difference. The difference is
that the size of the error that you will detect on any given case will in
general be different from the size of the error that I detect. And conse-

quently the learning trajectories will be different. You think that you can imagine a case in which you're rewarding for schness success and I'm rewarding for chess success, in which all the error signals turn out to be so close that there's no difference in the learning trajectories, you're kidding yourself. There ain't no such animal.

DENNETT Well let me give you an example. Some computer chess program recently found a mating net which is, I think, 232 moves long. Now that means that the rule declaring stalemate if there are 50 moves without a capture is now jeopardized because there's a situation that can come up in the game where White, say, can achieve checkmate—a *forced* mate—but it's 232 moves long without a capture. So the rule should be adjusted. We should change the stalemate rule to 250 or 300, because intuitively this is a win for White, not a stalemate. Suppose the difference between chess and schness is just this: chess is chess and schness is the game with the enlarged stalemate rule. It just never comes up in the whole selectional history of these experiments. You're selecting for schness and he's selecting for chess, but the difference never ever comes up. And so, although in your head you always have this thing ready to go if it ever comes up, it never comes up, and he has a different rule that never comes up. There's no difference in the error signal, there's no difference in the selectional history, and so, as far as that case goes, although there is a historical fact because of the curious way we told the story, it's hidden in these heads and never plays any role in the selectional history, right?

CUMMINS Yeah, OK.

DENNETT If it's like that you agree with me there's no fact of the matter?

CUMMINS That's right. Well, I think there's a fact of the matter, it's just a smeary fact. It's a fact that doesn't make the distinction.

DENNETT There's a sort of weird boring historical fact that these entities were selected for their ability to play schness, these were selected for their ability to play chess, but the fact has left no trace at all.

CUMMINS It left no trace, yeah, and there's only these counterfactuals which neither of us cares about. I agree with that. I'll grant you that.

SMITH Just for clarification, because we were talking about reflective... What if one of them, say Rob, realized in fact there was this rule and was keeping an eye out and wondering whether in fact anyone would discover a forced mate that took longer than 50 moves. If that was all there, would there be a fact?

DENNETT I think the point is, that when you've got people with brains and minds, who are thinking, so that one of them can be selecting for chess and the other one for schness, then you've got these agents that can settle all sorts of facts of the matter that in natural selection don't get articulated anywhere and don't get settled.

CUMMINS Well, this is natural selection, though, it's just...

DENNETT But, natural selection with a very special sort of environment. The sort of environment where, as it happens, something gets articulated that doesn't normally get articulated.

CUMMINS But I agree that in the case you said, that there's no difference in the targets. I agree with that. There is a historical fact of the matter about what was being... but I don't think that fact is, as it were, thick enough to support the claim that the two populations evolved different targets. That's just too precious.

DENNETT This morning you took John's example of a knight fork and the difference between that and a schnight fork. [See Part 3—ed.] My diagnosis of why you are so sure that you can draw this biological line that John does not think you can draw, is because you are covertly putting agents in the selective position. You're thinking this way: I'm playing chess and I break down into a functional decomposition the job that faces me. Now, knowing chess, I know what a knight fork detector is in John's sense where you have to be able to tell it from any media. You know I'm a savvy chess player. But, life is short and I don't have much money, I'm quite prepared to install in my design here a cheap knight fork detector which only works on a few media. It'll miss some cases. I don't care, I don't care how good it is. But I, the designer of this system, know what the project is. I know that that thing's a knight fork detector not a schnight fork detector. But natural selection isn't like that. Natural selection doesn't have the big picture. And so, precisely the indeterminacy that you insist is not there in the biological case and I say is there in the biological case, because mother nature doesn't tell the difference between the knight fork and the schnight fork.

CUMMINS But mother nature does know the difference between shadow detectors and predator detectors. [See Part 3; the example is introduced in s. 3.1.5 of 'Haugeland on Representation and Intentionality', and discussed throughout that Part—ed.]

DENNETT No.

CUMMINS There my point about looking at the error sizes really does make a big difference. You get very different kinds of learning curve in the two cases, particularly if we know some more details about the downstream consumers. You may not get learning at all in one of those cases.

DENNETT Now, you're going to have to prove that to me. Here's a case I want to imagine, and you've already helped, in a way. We have these two subvarieties. One of them gets a cheap shadow detector on a hair-trigger. The job is for you to say what the difference is between them. That is to say, if somebody comes along and says, well, you dummy, the reason this subspecies isn't doing too well, is that you put a shadow detector in there instead of a predator detector. And he says, no, there's a predator detector in there; it's just not a very good predator detector. You and Millikan and anybody who's thought about this realizes that you want to have room for a not very good predator detector, but good enough. But the trouble is that a not very good predator detector and a shadow detector are, as far as I can see, indistinguishable. And the challenge is for you to show how, without putting a big scheme in mother nature's head, you're going to tell the difference.

CLARK But what about a Fodorian move. What about just saying in worlds in which there are shadows but no predators that doesn't...?[8]

CUMMINS No I don't...that's one possible move, but...

CLARK But the only move that could possibly work...

CUMMINS Well, if that's right then I'm prepared to surrender because I think you'd disappear without a ripple into that swamp. No, I would much rather go back to the point about how you have to think of the error signal. And I think that it's an empirical issue. I don't think it has to be this way, but I think it can be this way. I think there's a real distinction between a situation in which what we've got is, as we usually say, something which is giving us a lot of false positives. Which, on the shadow detector version, we don't. Why talk the one way rather than the other? Because it depends on which error measurement is the one that tracks the learning curve. Let's think of the rewards as opposed to the errors for the moment. There's a sense in which nature isn't rewarding you for getting the shadows right. Those are waste cases. And so when you think about the regime that's driving the evolution of this detector, if you think of it as a shadow detector you lose sight of the fact that false positives carry a cost.

CLARK When you say nature isn't rewarding us for getting the shadows right, that just is the Fodorian move.

[8] [See Fodor's 'A Theory of Content II' in Fodor (1990)—ed.]

CUMMINS No, I mean historically, as a matter of fact, you actually burned calories every time you jumped down a darn hole and it was a shadow.

CLARK But you're saying, as it were, in worlds in which there are the shadows but no predators, you won't be rewarded for this—

CUMMINS In the real word there were both. I have no objection to the idea that the solution is, in some sense or other, to recognize predators by means of reacting to shadows or something like that.

CLARK Nature is rewarding you for shadow detection. Just like when something detects food by detecting the presence of some chemical in the food, nature is rewarding it for detecting food. It does so by detecting this other thing, chemical, whatever it is. Why is the shadow case different to that?

CUMMINS I'll have to think of another way to say this.

SMITH I have a question for Dan, which is that language seems a representational vehicle, that, at least especially as we philosophers imagine it, we think has conceptual content or propositional structure—roughly taking the world to consist of objects and properties that hold of it. With respect to the things you were saying at the beginning of your comment about what you think is distinctive of a certain kind of human capacity: is it language in the sense of a communicative structure that you think is critical, or is the conceptual structure of that representation— productive, systematic, object-property structure—the thing that's crucial, and language is needed because otherwise we wouldn't get that kind of conceptual structure? What's the division of labor between these two facts about language, which seem to me at least logically separable?

DENNETT That's a very good question, and I wouldn't have even understood the question before I read your book, but I think I do now understand the question, but I don't know what the answer is. As you'll hear more tomorrow, I want to add natural selection, evolutionary considerations, as a friendly amendment to Brian's story, though he doesn't think it's a friendly amendment. [See Part 5—ed.] But we'll see how that goes, because if I could add that as a friendly amendment, then I could say, look, the object–property distinction, the whole metaphysics that Brian elaborates in the book, and the emergence of this conception, is what I call a Good Trick [Dennett 1995a]. It's a trick we would expect to find on other planets, wherever there was intelligent life. We would expect that once you get above the fish and the microbe to complex life-forms that are social—this is where the communication comes in—then, you would expect objects and properties to become the reigning ontology everywhere in the universe where social communication emerges by evolution. And that would take your question and answer it but not by siding with one or the other but by saying that, as you yourself suggest, it is not really accidental. It's not an option to have a different ontology. The world's too hard. The world pretty well obliges us to hit upon this ontology. But the only real way the world can oblige us to do anything is by killing us if we don't. And so it's the evolutionary pressure that provides the dynamics that gravitates to the ontology. And of course I want to say something similar about John, and say, it's the social evolutionary pressure that he comes so close to articulating. He has memes right there, and then he backs off. [See Dennett (1999)—ed.]

CLARK   It obliges us to have that ontology if we're going to think about it at all.

DENNETT   That's right. We may not think about it at all, we may just be like trees or clams, but if we're ever going to go down the guerrilla warfare path of being mobile, distal, knowing, future interested, devious types, then we're going to hit upon objects and properties as the cool way of organizing our task.

HAUGELAND   Are you going to talk some more about what it is that makes that trick a Good Trick?

CUMMINS   Yeah, as opposed to say, a better trick than the other ones that happened to get tried.

HAUGELAND   Yeah, your counterfactual hypothesis about other planets has to be a Good Trick as opposed to the best one tried so far.

DENNETT   I don't have a good story about how we get from 'well, we're doing pretty damn well here' to 'it's a universal Good Trick'.

HAUGELAND   I think that's probably a case where combinatorial explosion is your friend.

DENNETT   I think so too, and I think the only person who has come within a country mile in trying to put together this kind of argument is Marvin Minsky in that paper of his about the space of possible formalisms.[9] He gets the idea that in the huge space of possible formalisms, there's only a few Good Tricks. And so they're going to be discovered—base 10 arithmetic's great, base 2 arithmetic's great, and base 16 arithmetic is great, and there isn't a schmarithmetic. There just isn't anything that is

---

[9] [Minsky (1985), discussed in Darwin's Dangerous Idea (Dennett 1995a: 129–30)—ed.]

good for a damn thing in the neighborhood of arithmetic. There's just arithmetic. It's a Good Trick. And at least that gives us a sort of a schema, an argument type. We could think about whether we can make the same sort of move with ontology.

HAUGELAND That's something like what David Lewis [1971] claims is important about digital systems.

DENNETT Yes, I like that idea.

SMITH There's more to be said, I think, because there's the coreferentiality of names which allows you to get arbitrary graph structures into linear form. There's actually more than one trick at play. There's the subject–object, the ability to use abstraction as a form of getting stability, so as to get a sort of context independence. I think actually it's a—I don't think Dan would disagree with this—even if there's nothing in the vicinity, it's actually still a bit of a Rube Goldberg trick. It's not an elegant idea. I suspect it's culled together from a variety of things such that the mess works.

CUMMINS But aren't you suspicious of the idea that it's such a Good Trick that it enables us to survey the space of tricks?

DENNETT One can be modest and be a little bit anxious about that. Yes.

CUMMINS When the aliens come and say, poor slobs there they are mired in arithmetic. Not bad for *Homo sapiens* but pretty primitive stuff. Of course they won't say that. I think the reason it's hard to make the argument you're talking about is—

DENNETT You can't adopt the vantage point from which the argument—

SMITH Well, I think it's a stunningly bad ontology for getting around the world. And I don't believe it actually is the reigning ontology that Dan thinks. I believe that about 5 per cent of my content is actually in this form, and that you would die within minutes were your other forms of content reduced to it. So that's not to say that you're not right, but there may be other forms, incommensurable with it that we haven't imagined, which in fact have transcendent power with respect to it. But it sure is bad in lots of ways. I guess I do think there is somewhat of an argument of the sort Dan said. But in a way, what I find compelling about it is it's such a manifest failure for so many purposes. You can of course see the trade-offs.

DENNETT It would be a lousy trick if it weren't for these damn historical constraints. This is the best trick that we can do. And, of course, if we had seventeen mouths so that we didn't have to have this linear stream of communication, coming out of one source, for instance, or if we had

some other sense organs, then of course we wouldn't have to have this
ontology. But given the constraints of our species, then...yes it's a
Goldberg machine, but, it's like the America's Cup, the original race.
Yes, there's not only a first, but there is no second place. Second place is
below the horizon it's so far away.

SMITH To go back to the point you were saying, Andy, I think one of the
reasons that it's powerful for us is that we've figured out how to
coordinate it with all the rest of our capacities (which have contents
of a different form), such that we are actually able to integrate them.

CLARK That's what makes it powerful, but, still I think there might be more
to be said for it than the order of 5 per cent or whatever. That it makes
possible something like the search for higher-order patterns. It seems to
me a lot of thought is concerned with spotting higher-order patterns.
And without something like digitization, something like the imposition
of a system of concepts onto the world—where you say, OK, this applies
here but it doesn't apply there—that you just don't make that space
available. Making that space available is, roughly, opening up the
realms of thought, as far as I can see. It may only be 5 per cent of what
gets you around the world on a day-to-day basis, but it may be 90 per
cent of what opens up the space of thought about the world.

SMITH I'm not sure that I disagree. I don't think conceptual representation and digital representation are as close as logic courses think,
particularly because of the higher-order digitality stuff of John's [Hau-
geland 1981].

CLARK But bringing the world under concepts. Something like that.

SMITH It's stunningly powerful, and this is one of the reasons I was asking
Dan this real question, because if I read what he was saying at the
beginning of his comments here, about this sort of conceptual formulation of the notion of language, then I actually think I agree with a lot
of what he said which is that it's damn important. But at the same time,
I think a lot about the cost at which it achieved that power. It's all so
very interesting. Because I think prowess with respect to conceptual
representation involves not only mastery of its powers but also knowing its limitations.

DENNETT This is exactly why I thought the Sperber paper [1982] was
worth reading. Because I thought he had some insight into the sort of
transition. How is irrational thought possible? Well, because, these
people are not actually fully competent to handle the mind-tools they
have, but they're doing the best they can with them, and they are

thinking about the world with tools that do not succeed in expressing propositional attitudes cleanly.

CLAPIN Is it the tools that are the problem or the use of the tools? There's something really odd going on if they've got these really good tools but they can't use them properly. These kind of linguistic tools are partly constituted by our ability to recognize and follow the rules. (I'm just thinking about the games in 'Truth and Rule Following' [Haugeland 1998a].) So we have to be good in some sense, in order for language to exist at all.

DENNETT But look at it from the point of view of the anthropologist. The anthropologist is out there, trying to figure out what the heck is going on . . . and trying to learn the rules of their game. And of course that is inevitably an idealizing . . . you can't sit there and try to learn the rules of chess with the assumption that there's something incoherent about the game of chess. You're looking for a coherent set of rules. You're looking for an unflawed practice. Well, suppose there isn't an unflawed practice.

CLAPIN Is there a difference, actually? There might be some reason to think that for you there actually is nothing to choose between the practice being flawed and the tool being flawed. That they kind of constitute one another.

DENNETT They do, I mean, for the moment, I don't see what the difference is going to be. That is, it's their language, it's their conceptual scheme. I suppose that we could find the vantage point to make the claim that they are inept users of a wonderful conceptual scheme that they have somehow hit upon, and if they just got a little more adroit, they'd be off to the races. I suppose that's possible.

CUMMINS Sure.

SMITH Just to note that that valorizes conceptual takes on the world.

HAUGELAND And you're opposed to this?

SMITH Well, I think that they have their uses, but I wouldn't want to say that somehow . . . if only we would be better, we'd be more conceptual.

DENNETT Oh, I see what you're saying.

CUMMINS There's a sense in which I'm beginning to come around a little to this. And that is, my first thought was, well here's something to be said for Dan. After all, we're all sitting around . . . we can sit around and talk about whether, say, to graph or map something, but it's very difficult to imagine sitting around graphing about whether we should talk or . . . And then my second thought was, but that doesn't say anything about the sort of priority of language. It just says that, you know, we're trying to communicate about this problem. There's no particular reason why I couldn't think about... I couldn't, in thought, as it were, graph about whether to talk, or something else. But then my third thought was, on Dan's view, and on my view too, there's a sense of thought which is really essentially social. And really probably does require a communicative underpinning. And from that perspective it may not be language's extraordinary representational power, but its rather flexible communicative power that allows me to bootstrap up this sort of—

DENNETT I am quite content to take very seriously your last chapter about language being recipes, not representations [Cummins 1996a]. I haven't thought that through yet, but—

CUMMINS Yeah, but, I think that's a sort of interesting idea. This really... Andy likes not paying too much attention to the skin boundary. And one way to gloss your [Dennett's] claim is that there's a social conception of thought which is really unthinkable without a certain kind of communicative apparatus, not just any kind... and then, really there is a way of turning a kind of matter of degree into a matter of kind. When communication achieves a certain level of sophistication and a certain sort of direction, then you've got this sort of emergent—

DENNETT That's music to my ears—

CUMMINS I don't know if I believe any of this. I'm just saying it to see whether you nod.

DENNETT It's music to my ears.

SMITH Another argument for it is that at least in my view, the forms of representation that we by and large use, which aren't of this form, tend to have this kind of inexorable egocentric indexicality, which, as it happens, derives directly from physics, I believe. But one thing that language surely does is that it is a tremendously well-devised force for extricating one's thoughts from a first-person point of view. I don't know if it's necessary, but it sure as hell has gone to a lot of work to get views that are not as perspectival. And that may actually be necessary to achieving a certain kind of objectivity.

CUMMINS Any form of communication is sort of stuck with solving that problem.

HAUGELAND Maps, too, solve that problem.

CUMMINS Sure. There are a lot of different ways of solving that problem.

PART 3
On Haugeland

Texts

'The Intentionality All-Stars' (1990).
'Representational Genera' (1991).
'Mind Embodied and Embedded' (1995).
'Truth and Rule-Following' (1998a).

John Haugeland has a deserved reputation as an outstanding philosopher of the cognitive sciences generally, and artificial intelligence in particular. From an exceptionally well-informed perspective Haugeland has offered probing analyses and critiques of the foundational issues and the aspirational claims of cognitive scientists.

In thinking about mental representation, Haugeland has offered a number of groundbreaking analyses. In considering the distinction between analog and digital systems, Haugeland argues that while many analog systems may be simulated to any desired degree of accuracy by digital systems, this is only because they exhibit what he calls 'second-order' digitality. For example, a monochrome photograph, which is of course first-order analog, is second-order digital because it varies along only three distinct dimensions: horizontally, vertically, and the grey-scale (Haugeland 1981). There are some (first-order) analog systems, however, which may be second-order analog, and thus distinctively non-digital.

In 'Representational Genera', Haugeland (1991) takes a fresh and challenging look at different kinds of mental representation and different kinds of representational content. He argues that the differences exhibited by logical, iconic, and distributed representations are the result of different kinds of content and not the result of the different kinds of representational schemes (where a representational scheme specifies the kinds of vehicles and how vehicles and content are related). Beyond these differences, however, there is no essential structural basis for the variation among schemes of representation.

Haugeland argues for this by showing that it is easy—too easy—to recode a logical representation into an iconic one (and so on). For example, digitizing a picture or photographing a sentence is easy; however translation between genera ought be hard, as in *describing* a photograph. Here we see Haugeland attending to the intentional capacity to *understand* representations. It is this idiosyncratically human capacity that should guide us in identifying the true contents of a representation. We should not be distracted by superficial details such as linguistic or pictorial form.

In 'Mind Embodied and Embedded', Haugeland (1995) argues for the importance of embeddedness to understanding the mind, in contrast to the Cartesian paradigm where mind and body are radically distinct. Here Haugeland is looking for a model of mind–world relations that eschews discrete components connected by transducers, and takes seriously the continuity of mind with body and world. But Haugeland's picture is one where the mind is none the less very special in the natural scheme of things: 'Intelligence abides in the *meaningful*' (p. 230). But the meaningful is not to be explained by internal representations that broker the relationship between mind and body. The world itself is meaningful.

Already, in comparing these two aforementioned papers, we see Haugeland's unique contribution to the philosophy of cognitive science. He is better informed about the technical details than most philosophers, but harbours deep concerns that cognitive science tends to oversimplify the profound philosophical questions it raises. He acknowledges the centrality of mental representation to cognitive science, and makes an important contribution to understanding its vicissitudes. On the other hand he sees that often too much of the mind–body problem is thought to be solved as soon as such inner states are posited. Mental representations—inner sentences, pictures, or even distributed weight vectors—don't *explain* how the world is meaningful in the robust way ultimately required.

One of the driving ideas behind the Peak Research Meeting on Mental Representation was that you can't think long about mind and mental representation without coming up against fundamental questions about ontology and objectivity. Haugeland exemplifies this approach in his important recent paper 'Truth and Rule-Following' (Haugeland 1998*a*). Here he sketches an account of objectivity that has profound consequences for a theory of mental representation. The mind, we assume, represents the world as being a certain way. These representations obey norms of truth, meaning, and objectivity: their meanings allow them to contribute to propositions that are true or false, and that are about objects. This is one way to understand the traditional naturalistic accounts of meaning: conceptual role semantics, teleosemantics, asymmetric dependence, and the like are all attempts to explain the ability of mental representations to conform to the norms of objectivity.

Haugeland approaches this issue from a new direction: how do you know when you've got a system that conforms to the norms of objectivity? His starting-point is that objectivity and truth are *achievements* that require explanation—we cannot take objects for granted. Contrast this with the approach in the traditional literature on mental representation that assumes objects are given, and investigates what connection between object and representation gives rise to content. The latter approach embodies a straightforward realism, whereas Haugeland's approach is more cautious. According to Haugeland, being intentionally directed towards objects, qua objects, depends on a certain kind of practice or skill: a resilient commitment to certain constitutive standards of objectivity. For Haugeland, the world disciplines our representing practices, but only in conjunction with other aspects of being human.

As Cummins' commentary shows, this scientifically well-informed, but profoundly philosophical approach to human meaning makes fruitful demands on the traditional philosophy of mind approach to representation. Cummins embraces Haugeland's assumption that intentionality and objectivity are 'two sides of the same coin'. His concern is to maintain a robust realism despite recognizing the role played by an agent's representational resources in determining objects. Cummins worries that Haugeland 'over-intellectualizes' the requirements for objectivity. Wanting to maintain a clear separation between epistemology and metaphysics, Cummins argues that what a cognitive system knows ought not have any bearing on the objective world which causally affects it.

Haugeland on Representation and Intentionality

ROBERT CUMMINS

3.1.1 Targets and Objects

Haugeland doesn't have what I would call a theory of mental representation. Indeed, it isn't clear that he believes there is such a thing. But he does have a theory of intentionality and a correlative theory of objectivity, and it is this material that I will be discussing in what follows.

It will facilitate the discussion that follows to have at hand some distinctions and accompanying terminology I introduced in *Representations, Targets and Attitudes* (Cummins 1996a; *RTA* hereafter). Couching the discussion in these terms will, I hope, help to identify points of agreement and disagreement between Haugeland and myself, and perhaps help to build a bit of a bridge. In *RTA*, I distinguished between the target a representation has on a given occasion of its application, and its (representational) content. *RTA* takes representation deployment to be the business of *intenders*: mechanisms whose business it is to represent some particular class of targets. Thus, on standard stories about speech perception, there is a mechanism (called a parser) whose business it is to represent the phrase structure of the linguistic input currently being processed. When this intender passes a representation R to the consumers of its products, those consumers will take R to be a representation of the phrase structure of the current input (because of where they got it).

There is no explicit vocabulary to mark the target-content distinction in ordinary language. Expressions such as 'what I referred to', 'what I meant', and the like, are systematically ambiguous with respect to this distinction. Sometimes they mean targets, sometimes contents. Consider the following dialogue:

YOU: I used this map and got around the city with no problem.
ME: Which city do you mean? (or: Which city are you referring to?)

Here, I am asking for your target, the city against which the map's accuracy is to be measured. Now compare this exchange:

YOU: Here is the city-map I was telling you about.
ME: Which city do you mean? (or: Which city are you referring to?)

Here, I am asking for the content, that is, for the city the map actually represents.[1] The potential for ambiguity derives from the fact that there are two senses in which representations are semantically related to the world, the content sense and the target sense, but the distinction is not marked in ordinary vocabulary. The distinction is *there*, as the example just rehearsed makes clear, but it is marked only by different uses of the same expressions in ordinary language.

Representational error, then, is a mismatch between the representation produced and its target on the occasion in question. The obvious way to think of representational error, as Jerry Fodor once said to me in conversation, is this: Error occurs when a representation is *applied to* something it is not *true of*, for example, when one applies a representation of a horse to a cow. The distinction in this formulation between what a representation is *applied to* and what it is *true of* is precisely the distinction between a representation's target and its content. The crucial point is that what determines what a representation is *true of* must be independent of what determines what it is *applied to*, otherwise error is problematic. It follows from this that a theory of representational content—a theory that says what it is for R to be *true of* T—is only part of the story about representation. We require, in addition, a theory of target fixation, a theory that says what it is for R to be *applied to* T. Since the target of tokening a representation is, as it were, the thing the representation is intended to represent, I shall say that representations *represent* their contents, but that a use of a representation *intends* its target. *Intentionality* is thus different from *semantic content*. The former is part of the theory of targets, while the latter is part of the theory of representational content.

[1] The standard Twin-Earth cases simply trade on this ambiguity in semantic terms. See RTA: 126 ff.

The *intentional content* of R is therefore not the actual content of R at all, but, rather, the *intended* content of some use of R.[2]

I construe Haugeland's theory of intentionality and objectivity as a theory about targets. The theory has two internally related parts:

1. Intentionality: How are targets fixed—that is, what determines the target of a representation on a given occasion of its use?

2. Objectivity: What targets is it possible for a given system to have? (Because what will be an object—not a 3-dimensional piece of furniture, but something that is objective, something that exists and has its properties for a given cognitive system—will depend on what targets it can have, not on what it can represent.)

By definition, a target of a representing is normative for the accuracy, on that occasion, of the representation deployed. If you have targets that you cannot represent accurately, you get what I called forced error in *RTA*. Accuracy and error come in degrees, of course. A certain amount of error is tolerable, sometimes even desirable, as when accuracy is traded for tractability or speed. Moreover, a given representation may be an accurate representation of one target and an inaccurate representation of another. Accuracy, then, is not intrinsic to a given representation. Indeed, representational types are not accurate or inaccurate. Only particular deployments of a representational type can be accurate or inaccurate, and the degree of accuracy is just the degree of match between the representation deployed and the target at which it is aimed. *Discussion point 3.1*

To understand objectivity, then, we must understand how it is possible for a representing to be aimed at some particular target, and this is what makes intentionality and objectivity two sides of the same coin. To understand one is to understand the other.

Haugeland emphasizes that, in this inquiry, we must not take the objects for granted, and I agree. To see why, consider parsers once again. A parser is an intender whose function is to represent the phrase structure of the current linguistic input. Targets, then, are fixed by the representational function or functions of the intender mechanisms that produce or

---

[2] 'Intend' is a technical term here. I do not, of course, suppose that cognitive systems generally intend their targets consciously, i.e., that whenever T is the target of a use of R in Σ, Σ forms the intention to use R to represent T. But I do think the technical sense is a natural extension of this usual sense. In the case of conscious, deliberate use, intended content is quite literally the content one intends to represent. As always, one may not succeed in doing what one intends, hence one may fail to represent what one intends to represent.

deploy them. So, when we ask what targets a system can have, we are asking what representational functions it can have. *Discussion point 3.2*

Whatever your favorite account of functions, it is not going to be the function of any canid intender to represent chess positions. It follows that canids cannot have chess positions as representational targets, and hence that no chess position as such is normative for the accuracy of any canid representation deployment. In this sense, then, chess positions are not objects for canids. For exactly analogous reasons, it cannot be the function of any subcultural intender of which we have any experience to represent positrons. What representational functions something can have evidently depends in part on its conceptual sophistication and on its perceptual and inferential resources. This, then, is why the theory of intentionality cannot take the objects for granted. Nothing can be an object for me if I cannot have it as a target. I cannot have it as a target unless it can be the function of one of my intenders to represent it. But which intenders I can have depends, at least in part, on my so-phistication and resources. How I am designed—my functional analy-sis—puts constraints on what can be an object for me. *Discussion point 3.3*

Unlike representational content, function (and hence target fixation) is holistic in the sense that functions arise out of the organization of some containing system.[3] So, when Haugeland asks what perceptions are perceptions of, or what our thoughts are thoughts about, he is, I think, thinking of what I call target fixation. And he is right that target fixation is holistic. You cannot have chess positions as such as targets unless you have the sort of functional organization that supports an intender whose job is to represent chess positions. About intentionality and its relation to objectivity, then, we are in substantial agreement about the basics.

What about the details? Here, I am less confident. I propose to look at several different areas where I think that I must have misunderstood his position, or one of us must have misunderstood something about the phenomena themselves.

---

[3] Indeed, it is my view that holism in the theory of meaning is a response to the holism of target fixation. Since reference fixing, in *one* sense, is target fixing, and since Davidson (1967) turned the theory of meaning into the theory of reference, target fixation can look like the whole story about meaning. If you squint and don't move.

3.1.2 Seeing

I am pretty sure that Sheila, our canny Australian Shepherd cross, can see can-openers and tennis-balls. I am also pretty sure that it cannot be the function of any canid intender to represent tennis-balls or can-openers. How is this dissonance to be harmonized?

It seems impossible to explain how Sheila could chase and catch a thrown tennis-ball if she could not see it. But how can it make sense to say she sees it if it cannot be a target for her? Seeing is normative, an accomplishment. 'See', as we used to say, is a success verb. If tennis-balls cannot be targets for her, then they cannot be norms against which the accuracy of her perceptual representations are measured.

The overwhelmingly tempting move here is to say something like this: It certainly is the function of one of Sheila's intenders to represent the currently foveated thing, understood here as a coherent physical lump, and this thing could well be a tennis-ball or a can-opener. So, though she sees the tennis-ball, she doesn't see it as a tennis-ball. Realistically, she doesn't just see it as a coherent lump, either, since she can distinguish tennis-balls from balls of other sorts of the same size and color, and will pick one out of a pile of assorted balls when asked to get the tennis-ball. So she sees it as a ball (sphere?) of a distinct sort, pretty much as do young children who haven't a clue about tennis, but recognize the characteristic size, texture, and characteristic seam pattern of two interlocking bones wrapped around a sphere. In just this way, non-chess players can recognize standardized chess-pieces. Because of this, terms such as 'tennis-ball' and 'chess-piece' are ambiguous. There is a functional sense in which a salt-shaker can be the white queen (or any other piece) in a chess game provided it is played (used) like one, and any ball of roughly the right size and elasticity can be a tennis-ball in a game of tennis provided it is played (used) like one. But there is another sense in which these terms pick out objects with characteristic shapes and other intrinsic properties be-cause these are the standard occupants of the functional roles in question. Sheila can see tennis-balls in this latter sense, but not in the functional game-embedded sense.

The natural moral of this story seems to be that all seeing is seeing-as. Since seeing is an accomplishment, it must have an intentional object—a target—against which its accuracy is measured.[4] For a tennis-ball, as

---

[4] Representational accuracy should not be confused with perceptual or cognitive or behav-ioral success. Successful perception needn't be accurate perception. Indeed, to reiterate a point

such—that is, taking the term functionally—to be a perceptual target, you have to be able to see it as a tennis-ball. Hence, the only things against which the accuracy of your seeing can be measured are things that can be seen as something or other. Since all seeing is normative, if Sheila doesn't see the tennis-ball as a tennis-ball, she must see it as something else if she sees it at all. So all seeing is seeing-as. QED.

So what? It depends on what is built into seeing-as. Or better, it all depends on what it takes to have tennis-balls and chess positions as targets. The capacity to see something as a tennis-ball is just the capacity to have tennis-balls as such as targets. So the question is what it takes to have an intender that has the function of representing tennis-balls as such. Here, I think, Haugeland and I part company. I think his account over-intellectualizes target fixation and underestimates forced error. He writes: 'Surely no creature or system can see a given configuration as a knight fork without having some sense of what a knight fork is. To put it in a familiar but perhaps misleading terminology, nothing can *apply* a concept unless it *has* that concept' (Haugeland 1996: 247, hereafter OP). The respect in which Haugeland thinks this remark might be misleading is that it might suggest to some readers that seeing-as requires linguistic abilities. I am not even slightly tempted to think that having a concept—even a concept like the concept of a knight fork—requires having linguistic abilities, so I am not worried about being misled in this respect. My worry is, rather, the claim that having a knight fork as a perceptual target (or a target of thought, for that matter) requires having a concept of a knight fork, where this is meant to imply having at least a minimal knowledge, though perhaps not explicit knowledge, of chess in general and knight forks in particular.

To get a sense of why this worries me, consider a case of learning. What Haugeland's account rules out is a scenario such as this: before learning, you have *T* as a target but do not know enough about it to successfully hit it. The errors you make, however, drive incremental improvements in aim, as back propagation does in connectionist learning. If this is possible, you must be able to have targets you know next to nothing about. If the targets you could have were constrained by how much you knew about them, the

made earlier, accuracy can be expensive, hence undermine success. This means that no simple behavioral test is a test of representational accuracy. It also means that cognitive science has an extra degree of freedom to deploy in explaining success and failures. In particular, it can distinguish between those failures that are due to the representations, and those that are due to an inability to exploit them. I will return to this point at length below.

size of the error would not decrease as you learned more. Indeed, your early shots would not be misses at all, since they wouldn't be aimed at the target you ultimately acquire. *Discussion point 3.4*

Notice that I am not complaining about circularity here. It isn't that you need to know *about* T to have T as a target. I find this suspicious, all right, but I am sure some boot-strapping story, or co-constitution story, could leave me speechless, if not convinced. My complaint is rather that the account makes it impossible to articulate what it is that drives the learning process. NETtalk, for example, begins by knowing nothing about the phonetic values of letters in context (Sejnowski and Rosenberg 1987*a*, *b*). It learns the mapping by adjusting its weights as a function of the difference between its 'guesses' and the correct values. But this means that the correct values are targets right from the start, since it is the correct values against which the accuracy of the guesses are measured. Whether or not you think NETtalk is a good model of how letter-to-phoneme mappings are learned is not relevant here. If you think *any* perceptual or recognitional learning proceeds by adjusting one's knowledge to reduce the mismatch between one's targets and one's representational attempts, you have to have an account of target fixation that largely decouples it from what you know about the targets.[5]   *Discussion point 3.5*

3.1.3 Functions

How *can* systems have or acquire targets about which they know next to nothing? This is a question about representational functions, and hence depends to some extent on the theory of functions. I will discuss just two: Millikan's and my own.

On Millikan's (1984) account, an intender has the function of representing a T (for example, the phrase-structure of the current linguistic input) if it was selected for, historically, because, on various (perhaps rare) occa-

---

[5] A similar point can be made about representational contents. If you hold, as all use theories (causal theories, conceptual role theories, selectionist/adaptationist theories) must, that there can be no more content in your representations than you can exploit, then you will be at a loss to even articulate the process whereby a perceptual system learns to exploit the information in its proximal representations to identify distal stimuli. Think now of the input end of NETtalk. Its input vectors carry information about the phonetic value of the targeted letter. Its job is to learn how to exploit this information. Since it cannot learn to exploit information that isn't there, it must be there prior to any ability to exploit it. Hence, input content must be independent of the system's sensitivity to it, contrary to all use theories of content. (See R. Cummins 2000, for a fuller exposition of this point.)

sions, it did represent Ts accurately enough. How accurate is accurate enough? Enough to get selected. The point is that the intender got selected because, often enough (which might not be very often) it got however close it did (which needn't have been very close) to an accurate representation of Ts. Ts are the targets, on this account, because it is Ts as such, not something else, that are the standard you need to look at to see why the relevant intender was selected.

On this account it is plain that little if any knowledge of Ts is required to have them as targets. What is required is just that Ts were a good thing to get represented now and again, that the capacity to do that be heritable, and that competing lines didn't do it, or something even more important, better. Knight forks are bad candidates for canid targets because chess didn't figure in their evolutionary history, not because they don't have a clue about chess.

On my account of functions, an intender has the function of representing Ts if its capacity to represent Ts figures in a functional analysis of some capacity of a containing system (Cummins 1983). Consider, then, whatever complex capacity C of the whole organism made it more fit than the competition in the Millikan scenario. The capacity to represent Ts (to some degree of accuracy, with some reliability) figures in an analysis of C. And since Millikan's account didn't require knowledge of Ts, neither does mine.

3.1.4 Commitment

Let's rehearse the plot. Haugeland and I agree that what targets a system can have—what it can intend—and, hence, what can be objects for it, depends, in part, and in a more or less holistic way, on the sophistication and resources of the system. So an account of intentionality and an account of objectivity are just two sides of the same coin. So far, we are both Kantians. In my view, however, Haugeland's account of intentionality over-intellectualizes intentionality by assuming that you cannot have targets you know next to nothing about, and under-estimates the power of biological functions to make room for systematic error and therefore to ground targets and hence objectivity.

Given that Haugeland doesn't think biological function can ground targets, and hence objectivity, what does he think intentionality *is* grounded in? In a word, commitment; vigilant, resilient commitment. To see how this is supposed to work, we need to return to the chess example.

Nothing is a knight fork except in the context of a chess game. Nothing is a chess game unless the rules are in force. What enforces the rules? Nothing but a commitment on the part of the players not to tolerate deviations. You get a chess game, not when the rules are satisfied, but when the players take responsibility for their satisfaction.[6]

Thus, there are no knight forks unless there are players taking responsibility for the satisfaction of the rules and conditions constitutive of chess. When they do take such responsibility, and when the world cooperates well enough to make satisfaction possible—for example, by not having the pieces multiply and spread to adjoining squares—chess, and all that goes with it, is constituted. Haugeland thinks nothing less will do for objectivity generally, and consequently that mundane and scientific objects are on a par with chess positions when it comes to the grounds of objectivity. Hence genuine intentionality is possible only where there is not only the possibility, but the reality, of this sort of commitment. ***Discussion point 3.6*** Since something comparable to human intelligence seems to be required for this sort of responsibility-taking—at least in many cases that we often think about—it seems to follow that animal and machine intentionality is ersatz.

Once ersatz intentionality is distinguished and characterized, however, it becomes apparent that there are candidates for it besides GOFAI robots. In particular, I want to suggest that (as far as we know) the intentionality of animals is entirely ersatz (except for purely tropistic creatures, whose intentionality is at best 'as-if'). That is, we can understand animals as having intentional states, but only relative to standards that *we* establish for them.   (Haugeland 1992: 303, hereafter UDS)[7]

---

[6] Compare this passage from Alston (1964: 41–2). 'If we set out to analyze the concept of a serve in tennis, the problems we encounter will be very similar to those we have just discussed [in connection with the analysis of the illocutionary act of requesting someone to close the door]. To serve is not just to make certain physical movements, even given certain external circumstances. (I can be standing at the baseline of a tennis court, swinging a racket so that it makes contact with a ball in such a way as to propel it into the diagonally opposite forecourt, without it being the case that I am serving. I may just be practicing.) Nor are any specific effects required. A shot can have widely varying effects—it can inspire one's opponent with fear, despair, exultation, contempt, or boredom; these variations, however do not keep it from being true that one was serving in all these cases. Then what does change when, after a few practice shots, I call to my opponent, "All right, this is it," and then proceed to serve? The new element in the situation, I suggest, is my readiness to countenance certain sorts of complaints, for example, that I stepped on the baseline, hit the ball when my opponent was not ready, or was standing on the wrong side of the court. I take responsibility for the holding of certain conditions, for example, that neither foot touches the ground in front of the baseline before the racket touches the ball.'

[7] I think Haugeland underestimates the capacities of social animals, especially those living in a dominance hierarchy, to take responsibility for the satisfaction of social norms. See D. D. Cummins (2000) and the papers referenced there.

It is tempting to agree with Haugeland that nothing less than this will do for the objectivity of knight forks. Knight forks, after all, are, well, pretty conventional objects. So it is not too surprising that they can exist only on the supposition that the conventions are somehow kept in force. And what could keep them in force other than the commitments of the players of the game? But surely you have to have illegal concentrations of transcendental philosophy in your veins to think nothing less will do for sticks and stones, conspecifics, smiles, and threats.

But this is unfair to Haugeland's position. Chess has to be playable, and this requires, to repeat, that the pieces do not multiply, that they do not move (in the chess sense) unless moved, etc., and these are not matters of convention. To give a very crude summary of a subtle and nuanced position, physics and chess differ in the extent to which the constitutive standards are matters of convention, but not at all in the grounds of *objectivity*, which have to do with a commitment to seeing that the standards are satisfied, not with their conventionality or lack of it.

And yet, surely this position vastly over-intellectualizes what it takes to have targets. And targets are all that objectivity requires, hence all that a theory of intentionality needs to accommodate. Targets are grounded in representational functions, and representational functions do not in general require either conceptual machinery nor standard-grounding commitments. From this point of view, it seems it ought to be possible to see knight forks as such without having a clue about chess, and hence without being in a position to take responsibility for the satisfaction of its constitutive rules and conditions. It is tempting to give Haugeland knight forks, and hold out for stones, but I don't think this will do.

If target fixation is what I think it is, then, like Haugeland, I am committed to knight forks and stones being in the same boat. It is just that my boat is little more than a fleet of floating logs, while his is, well, the Titanic. *Discussion point 3.7*

3.1.5 Functions Again

To make this contention stick, I need to show how an organism could have knight forks as targets on the cheap, as it were. To do that, I need to explain how it is possible for a relatively cheap intender to have as one of its functions the representation of knight forks.

Haugeland (OP: 248) points out that perceiving knight forks is a pretty abstract capacity.

These complementary considerations, that chess can be played in widely different media, and that widely different games can be played in the same media, together with the fact that knight forks can occur (and be perceived) in all the former but none of the latter, show that the ability to perceive knight forks presupposes some grasp or understanding of the game of chess—at least enough to tell when it's being played, regardless of medium.

What I find interesting about this passage, and the argumentation that turns on it, is the idea that what you do doesn't count as perceiving knight forks *unless you can do it all*, that is, recognize them in various media, and distinguish them from schnight forks (configurations that look like knight forks but are part of schness, not chess) in the usual media. But this conflates two very distinct issues:

1. How good is the system at recognizing knight forks?
2. Are knight forks among its targets, that is, are some of its representational efforts to be assessed for accuracy against knight forks?

Discussion point 3.8

I can, for example, be arbitrarily bad at recognizing colors (I am color blind), and yet have the color of the vegetable in my hand as a representational target. I won't hit it reliably, but it does not follow from this that it isn't my target. In order to understand error in learning, you don't want to think that your targets somehow depend on what you can hit. *Discussion point 3.9*

Similarly, I can have the shape of the currently foveated thing as a target even though I always get it wrong to some degree (if, for example, I suffer from astigmatism). The mere fact that a dog or pigeon or novice human will be reliably fooled by schnight forks, and fail to see knight forks in esoteric media, is beside the point. You cannot, in general, argue that having T as a perceptual target is expensive because perception of Ts is expensive. Predator recognition systems tolerate a lot of false positives in the interest of speed. But when a prairie dog dives into its hole in response to a shadow made by a child's kite, this is a *false* positive, a mistaken predator identification, not an accurate shadow detection. This is not a point about the content of the animal's representations, which may not distinguish between shadows and predators, but a point about their targets. To understand what is going on, it is crucial to grasp that the targets are predators. Without this, you cannot even articulate the point about trading accuracy for speed.

In general, you are going to vastly underestimate the representational (and other) functions a system can have if you do not maintain a principled distinction between representational accuracy on the one hand, and perceptual, cognitive, or behavioral success on the other. This distinction is precisely what grounds explanations in terms of trade-offs between accuracy on the one hand, and speed and tractability on the other. I think Haugeland misses this point when he writes:

> But there is another important distinction that biological norms do not enable. That is the distinction between functioning properly (under the proper conditions) as an information carrier and getting things right (objective correctness or truth), or, equivalently, between malfunctioning and getting things wrong (mistaking them). Since there is no *other* determinant or constraint on the information carried than whatever properly functioning carriers carry, when there is no malfunction, it's as 'right' as it can be. In other words, there can be no biological basis for understanding a system as functioning properly, but nevertheless misinforming—functionally right but factually wrong, so to speak.
>
> (Haugeland 1998*a*: 309–10, hereafter TRF)

Biological norms *do* enable this distinction, because it can be crucial to understanding the biological role of an intender to see that it is accuracy with respect to *T*s that must be measured to judge its adaptiveness, even though it seldom or never gets *T*s completely right.

If you miss this point, or just don't agree with it, then, like Haugeland, you will be forced to look elsewhere to find the resources to ground objectivity. You will be tempted to deal with my astigmatism and color blindness, either by claiming that I don't see colors or shapes (implausible), or by pointing out that I will take responsibility for corrections aimed at bringing my percepts (or, if that is not possible, my beliefs) into line with independently accessed color and shape information. Since prairie dogs don't take responsibility for their false predator recognitions, you will conclude that they don't see predators.

On the other hand, if you are on a budget and in the market for esoteric perceptual targets, here is how to get weak king-side defenses cheap. Imagine someone who is trying to learn to recognize them. They start with some crude criteria that don't work very well. Still, the function of those criteria is to enable recognition of a weak king-side defense. This is their function because the trajectory of the learning is tracked by the difference between the student's guesses and the actual weakness of the king-side defenses. The student needn't even be conscious of this. Indeed, it may well be that teachers who treat this as like a chicken-sexer case will have better success than their more cognitively explicit competitors. ***Discussion point 3.10***

Whether or not such learning could be successful, leading to reasonably reliable discrimination from foils in a variety of media is beside the point. What matters is that the relevant error is the gap between student guesses and weak king-side defenses. Nor need the students be committed to keeping the rules in force. For one thing, they may be spectators, not participants. More importantly, however, it isn't their commitments that count. They may be committed to anything you like, or nothing at all, provided only that it is differences between their guesses and the weakness of king-side defenses that must be compared to track the learning.[8]

If we are not careful, this talk of what *we* must do to track learning will make it look as if I have tried to pass off some ersatz intentionality for the real thing. Not so. It is the gap between weak king-side defenses and the student's guesses that drives the learning, whether or not anyone realizes this. It isn't that we make the learning intelligible by establishing this standard. It is rather that the learning becomes intelligible when we realize what the operative standard has been all along. The only reason to resist this point is the mistake about functions scouted above, the mistake rooted in the failure to distinguish representational accuracy from perceptual (cognitive, behavioral, reproductive) success.

Perhaps Haugeland thinks that *that* distinction, if viable at all, is a matter of *us* establishing standards for *them*, so that the functions in question are themselves ersatz functions. But I don't think it is. There is a subtle relationship between the accuracy of a representation and the success of its consumers. Once we see that accuracy can be sacrificed for speed or tractability in order to improve consumer performance, we will no longer be tempted to say, with Haugeland, that biological norms cannot enforce a distinction between success and accuracy.

---

[8] I don't mean to suggest that tracking learning trajectories is always the issue. I doubt that prairie dog predator recognition is learned at all. But thinking about learning highlights the difficulty because it is in the nature of the case that the target one is trying to learn to see (recognize, identify) is, in the early stages, beyond one's abilities. The novice learning about knight forks, and even some experts some of the time, will be stymied by non-standard media and fooled by schnight forks, as will a dog or a pigeon. All three may do quite well with the standard cases. And they may never get any better. The training may be discontinued, or the student inept. But the fact that acquiring the 'full ability' may be beyond certain non-human animals, and beyond certain humans, for that matter, is beside the point. Having a target doesn't require being able to hit it.

3.1.6 Representational Content

There is no free lunch, especially on a fleet of logs. The distinction I have been urging between representational accuracy and consumer success will collapse if you have a use theory of representational content. I said above that use theories of target fixation are not only acceptable, but inevitable. I also said that, to the extent that representational content is not distinguished from intentional content, use theories of representational content will seem inevitable. Use theories of representational content seem inevitable to almost everyone anyway. What could possibly endow a representation with a content that is completely independent of how that representation is used? And why should we care about such contents? These are large questions, and I will not address them here. But I do want to explain why use theories of representational content threaten to collapse the distinction between representational accuracy and consumer success. If I am right about this, then everyone who assumes a use theory of representational content should follow Haugeland in thinking that genuine intentional content is rare and expensive, rather than following me in thinking it is common as dirt.

Use theories can be understood as applications of the following strategy:

1. Begin by noting that the content of R is whatever it is applied to in cases of correct application.
2. Provide a naturalistic—that is, non-question-begging—specification N of a class of applications that can be presumed to be accurate.
3. Identify the content of R with whatever it is applied to (its target) when N is satisfied.

The trick is in supplying the non-question-begging specification of a class of applications of R that can be presumed to be accurate. Use theories require that there be a sort of non-semantic natural kind of cases in which R is bound to be accurately applied to T. After the fact—with the definition in place—these will be cases in which application of R to T is accurate by definition.[9] *Discussion point 3.11*

But: there *are* no non-question-begging conditions that guarantee accuracy. The best one can do is to require success or effectiveness. These are normative notions, but not semantic ones. So, for example, you get the suggestion that the content-fixing cases are those in which the producer of the representation and its consumers behave in the ways that account,

---

[9] This is why all use theories give you some version of the analytic–synthetic distinction.

historically, for their being selected (Millikan 1984). This fails because, to get selection, what you need is more effective representation than your competition, and this might require less accuracy, not more. Turning this point around, we can see that the account will work only if it is sometimes OK to collapse accuracy and effectiveness. So that is how use theories undermine the accuracy/effectiveness distinction.

Do all use theories do this? I think so, But I haven't the space to argue it here (see *RTA*). What about Haugeland's theory of representational content? Does it do this?

Haugeland doesn't explicitly endorse any theory of representational content. His concern is with intentionality and objectivity. He certainly seems to endorse holism about representational content, but this is difficult to pin down because the distinction I make between representational and intentional content is not in the forefront of his writing. Still, I will risk being irrelevant and ask whether holism about representational content is likely to grease (or clear) the path to Haugeland's position on intentionality.

Holism about representational content is essentially the idea that a representation gets its content from its role in a theory-like cognitive structure. It is, in short, conceptual role semantics, the idea that a representation's content is determined by the set of epistemic liaisons it enables.[10] The theory T in which a representation R figures determines what R will be applied to. False theories, of course, will not determine accurate applications of R. But we cannot, without circularity, require that R applies to—is true of—those things a *true* host theory determines it will be applied to. So, what conditions *should* we place on T?

Notice that this is just the crux of every use theory, namely, specifying non-question-begging conditions under which content-fixing applications can be assumed accurate. What are the options here? If we say that every application licensed by the theory is content-fixing, we leave no room for error at all (Perlman 2000). Or rather, since the theory may license application of R to T yet be mismanaged or improperly deployed in some way, the only error allowed is whatever lives in the gap between well-managed and ill-managed theory.

---

[10] The term 'epistemic liaisons' is Fodor's (1990). It is important to realize that representations do not, by themselves, have epistemic liaisons. An attitude—an *application* of a representation in some particular cognitive role such as belief, desire, or intention—can be justified or rational in the light of others, but a representation cannot. So representations link to epistemic liaisons only via the attitudes they make possible. (See *RTA*: 29 ff. for a full discussion.) I am going to slur over this in what follows because I can't see that it makes any difference.

But misrepresentation should not be confused with improper deployment on the part of the using system, nor bad luck in the results. These can diverge in virtue of the fundamental holism underlying what can count as a representation at all: the scheme must be such that, properly produced and used, its representations will, under normal conditions, guide the system successfully, on the whole. In case conditions are, in one way or another, not normal, however, then a representing system can misrepresent without in any way malfunctioning.

(Haugeland 1991: 173, hereafter RG)

Well, what is proper deployment? Not deployment that licenses accurate applications, for this returns us in a circle again. It is rather something like this: all the inferences and calculations are done right. 'Done right' threatens circularity again. The only way out is to say something like this: *done right* means (a) done as they were designed to be done, which leads back to Millikan, or Descartes's God, or (b) done *effectively*, that is, done in a way that leads to cognitive, behavioral, or reproductive success.

I think it is safe to conclude that there is no way to carry out step two of the use theory schema above without assimilating accuracy to effectiveness. I don't claim that Haugeland has done this; only that whatever pressures there are for use theories generally, and for holistic conceptual role theories in particular, are pressures to assimilate accuracy to effectiveness, hence to underestimate representational functions and overprice target fixation and intentional content. I don't think there is much pressure for holism about representational content once it is distinguished from intentional content. But there *are* pressures for use theories of content if you think that representations are structurally arbitrary in the way that words are, that is, that any structure of formatives could, in a suitable context, represent just about anything.[11] If representations are like words in this respect, what could fix their content other than use? My own view is that this is a good reason to reject the idea that representations are structurally arbitrary, but that is another story.

---

[11] There are some hints of this in Haugeland's *Representational Genera* (1991). He clearly thinks that representational content is scheme-relative, and this suggests that a token with a given set of intrinsic structural properties could have arbitrarily different contents in different schemes.

Reply to Cummins on Representation and Intentionality

JOHN HAUGELAND

Cummins and I agree on a lot of things—including some that we've come to agree on only since I read his comments for this workshop. Among other things, we agree that the difference, and also the relations, between targets and representations ought to be closer to the forefront of my thoughts—starting today. (I even acknowledge that there's a lot of transcendental philosophy in my veins, but I'm loath to accept the insinuation that there's too much.)

Let me begin by summarizing how *I* understand what Cummins is up to with intentionality and representation (drawing from both Part 3.1 and *RTA*). The fulcrum, as I see it, is his idea of *intenders*: mechanisms the function of which is to represent things by 'applying' representations to them. In any such application, there are two *factors* that need to be distinguished: (1) what thing, or sort of thing, it is *supposed to* represent; and (2) what thing, or sort of thing, it *actually* represents. What the intender is supposed to represent is determined jointly by the *function* of that particular intender and the *situation* in which it is currently functioning. What it actually represents is determined by the representation that it applies. The former, what the intender is supposed to represent (on this occasion), is called the *target* of its representing; and having that as its target is called *intending* it. The latter, what it actually represents, is called its (representational) *content*; and having that as its content is called (of course) *representing* it.[12]

Note that the use of the word 'actually' here can be confusing. What an intender, on a particular occasion, 'actually' represents is *not* the actual thing to which it actually applies a representation; rather, it's what that representation is a *true* or *correct* representation of. On the other hand, the thing to which the intender *applies* the representation is the *target*. This is what it is supposed to represent—by deploying a correct representation of it—but may not actually succeed at doing.

For example, suppose you designed a robot to find its way around various shopping malls, by deploying and relying on maps of those malls. The maps, of course, are representations; and the relevant intender is the subsystem of the robot that selects some map and applies it to the current mall—say by supplying it to the route-finder mechanism that will rely on it. The target is the current mall; that's what the intender is supposed to represent. If it produces a correct map of the current mall, then it will have succeeded at representing it; but if it instead produces some quite different map, then it will *actually* have represented some quite different mall (or possible mall), not this one. In other words, it will have made a representational *error*—it will have misrepresented.

And this shows why Cummins thinks the distinction between target and content is so important: you need it in order to be able to say what *error* is (as opposed to other sorts of mishap). An intender makes a representational error when there is a 'mismatch' between its target and what it actually represents (the content of the representation it deploys). It follows that there are two distinct philosophical problems in the vicinity: (1) target fixation (intending); and (2) representation (having content). And Cummins makes a powerful case that many a familiar ill flows from failing to keep them distinct.

My work, however, he construes as a theory only of targets; so I stand cleared of *that* confusion. My account of intentionality, he says, is about target fixation (intending); and objectivity concerns which targets it's possible for a given system to have. Unfortunately, however, I don't think this is quite right. It may be extensionally right to say that what I call objects are what he calls targets—or, at any rate, targetables—but *not* vice versa. I'm prepared to allow that lots of creatures and systems can have

---

[12] In fact, I think Rob waffles a bit on whether the content of a representation is what it actually represents or some specification that is satisfied by what it actually represents. Nothing need turn on it; so I will stick with the former.

intenders with targets, in Cummins' senses; but I maintain that only a few—only people, I think—can have objects, objectivity, and intentionality in *my* senses. Of course, it's a substantive claim—with which Cummins may take issue—that my distinctive senses of these terms mark a real difference.

Thus, he complains several times that I over-intellectualize (and over-price) target fixation, while, at the same time, underestimating biological functions and representations. The short answer is that I'm not talking about target fixation, but rather objectivity—which really is expensive (and, in its way, intellectual). That can't be the whole answer, however, since, as I just acknowledged, the real question is whether I'm entitled to that distinction.

So, let's look at what Cummins says about animals, starting with prairie dogs, and see where the estimates fall.

Predator recognition systems tolerate a lot of false positives in the interest of speed. . . . [W]hen a prairie dog dives into its hole in response to a shadow made by a child's kite, this is a *false* positive, a mistaken predator identification, not an accurate shadow detection. This is not a point about the content of the animal's representations, which may not distinguish between shadows and predators, but a point about their targets. To understand what is going on, it is crucial to grasp that the targets are predators. Without this, you cannot even articulate the point about trading accuracy for speed.   (p. 132)

First, let me venture a bit of clarification. The larger point has to be about *both* targets and contents; for, by Cummins' own account, it's only in the relation between these that one can so much as make sense of falsity and accuracy. His more specific point, however, is that we *have to* understand the *target* of the intender that's activated by the shadow as predators (not shadows), or we couldn't even describe the accuracy/speed trade-off. The implicit reasoning is this: if the target were understood as shadows (or as whatever systematically triggers that intender), then the intender would never be wrong, and we wouldn't have a way to characterize the sensible design compromise that evolution has obviously settled upon here.

But I'm not convinced. In Cummins' terminology, this intender is going to produce a representation for some 'consumer'—a prairie-dog activity selector that takes it as a cue to dive. It seems to me that we could, with equal justice, attribute the 'error' (or design trade-off) to this activity selector. In other words, instead of saying that prairie dogs are easily fooled, we say that they are skittish or easily spooked. It's not that I think this alternative is preferable, but rather that there's nothing to choose between them. *Discussion point 3.12*

What we see is a consistent stimulus–response pattern, the evolutionary rationale for which—it's beneficial in the long run to jump on shadow detection (because it's fast)—is perfectly intelligible even without any targets or representations (compare houseflies).

Sheila and the tennis-balls, however, is more interesting. I expect that she really does intend and represent them, in some non-trivial sense. Let me quickly sketch three reasons for this. First, she can detect and track them in several ways (by sight, sound, and smell, say), and also deal with them in several ways (seeking, chasing, and catching them, say). But what makes this important is that the detections and dealings are all cross-connected: she can seek by any of the senses, sight can guide any of the actions, and so on. So there's plausibly some intermediary that's *common* to 'tennis-balls' (or something like them). (This is what I called *semantic intrigue* in my reconstruction of the intentional stance—Haugeland 1990: 144, hereafter IAS) *Discussion point 3.13*

Second, Sheila can engage in 'tennis-ball-related' behavior, even when none is within sensory range. (What I called 'not present and manifest' in RG: 172.) Third, she has fairly definite expectations about what tennis-balls are like. Thus, if she jumped up and caught what looked like a familiar tennis-ball, and it tasted like mustard, felt like putty, or screamed and bit her back, she would doubtless be surprised. (Compare the family dog at the end of OP: 262.)

So, how does all this connect with Cummins' apparatus? Pretty congenially, I would think. Surely he is right that Sheila doesn't have any intenders the function of which is to target *specifically tennis-balls*. Nor, likewise, can any of her representations have specifically them as their contents. Of course, if she has representations, then they must have contents; and then we face the familiar muddle about how to specify them, given that *all* our words are way too laden and sophisticated. But that doesn't strike me as a killer objection so much as an annoying limitation. (Indeed, I think that we ourselves have and use representations that we couldn't put into words.) So, taking the scare quotes suitably seriously, I think we can say things like this. If Rob were to throw a wad of paper across the room, such that Sheila caught it out of the corner of her eye and lunged for it, maybe she *mistook* it for a 'tennis-ball'. That is, maybe she *targeted* 'that projectile' and applied her 'tennis-ball' *representation* to it. And, when she caught it, she might even realize her mistake (and glare at Rob). Why not?

'But, *wait*,' you mutter, 'isn't this the same John Haugeland who is always down on animals, and wants to reserve all things "cognitive" for people?' No, there's no such guy, and never has been. What I want to say is rather this. *Some* human cognition is *qualitatively* different from anything that any other animals have—*so* different that, if they're both called 'cognition', then it's really in two different senses of the word, related only by a family resemblance. And, 'cognition', of course, is far from the only word in this boat—which creates a real problem of clarity and precision. What I would *like* to do is partition the vocabulary, so that some of it is used for what we and the animals share, and some of it is reserved for what is exclusive to us. But, since, in common parlance, the words are all interrelated, that can sound outrageous or incoherent. ('What do you *mean*: animals have representations, but only people have "genuine" intentionality? Representations are *by definition* intentional—as you yourself used to say!') The alternative would be, like the great Germans, to invent a bunch of new words. (It's hard to know which would put off my friends more.)

Anyway, the more important business is to convince at least a few people that there really is this huge difference that I'm on about, and to give some indication of what it amounts to; then, maybe, some of the terminology can settle down, one way or another. So, what is it that Cummins and I and the rest of you all can do that Sheila can't? Lots of things, of course; but here's one that I think is pretty basic. We can realize that we're *wrong* about things in a way—indeed, in two deeply related ways—that are fundamentally unavailable to her.

Now, let me hasten to insert three quick clarifications, so as to forestall needless miscommunication.

1. I just specified one way that Sheila *can* be wrong about things, and maybe even realize it. So, I'm not denying *that*.
2. One obvious way in which people can be wrong about things and Sheila can't is by asserting falsehoods; but that's not what I mean.
3. Another obvious way in which people can be wrong about things and Sheila can't is ethically or morally; but that's not what I mean either.

Actually, (2) and (3) may be intimately connected with what I'm going to describe. But I don't want to approach it by either of those two routes because: first, I'm not clear about how the connections might go; and second, it's too easy to think it's too easy. (After all, they're 'obvious', right?)

Here, then, is the first of the two deeply related ways that *we* (and *only* we) can realize that we're wrong about things. We can realize that it would be *impossible* for things to be as we think they are or represent them to be—and, *therefore*, they aren't. Once it becomes apparent that that would be impossible, it has to have been wrong. ***Discussion point 3.14***

Sheila—or, to raise the stakes, some higher primates—may be able to appreciate that things are strange, or baffling, or even too untoward to mess with. What they can't do, or so I'm saying, is confront something with the attitude: Well, it sure *seems* like X; but X would be *impossible*; so it *can't* be X. (Here, formulated in words, but verbalization is not the fulcrum.) This is one kind of appearance/reality distinction. So another way to put my point is to say that animals can't make that *kind* of appearance/reality distinction.

But, look, it's all too easy to concoct counter-instances. Thus, so-called 'theory-driven' perceptual mechanisms will only deliver percepts that meet certain 'reality constraints'—which is to say, they filter out 'impossible' ones, often replacing them with similar ones that are possible. Some of these filters are even learned, as when one learns the phonetic structure of one's native tongue, and then doesn't even hear minor deviations from it. Processors of error-correcting codes do the same kind of filtering; and it's one way of describing the much ballyhooed 'pattern completion' of PDP nets (which we all know can be 'learned'). And animals, surely, can do all of that.

So, what's the difference, in the case I have in mind? Well, there's this: in many cases the illusion persists—and yet one rejects it anyway. Can you imagine a dog (or a chimp) watching a magic show and *refusing to believe* that the smiling assistant is in two pieces, or floating in thin air, or what the duck just turned into—*on the grounds that* such things are impossible? If not, *why* not? For one thing, it's hard to imagine animals figuring out or deciding what to believe by adducing considerations, evaluating them, and then finding the remainder compelling. But maybe that's just a failure of imagination—it's hard to imagine what any *reasoning* would be like that couldn't be put into words by the reasoner. I even wonder whether any animal can entertain a *hypothesis*, in the sense of *deliberately* suspending judgment on something, pending evidence one way or the other.

Still, I think the essential thing is not the form of the reasoning but whether convictions about what is and isn't possible can figure among the considerations upon which its conclusion is based. My reasons for this are twofold. The first is that fairly young children can reason and entertain hypotheses, and yet be shaky about the appearance/reality distinction. That's why, at a certain age they come to love magic shows: possibility and reality becomes a real issue for them. Indeed, I wouldn't be surprised if Stone-Age adults were in much the position of contemporary children in this regard. That is, I think that convictions about possibility and their bearing on the kind of appearance/reality distinction I'm discussing are part of our *cultural*, not our biological heritage.

But my second reason for emphasizing convictions about what is and isn't possible is their deep connection with the second way in which people—and only people—can realize that they're wrong about things: namely, people can realize that their convictions about possibility are wrong. This is a more consequential realization than might first be obvious. For, given that these convictions have been governing what has been acceptable as real, they have also been contributing materially to the sense or content of the representations in use to represent the real. That's what makes M. C. Escher's architectural drawings so spooky: while abiding carefully by many of the conventions for representing three-dimensional objects, they subtly flout others, thereby seeming to represent impossible buildings. In other words, those conventions themselves depend on what is and isn't possible. In quite another context, the senses of the words 'mass', 'energy', 'space', and 'time' all changed when relativity changed our convictions about what is and isn't possible.

Generalizing, then, the conclusion is this. As creatures who won't accept as real anything they deem impossible, and who can realize that their convictions about possibility are wrong, we are also creatures who can realize not merely that their actual representations of things are defective but that their very representational resources are defective—and then can fix them. This capacity is certainly a cultural achievement, perhaps the highest so far.

As all of those here today know, I've tried to characterize it in recent years in various ways; and I attempted a new route into it today. But I still think the best way is to say that what distinguishes humanity—*not Homo sapiens*—is the capacity for what I call a double-edged commitment, which is equivalent to a distinctive kind of responsibility. The two edges of the commitment are, first, to *stick to* the convictions about what is and isn't possible, even in the face of ostensible problems (for otherwise the appearance/reality distinction has no bite); but, second, to find oneself *bound*, eventually (if the problems can't be resolved), to give them up in favor of more promising ones (for otherwise they degenerate into dogmatic orthodoxy). These two edges are exactly the structure of genuine—what Heidegger calls authentic or owned—*responsibility*. **Final discussion**

3·3

Discussion

HAUGELAND Can't you have, as it were, standardly intended targets for representational types, where you can then talk about their intrinsic accuracy, relative to that? I mean, you buy a map of Chicago, it says Chicago on it. Even though someone might misuse it by targeting St. Louis but—

CUMMINS I think those cases are funny. I think that they're intended to have Chicago as their targets when they are produced.

HAUGELAND Well, right, and you play on that same pun.

CUMMINS A little bit. I want to come back to that kind of case in a bit. In fact, I think it will loom large in the discussion between me and Brian [See Part 4—ed.], but for the time being I want to think about this fairly peripherally, so that that kind of option doesn't really arise. But I think in conventional representational systems it arises all the time. That is, you can generate these things with the intention that they have a certain range of targets.

CLARK What's an intender mechanism?

CUMMINS A parser would be an intender. Something that's identified in terms of some representational function. And these can be more or less architectural, or they can be produced on the fly in various ways.

DENNETT Always some representational function; aren't there other intender mechanisms? Digestive mechanisms and everything else?

CUMMINS I think grasping is a good example of a process that has a target but that isn't representational at all. But I think there's a close analogy with intentionality here. There is, as it were, an intended target of the grasp.

HAUGELAND Are you going to let him get away with digestion? Are there intender mechanisms in the immune system?

CUMMINS You got me. Yeah, I expect.

DENNETT I'm just trying to figure out whether 'intender mechanisms' is a very generic, functional term.

CUMMINS I don't know how generic it is, but I'm pretty sure that the kind of intentionality you get in representational systems is a special case of a more general kind of thing where the match, or failure of match between aim and hit is crucial to assessing the success of the endeavor.

HAUGELAND So there's an intender mechanism in the frog or toad's tongue—

CUMMINS Yeah, I think that's right.

CLAPIN So only some intender mechanisms have the job of representing, of having representations.

CUMMINS That's right, exactly. I think there's a lot more intentionality than is involved in representation, but I think that when you have an intender whose function it is to represent, then we can think of the resulting application of the representation to the target as something whose semantic content has two sources. It has its intentional content and it has this content that it gets from the representation and the two things come together in a certain way.

CLARK So intentionality is out there in the trees, it's all around, for you.

CUMMINS Oh yeah. We'll come to that.

3.3 SMITH You seem to say that if something is a target it's objective?

p. 125 CUMMINS I'm going to claim that the things that can be objects for me are the things that can be (in this sense of objectivity that I'm trying to get at, where there's enough commonality between John and me to have a meaningful dispute) determined by what representational targets I can have.

SMITH But does it go the other way—if something can be a representational target for you, are you suggesting that for you that's enough for it to be objective?

CUMMINS Yes.

HAUGELAND Once you have a representational target you have something against which the accuracy of a representation could be measured. So that's the ur-form of the true-false norm.

CUMMINS That's the normativity that it seems to me is important in objectivity. It's the idea that something independent of how I think of things or see things or represent them, or however you want to put this, is normative for the accuracy or truth or whatever you want. I tend to like graded notions better than truth.

HAUGELAND It's one of the many normativities involved.

CUMMINS That's right.

DENNETT So the Holy Trinity is an object, is objective for Catholics. If a novice Catholic who wonders whether or not he's got it right...

HAUGELAND It's not clear that the novice Catholic can actually go to the Holy Trinity to check whether...

DENNETT Well, that's why I raised the case.

CUMMINS That doesn't worry me. We will come to that stage.

HAUGELAND You have said that what representational functions something can have depends in part on its—the intender's—conceptual sophistication and its perceptual and inferential resources.

CUMMINS I think it depends on the conceptual sophistication of the system in which the intender is embedded. An intender's identity is holistic in the following sense. Whether they can be something whose business it is to, say, be a parser, depends in part on its neighborhood.

HAUGELAND Fair enough.

CUMMINS This just flows in part out of my story [Cummins 1975; 1983] about what functions are—they're contributions to the capacities of some larger system—if you could reach in there and pull out the parser and stick it under a door to hold the door open then you ask, well, what's the target of that thing, well it would change...

HAUGELAND Concepts and the things involved in inferential capacities, whatever they are, sound representational.

CUMMINS Well, they might well be. Since in general what identifies an intender is it's functional neighborhood, and since its functional neighborhood might be lots of other intenders among other things, it's not a bad gloss to say that, roughly speaking, systems that we would ordinarily say have high conceptual sophistication are likely to turn out to have a more finely grained set of intenders at their disposal than less sophisticated ones.

HAUGELAND So you can have circumstances—am I tracking you all right?—in which some of the concepts that a system has are being harnessed by the intender mechanism to fix the target, and then others are being applied to that target?

CUMMINS Well, I don't like the idea that they're being harnessed by it. I think it's just that because of the fact that functional notions are holistic in this way, that, it's merely the fact that it's, as it were, living and embodied in this ritzy neighborhood, that allows you to think of it as having this intention at all. But whether the thing actually goes and harnesses this stuff I think is a quite separate issue. And it's not the point I'm making here. I'm just making the point that functions aren't atomistically identified.

HAUGELAND I'm thinking of a case—I know language is a dicey one, but it's so handy.

CUMMINS And so misleading.

HAUGELAND If I say 'that guy from Davis is reading a paper now', it's easy to fall into saying, 'well "that guy from Davis" is picking out the target, and "is reading a paper" is...'

CUMMINS No, I don't like that.

HAUGELAND I thought you wouldn't.

3.4 HAUGELAND The size of what error?

p. 128 CUMMINS The size of your representational error.

HAUGELAND But you're just learning to have *T* as a target.

CUMMINS No. I have *T* as a target and I'm learning about chess—I'm learning to hit it.

CLARK Well, to have it as a target is just to be aimed at it for you?

CUMMINS That's right.

CLARK So targets are cheap.

CUMMINS Yes, the whole idea is that what drives the learning is some attempt to narrow the gap between content and target. So it must be that when you start out you can have a target about which you know next to nothing. That's how you articulate the learning problem.

HAUGELAND Well, it depends on what you are learning.

CUMMINS I agree. I want to be rough and crude here at the start.

CLARK As soon as you've pointed at *T* you have to hit it as a target. There's something odd about that analogy. If I've got something as a target in archery, and I move around, it's weird to think that the target moves to wherever I'm pointing.

CUMMINS Exactly. That's it.

SMITH No, but that's not a case where that's an issue. The question is whether John is denying it.

CUMMINS I agree that's an issue, so I'm being a bit perverse here, but bear with me and I think the perversity will bear fruit in the end.

DENNETT One problem with using the NETtalk example is that NETtalk 3.5 p. 128 only works because Terry [Sejnowski] knows what the target is, and he's the one that's providing the feedback.

CUMMINS That doesn't worry me. I think there's an epistemological point about how the information gets into the system in order to drive the learning. I'm not worried about that. I'm just worried about what conceptual framework do we as theorists have to have just to articulate what the learning problem *is*.

CLARK But how do we know, on your account, what the target is?

CUMMINS How do I know as a theorist?

CLARK Yes, how do we know, for a given case, you're aimed at something, you're adjusting yourself in some respect, in response to the thing. But, what aspects of that thing are you, as it were, aimed at?

CLAPIN So your question is, if you came across a network in the wild that was undergoing learning—

CUMMINS How would I know what it was aimed at?

CLARK What aspects of the thing it was aimed at. Because it's one thing to say it's aimed at that bit of space-time, or something. It's another thing to say, OK, it's aimed at phonetics, or something.

CUMMINS I think this can be a difficult methodological problem. And sometimes I think it can be quite simple and obvious. But I think it's one of these kinds of half-theory, half-empirical sort of issues where your hypotheses about what the targets are, are driven by, for example, attempts to understand the learning in a useful way.

DENNETT Do you suppose—this is a theme that looms large I think—that, I'll use it for the first time, not the last, there's a fact of the matter about what the target is, as it were *ab initio*.

CUMMINS Yes.

DENNETT Yikes!

CUMMINS I'm an unrepentant realist about this.

SMITH So what if Putnam says, 'Damn it, I'm retired now; I'm going to find out what the difference is between beeches and elms'? That's not the kind of learning you're talking about here?

CUMMINS Yes, it might be. I'd have to know more about it.

SMITH The question is, is the issue acquiring knowledge, or is the issue acquiring targets.

CUMMINS Look, let's take a much cruder version of the story that John uses. Suppose I'm a simple-minded conceptual role theorist. Then I think, I don't have a target-content distinction, but nevertheless, I'm going to think, in my terminology, that what targets I can have depends on what I know. So, changes in my knowledge can't be driven, can't be understood, even by a third party, as a narrowing of the gap between my targets and my knowledge, because every time I learn more my targets change. So it's hard to even articulate learning problems in that framework.

SMITH But neither you nor John is a conceptual role theorist.

CUMMINS I have a worry about John. Which is that I think that his theory, though way more sophisticated, still falls prey to this, but I'm not sure—

HAUGELAND It may, I'm not sure either, but I want to know what you're saying, so far. Now, how do NETtalk and the other examples bear on the question of the capacity to have tennis-balls as such as targets? NETtalk's target is just set by the fact that it's got certain nodes labelled 'input' nodes. It's like the parser. Whatever is in the damn inbox is the target. Period. There isn't a problem of having it as the target.

DENNETT I don't think you [Cummins] would agree about NETtalk as having that as its target.

CUMMINS I don't quite, but let's just make sure we get the structure of the argument straight. My worry is, as I say, the idea that knight forks can't be objective for a creature that doesn't know anything about chess. There's a sense in which I agree with that, but I don't think I want to go nearly as far as you [Haugeland] do about it. I think you can have things as targets that you know next to nothing about. In fact, I really think you can have things as targets that you know nothing whatever about. So that's why I think intentionality is intellectually cheap.

DENNETT But now, can we take the knight fork example? You've got a little kid that's just learning chess, and is learning by watching Granpa and Uncle Joe, not by being taught. It's as unintellectual as possible. He has a sort of recognitional capacity, of 'Oh! What are those named?' Of course he's got no name for it, he doesn't have to have much of a sense, even, of what it's for, but it has become salient for the kid.

CUMMINS Now on John's view that won't count as recognizing knight forks, because knight forks are things that are say, independent of medium—things that can happen in correspondence chess, or what he calls esoteric chess.

DENNETT But are knight forks the target?

CUMMINS That depends, as it were, on which gap the error signal narrows. If I'm a teacher, and you're trying to do these things, and I'm prepared to say yes to you when you recognize a pattern even though it isn't in the game, then knight forks aren't the target. Now let's take the teacher out of the picture. And now it gets a little trickier to see what the trajectory of your learning is, but we at least have to be able to articulate the possibility that the trajectory of the learning is going to converge on knight forks and not, say, a positional pattern.

DENNETT Well, I want to push that just one little bit more. So the kid has a sort of dawning recognitional capacity, and has acquired the goal currently of looking for another one of those. So now he has the target of finding another one. So now if he looks at a situation on the board, he can misidentify, he can say, 'oh, that's one of those', when it isn't. So there's the possibility of error. But now the question is whether there's a fact of the matter of whether the target is a knight fork or something which is, as it were, a weird gerrymandered subgenus of knight forks.

CUMMINS I'm going to come to schnight forks in just a moment.

CLARK I don't think there's an answer to the question, 'Which gap does the error signal narrow?' I think that there's no answer to that question.

CUMMINS I think there is.

DENNETT That's where the realism comes in.

CUMMINS I think that's an epistemological issue. I know how to caricature in a derogatory way the opposition: they're the village verificationists. There ought to be an equally derogatory way to caricature my kind of realism.

HAUGELAND There is. The village realist.

CLARK To take responsibility do you have to consciously enforce the rule? Do you have to kind of have them in mind? 3.6 p. 130

CUMMINS There are probably cases when you do and cases when you don't, but I don't think consciousness is important here. What's important here, is, as John says, a sort of vigilance and resilience thought of as a disposition to respond to untowardness in certain kinds of ways.

CLARK But you know so many systems have vigilance and resilience: the frog, when it's trying to get the fly rather than anything else is presumably resistant to—

CUMMINS But the question, 'What can it be vigilant and resilient to?' will depend heavily on what resources it's got. That's how his [Haugeland's] version winds up differing from mine.

HAUGELAND Yes, to use the other word, it's what you're taking responsibility for.

CLARK And how can you fix that without thinking about it?

HAUGELAND Well, I try to describe, as it were, the behavior pattern you'd see.

CLAPIN And that's enough for commitment?

HAUGELAND I haven't made a point of making that case, but I don't see why it couldn't be.

CUMMINS But I think it's important to see that in John's account of intentionality, and its correlative relation to objectivity, one of the things that he isn't taking responsibility for here is that his account should turn out to be reductive in the way that, say, a certain kind of naturalistic semantics has always insisted on. That's not one of the rules of the game that he's playing. So as I said before, it's not the looming circularity or failure to naturalize that worries me about this. It's something else. Well, the other thing worries me, but I don't think it's fair to be worried about it, because, it's not what he's after. I don't think that it's a good idea, at least at a first pass at understanding John, to worry about how you're going to sanitize it, naturalize it.

CLARK I was really worried deep down here about the relation to reasons, that you would think that taking responsibility requires being sensitive to reasons.

CUMMINS In certain cases it might be, but in other cases it might not. That's why, for example, probably in science, to play the positron game or whatever it is, it probably does require that kind of stuff, but in other cases maybe not. So it's not essential to his account of objectivity, rather it's the vigilance and resilience, the commitment, that matter. And what it takes to have the vigilance and resilience and commitment will vary from case to case, and his whole idea is that, well, what you can be vigilant and resilient and committed to depends on your resources, and hence what can be an object for you depends on those things and that's why we differ from canids, for example. Is that a fair gloss?

HAUGELAND Yeah.

CUMMINS Wonderful. And I don't believe it.

3.7 SMITH Can you elucidate why responsibility and commitment are intel-
p. 131 lectual?

CUMMINS In the case of knight forks, to take responsibility for the relevant stuff there, requires a fair knowledge of chess. You can't take responsibility for maintaining the constituent standards of chess if you don't know anything about chess. But I think that you can have chess positions as targets without knowing anything about chess. So, on his view I can have chess positions as objects only if I know about chess, and on my view, you don't.

CLARK But to have it as a target isn't to have a thought about it, is it?

CUMMINS 'About it' in the target sense, but not 'about it' in the representational sense. I think ultimately what makes it tempting to overprice intentionality is that slide.

CLARK But if John means you can't think about knight forks without, as it were, taking responsibility for the rules of chess...

CUMMINS I think you can think about them in the target sense if you don't know anything about them. You can't represent them if you don't know anything about them, but you can think about them.

CLARK Maybe I'm just so non-referential in the ways that I think about thought, that the idea that having a target could in any sense make it the case that you're thinking about something, is just weird to me. It's like, you know, you just turn around and there it is, you're having a thought about something.

CUMMINS If you think that, then you won't think like John and me that intentionality and objectivity are two sides of the same coin. I think he's right about that.

HAUGELAND Can I answer Brian's question? I think that the prerequisites for the possibility of being able to see knight forks, I guess *as* knight forks, are the same as the prerequisites for understanding chess pieces and chess positions. All these words are ones that one appropriates. So I want to appropriate 'understand' here, and that can be seen as a kin of intellection. But I don't intend 'meaning' to say something that entails cerebral cogitation, or—

DENNETT A sort of mental sophistication.

HAUGELAND Right. It's something like, I mean, I would like to evoke, at least, the suggestion that you understand hammers when you get to be good at driving in nails.

SMITH Well, that's what I would have thought you would think, and that's why the word 'intellectual'... it's exactly because of the kind of knowledge of carpentry that a carpenter has, that 'intellectualization' seems to me to be a misleading term.

CUMMINS It may be a misleading word here, but I want to be kind of provocative about this, because, let me proceed a little bit. I'm prepared to play quite fast and loose with what counts as having knowledge of chess, because on almost any construal of what that is, you have to have more of it on John's view than on my view. And it's that difference that I'm interested in highlighting, and I think it just gets in the way to worry too much about what the knowledge is.

SMITH Well, OK, that helps. As long as it's broad, because for some of the rest of us who aren't either of you—where we want to be on this continuum depends quite a lot on...

CUMMINS You may be orthogonal to a certain axis, and there will be a sense in which although we have this disagreement, from the point of view of some of the rest of you, it will be a kind of intramural disagreement. And so, in spite of being insulting, I may be trying to recruit an ally.

HAUGELAND It might work too.

3.8   CLARK Can a knight fork be a target in a system that's in principle incap-
p. 132   able of learning of that pattern?

CUMMINS Yes, I think it can, so I want to make this as stark as I can.

SMITH Knight forks qua knight forks?

CUMMINS Yes, yes exactly.

3.9   CLARK But if you go back to your sheepdog, suppose that it just couldn't
p. 132   track the ball at all. The ball could still be the target for you then?

CUMMINS Yes.

CLARK That's why the closet verificationists here are uneasy.

CUMMINS I know. Look, I'm prepared to give a little, but this is a negoti-ating position. I like doing philosophy in a way where you take the simple, extreme thing and try it. And then if you can push me around, that's fine. I'm fairly easily pushed, actually, but I'd like to start from a place so that even if you push me pretty far, I'm still pretty close to home.

3.10   CLARK That very same error signal could be teaching you about lots of
p. 134   other things. Exactly that error signal could be about many different things.

CUMMINS Could be. Needn't be.

CLARK OK, so what makes it about the weakness of the king side defense, rather than one of the other things that that very same error signal could be about?

DENNETT Because the teacher means it that way, that's the trouble here, he's got the teacher in there with all that understanding in the teacher's head.

CUMMINS No, we could as third parties look at the teacher–student interaction, and ask ourselves, how do we track the trajectory of the learning? And that will be an empirically grounded theoretical endeavor which I claim will sometimes settle best on, say, weak side defenses, and sometimes settle best on some other kinds of things. And I think there's an objective fact about this matter, but I'm not enough of a verificationist to think that I owe you an account of how I can be guaranteed to get it right any more than I owe you an account about how I could ever be guaranteed to get anything right.

CLARK But what is the notion of 'it will settle there' then? You allowed a minute ago that in fact the system could be intrinsically incapable of learning the pattern.

CUMMINS That's right, but nevertheless in tracking learning, I may get a much better account by picking a target that it doesn't hit, just as in the predator recognition case. It's important in that case. I don't have the whole story here but most of this seems to me substantive scientific methodology. How, as an evolutionary ethologist, do I actually figure out that what was adaptive here was predator recognition and not shadow recognition? Well, I don't know. But, I did figure that out, it seems to me.

CLARK But you figure it out because you were dealing with a system that was capable of learning it.

CUMMINS No, the system is never capable of actually hitting predators *per se* reliably.

CLARK But it was capable of learning enough of the pattern in order to hit them enough of the time for it to be plausible for you to say that that's what its about.

CUMMINS To do better than the competitors in its lineage, and that may be arbitrarily bad.

CLARK Sure.

CUMMINS Now, that's where John and I differ, because on John's view— in that passage that I read—it makes it sound as if I've got to be pretty good. In his view, I can't have knight forks as my target if, for example, I can't recognize them in alternative media.

CLARK But why don't you say, on John's view you've got to be good enough? And the question of what good enough is depends very much on what the problem is that you're dealing with.

CUMMINS Well, that I think is where I have an extra degree of freedom that he doesn't have.

HAUGELAND No. Why in this case, isn't it that all you can say is that the function of the trained-up recognizer, targetter, is to distinguish whatever it is the teacher or provider of the error signal was tracking? I mean, that's the only input you have to learn and process. This one wasn't right, this one was right, or maybe, a score. And that all the system does is get better, as better as it can, at, as it were, predicting the teacher's output.

CUMMINS That's right, and that's the thing to think about in the evolutionary case, when you think about sort of evolutionary learning if you like. In that case, we don't think of selection, as it were, knowing an awful lot about predators. It's predator avoidance that is responsible for the advantage—for whatever adaptiveness this intender contributes to its host. But, whether that's good enough to get it by his competitors depends on what his competitors are like, and they may be awful. So, all I'm saying is, to understand this kind of learning, you need to decouple how good you are at it from what it is you're aimed at. And I don't think that John's account decouples enough to make good sense of that. If you want to be more verificationist than I, you may not want to decouple quite as far as I do; so there's this kind of continuum here. I just want to make the contrast stark by starting way out on the other side of it, in a way. So that we can focus on that issue as opposed to others. Two points determine a line, but they determine it a lot easier if they're pretty far apart.

3.11   CUMMINS It's important, I think, to remember that your [Haugeland's]
p. 135   account isn't intending to be reductive. But I just think it's useful to see why if you do have a use theory, you're going to be naturally pushed into your sort of views about intentionality. I'm not saying that this is why you do it. I don't know why you do it.

HAUGELAND The thing that's wrong with my view is that other people can have bad reasons for it!

CUMMINS If that's right, I think it's important to see that. Because I think there are a lot of use theorists out there, and there are a lot of people who are agreeing with you without understanding what it is you're about. That is, for the wrong reasons.

3.12   CUMMINS Do you mean, epistemologically it may be very hard to tell
p. 141   them apart, or that there's really no fact of the matter?

HAUGELAND That there's no fact of the matter.

CUMMINS OK. Now, that worries me because it seems to me that there are a lot of compelling explanations in psychology that exploit exactly that difference. And I take it to be part of my job to reconstruct that. So I'm right in thinking that in this respect you really do think effectiveness and accuracy just collapse. You can't tell the difference, there's no fact of the matter about it?

HAUGELAND You allow us that there may not even be a representation that marks the shadow–predator distinction.

CUMMINS Yes, that's right.

HAUGELAND It could be reflex. This particular response in the prairie dog could be a reflex.

CUMMINS The underlying argument here is that being skittish, versus the other story, generate equally effective behavior, and that's all there is to go on.

HAUGELAND They generate the same behavior.

CUMMINS It's because the same behavior gets generated that you find no distinction.

HAUGELAND Well, they generate the same behavior and, moreover, you can, under either way of, so to speak, parsing the behavior and the intervening steps, either way of describing it, you can equally well give the same account of the evolutionary trade-off.

CUMMINS So in your view it couldn't happen that at some point I had the population of prairie dogs split into two subpopulations, one of whom as it were, realize the skittishness story, and one realize the other story, and one did better. That story is nonsense on your view. There's no content to it.

DENNETT Yes.

HAUGELAND If this is all the information we're working with, that's right.

CLAPIN I don't quite understand what the difference is between being easily fooled and skittish.

HAUGELAND I'm suggesting sort of simplistically that we have, on the one hand a mechanism that takes input from the environment and comes up with something depending on that input. And then this thing that it comes up with is passed on to another mechanism which is, as it were, selecting among the behaviors that a prairie dog could have, like diving and grazing and mating and so forth. The issue is, what is this thing that's passed along? And, if it's construed as a mention of a predator, rightly or wrongly, then you have a mechanism over here that says, 'Oh damn, predator, I'd better dive.' On the other hand, if you take that thing that it passes along as mentioning or pertaining to shadows, then you have a mechanism over here that says, 'Shadows, it's best in the long

run to dive, never mind whether it's anything else.' And that's skittishness in the action selector, right? You've got better safe than sorry in the
action selector rather than in the response to the environment.

CUMMINS And your point is that these two stories which you've just
carefully distinguished are actually not different.

HAUGELAND Yes, right, there is nothing to choose between those two
descriptions unless we've got other stuff going on.

CUMMINS That's right. I just want to identify the verificationism where it
is. That's OK.

3.13 HAUGELAND And its what about the intentional stance that I think Dan
p. 141   has never heard. And it would save you [Dennett] from what, alas, you
don't want to be saved from, which is the ridiculous supposition that
the intentional stance applies to thermostats and flowering trees. The
intentional stance is a much better idea if it's narrowed down, and this
is a way to do that.

CUMMINS And when you say that these are reasons, you mean, not that
these are as it were evidence for it. But these are as it were grounding
facts. I just want to get the epistemology and the metaphysics separated
here, because I'm worried. I have no problem with saying it's evidence.

HAUGELAND Well I think that these three reasons I'm going to offer are
the kinds of things that there have to be in order for there to be a
difference to draw—the thing that there isn't with the prairie dogs.

CLARK Presumably the metaphysical requirement is that there be some
evidence of some kind.

CUMMINS Oh I don't have any such requirement, no.

HAUGELAND Yes, but you said, marvelously, it's one of my favorite
quotes by a philosopher, that 'I don't have much of a metaphysical or
ontological conscience.'

CUMMINS I have none. I freely confess. I have no ontological conscience
whatever.

3.14 CLARK To realize it's impossible is much more than flat out rejecting. It's,
p. 143   as it were, reflecting that this and this couldn't both be the case.

HAUGELAND Well, I've avoided the word 'reflection', that can be loaded,
but I said realizing that it would be impossible, and on that basis, then
rejecting.

SMITH Entertaining it and then rejecting it. You actually have to entertain
it in some sense.

DENNETT Well that's what he wants to resist because he's trying to thread this needle without getting intellectual, and let us have all these propositions running through our heads.

HAUGELAND I'm thinking of a case where there is a representation or a how we think things to be, being vague about what that comes to, but that it has some content. And then appreciating that, 'No that couldn't be. Things couldn't be like that,' and so rejecting it.

CLARK So when the visual system can only see something like the Necker cube one way or the other. It's not, as it were, rejecting the possibility it could be both at once.

HAUGELAND I think that's actually rather difficult for me, and I'm going to acknowledge that in a minute.

CUMMINS All I really have to say is this. I think your reasoning is faultless. And I think your conclusion is wholly unacceptable, and so I want a Final discussio p. 144 *modus tollens*. What I want people to think is, look, if you're not prepared, like me, to abandon your ontological conscience, your epistemological scruples, and say, look, there's just a fact of the matter about the difference between the effectiveness and the accuracy, then you really ought to wind up just where you are. I think that's exactly right, and it seems to me that we should all be cognizant about where this particular route leads. What was really useful about your comments is that having a lot of different characterizations of where that endpoint is, is extremely useful, because different ones will resonate with different people, whether they want to be there or they don't want to be there, and why not. I don't want to be there, and the only thing I can say about why I don't want to be there is—I don't know whether it's true or not—I just don't see it as a position from which I can comfortably articulate what I think is the real dispute between, say, Piagetians and their contemporary opponents about development, and things like that.[13] Those are the kinds of issues that drove my particular position. But, I think it's really interesting the way that those issues bear on this question about what objectivity is all about.

HAUGELAND It's not clear to me that they have to bear. That is, it's not clear to me that you and I—were you only willing—could not divide

---

[13] [The dispute in this case concerns whether a child's developing ability to solve word arithmetic problems involves acquiring greater representational power (Piagetians), or simply learning better to exploit the representational powers they have. (See e.g. D. D. Cummins, 1991)—RC.]

the field in a certain way. I'll give you all the animals and half of what's true about people if I can keep the other half, crudely put.

CUMMINS Yes, and I will give you the stuff about people construed in a certain way. But I have a very hard time giving it to you when it's construed as an issue about objectivity.

HAUGELAND Does that mean you're not prepared to give me something distinctive about people for which I need a word, and objectivity might do? We're not quarrelling over just the word?

CUMMINS No, of course there are, as you said, a million things that are distinctive about people, starting with their morphology. That's not the issue. The issue is this notion of what it is for there to be a world independent of thought, which depends on, in a funny way, what your thought is like. And I just feel like, if you really think that there's a world independent of your thought, then you shouldn't think it depends on what your thought is like at all. And I just want us to start by establishing a crude position over here and see how the negotiation goes, that's all I want to do.

HAUGELAND So it really is the ontological conclusions that most rub you the wrong way.

DENNETT It's amazing for somebody that doesn't have any ontological conscience.

CUMMINS I guess that's right. I mean, maybe lack of ontological conscience isn't really the right way to put it. Maybe it's a lack of epistemological conscience. I tend to be very unimpressed by arguments that move from premises about what we can know and what we can tell and what we distinguish, to conclusions about what there is. I don't like that kind of move in general and that's why I don't want people to see your claim here as a question about what's different between humans and animals, because I really think that's misleading in a way. There's a certain kind of sense in which you think human mentality gives rise to a certain kind of reality, because of the way it works.

HAUGELAND Not 'gives rise to'.

CUMMINS Well, helps to constitute. I don't know what exactly the right sort of...

HAUGELAND Constitute means 'make sense of'.

CUMMINS Yeah, OK, that's all right.

HAUGELAND So, when I say that reality is constituted by commitment to a set of constitutive standards, I mean it's made sense of as reality. What matters to me is not how we can know what is and isn't real—a

good old-fashioned epistemological issue—but, how we can so much
as make sense of the idea of reality.

CUMMINS It's intelligibility, that's right.

SMITH It is true that your objectivity is ultimately empirical?

HAUGELAND Yes, it's, as it were, a constraint on the account, that the way
I make sense of reality, what we understand by reality, that it be
something that we could be on to. That's what we mean.

SMITH It's a little difficult for me to say this because I believe it so
strongly—I'm worried that I'm projecting it onto you—but my sense is
that you think that that's right. That when you give up your sense of
possibility, for example, in the second case, when you sort of revise it,
you're revising it because in fact something has happened which you
didn't think was possible, and it's really happened. And that's actually
critical, it seems to me, to your being able to distinguish between what
the world's like and how you represent it as being. In other words your
promise is that in spite of the use basis—I'm trying to put it in Rob's
language—in spite of the fact that how we find the world intelligible is in
part a function of how we live, nevertheless, you can in fact make room
for the gap which Rob thinks you can only make room for in his way.

HAUGELAND That's exactly right.

CUMMINS That's right.

SMITH It seems to me that that's the cogent issue here, and the challenge
back to Rob is: not all use theories have what we recognize as fatal
about the use theories that Rob thinks are fatally flawed, namely an
inability to name distinctions.

CUMMINS I think that's a good characterization, and what I would say in
reply is that I think that the gap that John ingeniously constructs is an
ersatz gap. It ain't the real thing. It's a kind of epistemological reconstruction of it which is really ingenious, but it just ain't the real thing.

SMITH Well, that's why I think the issue of how intellectual versus the
kind of understanding carpenters have is crucial. Because I'm worried
that if it were intellection in the ratiocinative sense, then Rob's view
would be right—that this is all ersatz and it's actually critical that it's
grounded in activity.

CUMMINS It's getting you on board when it's just implicit know-how
that's going to be hard, right?

SMITH Well, that's the move, that's where we are, which is the grounding
of know-how in activity is actually what rescues John from the challenge that you just articulated, I think!

HAUGELAND Well, I would be pleased if that were so, but you're going to
have to tell me how it works.

CUMMINS I think on your own views things can—just like Hugh said—
slide back and forth in a way between what's tacit know-how and
what's explicit and so on,[14] and so it's going to turn out that where this
gap is is going to be really slippery.

HAUGELAND It's the resilient skills that you're thinking of, isn't it? I see
the connection.

SMITH It's not the slip between tacit and explicit, because that can all
remain epistemic. It's the fact that it's grounded in concrete engagement
with the world and projects and so on and so forth, that's what I was
calling empirical. It's not a very good word, but it's a kind of in-the-world
anchoring of this activity, which in fact is what grounds objectivity.

DENNETT But that will ground biological—

SMITH Well, sure, we haven't got to the question of whether in fact the
introduction of the normativity that evolution provides is a strong
enough form of normativity to ground the kind of stuff that John
wants. I don't think it is, but I want to talk about that in my response
to you [Dennett]. But the point is: at least we're there. This is again
narrowing the points of disagreement. Even if the ways we render it
intelligible are use and project and contingent in lots of ways, but are
nevertheless grounded in the world and its activities, then the question
is: what is the normativity on activity that gives this thing bite? And
your [Dennett's] answer is: evolution.

DENNETT Yep.

SMITH And his [Haugeland's] is not.

HAUGELAND Not even cultural evolution.

DENNETT It's damn close though.

CLARK I think what I need is the knowing-how version of conviction. If
conviction is important, for the story that you want to tell, you don't
want conviction to be a kind of opinion-based (in Dan's terms) intellectualist achievement, then you have to have a notion of conviction
that isn't opinion based.

HAUGELAND I used conviction in the formulation today, but my preferred
word is resolute commitment. And what that amounts to is that you
have the—to echo Brian—the skillful ability to recognize an impossible
event or structure when you see one, that is, seem to see one.

---

[14] [See section 6.1.10, 'Explicitness and Redescription: Clark'—ed.]

CLARK to recognize it qua impossible, not just to recognize it . . .

HAUGELAND That's right, recognize 'that would be impossible', or 'that would be against the rules' (as impossible in chess as a rook moving along a diagonal)—you can tell it when it happens—and you have the disposition, the response, the response that you will stick to. The 'stick-to-it-iveness' of 'No I reject that.'

CUMMINS But what's that? I mean, here I am with all my practices and whatever and know-how and embodiment in the world, being what it is, and then something mega-untoward happens—I don't mean it's big but it has this special impossibility character to it. But that can't be, on your view, a case of recognizing an impossible object because of course, on your view, I don't at this point have the resources to even think about such a thing.

HAUGELAND Well this is the diciest move in TRF. The distinction between possibility and conceivability. Conceivability is that which you have the empirical resources to recognize when it happens. Possibility is that which you will not reject as impossible employing your constitutive skills. And the important move—this is the way that I can make, as it were, Kuhn's [1962] idea about crisis safe for metaphysics—is that those don't coincide.

CUMMINS I agree with that, that those don't coincide. There's a reason why I think this is an ersatz—this is what you call the 'forbidden zone'?

HAUGELAND excluded.

CUMMINS Excluded zone [Haugeland 1998a: 331]. It's a wonderful idea. The excluded zone is, as it were (this is going to be provocative) the verificationist ersatz for what I think of as the real thing. What, on your view you can't have is things that are not only outside of what's possible but things that are outside of the excluded zone.

HAUGELAND The inconceivable.

CUMMINS Yes.

HAUGELAND Well, all I say is you can't conceive them.

CUMMINS But, there's a certain sense in which there's nothing in the inconceivable zone, whatever that is, which could be, in my termin-ology, a target. I think evolution can drown targets, and I think evolu-tion can select for my ability, however bad, to represent things of which I cannot conceive at all.

HAUGELAND Or at least confront them and know you are confronting or something like that. Look, here's a thing I have never addressed and ought to be able to address and if it were demonstrable that I couldn't, that would be a problem. And that is, the question of how a whole new, what I call domain, could open up and gel for us—it's related to the issue of how there could be a replacement domain in a revolution—but what about a whole new one sort of emerging out of the muck? Oh, OK, then we can get some standards here and this is what these objects could be and then we can come to, in my sense, see them objectively, and know the truth about them. How that could emerge *ab initio*. And I haven't said anything about that.

CUMMINS Just to tie in here with Dan a little bit. On my view, evolution can, and even operant conditioning, can punish and reward you for failing to track things that you cannot, that you really had no clue of.

HAUGELAND I don't deny that. They may not be objects for us, even if they're targets, remember.

CUMMINS OK, this is really important, because that means that there is a sense in which there is a norm out in the world against which the accuracy of our knowledge and representation, and so on, might be measured, for theoretical purposes say, that doesn't involve what you're calling objectivity—they're not objects.

SMITH It's not the *norm* in the world, it's the world.

HAUGELAND Yeah.

SMITH I think this is where the games in John's account are not good, from my point of view. One doesn't defer to chess.

HAUGELAND Well, Rob is sensitive to this. There is this little bit of empirical content in chess, but I confess, one learns to rue the things one has said and how one has said them. This is the way I wormed my way into this and now I feel that chess is a bad example.

CUMMINS Oh, I think it was very good.

HAUGELAND There's a certain kind of susceptible person who will follow the same trajectory I did and see, 'Oh yeah there's something distinctive about chess, now just change this and this and this, and you can keep that distinctness without the other stuff.'

CUMMINS That's right, and I think that's a very good way of characterizing your view.

SMITH But at stake here at the moment, between you guys, is how can you, as it were, end up representing what wasn't for you before, at all. And you're [Cummins] getting evolution to do that work for you.

CUMMINS Not just evolution. There's a lot of other things that can do that work, but, what I'm trying to do is describe a framework in which you have a clear articulation of what that problem is. I think it's very difficult in John's framework to clearly articulate the problem faced by a learner that, as it were, needs to expand its conceptual resources.

SMITH See I guess—now I'll use my language not John's—I think stabilizing the world, getting there to be a world that you live in, which is part of objectivity, is harder than you think. I mean that that's the framing, from my point of view, of what you just said. There has to be a world you're in . . . And you defer to it, right? When you and it differ, it wins. That's a gap.

CUMMINS There's a big difference though, between getting the world to, as it were, seem to me stable enough to defer to it, versus there being a stable enough world to knock me off track, and those are really quite different. It seems to me that, I just feel a tendency to assimilate those two.

HAUGELAND In me?

CUMMINS Yes. Yes and no. It's a very subtle position.

DENNETT This is the tinge of verificationism. I like that tinge.

CLARK It's the difference between wondering about under what conditions you can have knowledge of an objective world, and wondering about under what conditions there is an objective world

CUMMINS That's right.

CLARK It seems to me that in a way John is interested in what it is to know a world that's objective. That's when you start to make appearance/reality distinctions and when you get the right notion of truth operative. But that doesn't involve actually taking a stance on whether or not—

SMITH No, I think there is, that's why I keep saying about this deference that it is empirical and that is grounded in skills, and so on. My sense is that there is a prior commitment that there is an objective world. And then he's talking about what it is to know it. You're right, but the ultimate normativity is grounded not in the knowing, but in the world.

HAUGELAND The world is the boss. This is Joan's [Wellman] way of putting it.

DENNETT If you believe that then you just have to let evolution be the teacher.

CUMMINS Or at least one of them.

DENNETT That's the way the world's the boss.

HAUGELAND That's the way the world is the boss when it comes to genetic formation.

SMITH Well, and also, you defer to the world, you don't defer to your teacher.

HAUGELAND Another way that the world is the boss is that gravity will hold you down. But when you're talking specifically about, is such and such a claim true about the objects, the objects that I understand as such and suches, then the way in which the world is the boss is as an epistemic kind of bossiness, that it seems to me is a late achievement on this planet.

SMITH This goes back to Hugh's question about the metaphysics of this. This is a reason why this story, this approach, is a metaphysical approach. Because the nature of objects that you end up with in this approach [Haugeland's] isn't the same as the nature of objects that you have in your [Cummins'] approach. It's no accident, in other words.

HAUGELAND I could substitute them, then, and talk about their objects.

SMITH No, I think it's a really critical difference, because if you were a naïve realist and you were to believe this story, then I think you might be subject to what it is that you [Cummins] think is fatal about this story. But in actual fact it's the world, not the objects, that is the ultimate ground. And I very strongly believe that you have to be non-pluralist about the world, even if you're pluralist about your objects, in order to anchor the deference, in order to anchor the objectivity, in order to anchor normativity ultimately.

HAUGELAND I don't even understand that.

SMITH No. I've noticed that. (*Laughter.*)

PART 4
On Cummins

Texts

'Content and Targets; Attitudes and Applications', *Representations, Targets and Attitudes* (1996a), ch. 2.
'Representation and Isomorphism', ibid. ch. 7.
'Target Fixation', ibid. ch. 8.
'Language and Communication', ibid. ch. 10.

Robert Cummins has written far and away the best introductory survey of the philosophy of mental representation, *Meaning and Mental Representation* (1989). He has made an outstanding contribution to the philosophy of psychology with *The Nature of Psychological Explanation* (1983), and has offered an important account of function in 'Functional Analysis' (1975). Cummins takes the approach of a philosopher of science when investigating cognitive science: What concepts do scientists use? What concepts do they need?

His most recent book, *Representations, Targets and Attitudes*, puts forward a radical account of mental representation and the role of language. Put starkly, Cummins' view is that the only phenomenon deserving of the name 'representation' is isomorphism: representations that represent by virtue of sharing structure with their contents. A second key aspect to Cummins' view is that languages don't represent. Rather, they communicate.

Cummins' fresh approach to the problem of mental representation begins with the development of an account of representation that solves the error problem by definition, and proceeds to an investigation into what other features such a cognitive system might have. The error problem has bedevilled naturalistic approaches to semantics for over twenty years, and there has been little consensus regarding the various solutions offered (including Dretske's learning period, Millikan's teleofunction, and Fodor's asymmetric dependence). Cummins begins by pointing out that representational error lives in the gap between what, on any given occasion, a representation actually represents and what it *ought* to represent. So my mistaken identification of a cow on a dark night as a horse makes use of a token representation that actually represents cows, but it *should* have represented horses (since that is what I'm actually looking at). Cummins then needs an account, for any token case of representing, of what the representation in fact represents and what it ought to represent. What a tokening ought to represent is termed the 'target' of the tokening. But the state must have representational content independent of how it is being used on a given occasion—in particular, independent of its target on that given occasion. The theory of targets amounts to an account of the function of a particular tokening. Any good general account of function (such as his in 'Functional Analysis' 1975, or Millikan's 1984) may then be employed in the explanation of targets.

Cummins concludes that the only candidates for a kind of representational vehicle that has its representational content intrinsically are those that are isomorphic to their contents: if representation *R* shares structure with content *Y*, then it does so regardless of how it is being used or tokened on any given occasion, and regardless of whether the tokening recognizes or makes use of that shared structure.

Cummins' approach amounts to an audacious redescription of the problem of representation; one that allows a division of representational responsibility. Acts of representation are composed of representations and targets. These acts of representation may constitute propositions that participate in propositional attitudes, which in turn may be the components of (quite sophisticated) knowledge structures. This gives Cummins four degrees of freedom in explaining representational abilities: representations, applications (of representations to targets), attitudes (toward applications) and knowledge structures (composed of attitudes).[1]

---

[1] Cummins provides a very helpful summary of his view in section 3.1.1 ('Targets and Objects').

Smith draws attention to important differences between his own broad approach—situated cognition—and Cummins'. The situated picture of representation emphasizes process and context-dependence whereas isomorphisms are typically static structures with intrinsic contents. A key issue raised by Smith is whether Cummins ought to generalize the problematic notion of isomorphism to the idea of a structure that generates *appropriate* behaviour.

Cummins—or Something Isomorphic to Him

BRIAN CANTWELL SMITH

4.1.1 Introduction

Everyone's right. Or anyway that's what I tell my students. 'Look,' I say; 'this paper you are reading was written by a dedicated, intelligent person, who has devoted their life to studying these issues. The author's had an insight, uncovered some subtlety, which they're trying to tell us about. Imagine that they're showing us a path through the forest. Problem is, people write in *words*; and words are blunt instruments: intellectual bulldozers, Caterpillar D9s—big bruisers, that cut wide swaths. Rare persons—poets, mostly—can wield words with enough finesse to clear a delicate trail, without doing too much collateral damage. But most of us, when we write, even when we think we are navigating an exquisite line, are in fact unwittingly mowing down trees, ripping up the earth, sowing all kinds of destruction.

'So here's my advice,' I go on. 'Don't assume this text is written in a language you know, and take your task to be one of figuring out whether what they've written is true or false. You will almost certainly judge it false. Be more generous! Assume what you are reading is true, and tell me what language it is written in. Ignore the ancillary damage; pointing that out is easy, and anyway that stuff will grow back. Figure out what the author was on to—what they were excited about, what wonder they have seen. Tell me, if we were to follow their path further, where it would lead.'

I rehearse these platitudes here because they prove so bracing in Cummins' case. Like many of us, Cummins has worried about representation for decades. He is full of deep insight, fine detail, penetrating analysis. Yet I confess in this book he also says things that, at least if interpreted in my own dialect, seem a mite daft. Such as that the word 'two' cannot represent *twoness*. In fact words can't represent at all. Representations, according to Cummins, have to be isomorphic to their targets—so the word 'two', being unary, can't represent duality. And that's not all. Cummins doesn't think that a picture can represent a left hand, as opposed to a right hand. Nor, if Igor and Isaac are identical twins, can a photograph of Igor represent Igor and not Isaac (or the other way around). And so on.

That representation requires isomorphism (and nothing more) is a strong claim—so strong, in fact, that once you reach it, in chapter 7, it's tempting to go back and read the book a second time, substituting the term 'isomorph' for 'representation', to see if the whole thing makes more sense. But that strategy, superficially appealing though it may be, doesn't, I want to argue, best illuminate Cummins' path. He isn't simply endorsing the cognitive utility of isomorphic structures. He's making a more substantive intentional claim. Needless to say, the question is exactly what that claim comes to. I am not sure, I confess, that I can quite discern the answer. So this commentary, rather than judging his proposal, will more be one of query. What I hope is that in his response, Cummins will be able to set us straight.

In particular, my strategy is not going to be to assume that we know what the term 'representation' refers to, and ask whether Cummins is right, that representation (so understood) is isomorphism. Rather, I want to figure out what Cummins could possibly think representation is, such that he thinks it is isomorphism.

4.1.2 Points of Agreement

Before getting to questions, though, I want to start with some points of agreement and appreciation.

First, Cummins is interested not in an abstract, idealized conception of representation, but in finite, resource-limited, concrete mechanisms. He is concerned with *engineering*, and with the consequences for design of real-world trade-offs between accuracy and efficacy (or efficiency). Better to suffer a few false positives in your predator detection routines, he says, and get the hell out of there, than to wait around until you're absolutely sure that that thing's a piranha. He's right: that's what animals do, that's how computer programs work, that's the right design stance. And he's right, too, that this kind of pragmatism has consequences for a theory of truth.

Second, Cummins is also entirely right, in my view, to fight for a serious, substantive notion of content—one that doesn't (vacuously) devolve into '*x* means whatever happens when *x* is used', or '*x* refers to whatever *x* is pointed at'. He also realizes (and this, being rarer, I especially commend him for) that sticking up for a serious notion of content will require rejecting the common methodological assumption that theories of cognition will necessarily be *causal*. I applaud him for making these commitments. It is quite likely, in my view, that intentional systems will ultimately prove to be theoretically distinctive, among natural entities, exactly in virtue of the fact that constitutive accounts of them will not (at least in any *local* sense) be causal accounts. It's not hard to see why this might be true: intentionality and content are precisely achievements, that allow systems to be existentially oriented toward that with which they are not causally engaged. So why should we expect constitutive accounts of them to be narrow?[2]

Third, at least in some places Cummins has a salutary, if somewhat inchoate, recognition of the normative character of intentionality. This is betrayed (among other places) in his insistence on focusing on representational *error*—on the gap that, in no small number of cases, comes between how things are, and how creatures take them to be. It would appear that Cummins is a straightforward (even promiscuous) realist, so for him acknowledging this gap, while crucial to his project, isn't horribly expensive. Since exploring the metaphysical consequences of representation is one of this workshop's explicit aims, however, and since I am not so blasé a realist as is Cummins, I want to go on record as saying that I take a recognition of the profound importance of the distinction between how we take the world to be, and what it is actually like, to be as critical (if anything even more critical) for pluralists and other varieties of irrealist as for standard-issue realists. So I welcome Cummins' placing error—and gaps—on center stage.

Fourth, befitting his engineering sensibilities, Cummins is interested in *use*—with *how representational systems actually work*. This is a critical point, on which it is important to be clear. As we'll see, he categorically rejects what he calls 'use' theories of content. Nevertheless, he *is* interested

[2] For more on this topic, see my response to Dennett in section 5.2.

in use itself. In fact I will tentatively suggest that his (curious) isomorphism suggestion arises from a combination of this mechanical, usage-oriented focus, plus a theoretical mistake. But whether or not my diagnostic suggestion is on target, his focus on use is surely correct.

4.1.3 Situated Cognition

Focusing on use is not unique to Cummins, of course; it is a theme of many other writers, including those interested in situated cognition. Cummins doesn't identify himself with (or even mention) situated cognition, and in situated company Cummins' proposal is quite non-standard. It seems to me helpful in triangulating on his account, therefore, to list five characteristics widely agreed by situated theorists to hold of real-world representation (that's their 'representational' bulldozer, not his).

1. Stemming from a commitment to use, it is characteristic of situated accounts to view representation as an *activity*—as a property of processes, not static structures. Many writers (but not Cummins) think that assigning content to an enduring structure (as opposed to a process or event) is a short-cut—something like a theoretically derivative recognition of a commonality that endures across, but is ultimately grounded in, activity.

2. Representation is often recognized not only as highly *context-dependent* in general ways, but more particularly as often, perhaps even always, *indexical*. As Barwise and Perry (1983) (among others) emphasized, words such as 'you', 'here', 'now', etc., are the norm, not complicated deviants. (This inexorable indexicality, I believe, ultimately stems from the ontological fact that leads physical laws to be expressed in differential form.)

These first two 'situated' properties of representation—activity and indexicality—go well together. For whereas general rules or patterns are often associated with (relatively static) word *types*—rules that Barwise and Perry label the 'meaning' of the representational type—the specific interpretation of an indexical word use cannot be identified with the type, *nor even of the token used* (as shown by Perry's famous example of two deaf mutes, so poor that they share a card on which is scrawled, 'I'm a poor deaf mute; can you give me some change,' which they alternately hand to passers-by). Rather, interpretation goes with *concrete situations of use*—with utterances, in the case of language; more generally, with *events*.

3. Going along with these issues of context-dependence, indexicality, and a focus on activity or events, situated representation is often seen to be largely *implicit*. What the stomach sends the brain is at best something like 'hungry!'—meaning 'I am hungry', of course, but the fact that it is the stomach's owner who is hungry need not be represented explicitly, since it is invariant across all signals from that particular stomach, being established by the inalienable context. In fact the stomach needn't even say 'hungry'; all it has to do, as every programmer knows, is simply to raise a flag, or send a one-bit signal along a dedicated wire. In that context, essentially all of an action's content—all of what Perry calls the 'issue' (which is to say, the full proposition minus only the polarity)—is established by the embedding architecture. All that needs to be flagged 'explicitly', as it were, is that residual bit of whether (or possibly how much) the agent is, at that moment, hungry.

In general, working out the division of labour across these four contributors to total intentional content—(1) what part belongs to or is determined by a use or utterance, (2) what part belongs to or is determined by the more long-term structural token or instance of a signal or structure that is created or employed (produced or consumed) in that use, (3) what part belongs to or is determined by the type of which that token or instance is an instance, and (4) what part belongs to or is determined by the general architectural setting in which the whole scenario is embedded—these are extremely interesting, intricate questions, that have yet to receive much systematic attention. There has been a little work on the linguistic case, and (as Cummins well knows) computer programs embody tremendously sophisticated but untheorized approaches to more general data structures. But a general story awaits philosophical reconstruction.

4. The engaged, dynamic, and architecturally fitted sorts of mechanisms that emerge from this sort of picture are often so purpose-specific that it is not clear that any *static* semantic evaluation is applicable (such as traditional notions of content, reference, or truth). Rather, the appropriate semantic evaluation may be governed by norms applying *directly to the activity in which the agent is engaged*. This focus on activity—as for example in Millikan's (1995) 'pushmi-pullyu' representations—has led some writers to believe that 'representation' is not even the right notion under which to understand the applicable form of intentional force.

This issue—by no means minor—ties into another central workshop topic. To give it a name, what is at stake is whether engaged activities are subject to what I call 'statical' norms: that is, norms on states, such as *true* or *false*, or whether they are subject to 'dynamical' norms: that is, norms on activity or process—such as *evolutionarily adaptive*, or *good*. In logic, the intentional system with which we are most familiar, the statical norms—truth, reference, etc.—are taken to be explanatorily prior, and the dynamical norms—truth-preservation, inference to the best explanation, etc.—are viewed as explanatorily derivative. What is happening, I believe, is a very important shift in explanatory priority, with people embracing various dynamical norms, and then defining more familiar statical norms (such as what a structure represents) in their terms.

5. This focus on dynamic, architecturally embedded, implicit representation (of the sort Clapin talked of[3]) has fueled an increasing interest in what is called *non-conceptual* representation: representations that, perhaps because of being so purpose-specific, and perhaps because so inexorably context-dependent, fail to meet standard notions of productivity, systematicity, etc. (that is, fail to meet Evans's, 'Generality Constraint', 1982: 100). No one denies (or at least not many people do—though Cummins, interestingly, is someone who would) that *some* of our human representational capacities are 'symbolic', 'linguistic', 'conceptual', recombinant, etc. (choose your weapon). But once one has embraced the idea of non-conceptual content, serious questions arise as to what *conceptual* content is for. Given his attitude to language, one is led to infer that Cummins may think that conceptual representation is *only* for communication.

Now I have laid out these five general characteristics of situated approaches to representation because Cummins' theory of representation (as isomorphism), in spite of sharing many of the same motivating concerns about concrete, pragmatically understood, real-world systems, is so markedly different from these familiar views. Just look at the contrasts. Representations, according to Cummins:[4]

1. Are structures, and have content qua structures, *not* as processes or 'in use';
2. Have what structural content they do *qua* types (not qua tokens or as used)—and for that matter (I think) also *represent* types, not particulars (that is, their content can be no more than type-specific);

---

[3] [See 'Tacit Representation in Functional Architecture' in section 6.1—ed.]

[4] At least this is how it seems; the book isn't entirely clear, but what he says and the examples he uses suggest this.

3. Are *not* implicit, nor context-dependent, nor indexical;
4. Are *neither* implicit *nor* architecturally-dependent; and
5. Are *not* governed by dynamical norms.[5]

Does this mean that Cummins is uninterested in the concerns of situated theorists—even if he doesn't identify his project with theirs? Not at all, I believe. Rather, he moves all these issues—indexicality, the determination of particular content by contingent local circumstances, architectural dependence, etc.—onto targets and applications. In that setting, I think, he would agree that they are important. For example, I suspect that I might be able to convince him that there are questions to work out in his account of targets, between what is true of particular tokens, what is true of particular *uses* of particular tokens, what is true of creations of tokens that differs from what is true of subsequent uses of previously created tokens, and so forth. For in different situations, different kinds of content go with different ones of these. (For example, imagine keeping a 'Don't erase this!' sign in your desk, which, from time to time, you place on the sill at the base of the whiteboard, to keep the cleaning folks from washing it. In this case, what matters to the interpretation of the word 'this' is its *use*; virtually nothing holds of the token qua token. Whereas in the case of an ordinary photograph, what most of us think of as the content is identified with the token, not with the use—presumably because referents are causally implicated in the process of creating photographs. And so on.)

In sum, many of the issues that other people who are interested in use have focused on under the heading of 'representation'—including many in the loosely affiliated situated cognition contingent—have to do with what Cummins calls targets, and their participation in applications, and attitudes, not with representations. So Cummins is using the term 'representation' for something else. Does he just take it to be a conceptual synonym for 'isomorphism'? No; as I said, in spite of this restriction, it remains a substantive thesis for him that representation is isomorphism. Yet it is clear that the word 'representation', in that claim, cannot mean for him what it means for some of the rest of us. So what *does* it mean? What is going on?

---

[5] Representations are also, as it happens, on Cummins' view, not conceptual; at least most of them won't be (since isomorphic structures are not in general recombinable into more isomorphisms); but nor are his forms of representation exactly what people interested in non-conceptual content are primarily focusing on.

4.1.4 Targets

The basic structure of Cummins' theory is that the phenomena (states, events, propositions, whatever) in the world that systems are directed towards—the phenomena that many of us would say they *represent*—are what he calls targets. In response to a review by Ruth Millikan (2000*a*), he says (at the end): 'I really have no dispute with her theory construed as a theory *whose target is target fixation*. My point is simply that the same machinery won't do as a theory whose target is representational content' (R. Cummins 2000: 128, emphasis added). He said much the same thing about John Haugeland: that his account of objectivity had more to do with target fixation than with what Cummins calls representation.[6]

Targets, that is, not representational contents, are what systems are intentionally directed towards; they are the things that the contingent particularities of agents' situations play a role in fixing; they are what is concrete and particular; they are what are indexically specified by (among other things) implicit aspects of system architecture. What representational contents are, in contrast, are *what the systems represent those targets as being like*. So representations, on Cummins' view, are not, as it were, 'what we talk about,' but 'what we say about what we talk about' (except of course it isn't *talking* and *saying*, but more general intentional directedness, that is at issue—more on that later).

Why is it that targets, not contents, are what in Cummins' theory have these properties (of concreteness and particularity, indexical specification, etc.)? Here I will hazard my first reconstructive guess at the path through the woods that Cummins is blazing. He realizes, I believe, in a way that may be uniquely perspicuous but nevertheless in broad outlines is familiar, that *the concrete, particular object of intentional directedness is not established by the content of the decontextualized, explicit, representational type*. At that level of generality, I believe, that is a thesis with which everyone at this workshop would agree. Whereas some of us (as Clapin suggests[7]) honor it by broadening or modifying the notion of representation to allow functional architecture, implicit structuration, local circumstances, etc., to 'represent', others by shifting our theoretical attention away from representation to more general forms of intentional directedness, and still others by invoking something like sentential structure (so that 'what is said' can be associated with something like the predicate part,

---

[6] [See Part 3—ed.]
[7] [See 'Tacit Representation in Functional Architecture', in section 6.1—ed.]

and 'what it is said about' can be associated with the subject part), Cummins is exploring a fourth alternative: of reserving the term 'representation' for something more explicit, and introducing a new category (target) for this kind of non-explicit, circumstantially particular object determination.

So that's one clue about the story. But what about details? How do these targets and representations actually work?   *Discussion point 4.1*

The way Cummins gets at these issues is via a discussion of error. At the beginning of *RTA* chapter 7, where he introduces his positive view, he says 'The central thesis of the foregoing discussion is that error is a mismatch between the content of a representation and the target of a particular use or application of it' (Cummins 1996*a*: 85). And error is ubiquitous— not universal, but always, according to Cummins (and I agree with him on this) potentially present. He strongly objects to the idea, implicit in various familiar causal theories, that there is *any* situation that can be non-circularly identified, even ideally (such as an 'optimal perceptual setting' or 'normal conditions'), in which error can be assumed to be absent, and representational content therefore *identified* with target. What the target *is*, roughly, is the situation in the world that it is the function of the system to represent when it 'tokens'—which is to say, I take it, when it *produces* or perhaps *uses*—a representation. And as we have seen, we won't go too far wrong if we assume that targets are fixed in a vaguely Millikanesque way (though he argues for a spate of alleged improvements to her account).

Now there is clearly something very right in the overarching idea that when an intentional system is directed toward some entity or state of affairs in the world, which I will call '*X*', and represents *X* as being a certain way, that its fix on *X* (as being the thing that it is saying something about) may outstrip in directness and surety the grip it has on *X* being how it represents it as being. It is also possible—and this may be something that has (perhaps overly) impressed Cummins—that the mechanisms by which the system 'attaches' to *X*, so as to represent it as being some way or other, may be quite different in kind from the meaning-bearing faculties at play when, given its fix on *X*, it then represents it as being a certain way. Traditionally, I take it, these differences would normally be allocated to differences in the reference-fixing mechanism for indexicals and in the semantic evaluation for sentences—on a model in which the system's representing *X* as being a certain way would be analogized to its entertaining a sentence-like structure of the form '*that X is* ϕ'.

But whereas I can grasp, or anyway begin to grasp, some of the intuitions that I think are driving Cummins to his proposal, I confess that I have many questions about how the story is in fact supposed to go. The questions I want to focus on today are rather general and abstract—though by that token I think perhaps more fundamental. I also have many detailed questions about how the machinery he sets up is supposed to work, though I will give them shorter shrift. So before moving to general considerations, let me quickly enumerate a baker's half-dozen technical queries.

The first question has to do with how we are supposed to explain targets that miss. Suppose it is the function of the intender in the prairie dog to target predators. Then when the child's kite flies by, casting the distracting shadow, one might informally want to say that the animal mistook *it* for a predator, where the 'it' was either the kite or the kite's shadow. But if it was the function of the intender to represent predators, it seems to me that there is an error, with a very Cumminsian gap-like structure, between the actual kite and the intended predator. But *this* gap cannot be explained as representation–target divergence, but an intended target–actual stimulus gap. So I'm not quite sure about the allocation of error between what happens in the target versus the target representation.   ***Discussion point 4.2***

Second, and this may be related, I found myself confused about the fine-grainedness of targets. Mostly it seemed as if targets have to be, as it were, *intensionally* fine-grained: states of affairs, objects *qua* some way of being or other. In fact it seems as if they must be this fine-grained, in order to anchor the notion of isomorphism. At other times, though, it seems as if they need to be coarse-grained. Suppose, for example, that on entering a room, my 'represent the large object in front of me' intender is triggered. But suppose what is actually true is that I am facing a mirror so large that I can't see the edges, and the threatening object is in fact behind me. If the target is fine-grained ('object in front') then it will miss, since the object is behind. Maybe the example isn't good. But I feel that, in order for the story to work, one is going to need a way of just saying (as it were) 'that thing,' *sans properties* (not qua anything), in order to be able to hypothesize as to what properties *it* has.

One way to say this is that names and indexicals have their uses. If both targets and representations are always sufficiently intensionally fine-grained to support isomorphisms, then I worry that there is nothing in the picture that can play the necessary role that names and indexicals do, of allowing us to *drop* property talk, and refer to objects 'nakedly', as it were.

Third, I feel queasy about the targets of desires—indeed, of almost anything except perceptual states. Suppose, believing it would help me to get more work done to be surrounded by hordes of young acolytes, I decide that I would like a dozen children. But suppose that a dozen screaming children would in fact block my chances of getting any work done at all. What is the target of my desire? Or for a different sort of example, what about the thing I said on the first night of this workshop, that 'one of us should pay for this dinner and then we should add up the amounts everyone has paid at the end of the week'. Once I realized that Dan had arranged for the Tufts Cognitive Science Center to pay for it, I realized that I should instead have said 'Thank you.' Was 'thank you' all along the target of my speech act? Not for naught was I raised a Calvinist; I know, a thousand ways to fail: faux pas, infelicities, foolishness, etc. It seems patently unlikely that gaps between targets and representations will be able to explain them all. Yet, once the target–representation gap is separated from falsehood, I am left unsure as to just what fraction it is intended to include.

Fourth, in spite of the appropriate distinction between falsehood and error, I am still not entirely clear about the relation between the distinction between targets and representations and that between subjects and predicates. For there is no doubt, as I have already suggested, that, at least on initial reading, Cummins' proposed distinction has something of a subject/predicate ring to it, to say nothing of the topic/frame distinction from linguistics. Suppose, for example, that I see John Haugeland crossing the street, but, not having previously encountered him with his new beard, I think, 'There goes Mickie Hart' (or some internal—or perhaps isomorphic?—representation of Mickie Hart). Now I take it, if I am looking at John, that Cummins would say that John is the target. And since there is a discrepancy between my (representation of) Hart and the real Haugeland, there is error. On the other hand, on a normal *linguistic* analysis, Haugeland would be the referent of the word 'that'; Hart would be the content of the (representation) of Hart, and the error would be error in the *sentential structure*. That is, my sentence ('that is Mickie Hart') would be *false*. Is the target/representation distinction an architecturally more primitive (and perhaps implicit) predecessor to what ends up, in assertive propositions, as subject/predicate analysis? More generally, while the two distinctions may be distinct, surely they cannot be unrelated? What exactly is the relationship between representation–target gaps, and sentential errors?

Fifth, I am not sure what isomorphic representations are like except in situations that are obviously topological. For example, what would it be for a prairie dog to have an isomorphic representation of 'predator'—unless there is something like PacMan running inside the prairie dog's head, which seems a tad unlikely.   *Discussion point 4.3*

This ties into a question that Ruth Millikan asked (in a recent review: 2000a), of how Cummins' 'Picture Theory', which inevitably invites comparison with the *Tractatus*, relates to that famous predecessor. Does the rough mimicking of in-the-world object–property relations by in-the-sentence subject–predicate relations count, in Cummins' view, as an isomorphism? If not, why not? If so, why is language not representational on his account?

Sixth, I fail to see how the target/representation distinction is handled over the course of a chain of thoughts. Suppose, after misidentifying Haugeland as Hart, I think to myself 'I really loved his last album.' Now what, according to Cummins, am I thinking? Is the target of the (mental analog) of 'his', in this thought, Haugeland or Hart? Presumably the answer is to be found by asking what it is the function of (this use or token of) 'his' to represent. To me, it seems most sensible to think that the content of the mental utterance of 'I loved his last album' is that I loved Hart's album, implying that the utterance is *true*—not that I loved John's last album, which is (as far as I know) semantically malformed. Yet my sense is that Cummins is committed to the target's being Haugeland.

But that is surely problematic. For suppose one entertains a whole sequence of thoughts, starting from a failed identification. It would seem, on Cummins' view, as if the entire sequence would be semantically malformed. But one can certainly start off on a wrong footing but then come to a very important realization; this often happens, when meandering in thought (for example, suppose, in the example just given, that, reflecting on that album, I realize that its rhythms are similar to those of some Indian chants I heard in college). Just because the thought *starts* with a false identification of Haugeland, surely that can't imply that all derivative realizations must fail. But I don't see how this would go, on a Cummins-like story.

Here, I think, is another way to put essentially the same point. Cummins agrees that the target content depends on neighborhood. But do intenders only reach out 'sideways', as it were, to exploit or acquire determinacy of target from the *targets* of the acts or structures they liaise with? Or do they reach out sideways and acquire determinacy from the *representational content* of (spatially or temporally) neighboring events? In strongly endorsing the thesis that targets must be determined 'completely independently' of representational content, Cummins seems committed to their reaching out only to surrounding *targets*. But I don't see how that is going to explain sustained reflection or dreaming. Surely what I am *aiming at*, now, depends on *how I took* what I was aiming at a moment ago to be.

Moreover, if target fixation depends on *no* representational content, even the content of surrounding events, I begin to lose my grip on the point of representational content. It starts to seem eerily epiphenomenal. Surely, I would have thought, the target T of an action A (if we believe in targets) would be a function of the representational content of representations leading up to action A, even if it is not a function of the representational content of the representation R applied to T. But if representational contents, as Cummins insists, are determined independently of use, then are targets determined independently of representational contents? Is this independence symmetrical? (More on independence in a moment.)

Seventh—and finally—I have a whole spate of questions about isomorphisms. There are just too many ways of parsing, too many kinds of mappings. The issue has to do with the general nature of (mathematical) isomorphisms, and how to establish the appropriate fine (intensional) grain that is necessary for semantic (representational) purposes: which properties and relations—and even objects—in the representation map onto which properties, relations, and objects in the content. There are lots of issues, here: for example, about how the right mapping is determined. To get involved in these questions would take us into quite technical considerations, which we might take up later. For now, I want to stay a bit more general, in order to consider the prior question, and presumably a question of more general interest, of whether isomorphism is the right subject matter. But I do want to record the fact that I have misgivings about whether, all the other questions aside, saying that 'representation is isomorphism' is anything like *specific* enough. These questions stand Cummins' comments that it is not problematic for a given representation to represent lots of things, and that only one of them need be the one that the target matches.

4.1.5 Use, Error, and Independence

But instead of pursuing these details, let's back up a bit, and turn to some more basic questions. As I said earlier, Cummins strongly objects to what he calls 'use' theories—theories that recruit the life or activities of the agent to fix the content of representational states. 'A theory of representational content that does not explain how R's content is fixed in a way that is independent of how R's targets are fixed is bound to mishandle error' (Cummins 1996a: 85).

That representational content must be *independent* of target content is one of the central themes in Cummins' book. Indeed, he repeatedly states that target fixation and representation content must be 'completely independent'. It turns out, however, that that is not the strongest way to state the thesis he is committed to. His real claim is that representational content must be specified (determined) *completely independently of use*. (Since targets *are* determined by use—targets are what it is that it is the function of a use to represent—the broader claim that representational content must be specified independent of use, in general, subsumes the narrower claim that it be specified independent of target, in particular.)

Now here we start to get places where I either fail to understand what is going on, or else strongly disagree. And so I look forward to Cummins' response. As I say, that representational content not be *identical* to either target or use I understand. If the representational content of every (or even any) micro situation or event is simply *identified* with either the target or the use itself (for example, the use's causal consequences), then there will be no gap—hence no error, hence no substantive notion of content, hence the project will fail. That I understand. But that representational content be *independent* of target and use I do not understand. For—and this will be the gist of my remarks in this section—there is surely a vast difference between non-identity and independence.

It is simply not true, in particular, in order for one thing X (representational content, in the case at hand) not to be *identical* to something else Y (either target or causal consequence), that X must be *independent* of Y. This is so even if we recognize that the term 'independent' is a bulldozer of its own—a veritable D10. There are as many flavours of dependence and independence as there are of possibility and necessity: physical, nomological, metaphysical, and logical—if you believe that modality comes in stripes, to say nothing of extensional and intensional forms (the former being symmetrical, the latter asymmetrical). But my point holds, I believe, on just about whatever variety you choose. Consider my arm. My arm is manifestly not *identical* to my body. But neither is it *independent of* my body. In fact notice that imagining my arm's being independent of my body is a rather gruesome thought—which only goes to show that you have to break the part–whole relation in order to get independence to apply. In general, that is, my arm is *partially constitutive* of my body. And modulo recherché machinations about mereology, part–whole relations are completely non-problematic relations to which *neither* identity nor independence applies.

For a more appropriate example, consider fitting a curve to a set of points. And ask about the relation between the curve and the points (at, say, each point's X-value). If you draw a random wavy line subject to no constraints except that it pass exactly through each and every point, then, sure enough, there would be no distance—no gap—between the curve and any given point (since, after all, it was stipulated to go right through them). But if, as usual, one fits a *constrained* curve—a straight line, say (or a Gaussian, or whatever), using a least-squares method—then there *will* be gaps. In fact the gaps are critical: they figure in the measure of the total error, the very error the minimization of which is used to determine the line. In general, a fitted line won't go through *any point*, exactly; there will *always* be gaps. But from the existence of those gaps can we conclude that the line is determined *independently* of the points? *Of course not!* That would be crazy. On the contrary, the situation is as close as possible to the opposite of that: *in spite of the gaps, the line is entirely determined by the points.*

Here's the point: while Cummins and I agree that content (and normative virtue) cannot be identified with 'whatever happens', I see no reason to suppose that one cannot put *constraints* on content so as to introduce the requisite tension between generic content (associated, say, with the type) and its target or use *in any particular case*. (This is one reason why I think issues of type, token, and use are so critical.) There is no reason, that is, why overarching use cannot constrain particular content, without sacrificing the possibility of substantial error.

For example, consider something that Haugeland and I, at least, are interested in: objectivity. My own sense is that normative virtue stems ultimately from a very rich sense of objectivity and 'stabilizing' the world: that what makes representations true, overall, is whether they add up to a picture of 'the world'[8]—or rather, more radically, whether they add up to an intentionally oriented form of living in the world, since I think the most profound norms are dynamical, not statical. But perhaps

---

[8] There are very substantial issues of how to reconcile this claim with the requisite respect for inexorable and ultimately ineffable pluralism. Solving that is one of the main things I try to do in Smith (1996).

someone else would prefer some other overarching constraint than objectivity (*some*, I know, would prefer evolutionary advantage). The point is merely this: if there is nothing to constrain the content of a given use of a representational token, then sure enough you don't have enough machinery to have a substantial gap. But if any operative constraints at all tie a particular use to the content of other uses, tying it to overarching constraints such as stabilization or objectivity, fitting it into a coherent scheme—any of these things could be exploited in order to make gaps (and hence error) *substantial. Independence* of use is simply not required.

In sum, Cummins' alleged *sequitur* from 'needing a substantive notion of error' to 'requiring independence of content and use' is simply a bad argument.

Let me make a methodological note, in passing. This is not an isolated or random inference of Cummins that I am questioning. Rather, the assumption that things that are different must be independent seems to me an instance of a regrettable but rather widespread tendency in analytic philosophy. It reflects a form of conceptual absolutism—a kind of 'forced clarity' (vaguely Cartesian) that, far from illuminating genuine issues, instead (in my view) takes leave of phenomena and encroaches on a worrying kind of scholasticism. In 'Analog and Analog' (a favorite paper of mine), John Haugeland talks about 'second-order digitality': an idea of concepts or types being perfectly clear, wholly distinct, and completely independent—in a way that charge and momentum arguably are, for example, and that chutzpah and braggadocio and self-confidence palpably are not (Haugeland 1981). Cummins' commitment to conceptual independence, which I am here indicting is, I believe, a case of mistaken (or at least over-eager) second-order digitality.

In my own work, interestingly enough, I have wrestled for many years with a similarly absolutist independence assumption: the thesis underwriting the formal symbol manipulation construal of computation, which claims that the effective operations of a computer proceed independently of semantics. For reasons with which Cummins would sympathize, syntax is not the *same* as semantics (the only way to hold that they are the same is to evacuate semantics of substance). But to believe that the non-identity of syntax and semantics warrants an *independence* claim is again (in my view) far too strong. It may once have been a useful theoretical idealization, but it has by now grown very theoretically misleading—again threatening us, I believe, with incipient scholasticism. I mention this, moreover, because I am not sure that the two cases (representational content and use, in Cummins case; syntax and semantics, in my own) may at root be the same: with 'use' being effectively syntax, 'content' effectively semantics. **Discussion point 4.4**

As far as I can tell, in sum, with respect to the intricate interplay of use, content, target, etc., the phenomena of intentional engagement with the world are nowhere near as 'clear and distinct' as is dreamt of in Cummins' philosophy.

4.1.6 Isomorphism

Where are we? Well, my reconstruction is two-thirds done. On the one hand, I think I understand what Cummins wants—an implicit, vaguely architectural, very concrete and particular way of determining the object of intentional directedness. Second, I feel as if I have a sense of why he thinks he needs something on which to ground a notion of explicit representational content that is independent of use (even though I believe it is based on a flawed inference). But I haven't yet said anything about the third part of the puzzle: why *isomorphism* should recommend itself as that independent answer.

To get at this, we need to look at Cummins' commendable commitment to use (not to use-based content, remember, but to use itself). This will allow me to hazard a guess as to why he is attracted to isomorphism. One reason I make this conjecture is because it seems to me to go some way toward explaining Cummins' stance (see his final chapter) on why language is purely communicative, and not, on his notion of 'representation,' representational at all.

The idea is this. Symbols, language, and the like are extremely abstract—very 'distanced' from the entities in the world they are about. If you are actually going to build something to do something, it has to *interact* with the world—physically engage with it. To do so (this intuition underlies some accounts of non-conceptual content, and I think it underwrites the humbling experience of programming) you need representations—activities, structures, whatever—that are massively more detailed than mere words. Even vastly interconnected word- or concept-based 'knowledge networks' aren't (in general) remotely detailed enough to do the task. (This is something that has been amply borne out in AI practice. And it is true of commercial code: there are something like 5 million lines of code—perhaps a million distinct identifiers—in high-end Xerox copiers.) And if, as a kind of *tour de force*, you hand-build linguistic representations that *are* sufficiently detailed to serve as the final arbiters of action, they will in general be so verbose as to fail the effectivity norm: too complex for simple mechanisms to handle. Imagine putting all the information on a map of London into words—allowing yourself talk of splines, bezier curves, *x* and *y* coordinates, etc. All you would get would be a useless tome of impenetrable axioms, which no one could reasonably use.[9] Maps are just *so much easier.*

One reason maps are easier is that direct physical engagement often involves physical *coupling* with the world. And coupling, it turns out, as a consequence of the way physics works, *itself tends to involve, at least locally, isomorphism.* Your route through London is isomorphic to the layout of the streets on which you are travelling—a platitudinous but substantial fact about physical travel. The shape of your hand, similarly, at least at the points of contact between it and the thing you are grasping, is isomorphic to that part of the thing you are grasping that your hand is in contact with. And so on.

So my hunch is that Cummins is motivated by the fact that real-world agents need structures that enable them to act in ways that are 'close to the details' of the worlds they engage with. Moreover—and this is important—agents don't give a hoot about whether the structures that engender appropriate behavior have a causal (or teleological or functional or whatever) history tying them to the part of the world they engage with. All they need is something that will steer them correctly. Not just use; *steerage.* And it is a consequence of physics that the *simplest adequately detailed structure for steering* is something that is isomorphic to the world it steers you through.

In sum, my guess about the basis of Cummins' isomorphism intuition is this: he thinks that he needs something *independent* of use,[10] that will nevertheless *guide* use. Isomorphic physical structures—free of teleological or design or other baggage—are the simplest candidate. Hence, I believe, his proposal. *Discussion point 4.5*

Now I've already said that I don't think the 'independent of use' requirement is right (because it is vastly too strong). Moreover, if I am right in my guess about steerage being the core motivating issue, then surely what ultimately matters is not that a guiding structure *itself* be isomorphic, as that it lead to *behavior* that is isomorphic. (I'm going to

---

[9] Unless, of course, they were simply to use it to reconstruct the map.
[10] Falsely, of course, as I have argued—but I am trying to follow him here.

relax the constraint that the behavior be isomorphic presently—but bear with me for a moment.) To see this, let me suggest a modification of the Autobot that Cummins describes in his chapter 7. In his original example, a cart is driven by a card that happens to contain on it a slit that is isomorphic to the track that the cart needs to follow, and the cart is engineered so as to exploit this isomorphism. The card, according to Cummins, is a representation of the track, because the slot on the card is isomorphic to the track.[11] But suppose we change things so that the track that the cart needs to follow has a repeating structure—say, a sequence of path fragments that all happen to be geometrically identical. Imagine as well that there is a grooved wheel—a little like the wheel in a music box, except with continuous rather than discrete markings—such that one rotation of the wheel is able to exactly lead the cart through one of the periods in the geometrically repeating pathway. Surely, I would have thought, in this particular case the wheel would be just as good a 'representation' of the whole path as the card—since it would lead to exactly the same behavior. And note that it would lead to the right behavior over the *whole* path, not just one period of it, because of being circular. By construction, however, the wheel is not isomorphic to the path. So on Cummins' account, it cannot be said to represent the path—or any multi-period segment of it. Nor can you say that one *rotation* of it represents one period—since rotations are kinds of uses. And so Cummins would be forced to deny that the wheel represents the path, even though, from a pragmatic point of view that I would have thought he would like, it is just as good as the card at driving the cart along the path. **Discussion point 4.6**

If this example cuts any ice with Cummins, it should suggest that (again, just for a moment) isomorphic *behavior* is what really grounds his intuition, not isomorphic *structure*. Behavior is use, of course—and Cummins is committed to eschewing use, even to being independent of use, so this is not a formulation that he will be likely to accept. But I've already argued that he needn't cut himself off from use so absolutely, and so I hope to have softened his allergies on that score a little bit. Isn't it just possible, I might suggest to him, that he should adjust his definition of representation so as to allow the wheel to be a representation of a periodic path?

[11] It is also a representation of every similar track, of arbitrary different scale, orientation, and reflection—to say nothing of all other objects of that shape, and so on *ad infinitum*. But leave that aside for now.

But of course Cummins is a savvy fellow, and he will recognize that I am offering him the eighth day in the Scopes monkey trial.[12] Because, as soon as he agrees to go down *this* path, it becomes easy to argue that it isn't *isomorphic* behavior that matters, but *appropriate* behavior. Except that 'appropriate behavior' is a big-ticket item—what does *appropriate* mean? What kind of bulldozer is *that*? But that takes us back into norms—and, for us here at the workshop, maybe into drinks.

4.1.7 Conclusion

Here, then, is my best shot at understanding the path Cummins is trying to lead us down:

1. He recognizes that the object of intentional directedness cannot be determined by general representational content, but is instead a function of (among other things) particular, concrete facts having to do with the agent's engaged interaction with the world;

2. He wants us to appreciate the overwhelming importance of the fine-grained causal driving of things, and yet

3. He recognizes that identifying the content of a representation with the fine-grained behavior that it engenders (without any other constraint) vitiates any attempt to have a full-blooded sense of content.

On the face of it, the last two requirements pose a challenge. Isomorphism is his proposed solution. My response is (1) that all three requirements are critical, (2) that the third doesn't imply that content need be *independent* of use, and (3) that if we exploit overarching dynamical norms, we can be open to vastly more intricate accounts of representational content that are both use-based and yet substantive.

What does this have to do with language and communication? Only this: that words, I agree, or anyway I think (I don't know whether *Cummins* would agree), need fleshing out into vastly more intricate and fine-grained form before they can actually let us engage with the world's virtually ineffable detail. That's in a way a corollary of the second of the two points just listed. I don't think he's right that words don't represent. But I do think he's right that words are a high-level, abstract form of

---

[12] [In the version of the Scopes monkey trial made famous in *Inherit the Wind* (Lawrence and Lee, 1982), Scopes' defence lawyer is able to get the opposition to agree that God's creation may have taken eight days rather than seven, from which it is a slippery slope to the billions of years needed for evolution—ed.]

condensing and summarizing intentional directedness—a high-level, abstract form of orienting to and describing the world that our capacities for intentional directedness direct us at. They are useful; on that we're agreed. And in order to use them appropriately, they need to rest on a vastly more intricate, sensitive, detailed capacity for physical engagement. A creature that had only words, without that fine-grained detailed way of steering its way around the world, wouldn't be able to do anything delicate—wouldn't be able to find or follow intricate trails.

Remember: words are bulldozers. They can do serious damage.

Comments on Smith on Cummins

ROBERT CUMMINS

4.2.1 Loopiness

Let's start with the personal stuff. Smith says that some of the things I say—for example, that the difference between a left and right hand cannot be represented—sound downright loopy. Well, I guess, having been 'outed', I may as well come clean. I confess, then, to having had intimate relations with loopy ideas for decades.

Smith is right, I suspect, in thinking that my claim that true representation is grounded in isomorphism is the loopiest idea in *Representations, Targets and Attitudes* (hereafter *RTA*). Several factors, however, combine to comfort me. The first is that the scientific truth is often loopy. Dirac was called far worse. The second comforting fact is tenure—a loopiness license designed to encourage creative thought in the full realization (often forgotten) that a one out of 1,000 hit rate is pretty good in any creative endeavor. These are long odds, but I'm not betting my job, only my reputation, and I have no reputation for sober, careful thought to lose. Finally, there is this: I was driven to it. I couldn't help it. Since ought implies can, it follows that I did nothing wrong, though perhaps what I said is false.

4.2.2 Driven to Isomorphism

Here is what drove me. I was sick of the disjunction problem and its kin. I resolved to reverse the normal order of things and begin with an account of representational error, then craft an account of representation to fit it. That way, I thought, however bad my theory is, it will at least be bad for a new reason.

My account of representational error is simple:

> R is inaccurate to the extent that it fails to apply to the thing it is applied to.

Several consequences follow immediately.

1. Only uses of R—applications of R to something—can be accurate or inaccurate. Representational types are never correct or erroneous.

(So a theory of error isn't going to fall out of a theory that distributes truth conditions over representational types. There has to be more to it than that.)

2. What R correctly applies to—its content—must not be a function of what users of R apply it to—the targets of those applications. Content must be independent of—i.e. cannot be a function of—use.

It is (2) that bothers Smith, and I'll get to that in a minute. But first, let me finish being driven to the loopy idea of isomorphism.

If you accept (2), which I think is a trivial consequence of the trivial account of error, you get the result that representational content (though not intentional content) must be intrinsic to the things that have it. Representations have to have their contents in a way that does not depend on what their users can or do apply them to. Moreover, and here Smith is right on track, they must be capable of steering thought and action. It seems to me that serious cognition, like finding your way home, is, unlike learning (or repeating) the alphabet or state capitals, something that requires getting a grip on the structure of the domain cognized.

So you have two constraints on serious representations: they have to be capable of steering thought, and that requires getting a hold of structure, and their contents have to be independent of use in the narrow sense of use that I've set out below and in *RTA*.

Surprisingly, these two requirements—independence of use and sensitivity to structure—converge. Primitive expressions in a language of thought—|cat|s say—could only have their contents as a function of use, because they are intrinsically arbitrary: any expression could mean anything so far as its intrinsic characteristics go. But this is just a way of saying that, in themselves, they bring nothing to the table. They are bookkeeping devices at best, pointers to something else that does all the work of informing and steering. A frame, or something.

So:

Representations need to have their contents intrinsically, independent of their uses.

They need to provide information about the structure of the world.

Isomorphism seemed like the simplest thing that fits the bill, so I stuck my neck out. Maps fit the bill, and occur in the brain. What more does a tenured professor with no reputation for sober carefulness require?

4.2.3 Various Responses

Now back to Smith.

4.2.3.1 *Use*

I was explicit about what I meant by 'use' in *RTA*. By a use of a representation, I mean an application of that representation to a target. My requirement that the content be independent of use is the requirement that the content of R not be a function of what its host system can, or does, or would-if-things-were-nice, apply it to. It is NOT the requirement that the content of R have no causal powers specific to its host. Indeed, it must cause steering in virtue of its form (syntax?), as Smith rightly insists. We isomorphismists (we should never land one at a time) think form *is* content, near as makes no difference, and I think Smith would agree, in a way. A physical steering controller steers in virtue of its structure, like the Autobot card described in *RTA*.

4.2.3.2 *Dynamical Representation*

Nothing in my account says representations need to be static. Indeed, I explicitly point out in *RTA* that processes can have dynamical structure, hence represent.

I've even made limited use of such representation in a connectionist counter-example to Fodor and Pylyshyn (1988) (Cummins 1991). Smith's rotating spool is fine with me. It is crucial to see that the rotating spool can be fine with me precisely because it isn't the spool or its groove or the structure of either or both that is doing the representing. It is the structure of the temporally extended process of repeated rotations that is doing the representing.

Having said this, I must confess that I am less enamoured of dynamical representation than some. Representations extended in time are not so good for predicting the future. The Galilean idea of representing time spatially was brilliant, and I suspect nature hit on the same good trick.

Think of the pictures in your high-school yearbook. They are not much help in identifying folk at the reunion. The dynamical solution would be pictures that evolve in time in a way that tracks the evolution of faces in time. That would be great at the reunion. But not so good for predicting what Haugeland will look like in twenty years, or how Smith looked twenty years ago.

For that, it is better to have a process that takes a static picture and the date it was taken and creates a new picture to correspond to a specified target date in the future or past. (The technology currently exists in this form.)

So: you can represent processes statically, and vice versa. And processes can represent processes, and things can represent things. But there is something to be said for static representation of a dynamic world. When decision time comes, you have the whole picture, not just a temporal slice of it.

4.2.3.3 *Appropriate Behavior*

Smith writes: 'isomorphic behavior is what really grounds his intuition, not isomorphic structure' (p. 188); 'it becomes easy to argue that it isn't *isomorphic* behavior that matters, but appropriate behavior' (p. 189). Two points.

(1) Behavior isn't use, in my sense, so I'm not allergic to it on those grounds.

(2) I AM allergic to behavior on other grounds. Here's why. I want a clear (scholastic?) distinction between representational error and other sorts of error: bad inference, malfunction, and the like. Inability to exploit an accurate representation can and should be distinguished from flawless exploitation of an inaccurate representation. This, as I pointed out in *RTA*, is what allows us to make sense of the dispute between Piaget and his contemporary critics.[13] I'm loath to collapse a distinction needed to articulate important theoretical and empirical disputes in psychology. I agree that a good representation is one that drives appropriate behavior. My point is that representations needn't be accurate to do this. Often accuracy gets in the way. It is expensive to produce, and often intractable to process.

---

[13] [See n. p. 159—ed.]

4.2.3.4 *Anaphora and All That*

I have no problem with targets being fixed by previous representings (though I don't think this is the basic case). Target fixation is typically indexical. Typical targets are things like 'phrase structure of the current linguistic input'. What that phrase structure *is* depends, of course, on what you just said, or what I just read, etc. Intenders can also be nested in a way illustrated by 'the thing on the knob on the door of the house that Jack built'. Getting targets fixed in such cases requires embedding intenders (vs. those embedded) to represent their targets first. This will, as Smith points out, leave embedded intenders at the mercy of embedding intenders. Smith finds this counter-intuitive because, when I misrepresent a piece of driftwood as John, my further anaphoric reference ('his' in 'his wife') appears to be a remark about (target) the driftwood.[14]

Cheap reply: this is language, hence conventional communication (a string of signals functioning as a recipe for assembling concepts in other heads), hence not a case of representation in my sense, hence not a case in point.

Moderately priced reply: cognitive systems, especially AI systems, *are* subject to this kind of error, which my account correctly predicts. Good ones can back out of such errors, but NOT because they are designed not to make them in the first place. You back out pretty quickly in the driftwood case because you know pieces of driftwood typically don't have names like 'John' and are not married. But you *do* back out, and that means there was an error to back out *of*. You'd have a tougher time in a thoroughly animistic culture. Make a system immune to the problem Smith raises, and you doom it in an animistic culture to an equally egregious mistake. ***Discussion point 4.7***

4.2.4 Intentionality and Representation

A central claim of *RTA* is that these are not the same. Smith often (as does everyone) speaks as if representations were intentional. But he knows better. Only *uses* of representations—applications of them to targets— are intentional. Smith would put this by saying that you get genuine intentionality only when you have a representational system actually engaging the world in some way. There is a regrettable but nearly universal tendency in philosophy to identify having semantic content with having

---

[14] [See also Smith's example of mistaking Haugeland for Mickie Hart, section 4.1.4—ed.]

intentionality. But representational types aren't, in themselves, directed at anything. They only get directed at something when they are applied. My word for the things they are directed at when they are applied is the target of that application. I don't think Smith really has any quarrel with this. But I think he is nevertheless in danger of thinking that representation cannot be grounded in isomorphism because he sees a lot of intentionality (hence content, hence representation) where there is no isomorphism. In indication, for example, or in communication. But we need some terminology to help us keep distinct what a system is applying a representation to—what it is pointed at on a given occasion of use—and what that representation accurately applies to—what objects, states of affairs (or whatever) in the world would actually satisfy that representational type. Indication, on my view, is genuinely intentional, but not representational. A system designed to light a particular light whenever a predator is near is like what I call a intender. Its function is to indicate predators (or their nearness). It therefore has what I would call a target—predator nearness—and so, when the light goes on, you have an event with an intentional content, namely, predator near. But you do not have what I would call a representation of a predator, because *all* the weight is borne here by who lights up. A different system can light an exactly similar light, and this means something entirely different. What I am calling representation is 'portable' in a way that indicators are not. A map of Tucson is a map of Tucson regardless of who produces it. But a light going on indicates predator nearness only if a predator detector lights it. The consequence is that indicators cannot be copied and retain their contents. (See Cummins and Poirier (forthcoming) for an extended treatment of this issue.)

Now you don't have to adopt my terminology. But you need some way to mark the distinction between portable content bearers such as maps and non-portable cases of meaningful signalling. And once you have portable content bearers such as maps, you need some way of marking the distinction between the content they bear, and what in the world their users actually apply them to. ***Discussion point 4.8***

4.2.5 Left and Right

OK, it sounds loopy to say that the difference between a left and a right hand cannot be represented. I plead the following three points in mitigation.

1. It doesn't follow that you cannot know the difference, or know that you are looking at or using your right hand.

This *would* be loopy. But, to repeat, it doesn't follow. You will think it follows if you think that wherever there is semantic content there is representation. You will be inclined to reason as follows, for example: you can have the belief that the thing you are looking at is a right hand, and that belief has the content that the thing you are looking at is a right hand, and so you can represent the proposition that the thing you are looking at is a right hand. And you can't represent that proposition as opposed to the proposition that the thing you are looking at is a left hand unless you can represent the difference between a left and a right hand.

Of course, you can use the word 'representation' to mean something like *state or process with a semantic content*. If you do that, you are entitled to the argument just rehearsed. But you will not be entitled to conclude that there is some portable copyable type that is satisfied by left hands but not right hands in virtue of the properties it has that do not depend on what it gets applied to.

2. Put a picture of a hand on a transparency and you will get a glimmer, I think, of how *perspectival* is your sense that your percepts represent right hands as such.

The point is that a large part of what goes into being a picture of a left hand or a picture of a right hand, is that you've got a perspective on the picture. But once you put things into your head, there isn't any perspective unless you adopt what Dennett calls a Cartesian theater story.[15] There isn't, in the relevant sense, a front and back side to a mental representation. I can certainly take a picture of a left hand. Since it is blank on one side, this fixes your perspective, so you can see it as a left hand. But that picture does not and could not convey leftness in a perspective free way.

3. As I said in the beginning, I was *driven* to this loopy conclusion. If you want something that has its content independent of its use and of who produces it, and which is therefore perspective free, you are going to have to give up the idea that isomorphs can be representationally distingui- shed. *Final discussion*

[15] [See Dennett's *Consciousness Explained* (1991a: ch. 5)—ed.]

Discussion

4.1
p. 178 CLARK If something has content but it's not representational content, that's because there isn't something there worth calling the representation on all our accounts, right?

SMITH Well, I thought you were disagreeing with Hugh when he was saying that the architecture can have content. [See Discussion point 6.1—ed.]

CLARK I'm happy with the architecture having content, I'm just not happy with it having representational content.

CUMMINS So we're on the same side. It's just a word to mark a distinction that we don't have.

4.2
p. 179 CLAPIN Can you just say that again?

SMITH Intenders can miss. So there's a gap sometimes.

CUMMINS What's the miss, beyond the fact that they conjure up a representation that doesn't apply to the target?

SMITH Suppose the kite goes by—what's the target?

CLAPIN Predators.

SMITH But there's no predator. It seems to me that the animal is intentionally directed toward either the kite or the kite's shadow.

CLARK Earlier I was hearing that the target was whatever the learning routine was in some sense converging on. [See Discussion point 3.4—ed.]

CUMMINS That's one way of pushing the intuition that there's more to targets than bluster. I don't want to take it as constitutive.

CLARK Because, at first I thought the target would be whatever the system was in some sense pointed at, but that seems cheaper than Rob wants it to be.

CUMMINS Whatever it is the function of the intender to represent.

SMITH That implies there can be a gap between whatever the system is actually at the moment focused on (the kite, I am assuming), and what it is that the intender is intended to represent (a predator). This strikes me as a crucial gap, but it is not a representation–target gap.

CUMMINS Well I think that we need to think about this 'focused on' stuff that you have here. I'm not sure what this means. Do you mean literally, lenses? You're willing to hand me that the business of the item in question is to chunk out predator representations?

SMITH Right.

CUMMINS And then if it chunks out a predator representation and what's actually out there is a kite then it's made a mistake.

CLARK But once he's said that its business is to churn out predator representations then you've got the target. That's just to say, that is a target, isn't it?

SMITH This is why I think this type-token-use stuff is actually really important, because, if it's the business of intenders to represent targets as predators, then the target has to fix on something such that it can be represented as a predator.

DENNETT No, but the business of the predator detector is to put up a flag when there's a predator, and, so it's just sitting there, all the time, hungry, waiting, and every now and then it gets turned on by a representation which it correctly or incorrectly identifies as a predator, right?

CUMMINS I think there's lots of brute indication that goes on, that I wouldn't call representation, but which I think is intentional phenomena. So, the case Dan imagines where you've just got a thing that's sort of sitting there idling along, and every now and then it hiccups, and because it's him that hiccupped we know that consumers will think predator. Now I don't think that's a case of representation. But it is a case of indication, and it's a genuinely intentional phenomenon, but it's significantly different from the case where what you have is something that's sitting around as it were, say, waiting around for some linguistic input and, instead of hiccupping it constructs a phrase structure representation, something like a parse tree. Now that's quite a different matter. Now I'm drawing this in stark terms, but I think there's a kind of continuum here really, but in that last case, as it were, way more of the information is in the product, and much less of it is in who hiccupped. And in the first case, the other extreme, it's all in who hiccupped, and none at all is really in the product. As you go toward the phrase structure end, you're more representational. As you go toward the hiccup end, you're more indicational. And then there's a whole kind of messy mush of stuff in between. And I just think it's useful to locate things on that.

HAUGELAND So does that mean, if we're trying to think about the prairie dog, we have to think of this intender, the one which deploys the representation 'predator' by your lights, sometimes including when a kite flies over, as an intender which has various other things it could also recognize.

CUMMINS Yes. If you want to think of it as a representation case, yes, that's right. The prairie dog case is really just there to make a point about accuracy–speed trade-offs. It's not there as a parade case of representation. [See also section 3.1.5—ed.]

DENNETT What if the intender doesn't just hiccup but it has, count them, seven different outputs, seven different shades of hiccup, and one of them is *mate*, one of them is *friend*, one of them is *foe*, etc. And, what it does is it sits there and whatever it is fed, it picks one of these, including one of them that is *null, don't know*. So now, those look ominously like terms in a language of thought because this is not isomorphism, we've got a basic vocabulary. And your line on this is?

CUMMINS My line on that is that whatever you call it is significantly different from the case of producing and consuming things like maps or frames or anything.

DENNETT It's not representation?

CUMMINS I wouldn't call it representation, no.

CLAPIN Do you get applications in that kind of case?

CUMMINS A device like that can apply a representation that's generated by somebody else.

CLAPIN Now I'm confused about what an application is. I thought an application is applying a representation to a target. It's when a representation has a certain role, has a certain function. And I thought the limiting case of that is when a flag goes up in a certain intender. A flag goes up—it's a predator or not. Now in that case, it seems to me, there's an application. The target is 'is it a predator?' the representation is 'Yes.' So, the application is 'Yes, there's a predator.'

CUMMINS Yes, that's right, but it's a really degenerate case.

CLAPIN Yes, of representation, yes, but it's a perfectly legitimate case of application.

CUMMINS Application, that's fine, yes. The thing that's interesting about Dan's case is you've got the producer and the applier separated, so it's really like the case of me rummaging in the glovebox for the map. I don't produce the representation in this sense, except in the sense that I produce it out of the glovebox. Now, in a sense I'm just a hiccupper. I just go through and pick one, and of course, when I hand it to you, that's an application. So, I do the applying.

CUMMINS I think that's a good reason for thinking that predator recogni- 4.3 p. 181 tion systems in prairie dogs probably aren't representational. I think that's right, and it's important, and I think people like Dretske and Millikan and almost everybody has got that wrong.

DENNETT They've got it wrong because they think those are representations?

CUMMINS Because they think those are representations and by saying that they assimilate to these other kinds of cases which really are an entirely different explanatory strategy.

HAUGELAND Yes, I think that's right.

CLAPIN And you think that they're really going to be indicators?

CUMMINS Yes, now I don't care what you call them, but all I'm saying is there's a big difference in how the thing goes and the subsequent kinds of errors that are available and the plasticity and all the rest of it that just gets slopped over if you just assimilate those cases. That's what I don't like and I don't care what you call it.

DENNETT I see the move, but what I don't see, then, is—what looks to me to be inevitable—when you start taking apart your representations, you're going to find them chockful of parts that are Millikanian indicator outputs and that sort of thing and we're going to be right back in the soup.

CUMMINS Only if you haven't been sufficiently inoculated against the idea that all meaning is Tarskian combinatorics.[16] If you really thought that you could figure out what even a complex data structure in AI was

---

[16] [See Tarski (1944) and Davidson (1967)—ed.]

about by looking at the referential semantics of its symbolic components and just combining them up à la Tarski, then I would agree with
you. But I think that's so patently not in the cards, and Brian I think
agrees with me about this.

DENNETT I want to know what's Tarskian and what isn't. Let's take one
of your best parade cases of representation, let's take a map, and let's
think about the implementation of maps in an actual system, whether
it's a computer system or a brain, and, suppose that the way that's
actually done is you've got all these little fovea indicators and non-
fovea indicators and position (X, Y) indicators and position (X', Y')
indicators, and together they all succeed in forming the map. Now this
one is saying what's at this retinal point, and that one is saying what's
at that retinal point, and each one of them is just a sort of indicator,
but, the consumer of this array of indicators gets a representation to
deal with. Now, it looks as if you're going to have to tell that kind of
story. I don't think that's a Tarskian story necessarily.

CUMMINS That's not even close. This is very close to John's case, a case of
recording. [Haugeland 1991] Sure you've got all these things that
indicate this and that. This is like pixelizing. I can pixelize and then
I've got, say, a symbolic language that is about pixels. But the picture
isn't about pixels. It's about my Aunt Tillie, and there's no way that
you're going to have a semantics of pixels that adds up via any kind of
combinatorial semantics to your Aunt Tillie. That's just not in the cards.

DENNETT But you're going to have to tell the story of how... let's just
remind ourselves, once you start getting into edge detection and all of
that, the dream is that you gradually transform the content from pixels
to edges to $2\frac{1}{2}$-D sketches, to 3-D sketches, and then, to Aunt Tillie.
Now, we may not like that particular story but we've got to tell some
story there.

CUMMINS But that you can build a picture of your Aunt Tillie out of pixels
is not an issue. That the building is semantic combinatorics is the issue.

4.4   CLARK Is there any value in distinguishing between the case where some-
p. 186   thing gets fixed independently versus the case where something, once
it's fixed, is independent? I could imagine very easily a kind of claim
that says representational content isn't actually fixed independently of
target content. They kind of do get fixed in a way that is interanimated.
But once they're fixed, they're independent.

SMITH Independent in...?

CLARK In the sense that one could go one way and the other could go in a completely different way. That's what you need for the gap.

CUMMINS Their subsequent trajectories are not functions of each other.

SMITH There are certainly cases where you fix one and that constrains what this can do, but then it can wander freely in its constrained region. So the point is I think we all need a real theory of dependence and independence. And we need better vocabulary—there's a lot of room in issues of partial constraint and subsequent wandering. And I think complete independence of use is too broad a hammer to get it.

DENNETT Brian, I've been trying to think of an example of this. I'm trying to take something which is a map, and, Rob takes it out of the glovebox. And over a period of time, however, in the context, it comes to be a signal for something else. Rob takes the map out of the glovebox, and it sort of started off being a map, and it has been turned into a family joke, and now, even though the map still has all these structural properties, nobody consults the structural properties, the structural properties are no longer used. All those structural properties are just beside the point, in a way, although historically it's very interesting, that that's what they are. But now it has become a completely different sort of thing. It isn't a representation at all. In Rob's term it is a signal.

CUMMINS Here's maybe a less extreme case which still uses maps. Every time you get out the map, you unfold it, you fold it up again, it gets a little crumpled. As a result of that, it's going to shrink. If you thought that part of what is represented in the map was distances, in a certain way, and suppose, because of the way it folds, it shrinks more along, let's say, east–west dimensions than north–south dimensions, then it's actually going to change its content. It's going to change it as a function of the fact that you keep using it all the time. If that's what I meant by use, then to say that use and content were independent would be demonstrably false. It isn't what I mean by use, but that's OK. And Brian makes a good point.

DENNETT But in my case you would say the content of the map is not changing at all.

CUMMINS That's right. I would say, it just came to have another function. But in my example you really get a case where on my own view about what content is, the content of the map actually changes. And I made it particularly crude in this case, but it changes as a function of getting

used. What doesn't change, though—and this is the claim that I meant
to make—it doesn't change its content as a function of being applied to
Chicago as opposed to Boston. It isn't as if you can change the content
of a map by, as it were, consistently applying it to X and not Y.

DENNETT But no, that's what I think Brian is getting at. I think that's what
Brian's inference-chaining cases are getting at.

CUMMINS Yes, those are challenging and interesting, and I want to talk
about those.

SMITH One of the things that's interesting is what's in the driver's seat
here, because if you take Rob's notion of structural isomorphism, then
he's pretty close to having his theory of independence of content from
use, except for shrinkages. But my intuition—maybe this is wrong—
was that having a notion of representation independent of use was in
the driver's seat, and then isomorphism was the solution. So, in that
way, I wouldn't want to allow you to stick with pure isomorphism
cases to show that this is reasonable, because of course it's reasonable
for those cases.

4.5 CLARK How substantial a claim is that? Could anything steer you—could
p. 187 something steer you through a world that wasn't isomorphic to that
world?

CUMMINS Yes, sure, it can. It just gets expensive. Sometimes expense isn't
a bad thing.

4.6 SMITH The point is—Rob would agree—that that thing represents part of
p. 188 the route. But it's a little tricky to get it to represent the whole route,
because isomorphisms—you can't reuse the same part.

CUMMINS Yeah you can, sure you can.

CLAPIN Don't you just smear it over time, I mean, the application is
dynamic over time.

CUMMINS That's right, it's just dynamic. It's a structural process, not the
structure of—

SMITH Great! That's what I wanted you to say! I feel like this is the eighth
day in the Scopes monkey trial[17]—that's what I was trying to sell you,
which is that it's the structure of the *process* that matters, not the
structure of the *object*.

CUMMINS I have no problem with that.

---

[17] [See n. p. 189—ed.]

CLAPIN But they're closely related, right? I mean the structure of the object will contribute immensely to the structure of the process.

SMITH Right, but I'm answering Andy—could a structure that is not isomorphic drive behavior, and what I'm saying is *yes*. The wheel is my example of a very simple structure that isn't *itself* isomorphic, but which can engender *isomorphic behavior*. And my feeling was the thing that really mattered to Rob was isomorphic behavior, not an isomorphic structure driving that behavior.

CUMMINS Actually, to make it even better, let's imagine that what the thing does is goes around and around the same course over and over again. Now in that case—

SMITH That makes it worse for me.

CUMMINS That makes it worse for you and better for me. But I think you're going to have a difficult time drawing a principled distinction between that and simply having the same route laid off sequentially. What difference does it make? Now, I don't know how to use this bulldozer word, isomorphism, to make that point, but it's clear the point can get made.

CLARK I keep thinking that you could drop all talk of isomorphism, replace it with talk of effective structure, and get what you need.

SMITH No, because the problem is those 5 million lines of code. That's what a program is: it's that effective structure that will cause a thing to behave the way that it behaves.

CLARK Where you have effective structure, you have a kind of isomorphism.

CUMMINS There are ways of getting the thing done without isomorphism, it's just expensive.

SMITH No, my claim was that Rob wants a more fine-grained category. The problem is that code is dirt. Code has some many different kinds of—

DENNETT But now, look. We admit that 5 million lines of code, which is not isomorphic, does the job, it's just very expensive. The isomorphism does the job, it's very cheap, it's very elegant, and, we've also agreed, that there's everything in between. There's every sort of rebus puzzle in between, which is 1 million lines of code and so much map and so forth. We get the whole spectrum of cases, but if we grant that, then it looks like an empirical question of how important isomorphism is.

CUMMINS Absolutely. And it's probably not very important in predator recognition in prairie dogs, I'm willing to bet, but on the other hand

I bet it is very important in the way prairie dogs find their way around prairie-dog town.

DENNETT So it's the limiting case. And it ties in with situated cognition. It's just one step away from Rod Brooks [1991] saying 'The world is its own best representation.'

CUMMINS Exactly, that was what the Autobot example was meant to conjure up in people; the good idea behind representation, as opposed to indication, is that if you think the world is its own best model, but the world doesn't happen to be around just now, then a good thing to do is to take something that looks very much like the darn world, and stick it inside. That was the idea.

SMITH Here's a question. I really have thought of this word as a phylum word and you've got a variety word, or something like that, but I think the phylum I would characterize is one that you would be prepared to be a variety underneath, which is: an effective structure that allows you to behave appropriately with respect to situations that you're not able to be driven by causally. That includes the whole gamut. And then the question is: what are the strategies for structuring effective materials so as to lead to appropriate behavior with respect to domains that you're not currently coupled with but you're nevertheless intentionally directed towards (taking a little debt on what it is to be intentionally directed towards)? I didn't think it did justice to you to just take your book as a celebration of the cognitive utility of isomorphism. I felt that there was more substance to it, and so here's my suggestion for more substance. Given this phylum characterization I've just given, what you're suggesting is that the first theoretically interesting chunk or step away from being driven by the world itself is being driven by effectively isomorphic structure. Structure whose stuff, whose effective structure is isomorphic to whatever structure in the world you care about. The stuff you care about doesn't need to be effectively structured. But the thing that's driving you has to have as its effective structure something isomorphic to that toward which you are directed. And the intentional thesis is that it's the first step.

CUMMINS I had a different take on it but that's an interesting claim. I'll tell you what my other take is in a minute.

CLARK What keeps bothering me, is, I don't have a sense of what effective structure could be if it's not isomorphic.

CUMMINS Good. Any port in a storm. I'll see if I can try and talk you out of that.

SMITH Andy, suppose you give me a network of 10^9 resistors, interconnected, that's just a maze. And you say, 'What's the voltage drop across this resistor here?' And I say, 'Look, Kirchov's laws say that the net energy dissipation in this thing is zero, and the energy dissipation in any resistor is I^2r, and r's have to be positive, and it doesn't matter about I—it's squared—and so therefore we've got a sum of terms and they all have to add to zero, and none of them can be negative and so none of them can be positive at all if they add to zero, so therefore all the I's are zeros so therefore the voltage drop there is zero.' That's an *analysis*. That wasn't a *simulation*. It seems to me that's a case where efficiency actually argues against, as it were, simulating this circuit. Isomorphism to the circuit would be hopeless, because by hypothesis there are 10^9 resistors. Whereas in this case conceptual analysis is devastatingly compact. For maps, it's the inverse; a conceptual analysis of the structure of London streets would be devastatingly complicated, and the isomorphic map is simple. I think that's what Rob is trying to impress on us.

CLARK But isomorphism doesn't have to be one-to-one. Indeed, the most effective isomorphisms are 'one to each salient unit', if you like, it's not one to every way that you could parse the target.

SMITH Let me see if I can sell you this example. You're a fox, you set out from your den, you chase some deer all over the place, endlessly, and you cross a river, and end up crossing it back and forth, back and forth, back and forth, and finally you lose track of the deer, or eat it, or whatever, but anyway your chase is done. And now you think 'I've got to get home.' And you say to yourself, 'I've crossed the river an even number of times, so I'd better not cross the river. I don't need to look on that side.' That would be an excellent thing to think. But it is going to be hard to do with an isomorphism.

CUMMINS Yes, it is hard.

SMITH But it might be effective.

CUMMINS A good case. Aren't you struck, though, that when you start thinking about real cases, it really turns out that, actually, you know, you have to work at coming up with these things. Until you get to language, and then they're ubiquitous, then they're all over the place.

SMITH Sorry, I just didn't understand that. The problem is that I would agree with everything that you said, so—the question is, what the error was. Was it that I thought the driftwood was married? 4.7 P. 195

CUMMINS Yes.

SMITH See, that's what I find counterintuitive.

CUMMINS That's because this 'of' notion really is ambiguous. There's a sense in which you thought of the driftwood thing that it was married.

SMITH Well, there is a sense, but the problem is, chain this twelve inferences down the line, and—

DENNETT Well, so what? It's like those damn doors in Shakey's pizza parlor.[18] Which one are you thinking about?

CUMMINS My point is that this is not the case where we want a story which doesn't provide a space to think that there are these errors, that we do make these errors. And what really happens in these cases, I think, even in language, is that we back out of them. It's just that we back out of them pretty darn fast. And sometimes we don't back out of them—

DENNETT And you would want to say 'Right.' The letter of the law is, yes, we can taunt Brian with that, 'Ha, ha, you thought a piece driftwood was married.' And there's a sort of sense in which, yeah, that's true but who cares, because it's the sort of error you just back right out of.

CUMMINS That's right.

SMITH OK. But, so here's the sort of thing that I guess I was concerned about, which is if I see the driftwood and say, 'Hey that's John, I should return his wife's library book.' Now the thing is, that could be a real recognition, that I should return Joan's library book. However, if it was the driftwood which I was thinking about, the driftwood has no wife, so therefore, I haven't thought a true thought. But the problem is I *have* thought a true thought. It was actually useful to go return Joan's library book. And I wanted to hang on to my having had a real recognition, which is that I should return Joan's library book. So, that needs to be in there too.

CUMMINS I think what you've got is, you've got a communicative signal here, which conveys a true thought. But I think that, until you back out of the representational error, you're still going to get something wrong here.

CLARK But the error you're backing out of is which error here? Just the original driftwood error, because you haven't actually made the other error. You haven't ever really thought the driftwood was married. That never happened. Otherwise you'd be backing out of an infinite number

---

[18] [See Dennett's 'Beyond Belief (1982). The section, 'The Ballad of Shakey's Pizza Parlor' is at pp. 53–60 in Woodfield, and pp. 167–73 in *The Intentional Stance*. Dennett constructs a poor man's Twin-Earth story using identical Pizza Parlors—ed.]

of errors, as soon as you made one, and we don't conceive of any physical system doing that.

CUMMINS I'm not sure about all the details of this. I only want to make a very limited point. I mean, Dan said almost exactly what I wanted to say. There's the sense that, good God, it's really unfair to taunt Brian with this, or not to notice that, as you put it, there is this other sort of true thought here, right. You don't want to put that insight in the driver's seat here, because that just completely obscures the fact that there really was something to back out of here in the first place. Now, exactly how you want to handle that is another sort of question. But it isn't an objection to my account that it says there's something to handle.

CUMMINS And so, a better way to locate the dispute between us is this: 4.8 p. 196 I think, like Millikan, he doesn't think really anything of semantic interest attaches to the types. And that might be right, but I think the right way to report that result is representation, as opposed to what I'm calling intentionality, just isn't a major player in understanding how the mind works.

SMITH Hang on a second. I did not follow this. Does anything of semantic interest attach to types . . . ? The word 'I', for example, is a type.

CUMMINS Now, be careful here, because on your own view, what types are semantically, is their uses. Not their internal structure.

SMITH No, wait. A simple example is to attach to the type, or word *I*, that it refers to whoever speaks it on an occasion of use. That's what indexicality is—generalities across uses, that can attach to the type which gives you a kind of productivity so you can understand, when someone whom you've never met before uses it, whom it is that they're referring to. So it's absolutely critical that something attaches to the type, otherwise every new token would in fact be . . .

CUMMINS That's right. I do believe that now it starts to get important to distinguish what I think of as representational systems and representational functions from communicative systems. Mind you, I think almost everything is a little of each. But, I think it's really important to know which one is doing the explaining on any given occasion. The two funny things about language, I think, is that it's primarily in the communication business and got exapted for representational purposes. But I think that its representational capacities are not to be understood by, as it were, compounding up the communicative meanings of the words.

Final
discussion
p. 197

DENNETT Can you make a model of a left hand? Fill a left-handed glove with plaster?

CUMMINS Not in the way that distinguishes it from right hands in a perspective-free way.

CLARK Can you make a picture of anything, then, that is perspective free?

CUMMINS My point is this: if what you're interested about in the model is the way structure drives behavior, then it won't matter a darn which one you have.

HAUGELAND It will, depending on which processor you've got.

CUMMINS Oh, no, that's right. But the point is that, both of them have all the structure you need. All the information is there. You have to have a different way of exploiting that structure in the two different processors, just like turning the card over in the Autobot. But the stuff is there to exploit. So my point is that when it comes to steerage, it's the isomorphism that matters and not this extra thing, whatever it is, that makes you think that the picture up on the ceiling of the Sistine Chapel has God reaching out with his right hand not his left hand. I don't have any desire to deny that.

CLARK The right and left hand case isn't a special case here, is it?

CUMMINS No it's not at all. It's the structure that matters, and since this is a paradigm case of shared structure, on my view, the two can't have different representational contents. They could certainly have different cause and effects in a given system because one might be able to exploit it and another might not. But—I didn't say this in *RTA*—I think it's enormously important to have a conception of representation in which it's possible for a system to learn to exploit structure in its representations that it was previously unable to exploit. This is another reason I like distinguishing it from use in my narrow sense of use.

SMITH Oddly enough I think that's your most powerful argument. But is this just word games, in the sense that you're using a word starting with 'r' for isomorphism? Because it's very hard to deny everything you say about isomorphisms—the cognitive utility, the closeness of fit, and so on and so forth. And the problem is, the attitude and application structure is so powerful; and you carefully place over here in targets and applications everything Ruth [Millikan] does and everything John does, and actually, everything else. So I say, look, I'm in the piano store and I want to know if this piano fits in our house, so I get a little piece of string and I just cut it and I come home and so on and so forth. Well

I think this is a representation, but of course it's a representation of how tall Dan is, and the circumference of a wine cask, and a zillion other things. That may be sort of coincidentally true, but what it really is, is the representation of the length of the piano. And you just do all that work over on the use, application, target side.

CUMMINS No, I don't think so. I think I'm dividing and conquering, I mean, I think that's the whole beauty of the thing, that of course it does represent all these things. Strings are pretty darn unstructured, OK, so, for me they're kind of toward the indicator end, OK, but let's let that go for a moment. Of course it does represent all these things. A better case is, there's a highly simplified map. It'll match a lot of cities around if you could rotate it enough or something like that. Of course it fits all of these things, right? And equally, I think, through the lens of language the targets of non-linguistic animals turn out to be pretty smeary-looking kind of things. But what actually matters in getting things done is in the match between the two. So the fact that you've got a kind of simplified map that a zillion other things would match pretty well, is just neither here nor there. The point is it does pretty good *here*. Well what's 'here'? That's the target issue. 'Here' may be pretty darn smeary in a sense, right.

SMITH Why should we give you the word 'representation' for this very interesting thing?

DENNETT It's just stuff that has information in it because of its structure.

SMITH It's non-information on most prevailing semantic accounts of information, because you don't have the counterfactual-supporting correlations.

CUMMINS No you don't have any correlations, you don't have any causal stuff, right. So that's why I resist your way of putting it, because I think that there really is a big difference between, as it were, exploiting these kinds of structural matches and mismatches, on the one hand, and exploiting informational correlations on the other. They're both good ideas in their place, but they're different ideas. And it's true, I've stolen the R-word, but I think historically I have some right to that. I think the real thieves are Dretske and Stampe and Fodor. They're the ones who are the thieves, I'm just kind of taking back our rightful property. If you tried the representational theory of art and aesthetics, and tried to gloss that as indicator semantics, it'd be laughable.

HAUGELAND Or verbal semantics.

CUMMINS Yes.

CLARK But it is true that within cognitive science it's totally weird, the way that you're using it.

CUMMINS I confess that I stole the *R*-word.

SMITH But it's not just arbitrary labeling.

CUMMINS No it isn't just arbitrary labeling, but there surely is a big difference between the indicator kind of case, where what really is important to making the explanation go is the degree of correlation and causal coupling on the input side, versus the kind of situation where you have a map, especially a steery kind of map like my Autobot case, where the causal coupling between the terrain and the car is just utterly irrelevant. You've got to mark that distinction somehow.

SMITH I actually think mental conceptual representation is extraordinarily powerful, so I think it's important, in being impressed by the communicative aspect of language, not to lose sight of the mental power of conceptual representation.

CUMMINS Let me say one thing about language. The way I think of it, spoken language was a biological adaptation, like Dan says. I think it was one of the great ideas that nature had, as it were. But I think it is, in the first instance, an idea to facilitate communication. Now, I think that, in 'Truth and Meaning', Davidson [1967] made this bold conjecture that you could understand the communicative functions of language by looking at their representational functions. And I think that's exactly backwards. What I really think is that you've got a communicative medium that got exapted for certain kinds of representational purposes. Or better, which got used to communicate about representational structures which sometimes are built out of words. But when they're built out of words, the words don't contribute to the representation their communicative meanings any more. The idea that you could cook up the representational content of a complex verbal structure out of the communicative meanings of its components is, it seems to me, a bold but false conjecture. In just the way that I think the idea that you could construct the communicative contents of a complex verbal signal, out of the representational meanings of its components—that was Davidson's conjecture—it was a bold but wrong conjecture.

DENNETT When I tell my students about DNA, I say, what you have to understand about DNA is that it has this sort of deictic semantics. What's this a recipe for? Go in the kitchen, reach up with your left hand and take a cup of this stuff that comes to hand there. Now, take two cups of the stuff that's nearest to your right hand, put those in a mixing bowl, blah blah blah and so forth. That is, it all depends on what's there when you go to reach, its deictic. That's why, even if you have a woolly mammoth genome and you put it in an elephant womb, you'd probably get more of an elephant than a woolly mammoth because the kitchen's wrong. Now what I'm getting from you is that you have a sort of deictic recipe view of language.

CUMMINS Yes.

DENNETT That basically you're saying that what I'm doing right now is giving you a recipe for making something in your head, and what you make in your head, that's the representation. The recipe isn't a representation at all. Weirdly enough because one might think that recipes were just paradigmatic representations, representations of processes . . .

CUMMINS I think that fudges the recording—what's the other side of that distinction that you [Haugeland] make?

HAUGELAND Representation!

CUMMINS representing distinction [Haugeland 1991]. I think that fudges that in a really serious sort of way. I mean, in just the way that a recording is, as it were, a recipe for reconstructing or constructing, the representation. But, imagine this: suppose the things that it was a recipe for going and getting weren't there. And what you have to do is figure out a way for the recipe to do the whole job. What are you going to do? Now that's actually, on my view, the problem of exapting language for representational purposes. I'll tell you what you do. You do something—and this is really a crude caricature—but you do something like this: it's as if you had—you know these little magnets with words on them, you put them on the refrigerator, and you make up sentences. So what you did is, you took all these things and you arranged them in a mosaic to make a picture. And then Donald Davidson came along and said, 'You know, I'll bet what the picture represents could be computed from the meanings of the words.' And I would say, 'Baloney'. You know? The magnet case is not really very good because there's not much internal in the way these things can go together. So if he said, 'Okay, but, in making the picture you had to honor certain constraints about which things can go which way . . .' But still you make a less serious error about all this if you start by thinking the extreme thought that 'What I'm going to do is I'm going to build a different kind of thing, a thing that connects with the world in a quite different sort of way, out of the old stuff,' and your recipe example I think is wonderful for that. That's exactly how I think about it. That's exactly what the language of thought people don't think, you see. They think its translation. Yeah, right, but that seems to me completely wrong.

SMITH Yeah, although these two options—you and Jerry [Fodor]—don't exhaust the possibilities.

CUMMINS As usual I'm being provocative by drawing this in a very exaggerated sort of way. But do you understand why then when people give me linguistic examples with which to test the target/content stuff, I get nervy and upset?

CLAPIN OK, but let me try to hoist you on your own petard. You've got this whole big deal about Tarskian semantics which just sounds right to me. But, what I want you to tell me is why is your story about embedded intenders any different?

CUMMINS Because, look, combinatorics is also a good idea. Semantic combinatorics of a sort, where we're talking about communicative meanings, is a good idea for language. There's lots of other kinds of combinatorics around, OK? Among which intender embedding is a case in point. I don't have anything against combinatorics. It's another one of nature's good ideas, and I'm prepared to exploit it wherever I think is necessary. It seems clear that one of the sophistications you get, as it were higher up on the phylogenetic scale of one thing and another is the ability to, as it were, acquire targets on the fly.

CLAPIN How?

CUMMINS Because of just the sort of things that Brian was saying, namely that the previous course of my representing and intending and activity and God knows what else—my thrashing around, right, can make it the function of a quite ephemeral process to represent a whatsit. And this kind of function, by the way, Millikan stories will never even touch because the darn thing only probably lasts about ten seconds. So, for that ten seconds the function of that process is to represent this thing.

DENNETT But now it looks for all the world, Rob, as if you've not only got a homunculus, but—I can't be understanding this right because it looks like—a very particular sort of homunculus, namely a programmer. Because, what a programmer does is: uses a programming language to build structures—to build intenders. And you granted that what a human brain can do is generate and make, acquire intenders, can build, acquire targets, can build intenders on the fly, out of something. And the something that it's building them out of includes the recent uses with their representations attached. So it looks as if your model of the process of intender embedding is a sort of continuous reprogramming. Creating new programs to meet special circumstances. And, one wants to know, who does the programming?

CUMMINS   All right, well, I have exactly the same answer to that, as you have when people say the same thing about you and selection. Who does the programming? It does itself. That's why I use the word 'acquire' instead of 'build'. Now, I do think that one of the things that language and conscious reflection gives you is the capacity quite literally to build them and be in this sense a programmer, but I think its darn rare. And I agree with you. It probably only happens when you have this sort of cultural technology at your disposal, and not just spoken language.

DENNETT   Lots of virtual machines.

CUMMINS   Yes, something like writing, even, or, maybe not. I don't know. But I think there are much simpler cases than that—it just is a feature of certain kinds of system, that functions don't always attach to permanent structures. They sometimes attach to rather ephemeral things. And, actually we all know this—when people say, 'Why are you doing that?' sometimes they want the motive and sometimes they want the function of your doing. And that doing may be quite ephemeral and quite unique, and, as it were, totally constituted as the function of the type it is by this sort of historical funnel that put you there. That doesn't require a programmer. 'Nesting' may have been a bad word for this.

DENNETT   OK, now all of this context, and now, right now, each one of us has a lot of knowledge and a lot of misinformation. Does that misinformation in us take the form of applications? I mean, all the things that I'm not now thinking about, but have false beliefs about. All those long-term misapplications of representations and targets and . . .? Have I got a zillion of those in my head?

CUMMINS   You gave me this disjunction and the answer, as usual, is 'Yes.' Both, in this case. There are I think cases, and psychologists call this episodic memory, where you quite literally store the application. There are other cases where what you've got is the disposition to make it in a relatively permanent sort of way because of say, the way your weights are set. Now in that case, is it an application? No, but what you have is, you have all of this misinformation in the sense that you are disposed to misapply certain of your things in your representational repertoire under certain circumstances.

DENNETT   Are those dispositions—

CUMMINS That counts as misinformation and that misinformation will show itself, if I get you into a situation where I can get you to do that.

DENNETT And is it a mistake to think of modeling those dispositions as data structures?

CUMMINS It's a mistake in a way. Yes, it is a mistake. I'm much more happy modeling those dispositions as facts about weight space or something like that. OK? It feels more comfortable to me. I'll tell you why I want to resist that data structure idea. And this gets into something else. What I said about language a minute ago, getting exapted, is exactly what happens to symbolic structures in AI. That is, you build these complex data structures out of these symbolic parts, but then it turns out that what the structure represents isn't, any more, semantic compositions of the meanings of the symbolic parts.

SMITH But that's why I think we should forget AI and look at commercial programming. And that's an answer to you, Hugh [see Part 6—ed.], which is, my worry is that, if you were to survey commercial data structures, let's say 3 per cent would turn out to be isomorphic, and 1 per cent would turn out to be linguistic, and 96 per cent would be some other category that is neither of these cases. For example, anything that involves counting, which is a hell of a lot of data structures, isn't an isomorph. Because numerals are not isomorphic to the numbers they represent, so anything that has a numeral in it where the semantic content of a numeral is a number, falls outside the isomorph case.

DENNETT Well, that's because those numerals are deictic recipes for making counters.

SMITH The point is that thinking that this map of the space of types underneath the phylum representation or something, is in any way spanned by isomorphs and language—I think that's a very dangerous meta-theoretic assumption that's on the table. I think that these are too small—we've got Liechtenstein, we have Upper Volta.

CUMMINS I don't think it's quite that bad myself. I don't like arithmetic and I don't think you should either, and the reason is because numbers don't have any mass. One of the things that makes it really easy to screw around with numbers is that you don't have to worry about the physics.

SMITH No, no, cardinality is not numbers.

CUMMINS Okay, I agree.

SMITH So, if somebody counts how many papers are still in the output tray, and gets to 50 and stops and says 'empty the output tray'—that's not a number in the sense that anybody could multiply it by 17, or relate it to anything else. It's this absolutely purpose-specific—

CUMMINS One last footnote about your recipe case. If I'm right about this then there's a fundamental problem about language understanding that we've never addressed at all. Suppose it turns out that the things that your recipe tells me to grasp are theory-like things, which may be implemented as points in weight space, but they aren't terms. So, you say 'dog' and what I go get is my theory of dogs. Then you say 'big' and I go get my theory of size, and so on. The trouble is that theories don't semantically combine in the right way. For example, a non-dog is not something you get by denying your theory of dogs, right? So, there's this problem about how, when I get all the stuff down off the shelf, I combine it into any kind of a coherent thought. And I think the beauty of the Davidsonian kind of story is that you get that for free. It's just that what you get is so thin it couldn't possibly steer anybody any-where. My story is something really thick that will steer you all over the place but the combinatorics become really problematic. If you think concepts are terms of the language of thought, then combining them is easy, you just don't get anything worth having. If you think they're what I think they are, they're really worth combining but nobody has a clue how to do it.

SMITH And this is what I think is the Evans generality constraint issue with respect to the flaw in concepts, which is, if you've only got a hammer, you treat the world like a nail. If all you've got are represen-tational structures then you're forced in fact to have this kind of clean combinatorics, you do enormous injustices and abstractions over the world to force-fit it into something you can combine.

CUMMINS What I can't understand is how to take the things that I think that the recipe assembles and assemble them into an action plan. Now I think that what you're calling conceptual thought isn't like that. But in a more primitive area, I think I can understand how to do what Andy wants to do. At least I got a glimmer about how that might work.

PART 5
On Smith

Texts

'Rehabilitating Representation' (forthcoming *c*).
'One Hundred Billion Lines of C++' (1997).
'Registration—I' (*On the Origin of Objects* (1996), ch. 7).
'Registration—II' (ibid. ch. 8).

Brian Cantwell Smith holds a rare and valuable intellectual pedigree for a philosopher of mind. As principal scientist at the Xerox Palo Alto Research Center (PARC) and founder of the Center for the Study of Language and Information at Stanford University (CSLI), he has studied foundational questions in computability and computer programming. Through this work he has come to the conclusion that the representational capacities of artificial systems such as computers raise profound metaphysical and epistemological questions.

In 'One Hundred Billion Lines of C++' (1997) Smith illustrates how misleading is the ordinary philosophical conception of computer programming. Standard programming practice is not (as is often assumed) committed to classical cognitive architectures. In particular, the processes implemented by executing programs have nothing like language of thought structure; none the less they make use of representations successfully to negotiate the world. They provide a rich resource of physical representation systems that are *effective* but don't fit the ordinary analyses of the philosophy of mind.

Smith's work may be aligned with the situated cognition tradition due to Barwise and Perry (1983). This approach emphasizes the importance of context in determining meaning. The situated semanticist is inclined to begin her theory of meaning with indexicals and other radically context-sensitive representations. Tokens of 'I' have very little meaning independent of how, when, where, and by whom they are used. More generally, the situated approach to cognition places significant emphasis on the contribution of the situation of the organism to that organism's cognitive processes.

Smith argues that as soon as we register the world using a system of representation, we make a set of strong assumptions about the way the world is. His task has been to show the profound consequences of this insight for the study of systems of representation.

Smith makes use of an engaging imaginative strategy to draw attention to the theoretical moves required to explain the occurrence of representation using only the resources of a representation-free physical world. Smith urges us to consider whether we need to think in terms of objects at all. Might an ontology consisting only of Strawson's (1959) 'features' be sufficient? When we declare that 'It's raining' we are drawing attention to a feature (raining) without being committed to any particular object that has that feature. Smith suggests we begin by thinking of the physicist's world as populated not by objects but field-densities. This field-theoretic description can be comprehensive while admitting only of field-densities for a small range of properties (for example, gravitational fields, electromagnetic fields, etc.).

Smith suggests that the common-sense world of middle-sized objects is an achievement of our representational practices. Representation is achieved when one aspect of the mish-mash of fields is able to *separate* in a certain way from the rest of the mish-mash. This region, the 's-region', is (or is becoming) the subject—something that represents the world. Smith first emphasizes the *distance* required between the representation and the represented, and secondly the need for coordination between the two. This coordination is likened to the actions of an acrobat who dances around a stage, but keeps a torch beam focused on one spot. The torch must undergo dramatic changes in orientation to maintain its focus at one point. The *intentional* acrobat is similarly dynamic in keeping its intentional objects stably registered.

Smith builds on this fundamental picture to argue that all representation is partly context-dependent, or deictic. Smith is scrupulous about the reflexive morals which thus apply. Acts of representation bring the world's objects and properties into being (as objects and properties), and any attempt to talk about the world will be an act of representation, and thus an act of object-making. This makes likely what Smith calls 'inscription errors' or 'pre-emptive registration'. For example, it is difficult to talk about the world except as containing objects with properties. But if this is due to the subject–predicate structure of language, then it would be an error to infer that the world must be so constructed.

In short, Smith says that representation is an immensely complex, powerful, and sophisticated achievement of the physical world. We are so adept at representing that we are apt to neglect this point and think it an easy and simple procedure.

The paper 'Rehabilitating Representation' (forthcoming *c*) amply illustrates what Smith takes to be the more practical implications of his view. Both classical and embodied/embedded approaches to cognition misunderstand representation. The former places too much emphasis on formality and the non-semantic; the latter places too much emphasis on the causal, local interactions between the system and the world, underestimating the importance of *disconnection* to intentionality.

The rehabilitation required involves acknowledging that representation is about causal connectivity to the world, but not a direct, local, or simple connectivity. Representing subjects, by virtue of their representations, participate fully in the world (not just the skin boundary of the world), help constitute the world (by virtue of the entanglement of ontology with representation), but are able to maintain a separateness from the world.

Dennett, despite being a self-proclaimed 'reluctant metaphysician', is sympathetic to Smith's metaphysical project (though perhaps is not completely converted). His dispute with Smith concerns the role of evolution in explaining the difficult achievements of representation and objectification. Objectification, says Dennett, is an evolutionary 'Good Trick', which was likely to be stumbled on because it provides significant selective advantage. Dennett also objects to what he takes to be Smith's commitment to the determinacy of mental content.

Brian Cantwell Smith on Evolution, Objectivity, and Intentionality

DANIEL DENNETT

5.1.1 An Original Account of Intentionality and Objects

Like the rest of us, Smith wants to steer between the Scylla of GOFAI and the Charybdis of Dynamical Non-Representational Systems, and he adds to the feast his own bounty of acute observations and tempting proposals about how such a rehabilitation of mental representations would go. But he and Haugeland, unlike the rest of us, are *ontologists* who think we need to reach *way* back and rehabilitate the whole of metaphysics in order to do this job right. Yikes.

What are the less radical alternatives? One might have thought we could safely presuppose the usual catalog of *physical objects*—ranging in size from sub-atomic particles through tables and mountains to galaxies—and their *properties*—mass, charge, location, shape, color... and then simply explore the question of which complicated organizations of such objects count as believers, or representations, or symbols... and why. That is the strategy that has worked so triumphantly for magnetism and metabolism, photosynthesis and jet propulsion. Why not for mental representation, too? If we can explain growing an apple, and eating an apple, why not seeing an apple and wanting an apple and reidentifying an apple?

Why not indeed? I have always been a reluctant metaphysician, and Rob Cummins and Andy Clark seem to me to have shared my optimism about the innocence of the standard inventory of what we might call the ontology of everyday life and engineering. We happy sailors on Neurath's ship resist the alarm calls of Smith and Haugeland.[1] Do we have to put on our life-jackets and jump overboard and get all wet doing a lifeboat drill? Maybe, and maybe not. But it can't hurt. A lifeboat drill is a great way to reassure ourselves that we know what we're doing. And actually going through with it—not just imagining going through with it—is the only way to get this reassurance. If we end up with pretty much the same inventory and explanations we thought we were going to use in the first place, it will be a sounder ship that continues the voyage. And *maybe* we'll discover something important that has been distorting all our other projects.

For anyone who shares my conviction that traditional or 'pure' metaphysics is a played-out game, a mandarin pursuit so isolated from the rest of human inquiry that it is extremely unlikely to find enough leverage to move us from our comfortable habits, Smith's project is apt to be appealing. Only somebody coming from outside philosophy, somebody whose driving problem is *not* philosophical but somehow more 'practical' (however abstruse and theoretical relative to farming or building bridges) could hold my attention in a metaphysical exercise, and Smith has been led to his metaphysical vision by decades of struggling with problems that are eminently practical—problems arising not just in the crypto-philosophical arena of AI, but in engineering, for heaven's sake, in the design of hardware and software for all manner of applications. His title '100 Billion Lines of C++' sings to me, then. If disk operating systems, word-processors, and web-browsers confront problems of reference and meaning that can only be alleviated by some revisionary metaphysics, I am all ears. But still, dragging my feet. Constructively, I hope.

Let's start with what Smith calls The Representational Mandate:

5.1.1.1 *The Representational Mandate*

1. Conditions
   a. A representational system must work, physically, in virtue of its concrete material embodiment (the role of effectiveness).
   b. But it is normatively directed or oriented towards what is non-effective—paradigmatically including what is physically distal.

---

[1] [According to Neurath's analogy, philosophers attempting to shore up the foundations of science 'are like sailors who must rebuild their ship on the open sea, never able to dismantle it in dry-dock and to reconstruct it there out of the best materials' (Neurath 1932/3: 201)—ed.]

    c. Being neither oracle nor angel, it has no magic (non-causal, divine) access to those non-effective situations; just caring about them is not enough (physical limitations bite hard!);

2. So what does the system do?
3. It

    a. Exploits local, effective properties that it *can* use, but doesn't (intrinsically) care about—i.e. inner states of its body and physical make-up, in interaction with the accessible (effective) physical aspects of its environment.

    b. To 'stand in for' or 'serve in place of' effective connection with states that it is not (and cannot be) effectively coupled to

    c. So as to lead it to behave appropriately toward those remote or distal or other non-effective situations that it *does* care about, but *cannot* use. (Smith, forthcoming *c*, hereafter: RR.)

I will be surprised if anybody here has any serious quarrel with Smith's Representational Mandate (though it is easy enough to think of absent theorists who would squirm or rage). But some of us may be taking Smith's Mandate and *interpreting it down*, understanding it in a less radical way than he would wish. In the hope of giving his vision of it a proper outing, I will first try to give a summary of what strikes me as the dozen or so main points in Smith's work *that bear on the issues of mental representation*. (Much of the most interesting stuff in his book I'm going to set aside, reluctantly.)

5.1.2 A Dozen Important Points

1. Why re-tool our ontology? If we don't, if we complacently (or opportunistically) cling to the standard inventory, we will commit what Smith calls *inscription errors* or *pre-emptive registration:*[2]

a tendency for a theorist or observer, first, to write or project or impose or inscribe a set of ontological assumptions onto a computational system (onto the system itself, onto the task domain, onto the relation between the two, and so forth), and then, second, to read those assumptions or their consequences back off the system, *as if that constituted an independent empirical discovery or theoretical result.* (Smith 1996: 50, hereafter: OO)

---

    [2] The term 'inscription error' is from Smith (1996). Since writing the book, Smith has shifted to using the phrase 'pre-emptive registration,' on the grounds that it is more illuminating (based on 'pre-emptive representation', from Cussins, in preparation).

Pre-emptive registration is a sort of metaphysical anachronism, back-projecting onto our vision of ultimate—or at any rate more fundamental—reality a category or assumption that is in fact the effect or artefact of some later, higher-level, more 'expensive' development. ***Discussion point 5.1***

2. The granddaddy case of pre-emptive registration is imagining we can parse the universe *primordially* into objects, which may or may not be appreciated in their object-hood by any (psychological) subjects in the neighborhood. By objects, Smith means what we (now) mean by objects—things that have spatio-temporal boundaries (at least roughly), that have careers, that can be reidentified, and that can, on occasion, be *present to subjects*—as objects to be perceived, sought, remembered, thought about, moved, destroyed, gathered, and so forth. As he puts it in RR, the world doesn't come 'pre-parsed' into objects, properties, relations, and other 'formal' categories.

3. The antidote to this form of pre-emptive registration is hard to swallow, but Smith gives us lots of help with various imagination-aids, temporary ploys, and other delicious candy-coatings. If I understand him right, it is actually strictly impossible to *describe* the primordial state without committing some sort of pre-emptive registration, since words—any words we can use—already bias us in favor of objectification of just the sorts he wants to describe the birth of. If I understand *both* Smith and Haugeland (unlikelihood squared) on this matter, they both think one can tiptoe past this problem (of the apparent *inevitability* of inscription *errors* in our attempts to do metaphysics). Here is how I put it in my review of Haugeland's book:

The task facing any 'Heideggerian/Kantian' theorist is to do justice to the role of *us* in *constituting* the denizens of 'our' world without lapsing into awful relativism/subjectivism on one side or caving in to *noumena*, or a 'God's eye view' on the other. Haugeland's solution, which grows on me, is to show how and why it is *hard* to 'constitute' a world (that takes care of anything-goes relativism) but not because there is a privileged way that the world—the *real* world—has always been constituted. His view is a close kin, I think, of my view of the evolution of colors: Before color vision evolved on this planet, sunsets and cliffs and volcanic eruptions had the reflective properties they did, but *it makes no sense* to ask if those sunsets were, say, red—since that question has no meaning independently of a reference class of normal observers. We can of course extrapolate back from our current vantage point and fix and answer such questions, using ourselves as the touchstone for colors, but we must recognize that we are doing that. [That is, as it were, acknowledging the pre-emptive registration that you're doing, and just keeping track of the fact that you're doing it. You're keeping yourself and your own categories somehow as a touchstone to talk about something to which they're not really directly appropriate.] Were there dinosaurs before *H. sapiens* came along and invented censoriousness and then ontology so that dinosaurs could be constituted? Of course there were, but don't make the mistake of thinking that this acknowledges a fact that is independent of *H. sapiens*.

(Dennett 1999: 433–4)

I don't see that Smith's view of this is different, and that's fine, since I think this is a good and defensible view. ***Discussion point 5.2***

4. With that *apologia* (or is it a caveat?) in place, I can now (pretend to) describe the primordial basis, the out-of-which that objects find their origin in. It is (very roughly) a Heraclitean world of flux, dynamically flowing and concentrating and dissolving. What is it composed of? Well, you really shouldn't ask, barefaced, since any answer will involve registration that is to some degree pre-emptive; but since we must advance the discussion, let's just speak of *features*. Don't worry; this is just a temporary stopgap: 'That the distinction between features and properties and objects is not sharp, on the other hand—that logic is messy, not just finger paints—will not ultimately be a problem, at least not for us' (*OO*: 127).

Features, I take it, are ways one *region* can be different from the neighboring region. Here 'neighboring' means, constitutively, *in effective interaction with*. One of my favorite dicta in a work filled with arresting phrases: 'Distance is what there is no action at' (*OO*: 200 n. 11).

5. This idea of locality underlies Smith's account of another kind of pre-emptive registration, highlighted in RR: the family of errors that occur when we persist in casting what really ought to be a theory of effective processes (or just effectiveness) as a theory of effective computation. The idea is that the truly important phenomenon of effectiveness is not a particularly computational phenomenon—it is a sort of historical accident that our first intellectual grip on effectiveness came via the work of Turing, Church, and their kind. Smith suggests that all kinds of mechanisms are effective without being *computational* in the ways that foster spurious connotations (of semantics, of proof in formal systems, etc.). This then seduces us into further pre-emptive registration and more inscription errors, taking 'logicist' baggage along for trips where it proves worse than useless. The central idea of effectiveness, Smith claims, has to do with local, non-distal causation.

6. The importance of 'flex and slop': Interactive effects dissipate, diminish with distance and time, due to what Hume once called 'a certain

looseness' in the world (Hume 1739/1978: 408 (II. III. 2)). If the whole universe were like a gigantic interlocked gear-world, in which nothing could move without propagating effects *ad infinitum*, nothing could be out of touch with, or inaccessible to, anything else; nothing could be alone, or individual. Nothing could 'keep its distance' without flex and slop, which is a heretofore unremarked precondition for intentionality, because it creates the distance that then creates the problems that the varieties of reference-negotiation solve. *Discussion point 5.3*

7. Particularity is not individuality. The primordial physics world is everywhere particular, but contains no individuals (*OO*: 124–5). *Discussion point 5.4*

As I said at the outset, what appeals to me about Smith's project is that he's coming to this from a career in computer science, not from a career of teaching metaphysics. I'm trying to reconstruct the head-scratchings in computer science that make this seem so attractive, and it seems to me that they are something like the ultimate Y2K problem. The Y2K problem was not having enough bits for the year—settling for 2 when you should have 4, or, if you want to take a longer view, 5, or if you want to take Smith's view, many many many more. That is, when you start representing the world, if you're using any sort of data structure, you stop short with n fields, and n fields is in a certain sense never enough for a concrete thing, even something as simple as a cup.

The reason we make something a cup is that we have to create our little Y2K problem. There are only so many fields that we can carry along in our representation of the cup. We realize that if we want to keep track of that cup, there are all sorts of futures that we're going to have real trouble tracking if the cup gets smashed and then reconstituted, if it gets sold, if it gets repainted . . . There are so many different things that can happen to that cup. If we want to have a data structure that refers to that cup—come what may—it's going to have to have too many fields. We just can't do it. This is Haugeland's point, I think: a description of a person can't go into everything that's determinate about that person. [See Discussion point 5.4—ed.] It simply leaves out a lot of fields. There's a lot of bits that just aren't fixed and there's no room to fix them. *Discussion point 5.5*

8. Chiming a point also made rather differently by Cummins (1996a), Smith offers several arguments to show that reference, and semantic relations in general, *cannot* be effective or causal relations. We can refer effortlessly to things outside our light cone, for instance, and the whole point of having something local by which you keep track of something

distal is to overcome (without guarantee) the non-effectiveness of all such distal relations (*OO*: 157, 210–11, 228; see also the Representational Mandate 1c, above). And, like Cummins, Smith sees this as providing the elbow room for error (*OO*: 223).

9. The sort of 'non-effective tracking' exhibited by Smith's imaginary supersunflower is the forerunner of semantics, the basis of intentionality.[3] It is not what Smith calls *registration*, but it is the competence out of which registration can ultimately grow.

In all these situations, what starts out as effectively coupled is gradually pulled apart, but separated in such a way as to honor a non-effective long-distance coordination condition, leading eventually to effective reconnection or recon- ciliation. There is a great deal more to intentionality than that . . . but in various forms these notions of connection, gradual disconnection, maintenance of co- ordination while disconnected or separated and ultimate reconnection or recon- ciliation permeate all kinds of more sophisticated example.   (*OO*: 206)

10. 'The retraction of responsibility onto the s-region [forerunner of the subject] is the origin of registration's asymmetry and directedness' (*OO*: 223). (I'll have more to say about this later, mostly critical, but reluctantly so, since I love the pedagogical uses to which he puts this mythic image of the s-region *parting* from its partner.) Smith's ulterior aim in this imagina- tive theme is to highlight the importance of the perspective shift he advo- cates in the next point.

11. It is the emergence of dynamically coordinated variation-systems (illustrated winningly by the intentional acrobat's flashlight, and the 'col- umnar'-shaped 'sustaining physical field' that unites the frog to the fly, *OO*: 217) that explain 'why we see trees, not electromagnetic radiation'. I think this point is strongly related to some of Ruth Millikan's (1984: ch. 15; 2000*b*: §§7.1–2) observations on identifying the reference/function of some- thing by finding what holds constant across occasions, when we 'turn the knobs'. It is not just co-variance but *systematic* co-variance—which won't be perfect since systems are costly and may have weaknesses—that under- lies our identification of objects of experience.   ***Discussion point 5.6***

12. There are a variety of instances in which philosophers have trad- itionally dealt with dichotomies and Smith shows us how to see these as extremal points along some axis of variation. Thus the philosopher's ideal

---

[3] [The Supersunflower is a sunflower which continues to track the sun by moving at the necessary rate even when the sun is obscured and thus not in causal contact with it. See Smith (1996: 202–3)—ed.]

of a purely non-deictic registration is a myth (OO: 249). We have cases that are halfway between implicit and explicit, halfway between 'pure' reference and intension (e.g. OO: 251), and so forth. These middle-ground cases are very important in Smith's larger scheme of things, since as he eloquently says (OO: 254–5), the main lesson to be learned is 'not to be seduced by limit cases'. (See also the end of ch. 8 (and of the book): Life—what matters—happens in the middle ground.)

These strike me as the main things I have learned from Smith's book and RR. Let me add what I take to be the main point of 'One Hundred Billion Lines of C++' (1997), to make a baker's dozen:

13. The productivity, the compositionality of programming languages (such as C++) should not lead us to suppose that in general the processes such programming languages permit us to design and implement are similarly compositional. The fact that the programmer can create indefinitely many identifiers (and indeed can create nonce-systems of compositionality on the fly as he goes) does not at all imply that the identifiers thereby created can be treated as manipulable, composition-friendly items by the program itself. The compositionality is in the syntax and semantics of the source code but not in the structures that then get built and then actually get implemented and then run.

This insight, restored to philosophy, shows not that Fodor's language of thought is not the way we work, but does show that there is nothing remotely like a plausible inference to the conclusion that there is a language of thought from the premise that the brain engages in computational-like processes whereby it extracts apt behavior from the information it extracts from the world.

Now I take the upshot of all this to be a multi-path attack on the 'classical' ideal of mental representations as well modeled by 'propositional' symbol systems that obtain their intentionality by composing something like Fregean Thoughts out of Terms with Extensions and Intensions. Every tractable theory has lots of idealizations and simplifications, but the idealizations of *that* family of theories are trouble-makers, not helpers—largely because of pre-emptive registration: they create the illusion of sharp distinctions where in reality there is something of a spectrum, from 'non-effective tracking' to the most intellectual of opinions (e.g. my opinion that the shortest spy is a spy). What Smith calls registrations—occupants of the right-hand region of this spectrum, you might say—only work in contexts of 'coordination conditions', in adjustment or

compensation (what Smith calls 'intentional dynamics', OO: 262), processes that philosophers have tended to overlook or underestimate the
importance of. Smith puts to good use one of my own images to skewer
the false view: the classical system of uninterpreted symbols is seen as
wearing a thin 'overcoat' of transducers and effectors as the interface
between symbol and world. **Discussion point 5.7**

Now I want to offer what I take to be a friendly amendment, but I expect
Smith will view it askance. If my expectation is mistaken, hurrah; if it's
right, there is no question I am more than eager to explore than why he
resists this (to me) obvious improvement.

5.1.3 The *Origin* of Objects?

For me, the ghost at Smith's banquet is—surprise, surprise—Charles
Darwin. Evolution is hardly mentioned in his book, whose very title trum-
pets its likely affinity to Darwin's great vision. How can we have a story—a
Just So story, in fact, eloquently brandishing its own unavoidable metaphors and anachronisms—of the *origin* of objects, of their emerging onto
the contemporary landscape from some primordial scene in which they
were absent—and not have it rely on the fundamental Darwinian principle
of natural selection? What alternative shaping forces could do the work that
needs to be done? Smith does a wonderful job of showing us the 'expensive-
ness' of objects and subjects; something has to pay for all this R&D!

Let me draw your attention to a few crucial points in his account where
I, Darwinian Fundamentalist that I am, feel an irresistible urge to insert
evolutionary considerations. Look again at the Representational Mandate:
a representational system is '*normatively* directed'(1b); it '*exploits* local,
effective properties' (3a) 'so as to lead it to behave *appropriately*' (3c).
Smith's examples—the supersunflower, the frog, and (most important) the
unnamed simpler organisms who pioneer the passage from proximal
irritation to distal 'non-effective tracking'—all bespeak his interest in
evolution, in simple minds and their successors, but he strangely eschews
the evolutionary perspective. Why? Because, I think, he wants to avoid
what he takes to be the pre-emption error of what we might call *premature
teleology*, or premature function. But he overdoes it, methinks. He wants
to introduce normativity in *his* way, not riding on the coat-tails of evolutionary normativity. But I think this is a mistake, too. All normativity *does*
ride on Darwin's coat-tails. In trying not to be 'expensive' Smith goes too
far here. Consider, for instance, his excellent summary (OO: 241):

The underlying spatio-temporal extended fields of particularity throw tufts of effective activity up against each other, and let them fall apart, fuse them and splinter them and push them through each other, and generally bash them around, in ways governed by the pervasive underlying (physical) laws of deictic coupling. [So far, no hint of teleology; this is all just Heraclitean flux, signifying nothing.] For a subject to begin to register an object as an individual is, first, for a region of the fields (the s-region) not to be connected to another region (the o-region), but *in the appropriate way* [my italics] to *let go* of it. . . . The coordination requires establishing *appropriately* [my italics] stable (extended in the s-region) and abstract (extended in the o-region) focus on the o-region, while remaining separate. The separation helps in maintaining the s-region from being buffeted by every nuance and vibration suffered by the o-region.

Notice how we end with pure engineering: protection of the s-region from buffeting, in order to maintain a 'focus'—on an *appropriate* object. The fact is that s-regions that happened to begin to register inappropriate o-regions (don't-cares) or to register suitable o-regions inappropriately (inefficiently, counter-productively, etc.) would not last long in the buffeting flux, not long enough to out-reproduce the competition in any case. Once we add this evolutionary point, we can emend Smith's account, adding what strikes me as its most important theorem: the world *doesn't* come 'pre-parsed' into objects and properties (just as Smith says) but objectification is what I call an evolutionary Good Trick (Dennett 1995*a*, hereafter: *DDI*), an elegant solution to the problem of staying alive in the world of flux, flex, and slop, a solution we would expect to find, for instance, in other galaxies in which life had evolved.

Will Smith want to go that far with me? I hope so. His pluralism is sane and temperate. By taking pluralism (and postmodernism more generally) seriously (and not just pre-emptively dismissing it with a sneer, as it is extremely tempting to do) he allows it to tame itself. *Yes*, there are real problems of pluralism, and *yes*, there is no guarantee at all of a single, pre-given ontology to which we can anchor all reference, but reference-preservation, or reference-negotiation, is a problem that we can solve, and routinely do solve. (Don't patronize the Others. You can be brought to understand their ontology and they can understand yours, with a little effort.) There is a Good Trick (*maybe* two or three, but we know of one for sure that works well) that has been discovered again and again by evolution, and Smith has a deeply insightful account of how it works to generate our ontology.

I think this evolutionary perspective on the birth of intentionality is preferable to the charming myth that Smith puts in its place: 'In all these situations, what starts out as effectively coupled is gradually pulled apart, but separated in such a way as to honor a non-effective long-distance coordination condition, leading eventually to effective reconnection or reconciliation' (OO: 206), which ignores the fundamental evolutionary facts: we only 'want' to be coordinated to the things that matter to us, and these are not necessarily things we *used* to be attached to. The food I hope to coordinate with has never been within hailing distance of me till now, but I pounce on it just the same. I love Smith's imagery—especially his Country and Western song sound bite: 'How can I miss you if you won't go away?'—but it reminds me, I fear, of another cool idea (Freud had a lot of fun with it) that we evolutionists have shown how to replace: what we might call the Siamese-twin theory of sexuality, which imagines a primordial time when male and female were happily united, later cruelly sundered, and spending the rest of eternity as 'halves' trying to reunite. The evolution of sexuality is a deep and fascinating problem, since it, too, is expensive and needs to be paid for, but we don't solve the problem by imagining that an m-region and an f-region gradually got pulled apart and are striving to reunite.

Smith says at one point: 'Third, the retraction of responsibility onto the s-region is the origin of registration's asymmetry and directedness' (OO: 223). This serves to balance his various claims about the *shared* roles of subject and object. As he says, the dance has two partners but is not symmetrical. By leaving out evolution, however, he leaves out what I take to be the deeper reason for the asymmetry. The sun doesn't give a damn about the sunflower, but the sunflower needs the sun. You need something more like predator–prey (or mate) asymmetries to make sense of the asymmetry of registration.

I think Smith ought to accept all of this, and in some passages he sounds just the right notes. For instance, he notes that 'a distinction takes hold between *what the s-region is doing* (tracking the coyote or incident sunlight) and *how it is doing it*. The former gets at a non-effective regularity; the latter, at an effective mechanism whose "job" is to implement or sustain it. Among other things, this split provides a toehold for normativity to attach its tentacles' (OO: 222). Exactly: An evolutionary toehold for normativity.[4]

What might be fueling his resistance, then? In his account of what he calls 'intentional dynamics', his name for the theoretical basis of situated

---

[4] See also his good footnote about Gibson, OO: 225 n.: looming is not registration/representation. It does good (evolutionary) work, however.

cognition, he tells us he wants to keep the normative at bay (*OO*: 262): he doesn't want to build the normative condition into the name (by calling intentional dynamics something like 'rationality' or 'reason'). Fair enough; we need to understand the underlying physics, if you like, that any representational scheme, good, bad, or indifferent, must cope with, so we must be careful to describe not just the (presumably) optimal mechanisms, but also the junk that might be lying around interfering. Bad engineering and good engineering live in the same world, and that world should be clearly described without the bias of pre-emptive registration, if possible. I also think he wants to avoid what might be called 'premature agency' a sort of inscription error in which one breaks the world up into *things* doing *things* to *things*, as if this were the primordial catalog. See, for instance, his nice image of getting rid of the potter, *OO*: 270. But in the end, I gather—mainly from the strong claims in *RR* (p. 29) about a distinction between *static* and *dynamic* norms—that Smith's reasons for resisting an evolutionary treatment of representation come from . . . Pittsburgh. The 'dynamic norms' claims ring a Haugelandian, Brandomian, McDowellian bell for me, but I don't buy it. Not yet. I think I'll stand firm and ask to be shown what's wrong with my Darwinian fundamentalism, whose motto is *All normativity is grounded in evolution and emerges from the cascade of Darwinian algorithms.*

5.1.4 Coda: Three Reservations

1. *Indeterminacy of Content.* I see a tension between 'There may not be any compelling reason to believe there is even a metaphysical fact of the matter' (*OO*: 55) on the one hand and, 'We may not know what it is, but that does not mean God leaves the content indeterminate' (*OO*: 62) and, on the same topic: 'Somehow or other—and this I take to be the most important and difficult task facing the cognitive sciences—it must be possible to have determinate representational content, that is, for there to be a fact of the matter as to how the world is represented' (*OO*: 68). I ask, 'Why?' Smith says 'it will have to be an answer that does not depend on how anyone registers or individuates those mechanisms—again, for the simple reason that it happens in people, for example, without anyone doing that.' I don't see that as a good reason. This is like Cummins' similarly staunch line on determinacy of content, and I am not yet persuaded. Why can't God leave content indeterminate?

In this tug of war, I tug on the former side, of course. It helps us escape what might be called Cartesian (or 'from the inside') ontology, the view Quine calls the 'museum myth of meaning'. We must not *assume* that there will be an 'inner' perspective from which semantic facts of the matter can be mined. (See also Ruth Millikan's (1984) critique of 'meaning rationalism'.)

I don't see what's wrong with (my) perspectivalism about this. After all, it is flat true of some computer applications that they can be adopted wholesale for use in another domain (the old chestnut of the chess machine that can play war games, or whatever). See 'The Abilities of Men and Machines' (Dennett 1978*b*) for an ur-example. Why should it be different when we then look at animals, say? What if the fly-detector machinery is reused (exapted) intact in some later beast? I think Smith is right (and it's a good point) that the semantic/syntactic distinction is *not* the external/internal distinction, but I don't think that this further point follows. *Discussion point 5.8*

2. *What about Animals?* In spite of all the good discussion about frogs (OO: 197, 216–18, and other places) and coyotes, we are left wondering: do clams register? do amoebae? do they objectify? (see OO: 149, 193, 232). Smith (OO: 195) says that larger corporations and communities may be implicated in intentional achievements, but he downplays the role of proper parts of organisms. Why? Smith's bias in favor of human beings is largely uncharted (see my 1999 review of Haugeland on the same topic). Yes, only whole human beings living in whole societies, with slathers of normativity laid on, ever really refer to anything, but then there is lots of quasi-reference. And Smith is the master of pointing to just these facts. I wish he'd said more about whether dogs reidentify individuals, for instance (a question I take up, and don't answer properly, in *Kinds of Minds* (1996: 113–16), where I explore the case of Ulysses' dog Argos, who seems to recognize him when he returns. Does he? Really? [See also Discussion point 1.4—ed.]). In Smith's brief remarks on ethics (RR: 31), there is a clear link to my concern with Smith's silence on evolution. What if there were no people, only animals? There would be no ethics, I gather, but wouldn't there be lots of *mattering*? There would be lots of survival and extinction for cause, lots of *biological* norms.[5]

3. *C + + and Searle on Programs.* First, I give Smith's essay an *A + +*, and express my main objection: he should have written it twenty years ago

---

[5] ['Extinction for cause' is contrasted to random extinction, the result of catastrophe or 'sampling error'. See Dennett (1995*a*: 304) for a discussion—ed.]

and saved us all from a series of dubious battles that have gained precious few insights as by-products. But I also want to add to his concluding point 3 on Searle, about which a bit of clarification is in order: 'Searle's analogy of the mind to a program is misleading. What is analogous to mind, if anything, is process.' Smith adds: 'it is unimaginable that evolution constructed us by writing a program, a syntactic, static entity, which specifies, out of a vast combinatoric realm of possibilities, the one particular architecture that the mind in fact instantiates'.

In his uncharacteristically ill-considered *Daedalus* article on AI, Hilary Putnam (1988) speaks of the Master Program—which is perhaps the closest anybody has ever got to imputing this view to AI or to anybody. (See my critique in the same issue of *Daedalus*, reprinted in *Brainchildren*, 1998.) Smith is right in what he says, but let's see what this leaves available: the mind is, as Smith says, process (or a bunch of processes conspiring together), and while there is—need be—no programming language that specifies that family of processes in nature, that plays the causal role played by the source code in the genesis of new processes inside computers, those processes may nevertheless be usefully specified as if they were implemented programs. That is, to take the Searle case very much to heart, Searle has claimed that whatever consciousness is, it is not like a program in this sense: take a brain that is unconscious, and make it conscious by installing/implementing that program on it.

Now I continue to believe with all my heart and soul that this is exactly what consciousness is! Consciousness is a set of behavioral competences that depend not so much on the organicity of the brain's neurons as on their global behavioral roles, so that you could in principle have live, healthy neurons by the billions subserving no consciousness at all—a comatose or otherwise utterly demented person—and you could turn that brain into the brain of a conscious person by 'simply' revising the behavioral microdispositions of those neurons, turning them into organelles and tissues that accomplished various 'computational' and 'communicative' tasks. In fact, when people recover from strokes, the resumption of various parts of normal conscious competence is very much a matter of the reutilization of healthy neurons to play new computational roles.

Moreover, of course, I've argued (and here is where my view is most radical, most embattled) that there is something that plays a causal role similar to that of source code in the genesis of much of this behavioral microcompetence: there are virtual machines that are installed by cultural imposition, learning, imitation, and memetic infestation, and whatever it is that hops from brain to brain is, in some no doubt hugely indirect way, a specification of a set of habits of thought. A bit like Java applets. Thus, you encounter Tetris, and find yourself executing shadow Tetris-moves involuntarily for some minutes or hours. Or you learn bridge, and find yourself putting yourself to sleep doing shadow-finesses, or you learn about agreement of adjective and noun in Italian and execute hundreds of agreement-checks ... until it becomes second nature. The culture has driven a little rule into implementation in your head, and it is the same rule that all Italian-speakers have somehow or other implemented in their heads. Perhaps, to continue the analogy up to if not beyond the breaking point: native Italian speakers have the rule compiled in their heads, a much 'sleeker, more efficient machine' (as Smith says) than the interpreted version that still occasionally rises to the level of consciousness in my own operating system.

My point here is that nothing Smith has said about the non-compositionality of most executable programs casts doubt on the utility of such treatments. On the contrary, it helps mightily to clarify them, and to ward off likely misinterpretations.

Reply to Dennett

BRIAN CANTWELL SMITH

Let me start by thanking Dennett for two things.

First, I'm grateful for the effort he has put into understanding this project—a project, I admit, that can seem a little like a fire hydrant: the content comes out in lots of different sprays. I learned from his comments, and that's great.

Second, I want to thank him for mentioning the issue he identified as number 12: domestication of the 'middle ground' opened up by all sorts of traditionally dichotomous theoretical distinctions. That focus on the textured intermediate territory, rather than on limit cases, is very important to me. I think of it as the philosopher's analog of *in vivo* rather than *in vitro* analysis. In my experience, people who don't appreciate the importance of this kind of middle-ground stance find it hard to hang on to, especially at first. It is a well-entrenched intellectual habit (especially in analytic philosophy) to think that theoretical rigor demands 'clear and distinct' ideas, even clear and distinct *cases*. But just as there are dangers of drowning in complexity and detail, so too there are dangers of excessive (especially formal) abstraction, particularly for subject matters—of which I think epistemology and ontology are instances—whose stuff and substance only emerges in these often messy middle regions. Doing such phenomena justice requires a distinctive theoretical style. Although hard to get, initially, this middle-ground approach is also hard to lose once you've got it—particularly when you see its not being appreciated all over the place. So I thank Dennett for noting that right up front.

Needless to say, I can't respond to everything he has brought up. Instead of giving a point-by-point response, I want to make six general remarks bearing on the issues he has raised. In conjunction with his comments, I hope these will clarify what is going on.

5.2.1 Naturalizing Ontology

The first remark has to do with the project of naturalizing ontology. 'Why bother?' asks Dennett. The main reason, of course, is because I believe the subject matter demands it. What ends up as a methodological commitment is grounded in an empirical claim: that the theory of ontology and the theory of representation and intentionality are about intrinsically inter-connected phenomena. To study one without studying the other would be like studying time without studying space. Time is not space, of course; no one thinks they are identical. But you would not get an adequate account of either space or time by studying it on its own. So too, I believe, for representation and ontology. *How things are* and *how we take them to be*, though by no means identical, are co-constituted in intricate ways.

I might say that I haven't always believed this.[6] During the 1980s I spent a long time trying to develop a theory of representation independent of ontology.[7] I was particularly interested in taxonomies of representational types (symbols, icons, descriptions, models, simulations, etc.)—a theory, I might say, in which isomorphisms figured.[8] Now I didn't have the smarts to invent targets to do the work that representations couldn't do. But my fundamental problem was that I couldn't hold the ontology fixed—couldn't stabilize it adequately—in order to develop satisfying accounts of the plethora of correspondences that held between them. I was unable to determine (except by fiat, which didn't satisfy me) which items were objects or basic elements, which were properties of those elements,[9] and which were relations among them. Small variations in how I registered the basic domains wreaked havoc with how I ended up classifying the repre-sentations defined over those domains. In the end I was forced to admit

---

[6] That's not quite true. What's more accurate is that I haven't always approached the subject, in my intellectual work, from an integrated perspective. Even in graduate school, I believed that ultimately they would have to be understood together. In fact my doctoral dissertation (1982) started out as one chapter in an integrated but unwieldy metaphysical project that, at the time, I was hopelessly unprepared to complete. OO is essentially what that project turned into.

[7] See e.g. Smith (1987).

[8] See Cummins' project (Part 4 of this volume).

[9] That is: which were 'exemplifications' or 'instantiations' of properties; the problem wasn't so much one of distinguishing the concrete from the abstract (particular from universal), though that wasn't unproblematic, either.

that the (ontological) question of whether something was an object could not be answered except with reference to the (epistemological) question of whether it was being *objectified* by a representing or cognizing subject. That is: my independence assumption did not work. So there is a lot of failure behind this claim that representation and ontology are parts of the same subject matter. That really is the bottom line.

So I started over, to reconstruct ontology and representation together. It is not just an exercise, at the end of which you end up with the same recognizable parts. The theory that comes out—the benefits it gives you—are different.

Perhaps the simplest benefit is that it gives you more resources to describe intermediate cases. The notion of *feature placing*, for example, turns out to be extremely broad and useful—and relevant, I think, to the issue Dennett raised about animals. The basic idea of a feature, which I take from Strawson (1959), is of something logically simpler than a property. Like properties, (concrete[10]) features are spatio-temporally instantiated, but, unlike properties, they do not involve a commitment to a discrete, individual, reidentifiable object, complete with unity or identity or individuation criteria, to serve as the exemplar or 'holder' of the property or feature or abstract type. Paradigmatic commonplace features are fog and other meteorological phenomena. The truth of an utterance of 'it is raining' requires only that there be raining going on 'around here, about now', as is sometimes said. There is no object to which the term 'it' refers.

Take another example. Suppose Dennett visits my California house, and on the second day remarks that the fog's come back. 'You are a philosopher,' I ask, 'has the same individual fog returned, or is it new fog, of the same type?' I don't know what Dennett's answer *would* be; but I know what it *should* be: 'Go away!' Similarly, suppose you and I go camping,[11] and you, getting up early and looking around, stick your head back in the tent and say 'It's amazing; we're camped right next to a whole ridge of mountains!' Again, suppose I pedantically inquire, 'You've used the plural "mountains"; just how many mountains are there?' There is no reason to expect that an answer is possible. The problem is not epistemological: that

---

[10] By a 'concrete feature' I don't mean a feature that is itself concrete, but rather one that is *instantiated in a concrete realm* (parallel terminology would use 'concrete property' for a property instantiated by a concrete object). I am not here making any commitment to the existence of 'abstract features'—that is, features instantiated in an abstract realm.

[11] These examples are from OO.

you don't *know*, that you can't *count*; that you can't *see*. Suppose the air is crisp, the view clear, and that we have all the time in the world. It doesn't help. The point is that there is *no metaphysical warrant*, at least no metaphysical warrant up there on the ridge, for one answer over another. Criteria for mountain individuation simply don't apply to such situations with anything like exact enough grip.[12] Similarly for a host of other examples. The point is simple: pre-theoretic philosophical intuition notwithstanding, much commonplace registration of the world does not require parsing it into discrete individuals.

Philosophers are a rarefied class; many of us, at least since our first course in model theory, have been persuaded that we *do* take the world in terms of discrete, reidentifiable objects exemplifying properties and standing in relations. Or anyway that that is the right idealization under which to pursue philosophical topics. I myself suffered under this misconception for many years. But I no longer believe it. (This is another of those things that are hard won. At first it is difficult to credit, but then, once you come to see that it is true, it is hard to imagine how you ever believed the traditional story: that it is a precondition for finding the world intelligible that you first parse it into discrete individuals.)

Feature placing is just a stepping-stone, of course. Adopting a *richer* ontological framework doesn't require the stronger thesis, that ontological facts are in part *intentionally constituted*. But examples of feature placing are useful because they suggest why that stronger claim is true. If pressed to supply answers to individuation questions in such cases (for example, to decide how many mountains there are), you will notice that the only way to do it is to make recourse not simply to the structure of the world (the details of the shape of the ridge), but also to the *demands and contingencies of the projects you are engaged in*. If we were committed to climbing all the mountains on the ridge, for example, that might affect our answers as to what distinguishes 'one mountain' from 'two.' If we were geologists, our answer might be different. Likewise, airplane pilots might arrive at judgment different again.

One common way to handle such variation in individuation practice is to claim that the word 'mountain' is ambiguous; that climbers use one sense, geologists another, pilots a third, and so on. But this strategy doesn't work. Senses multiply too profusely—varying per speaker, per occasion,

---

[12] Note that the use of the plural is fully warranted (both epistemologically and metaphysically), in spite of the absence of criteria for definite counting.

per project. Eventually one is forced to admit that sense is indefinitely variable, and subject to factors anchored in the intentional projects of speakers. But this is an expensive admission: it reduces the 'multiple sense' proposal to no more than a relabeling of the original problem.[13]

In the long run, I believe, there is no credible alternative except to recognize that intentionality is implicated in individuation. Let me put it as succinctly as I can:

> The identification and reidentification of objects involves an epistemic process of abstraction over the infinitely rich (and often surpassingly messy) ur-structure of the world. Among other things, the normative character of the intentional projects that agents are engaged in, when they commit these acts of abstraction, figures in the resulting 'clumping' of the world's effectively infinite detail. To be an object is to be a region or patch of the world that is *successfully abstracted*—where the issue of 'success' is tied into the normative conditions governing the dynamic project of which the act of abstraction is a constitutive part.[14] The fundamental character of (what it is to be) an *object* is thus intrinsically hooked into the intentional life practices of the objectifying *subject*.

One more point on this topic. As a way to muster support for simply availing ourselves of 'common-sense ontology', Dennett says 'Look, why not just assume sub-atomic particles and tables and mountains and galaxies, *in the way that science does*?' This leads me to mention a radical thesis that I hold, although I can't give it much defence here: namely, that *science may not be committed to objects at all*. Consider: an amoeba splits. Biology doesn't care about the individuals in the situation: whether one amoeba died and two new ones were born; or whether we now have a spatial distribution of unitary amoeba-ness; or whether one of the two emerging amoebae is the original one, and the other one is new; or any other possibility. Another example: in California I own an ancient redwood tree that has clumps of very substantial shoots (some as much as 50 feet high) sprouting around its base. How many redwood trees are there? Science doesn't know, and *science doesn't care*. Similar conclusions hold for fog, for the units of selection, for a myriad other examples. What this leads me to believe is that scientific laws (like animals) may in fact deal

---

[13] One way to understand this is as a claim that *meaning*, not just *interpretation*, is context-dependent (see Barwise and Perry 1983).

[14] These norms may include what in Smith (RR) I call *dynamical norms*; see section 5.2.6.

only in features;[15] and that the objects we *think* of as constitutive of science may merely be *simplifying epistemic devices that allow humans to calculate.*[16] Objects in science, that is, are in my view properly understood as part of the epistemic apparatus involved in the conduct of science as an intellectual activity (on a par with mathematical models); they are not ontological commitments of the theory as a whole. *Discussion point 5.9*

Put it this way: *ontology* and *abstraction* need naturalizing as much as *meaning*, *semantics*, and *content*. Assuming a 'standard ontological inventory' for purposes of giving a naturalistic account of intentionality, as Dennett suggests, is thus a doomed project: it is viciously circular. Think about how appalled we would be (or anyway naturalistically unsatisfied) if someone were to propose a theory of representation that dined out on intentional notions, as if they were freely available. The naturalistic challenge is to *explain* intentionality without viciously *presuming* intentionality. A similar moral holds for ontology, in my view. Because ontological categories are in part intentionally constituted, attempting to explain representation while dining out on ontology is, for analogous reasons, fatally circular.[17]

5.2.2 From E&M to M&E

Second, I wanted to make a remark about the role of physicality in the metaphysical project.

I remember talking to Fodor once,[18] trying to convey my amazement that reference could point outside a speaker's light cone. His response stunned me. 'Look,' he said; 'it doesn't matter what physics is like. Physics could be arbitrarily different, and it wouldn't have a shred of impact on the theory of intentionality.'[19] It is hard for me to say how deeply I disagree with this sentiment. There is a sense in which I am something of a

[15] That is, the only ontological commitment that the scientific theory makes may be to the features that are instantiated, or to what happens when certain features are instantiated.

[16] See OO: ch. 5, on physics.

[17] I am not claiming that nothing interesting can be said in a circular frame; one might learn how different aspects of the subject matter were interrelated. The point is just that such an account would not count as naturalization.

[18] At the Ernan McMullin Symposium on Jerry Fodor's Philosophy of Mind, University of Notre Dame, South Bend, Indiana, 12 April 1997.

[19] I have often thought that I should dedicate some of my writings to Fodor, because he incites such bracingly clarifying reactions.

physicalist.[20] Not, mind you, a *reductive* physicalist—but someone who takes the character of the physical world to be essential in determining what intentionality is like. As a result, I take the consequences for a theory of intentionality of the structure of the concrete, material world to be enormous (as, I might add, must anyone who takes material embodiment seriously). The trick is to spell this out in a non-reductive way. Note that the issue is not merely one of engineering: that intentional subjects be physically *implementable*. The connection is much stronger than that. As I tried to show in *OO*, the structure of the physical world actually establishes the problem that intentionality solves (as well, fortunately, as supplying the wherewithal for its solution). *Discussion point 5.10*

For various pedagogical reasons, I take field-theoretic interpretations of physics especially seriously. I'm a complete amateur at physics (as my readers will know), but for purposes of understanding intentionality, field-theoretic interpretations have a decisive advantage. They make it evident that physics does not involve a metaphysical commitment to discrete fundamental individuals. *Discussion point 5.11*

To see this, assume a field-theoretic interpretation of classical, high-school (Newtonian-Maxwellian) physics: spatio-temporally extensive fields of force, mass, charge, etc., subject to various dynamical regularities. And consider what is involved when we talk about individual bodies, as for example we might if we were to ask about the gravitational force exerted by this cup on this pen. In calculating the answer, we might be tempted to characterize the problem as a mass of 200 grams and a mass of 30 grams standing one meter apart. My point is simply that, as everyone knows, this characterization involves some simplifying idealizations. It makes two acts of abstraction over the raw fields: one to collect up the region of space-time we call 'the cup' into a dimensionless unity; the other to collect up another region, which we call 'the pen', into a similar dimensionless unity. That is, we *objectify* both cup and pen: treat them as discrete, individual, infinitely dense space-time points.

Why do we do this? For a very good reason: the simplifications are necessary in order to yield a problem that is epistemically tractable. Staying true to the field-theoretic interpretation would require treating the cup as a

---

[20] Some might expect me to say 'materialist' here—but I make a strong distinction between the predicates 'physical' and 'material'; see *OO*. Note: the non-reduction commitment is very deep; I don't believe that *even if we knew all there was to know about physics*, that we would necessarily have the raw material out of which to assemble an intentional science. Physics, like any other registration project, is drenched in loss. See *OO*.

full three-dimensional mass density manifold, the pen as another three-dimensional mass density manifold, and formulating the question as one about the gravitational attraction between two solid regions. Setting up the problem in this way (that is, without any abstracting simplifications) would require an infinite amount of information. And solving the resulting problem (a double triple integral of point-wise gravitational attraction between two regions) would require an infinite amount of work. Neither, in general, will be feasible.

In sum: working with solid 3D regions, which is all that physics is really ontologically committed to, yields epistemically intractable problems. So we simplify, for purposes of calculation. *That is where individual objects enter.*

Once the distraction of individuals has been set aside, one can see that the features of the physical world that most affect the nature of intentionality have to do with distance, coupling, and the locality of physical force (this has already come up in discussion, and I will say more about it in a moment). In particular, the 'point' of intentionality and reference, on my view, is to allow agents to be directed toward (ultimately, to care about) the world as a whole, beyond the (causal) limitations of that $\frac{1}{r^2}$ envelope with which, at any given moment, they are causally engaged. There are additional detailed connections as well. I mentioned an important one yesterday:[21] the differential character of physical regularities[22] engenders a kind of in-the-world deixis, which engenders an ineliminable indexicality in all representation and reference, which in turn underwrites the first-person qualitative character of phenomenological experience.

These are just a few examples of how I mean to take the physical world seriously.

5.2.3 Effectiveness

The third remark I want to make has to do with the relation of semantics to these issues of causation and local effectiveness. I subsume this under what I view as the problem of physical or material embodiment:

> How can small patches of the physical world (for example, us) exploit a small fraction of the sum total of ways of being that the world supports

[21] [See Part 4—ed.]

[22] That is, the ontological character of physical regularities that warrants our expressing them in the form of differential equations.

(namely, that fraction that is causally potent or causally effective), so as to allow them to register the whole world (not just the part they are in or constituted of) as exemplifying an almost limitless variety of properties?

How, in other words, do we exploit a *small fraction* of the properties of a *small part* of the world to gain access to *all* properties of the *whole* world? This, I would argue, is the problem to which reference and semantics are the solution.

I hope this formulation clarifies my disagreement with Fodor. For if my characterization is right, then understanding the character of what I am calling the 'locally effective' (that is, those properties of local situations that can do causal, effective work) is essential to the project of understanding intentionality. And this for two reasons. First, the effective properties are what an agent gets to *use*; they are the 'material', as it were, from which an agent can construct its intentional solution. Understanding them is thus necessary in order to understand how intentionality 'works'.[23] Second, we need to understand what these properties are *not*—that is, the vastly larger fraction (99%) of the world's features and properties that aren't effective, or don't hold of the local situation, and hence that the agent can't be coupled to 'directly', by physical coupling—since that is what constitutes the 'rest of the world' toward which the agent is intentionally directed.

One question that inevitably comes up, when I put things this way, has to do with the relevance of quantum mechanics. If intentionality is intrinsically related to physicality, then is the character of the intentional affected by the fact that the physical world is not ultimately classical? The answer may be 'yes', though I confess I am not prepared to say very much about this yet. To date, I have constrained my study of the locally effective to phenomena that, as far as I can see, could supervene on a classical base.[24] I've done this in part because I have yet to see any compelling argument that the human brain reaches further.[25] Even though I take my subject matter to be intentionality full bore—that is,

---

[23] I mean 'work' here in the sense of efficacy, mechanism, causal powers, etc. (This is the sense of 'work' in the formal symbol manipulation thesis about computing: that formal systems 'work' in virtue of the manipulation of purely formal properties of their ingredient symbols.)

[24] Except that I try to avoid completely unrealistic consequences of classical physics, such as that traces of every motion in the universe can theoretically be detected in the vibration of a single particle.

[25] Other, of course, than ordinary facts—such as that ice floats, that the folding of proteins and the like depend on quantum properties of the atoms, etc.

intentionality in any possible material manifestation, not just its human projection—nevertheless, the sheer magnitude of human accomplishment convinces me that basing such an account on classical physics is not too severe a constraint.[26]

In the long run, though, I admit that the study should probably expand to include quantum efficacy. But the nature of quantum influence may be quite subtle. For example, one place where quantum mechanics may bear on the nature of human experience, at least indirectly, is in issues of long-distance coordination, of the sort that violate traditional locality constraints (for example, as characterized in Bell's theorem). Note that the fact that we can register the world, see things, think, remember the location of Dennett's house in Blue Hill, and so forth, is because there is a tremendous amount of long-distance relatedness in the world. Maintaining a (moderately stable) conception of the (moderately stable) world depends on this (moderately stable) relational regularity. Is quantum non-locality a necessary precondition for such long-distance regularity? In informal conversations, some physicists have suggested that the answer may be 'yes'. If that is so, then that is surely one way in which the human condition may be crucially non-classical.

Other than speculative questions of this abstract sort, however, I doubt that quantum mechanics has much to say about our middle-scale intentional lives. So I lack sympathy for writers (such as Penrose) who feel that in order to penetrate the mysteries of consciousness we need to understand mind in quantum-mechanical terms. In 'Who's on Third?' (forthcoming *a*) I argue to almost exactly the opposite conclusion: that (again) using no more than a field-theoretic interpretation of high-school classical physics, one can see how the first-person, subjective, qualitative character of phenomenal consciousness must arise in any physically embodied agent that achieves an objective conception of the world around it. *Discussion point 5.12*

But return to the issue of simple effectiveness: how an agent can exploit what is effectively available to stand in for, care about, and otherwise direct it toward, that which is unavailable. This, in my view, is the best way to frame the question of intentionality. As you will predict, I ultimately locate the syntax/semantics distinction as a special case of this more general issue. But for pedagogical purposes, logic is not always the most

---

[26] One could imagine creatures in radically other places (on other planets, say) exploiting the efficacy of quantum mechanical reactions as their 'solution' to the intentional problem.

illuminating place to start, in order to avoid being distracted with inessential aspects of the formalism.

In my undergraduate teaching, I start by studying clocks. I choose clocks for several reasons: (1) because they are familiar, (2) because they have a clear mechanism (clockworks), (3) because clock faces raise issues of interpretation and content, and (4) because clocks are so manifestly dynamic. Suppose we want tea at 4 o'clock. I assume that '4 o'clock' is a non-effective property exemplified by passing metaphysical moments (one every 12 or 24 hours). If '4 o'clock' *were* effective, it would be simple to build a tea-making device: you would construct a detector to respond to a moment's exemplification of that property, and connect it to a switch. When 4 o'clock arrived, the detector would respond, the switch would flip, the kettle would boil, and out would come tea (or whatever). But of course—to make a point so obvious that we typically don't realize how crucial it is—*you cannot get a metaphysical moment's exemplification of the property of being 4 o'clock to turn a switch*. You can't do that because 'being 4 o'clock', as I keep saying, *is a non-effective property*. So what do you do instead? You construct a mechanism that uses properties that *are* effective, out of stuff you *don't* otherwise care about, and arrange it to be coordinated with the property that *isn't* effective that you *do* care about (a moment's being 4 o'clock). If the coordination is established properly, the former effective mechanism can stand in for the latter non-effective goal.

As Cummins just said [in Discussion point 5.12], one metaphorical way to understand this is to realize that intentional creatures have just a tiny keyhole through which to access the world. How far does their effectiveness reach? Because of proscriptions of locality, it reaches only to the surface of their skin. Strictly speaking, what is absolutely proximal—what impinges on your surface—is all you have to interact with. This is true of any conceivable physical agent: the infamous locality of physics restricts all engagement with the world to coupling with what is immediately present. Here we are, at this very moment, sitting in the living-room of an inn; our coupling to Dennett's farmhouse, even though it is only a few miles away, is at the moment very weak. So weak as to be 'undetectable'. When we want to go to Dennett's place for lunch, we cannot be driven by effective coupling to it (as a Gibsonian might imagine we are directed to an opening in a wall by effective coupling). So what do we do instead? We arrange the situation so that we can be driven by things that *are* effective, in the here and now (such as maps), that will enable us to get us to his house, there and then. The dance that this strategy engenders—of exploiting what is local and effective in order to be directed toward what is non-local or non-effective—this is the phenomenon I am talking about. ***Discussion point 5.13***

5.2.4 Computation

I trust that it is clear how this effective/non-effective dance relates to issues of mind, reasoning, and logic. My fourth remark has to do with its relation to computing. To explain this, we need to look at the history of computer science.

For almost a century people have been developing a so-called 'mathematical theory of effective computability'—or, as it is often simply called, the 'theory of computation'. In spite of its name, however, I do not think it is a theory of computing, because it doesn't deal with computing's essentially intentional character. Nevertheless, I still consider it an amazing achievement. What it is, I believe, is a *mathematical theory of causality*—that is, a theory of exactly what I have been talking about: *physical effectiveness*. This theory will not capture everything that matters about our pre-theoretic intuitions about causality, such as how you can cause things to happen after you've died. But that's fine; scientific theories never exhaust the pre-theoretic intuitions on which they are founded.[27] What this theory does capture, in the long run, I believe, is what we will end up taking physical effectiveness to be.

So the 'theory of computing' supplies half the intentional story: the effective half—the part about what you can *use*, what you can *do*, what *works*, how hard it is to change one physical arrangement into another.

A brief historical caricature may help explain why things developed this way. At the end of the nineteenth and beginning of the twentieth century, following the impressive achievements of the Industrial Revolution, there was a tremendous sense of the power of machines. Some of these machines were bluntly physical (steam engines). Some were targeted at very specific material concerns (smelting iron ore). Clearly, however, some very useful mechanisms, such as clockworks, weren't so concretely specified. Although it was crucial that they be physically constructed, it didn't matter what specific materials they were made of.

---

[27] See Paul Churchland's (1989: 238–41; 1995: 208–10) discussions of pre-Maxwellian intuitions about light.

People realized, from examples of this sort, that if you want to know 'what can be done', you can abstract from purely physical considerations—how big the mechanism is, how much energy it uses, etc. Paradigmatically, such mechanisms are used for detection, tracking, and other (at least inchoately) intentional tasks. Suppose you want to know when some particular train passes a spot on a railroad. You might put a sign or indicator on the train, and install a detector next to the track, to signal when the train passes. Sign and detector will obviously have to match, in physical characteristics, so that the latter can respond to the presence of the former. But beyond this, there are no requirements on what they should be made of, how big they have to be, etc. Because, of course, all we *really* need is to detect one bit of information: 'the train is here'.

Many such mechanisms can be imagined, of an essentially physical yet 'multiply realizable' sort, from simple detectors, to clocks, to what has seemed like the most powerful mechanism of all: one that could calculate, reason, do mathematics or logic. What people realized (to continue this glib story) is that, to get a theory of such devices, you have to let go of specifically concrete concerns. So what did they do? *They went to the other extreme*, and considered devices as completely abstract. Since what could be done (for example, by Turing machines) seemed not to have to do with specifics about particular materials, the theory took the opposite pole, and assumed that what could be done had *nothing to do with materiality at all*. This is why the theory of effective computability is framed as if computability were a purely abstract notion.

We are still living in the shadow of this history. The idea that the fundamental results of computability theory might be anything *other* than completely abstract is far from universally acknowledged. Many academics treat theoretical computer science as a branch of logic or mathematics.[28] And challenging this assumption bends some people out of shape.[29] Nevertheless, I believe, helped by people studying the powers

---

[28] Thus the current *Encyclopedia Britannica* claims 'As the result of . . . investigations by Turing, Church . . . Curry . . . and others, computer science has itself become a branch of mathematics' (Lambek 1999–2000: the subsection on 'computers and proof': http://www.britannica.com/ mathematics, foundations of > the quest for rigour > formal foundations > computers and proof (last accessed 13 August 2001)).

[29] I once taught a course on these questions, attended by the eminent (late) logician Jon Barwise. In it I argued that computability and complexity limits were ultimately grounded in material considerations of concrete mechanism—and hence that computability theory should be recognized as part of *physics*, not *mathematics*. Barwise didn't like it, and put up quite a fuss. Other people got involved, and started coming to the lectures. It developed into an intense,

and limitations of quantum computing, it is going to become increasingly apparent that computability limits are fundamentally material.

In terms of long-range intellectual trends, in other words, we moved from the completely concrete steam engines of the nineteenth century to the completely abstract inaccessible ordinals of the early twentieth century. Now, on the verge of the twenty-first century, we are settling somewhere in the middle. But through it all, the study has been a study of *mechanism*—of what can be done by concrete, material processes. As I say, I still don't think it is a theory of *computing*; real-world computation involves relationship, semantics, non-efficacy. But even if it doesn't explain our main subject matter, a theory of pure efficacy is a phenomenally important intellectual project, for which I have the greatest respect.

What is distracting—the reason this is not all universally realized—is that, because of its history, the theory of computability is still framed in semantical terms (computing *functions*, coming up with *answers*, representing *numbers*, etc.). Thus consider the standard practice of taking marks on Turing machine tapes to denote numbers. Though historically comprehensible, this practice, I argue, is actually wrong. The marks don't denote numbers, in spite of what everyone thinks. Rather, the numbers denote the marks. Computability and complexity theory, in my view, are *mathematical models of complex configurations of marks*. All the regularities captured in the theorems have to do with these marks and their arrangements, not with the numbers we associate with them. Why this is true, why you have to understand it this way—that is a story I can tell you over drinks.[30] The bottom line is that the role of the mathematics, in

multi-participant argument. The most interesting aspect of the debate was its sociology. Virtually without exception, everyone over 50 years old, and all of those who were trained in mathematics and logic, fell on the side of mathematics, on the side of pure abstraction. All the programmers, and all the younger computer scientists, fell on the side of concrete mechanism, on the side of 'somewhat abstracted' physicality.

The age issue is by no means irrelevant. If you track theoretical computer science, you will find that it is rapidly dealing more and more explicitly with concrete aspects of mechanisms. 'Time' and 'space' figure essentially in complexity theory, and not in a purely metaphorical way (like physicists' use of 'charm'); they have to do with genuine physical time and physical space. Increasingly, complexity theory is starting to deal with 'real time' and real three-dimensional space. And it is clear why. Consider microprocessor design. It turns out that transistors aren't what is expensive and limiting; what is expensive and limiting are *wires* (transistors are just where wires cross). And the ultimate constraints on wiring derive from limitations imposed by physical space.

[30] See 'Semantics in the Time of Computing' (Smith, forthcoming *b*).

computability theory, is just like the role of mathematics (and of objects!) in physics: it's a classificatory, epistemic device, employed by theorists. Like all theories, the theory is *semantic*, but it is not semantical;[31] it is not *about* semantics. What the theory does is to *use* semantics (not just terms, equations, variables, etc., but also mathematical modeling relationships, like physics) to classify concrete, in-the-world, non-semantic regularities.

Thus consider the results of computability theory, such as the unsolvability of the halting problem, or the difficulty of factoring products of large primes. Both problems are framed semantically: that you can't *decide* whether an arbitrary machine will halt, on an arbitrary input, that you can't figure out what *numbers* are prime factors. As any good theoretician knows, however, if framed in purely non-representational terms, as issues of yes/no decisions, or of pure numbers, these problems can be solved, trivially, if you employ what are called 'non-standard encodings'. For example, if you represent numbers as lists of their prime factors, then factoring them takes no work at all! Given this vulnerability, which applies to all complexity results, my argument has three steps: (1) the only way to bar such non-standard encodings is by bringing into explicit view constraints on the representations (constraints on the marks), not just on what the marks denote; (2) once you bring in the minimal constraints on marks needed in order to preserve the theorems, you have brought in everything you need; there is no more work for the 'denoting numbers' aspects of marks to do; and (3) what happens, in the traditional practice, is that these entirely concrete constraints are implicitly modeled by numbers, the numbers that the marks are taken to denote.

But enough technicalities; this is not the place for details. The point is merely that what is today called the 'theory of effective computability', in spite of the way it is framed, has *nothing to do with semantics*. It is a mathematical theory of physical effectiveness, pure and simple, of exactly the sort that we need for half the intentional story. It is a mathematical theory of Cummins' keyhole. *Discussion point 5.14*

Before concluding this topic, I should admit one thing: how much work is opened up by the reconstruction I am proposing. If I am right that complexity theory is really about the capabilities of pure mechanisms, independent of semantic interpretation, I am committed to reformulating its results in non-intentional terms. The theorems cannot be framed in

---

[31] See n. p. 261.

terms of decisions, or numbers, but as statements about how certain configurations of the world (that is, certain machines), if started off in given effective arrangements, will or won't or can't get into other effective arrangements, or about how, if you give a machine two different input marks, sufficiently complicated, these inputs will essentially 'drown' the machine, so that it won't be able to produce one kind of output mark from one, and another kind of output mark from the other. In other words, I am committed to reformulating all the theorems as claims about effective arrangements, *simpliciter*, without regard to anything those effective arrangements *mean*.   **Discussion point 5.15**

5.2.5 Objects

Fifth, I want to say a few words about objects—the subject matter of the book (*On the Origin of Objects*, 1996).

If you take logic, or introductory philosophy, you might think that there are two fundamental kinds: (1) concrete, individual, particular objects (called *tokens*, if they are linguistic or semantically interpretable); and (2) abstract, perhaps Platonic, *types*, which the individuals instantiate. In the general case, a type will have multiple instances: there will be a one-to-many relationship between types and their instances. In this sense, the abstract type acts to 'bind together' what is similar across the (extensional) set of objects of a given kind.[32]

One of the things that a career in computing has given me an extraordinary appreciation of is the sheer complexity of real, in-the-world, material objects. Among other things, this has in turn led me to appreciate the profound inadequacy, as an account of reality, of this simple picture of types and their instances. There is nothing magic about computing, in this regard: librarians know it too, in their efforts to catalog copies, editions, translations, reproductions, templates, and so forth. But I came to the lesson through computing.

Here is just one example of the kinds of practical issue that drove me to the story I report there. I normally download my e-mail to the hard disk on my home computer, where I have several hundred megabytes of files, folders, pointers from files to folders, and so on. When I travel, I copy the

---

[32] Obviously there are complexities: abstract individuals (such as the types themselves), types with only one—or even no—instances, and so on. But it is surely uncontroversial that the main, motivating case is of an abstract type holding of a set of concrete particular instances.

whole mess onto my laptop. Suppose I come here to Maine, dial in to a local ISP, and get a message from Dan Dennett. Intending to file it, I follow a link I have set up to the folder reserved for messages from him. This would have worked fine, at home. But when I try it here, on my laptop, a system message is displayed, asking me to mount the hard disk I left in California. Why does it do this? Because I copied the pointer from my home machine onto my laptop, and on my home machine this pointer pointed to the copy of the Dennett folder stored on that disk. Of course my laptop has a copy not only of this pointer, but also of the folder in question. The problem is that the system wasn't smart enough to know that the pointer should be adjusted to point to the copy of the Dan Dennett folder that now resides on the laptop.

What I hope this tiny example shows, or at least evokes, is the messiness of real-world issues of concreteness, abstractness, and multiple versions of 'the same thing'. Pointers are normally taken to point to individual files, but my intent, for this pointer, was that it point to something slightly more abstract: the Dan Dennett folder, of which I have multiple copies. You could say that this abstract Dan Dennett folder is a *type*, of which the individual copies are instances; but other than dressing the situation up in formal guise, that move doesn't much help. The problem is that even an ordinary desktop contains an astounding proliferation of highly related objects, of various sorts, many of which stand to each other in analogous one-to-many or many-to-one relations. Copies, virtual copies, pointers, caches, back-ups, editions, versions, replications, and so on—seemingly without limit.

Similar issues arise *inside* programs. Suppose you call a subprocedure with a matrix as an argument. And suppose the subprocedure changes the matrix. Was the original matrix changed, or did the subprocedure modify a copy? It depends on whether you passed it, as they say, 'by value' or 'by name'. Some other examples: one variable, multiple values; one IP address, multiple CPUs; one procedure, multiple call sites; one program, multiple copies, each of which can be run multiple times; one web page, multiple servers; one web page, multiple translations into different languages. And so it goes. Templates generate multiple copies, generators spawn new instances every time they are called, etc. And when the proliferating objects are *interpretable*, the situation gets even more complex. For example, there are problems of context-dependence: something that means one thing, in one context, can turn up in another context, or a copy of or pointer to it can turn up in another context, and mean something different (the Y2K problem is one especially famous example of context-dependence gone awry).[33]

Needless to say, if you work with these systems, you have to keep things straight. Some properties (the number of messages I have received from Dennett, say) hold of the abstract 'one' of which there are multiple instances or versions or copies. Some properties differ across each member of the group, in systematic ways (as we will see, this has to do with indexicality). Other properties (such as the location of a file on disk) may differ across the 'many' in no systematic way at all.

You might think that the way to avoid confusion would be to be extremely, even agressively, clear—always knowing exactly which object type you are referring to. You might even want to have different names (for example, to distinguish the program, considered as an abstract object, from concrete copies of the program, from temporal runs of the copy, and so on.) Let me simply report that all attempts I have made at being extremely clear in this way have failed miserably; they drown in inscrutable complexity.

Humans apparently handle such situations in a very different way. They seem to have a feel for the sort of things different properties can hold of, and to infer the appropriate instance or entity or individual for any given property in question.[34] In a way, you can tell that the term 'program' refers somewhat differently, in different cases, because a kind of zeugmatic infelicity arises from combining different types of reference under a single conjunction: 'Is that program recursive and corrupted?' sounds 'off'.

For many years, behind the scenes, I have been trying to develop a calculus in terms of which to understand this kind of proliferating objectification practice. I call it a 'fan calculus'—a calculus of the 'one' and the 'many'—because so many of these situations involve one thing (what

---

[33] Another example of context dependence. In the early 1980s, a friend used one of the first distributed file systems. He lived in Britain, but one day, while in California, he needed to work on a file he'd left back home. Rather than going to the trouble of explicitly bringing it over to California, he connected his California computer to the British file server. A day of work seemed to go fine; the file was loaded into his machine from Britain, and cached on his local disk. At the end of the day, when he logged out, his local computer sent the updated file back to the British file server. What skewered him was that he worked for less than 8 hours. The original file, which had been written in Britain, was, in the British time zone, more recent than the one he had just written in California. So the file system threw away his whole day's work. It had not occurred to the system designers that a caching computer and its file server would be located in different time zones. They had to modify the system code, to record time zones in memory explicitly.

[34] This process is reminiscent of what computer scientists call 'type-coercion'.

I think of as the point or root of the fan) that devolves or engenders or creates or spreads out into or is exemplified by or holds of multiple copies or versions or instances or tokens.

The classical type-instance distinction is a single fan, on this generalized scheme: what we call the 'type' is at the point of the fan; the (extensional) instances constitute its fringe. Even in the case of simple language, however, it is clear that a more complex classification is needed. Yesterday, in a discussion about indexical utterances, I made a three-way division, among *type*, *token*, and *use*. [See Discussion point 4.2—ed.] Very roughly, you can think of one fan connecting the type to each different token, and another fan connecting each token to the set of all its uses (if it is used more than once). To see the utility of this double-fan characterization, note that the mentalese word 'I' is indexical on the first fan, but not on the second. Your mentalese inscription of 'I' (if there is such a thing) and my mentalese inscription differ, systematically, in their referents. But unless I am deranged, all my different *uses* of my (single) mentalese inscription of 'I' refer to one and the same enduring individual.

In the case of types, tokens, and uses, we typically think of the types as abstract, the tokens as enduring and concrete, and the uses as concrete *events*. What is interesting about the proliferation of computational examples I cited, including files and copies and versions and editions and templates and copies of templates and generators and so on and so forth, is that much more complicated hierarchies seem to exist in which *all the entities are apparently concrete*. (Whether that is actually true, however, is not so easy to say. As the case of the Dan Dennett mailbox indicated, there may be slightly abstract unities in terms of which some regularities hold— whatever it is to be 'slightly abstract'.)

I mention all this only to say that considerations of this sort, involving complex relationships between 'one' and 'many', have influenced the account of objects (or perhaps I should say of objectification) presented in OO. One question that is of considerable interest, as I have already indicated, is how issues of concreteness and abstractness play out across these hierarchies. And as usual my answer is the predictable one: the most interesting cases, I believe, are somewhere in the middle.

If one is strict about laying out the hierarchies, moreover, intriguing patterns emerge. Even the simple case of a proper name, standardly described as 'one name, one object', involves two fans, as indicated in Fig. 5.1: one spreads out from the name qua type to its various utterances or uses; another fans back in from these different uses to a single person.

Similarly, the fan structure of the mentalese indexical described above is given in Fig. 5.2: one fan from type to tokens, individual fans from each token to its uses; and finally another set of fans back in from those uses to the holder of the token.

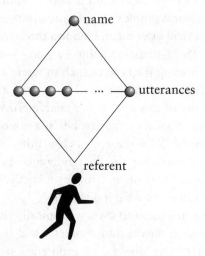

Fig. 5.1 Proper name

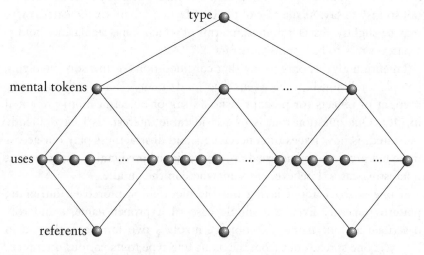

Fig. 5.2 The mentalest 'I'

With respect to the overarching project of naturalizing ontology, perhaps the most important observation is the following: *there are similar patterns of complex fan-ins and fan-outs underneath or 'within' the notion of an object* (as above objects, having to do with particulars and classes or types). Suppose we lay out any given concrete object in 4-space, as an extensive space-time worm. If I touch you, in a certain sense my hand will touch one part of you, say, your shoulder, at just one point in time. In saying that *I* have touched *you*, not just your shoulder, and not just now, I am saying that the touch, as it were, 'fans out' across space, to all of your body, and also across time, to make contact with you as an enduring individual. Suppose I touch you again, ten years from now, and for some reason ask 'Have I ever touched you before?' The positive answer that this question warrants can only be defended by noticing that the two spatial and temporal fan-outs end up being coincident, on one and the same enduring object envelope—an envelope, as I hope is obvious, that bears some resemblance to the result of the act of abstraction that we talked about earlier, in the case of the cup or the pen.

What I find intriguing is that so many cases, from the epistemic structures of reference to the ontological structures of individuals, involve various kinds of abstraction: 'gathering up' of a bunch of that which is in some ways different, and taking the result as a unity—as that which is one. Getting to the heart of this practice is an essential part of the story I want to tell. Moreover—and in a sense this is the heart of the metaphysical story—my ultimate claim is that there is no technical way to deal with the stunning complexities of these interrelated fans except by a single, integrated account that makes simultaneous reference to the aboriginal structure of the world and to the normatively governed intentional projects of the objectifying agent. One can only make sense of these structures, that is, via a 'blended' epistemological-cum-ontological account.

Finally, let me say a little about the subject Clark has brought up (in conversation): the role of indexicality and deixis in all this, and how that ties into issues of effectiveness (as you know, I have a claim that the intrinsic indexicality of reference stems from the fundamental character of physical law). Consider a single person's multiple utterances of the word 'now'. And assume, again for simplicity, that each utterance is used to refer to instantaneous moments, so that a sequence of utterances ('now! now! now!') would be used to refer to a corresponding sequence of (very short) passing moments.

What is evident in this case is that the referential pattern involves something I call 'point-to-point correspondence'. One concrete use refers to one concrete moment; another concrete use refers to another concrete moment; and so on. Moreover, the temporal sequences line up. As regards the link between deixis and physical effectiveness, the fundamental insight is very simple: *physical interactions have exactly the same point-to-point correspondence structure.* What takes place *now* affects what is happening *now*; what took place *then* affects what was happening *then*; what will take place *next time* will affect what is happening *next time*. In effect, this point-to-point correspondence (both spatial and temporal) is intrinsic to the structure of physical law.[35]

What happens when we *objectify* is that we gather a region or patch of the world into a unity. To do that requires extending these patterns of correspondence from simple point-to-point relationships, of the sort that underwrite physical regularity and simple indexicals, to much more intricate and hierarchical fan-ins and fan-outs. Feature placing, of the sort I described earlier, involves more complex forms of correspondence than simple point-to-point, but simpler than what is characteristic of the exemplification of properties and relations by full-fledged objects. To get to these more sophisticated cases, one needs to start getting involved with types, instances, and so forth, which involve complex, cross-cutting fans.

For example, suppose that last week I thought about Clark, and made a mental note to ask him, when I saw him this week, how his wife Pepa is doing. As indicated in Fig. 5.3, a complex set of fan-ins and fan-outs governs this successful ability to refer to Clark as an enduring unity. Both Clark and my mental token are temporally extensive, for starters. However, unlike the case of 'now! now! now!', and (similarly) unlike physical connection, the two temporal sequences don't line up, point by point. On the contrary, it is essential to the logic of the situation that when I thought about Clark, last week, at time t_1, I didn't think only about the temporal slice that was him-at-time-t_1–that is, about him *then*. Rather, I thought about *him*, which is to say, I thought about him as a temporally extended person (the whole lower space-time worm). By the same token,

---

[35] When a magnet attracts an iron filing, to return to that example, it is as if it is repeatedly calling out to the iron filing: 'You, come here, now!' 'You, come here, now!' forever. It is not at all incidental that this statement contains four paradigmatically indexical linguistic types: three indexical referring terms, plus the indexical present tense.

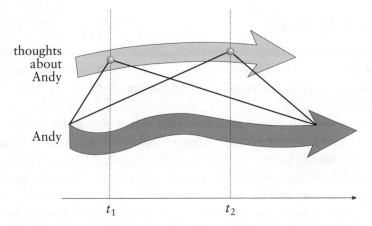

thoughts
about
Andy

Andy

t_1 t_2

Fig. 5.3 Reidentification

when I met him here at the workshop, at time t_2, the person that I greeted and talked to was again not the temporal slice him-at-time-t_2, but the same complete temporally extended individual. So my mentalese token fans out into individual uses; each of which fans out to cover the *whole singleton person*. In order for the reidentification to work, they must be coincident in that temporal extendedness.

Reidentification, in sum, requires this kind of cross-cutting gathering up and spreading out. This is in sharp distinction to the vastly simpler point-to-point correspondence that is true of all physical interaction, and that is true of at least limit-case indexicals.

Needless to say, this is just a whiff of a picture. What I am really doing, I suppose, is diagramming the field-theoretic structure of simple reference to concrete individuals. My point is only that if we are serious about our naturalism, something like field-theory[36] is all we have to start with. Somehow or other, we objectifying creatures are able to do a sophisticated enough dance to parlay our simple, effective, local, point-to-point field-theoretic coupling with our immediate physical surround into these complex patterns of cross-cutting fan-in and fan-out that characterize objective reference to the world. I don't claim to understand more than 1 per cent of how it goes. But it is something that I want to figure out.

Enough about objects. I have just one more general remark to make. *Discussion point 5.16*

---

[36] That is: the spatio-temporally continuous physical plenum that field-theory describes.

5.2.6 Evolution

Sixth and finally, let me say something about evolution. In brief: I don't want to accept evolution as a rock on which to build my church. But I will accept it as a flying buttress—as something that supports my church from the outside.

I agree with lots of things that Dennett says. For example, I think he is right to say that nothing but evolution could have gotten us here, could have done all this work. If evolutionary biology is right, which I presume it is, then sure enough, evolutionary adaptivity must be the means by which we learned to register the world. The causal history (of the emergence) of our registrational capacities, the causal history of our opening up into normativity, the causal history of how and why we take the world to be significant—all these causal histories undoubtedly unfolded along evolutionary paths, especially originally (for the last 10,000 years, social and cultural and political histories have presumably carried more of the developmental and explanatory weight).

Dennett is also right to suggest certain corrections of emphasis. Of course it is true that what we want to be intentionally directed toward is what *matters* to us, not what we used to be connected to. I certainly don't want to be sentimental about primordial or aboriginal union.[37] I also agree that processes of connection and disconnection, processes of registration of that to which one isn't (and maybe never was) connected, and so on and so forth—these constitute an Extremely Good Trick, which evolution discovered and exploited.

Finally, let me say that I am completely open to being instructed, as regards the details of evolutionary affairs. I am no expert, and look forward to knowing more. Moreover, I feel ready for the handshake. I believe that the constructive tenor of my account ('constructive' in an engineering sense), starting from very simple patches of the world and progressing up through mechanisms of simple non-effective tracking, to featural registration, to full-blown conceptual registration in terms of objects and properties, to a form of situated objectivity—this story of 'building up' registrational capacities seems to me very compatible with evolutionary history. And I look forward to understanding better how such capacities evolved.

---

[37] Though with this caveat: I do think that, even if it is riotously variegated throughout, the world's being 'one' is metaphysically prior to our 'carving it up' (to use the hackneyed phrase) into discrete objects, properties, etc. But this 'oneness' is a kind of existential 'being here with'; it is not a oneness of fusion or connection, of the sort that disconnection lacks.

If I agree with all these things, then why don't I talk about evolution?

The answer is essentially this: while I will admit that evolution is the means by which we learned to register, I don't believe that registering is itself an intrinsically evolutionary process. The explanation of *how we came to do it* may be evolutionary, that is, but the explanation of *what it is we do* is not.

To go back to Cummins' metaphor, I think of registration as a way of exploiting the 'keyhole' of what is effective, so as to end up being oriented toward what matters, including (largely) what is not effective—in order to be oriented to the world, to take the world as mattering. I see no reason to believe that this is an intrinsically evolutionary thing to do; that non-evolved creatures could not do the same thing. Moreover, I do not be-lieve—and I suspect this may be a point on which Dennett and I substan-tively disagree—that the fundamental normativity on which registration rests is intrinsically evolutionary, either. Again, *that we take the world to matter* may have evolved. But *that the world matters* is not by itself an evolutionary claim. If creatures were magically placed here, or emerged via a different means (say, on another galaxy), the world could matter to them—just as much. *Discussion point 5.17*

So that's the claim: that this intricate, sly, surreptitious strategy for exploiting what's effective in order to stand in relation to what's not effective is a Phenomenally Good Trick. It is a trick on which evolution stumbled, and made out like a bat out of hell. It is even clear why it is so evolutionarily useful. So there must be an evolutionary story about how it was discovered, what kinds of registration it evolved first, how it worked, what advantages it conveyed, what was tried and failed, and so on and so forth. In order to make good on the claim that it is an Evolutionary Good Trick, however, the character of the trick cannot itself be defined in evolu-tionary terms. In order of explanatory priority, registration must be under-stood antecedently to evolution, if we are to understand *how* it is a trick—a trick that the universe supports, that evolution could pick up and make out with. *Discussion point 5.18*

To make this concrete, let me talk a little more about norms, because I think norms are the place where the issues become most urgent.

In RR, as Dennett pointed out, I made a distinction between 'statical' and 'dynamical' norms.[38] Think about normative notions in formal

---

[38] 'Statical' isn't an ordinary word of English. But I call these norms *statical* and *dynamical*, as opposed to *static* and *dynamic*, in line with a general (if often unremarked) distinction

systems—the norms we apply to processes of inference in logic, for example, and analogs in such related fields as economics and game theory.[39] What we traditionally encounter are norms such as *truth preservation, inference to the best explanation, utility maximization,* and so on. What is interesting about these norms is that, while they apply to processes (and hence, in my terminology, are *dynamical*), they are defined in terms of explanatorily prior norms, such as truth, reference, explanation, utility and so on, that are defined on states (and hence are what I call *statical*).

My point in RR was that an extraordinarily important intellectual shift is taking place, across the intentional sciences: the explanatory order is changing. For a variety of reasons, ranging from evolutionary considerations, to the sheer difficulty of characterizing such age-old statical norms as truth and reference, to concrete experience building and maintaining and using computer systems, people have come to realize that the only way to define norms such as truth and reference in a useful and non-question-begging way is to base them on *how things are used.* In a sense, we are all becoming closet Wittgensteinians. It is not so much that statical norms are being discarded (truth, function, utility, etc.), as that they are being understood as derived from dynamical norms.

The reason why this shift in explanatory priority from statical to dynamical is so important is that it puts pressure on a source of dynamical normativity. If you are going to define your statical norms in terms of your dynamical norms, then you cannot define your dynamical ones in terms of

---

between '-ic' and '-ical' forms, in which the '-ic' form marks predicates that apply to phenomena that are *themselves* exemplars of the property in question, whereas the '-ical' form marks predicates that apply to phenomena that are *about* things that exemplify the property in question. Thus a 'historic' meeting is one that *itself makes history*; a 'historical meeting' is a meeting that is *about* history (no matter how insignificant the meeting itself should turn out to be).

Thus by a *dynamic* norm I mean a norm that itself changes, over time; whereas by a *dynamical* norm I mean a norm that applies to temporal things, such as processes. Similarly, a static norm is one that is fixed or unchanging; a statical norm is one that *applies to* (atemporal) states.

Two notes: (1) All entities to which the '-ical' adjective apply are by definition *semantic*; whereas only those semantic phenomena that are about semantics can legitimately be called 'semantical'. (2) There is only one adverbial form ('-ically')—historically, strategically, semantically, etc.—and so in adverbial position the distinction must be inferred from context.

[39] Some will argue that while inference may be a process, pure logic doesn't study inference, but only material implication—which is a (static) truth-theoretic relation, not an active 'step' in an inference process. But I don't agree that logic doesn't study inference. *Modus ponens*, natural deduction, etc., while characterizable at a level of abstraction that ignores time (as we often do, for example, when studying a proof as an abstract object), undeniably have their home in active processes of rational deliberation.

the statical ones, on pain of circularity. You need something else as a source of dynamical normativity. What is that going to be? Especially for a naturalist, this is a very urgent question: what naturalistically palatable source of dynamical normativity is available, on top of which to construct the entire normative edifice necessary for full-blooded intentional characterization?

This is the role that evolution is playing, I believe, in many of the intentional sciences. Evolutionary advantage is an extraordinarily convenient candidate on which to rest an intentional story. Ruth Millikan and the general project of teleosemantics can be seen as one example of this trend. And I take it that Dennett is proposing something similar, when he says all normativity rides on Darwin's coat-tails. He is basically asserting that evolutionary advantage is the 'mother of all norms', the ur-dynamical norm.

Unfortunately, I don't believe evolution is a strong enough base on which to rest all of human normativity. For think about how much the general issue of dynamical norms includes. Ethics, for starters; and even more generally, how to live. I cannot muster arguments here, but I simply don't see how one could milk evolutionary survival for this full range of normativity, for all that has inspired individuals and cultures, led people to distinguish good from bad, and so on and so forth, over the ages. Remember: I am not denying that human normativity may have *emerged* evolutionarily, at least at first (that is, to the extent that there was substantive normativity prior to the development of culture and civilization—something on which I have my doubts). All I am denying, to repeat my standard refrain, is the claim that normativity is an intrinsically evolutionary notion. *Discussion point 5.19*

So I have said that evolution is not strong enough to be a *basis* for all substantive norms. Clark and Dennett ask [Discussion point 5.19]: 'Is it strong enough to *give rise* to them?' The answer depends on what you mean by 'give rise to'.

If by 'give rise to' you mean *causally, historically,* how did these norms emerge? What engine could have done all this work to get us here? Isn't this the only mechanism through which normativity could have emerged? My answer to that question is 'yes'. *Evolution may have been the train on which norms arrived at our present station.* And as I said before, you can see why it would have arisen, evolutionarily: the ability to care, to register their world, to take things as significant, confers a huge evolutionary advantage.

But if by 'give rise to' you mean (as I do) something more metaphysical, something more explanatorily substantive—and something more like the word 'origin' in the title of my book—then my answer is 'no'. Even if it is an a posteriori necessity that, given basic material facts about the universe, about the origins of life, etc., evolution is the only means through which normativity could have arisen in registering creatures, nevertheless, it is not constitutively intrinsic to our normativity, I claim, that we have an evolutionary history. Remember: I want to be able to explain *what normativity and registration are*, such that we can say of evolution that it stumbled on them. But the fact that evolution stumbled on them merely makes evolution the implementing mechanism whereby we came to be normative.[40]

In detail, I should admit, there is undoubtedly tons to be learned from our evolutionary history—about what kinds of normativity there are, what kinds we have evolved to be attuned to, etc. And (perhaps even more so) there is tons to be learned about what our registrational capacities are, what constraints they have evolved to satisfy, and so on. All those things are interesting and useful. I just don't want to allow the interest and urgency of asking those questions to seduce us into what I think of as a kind of *nonreductive causal foundationalism*: wherein we confuse what things are with the causal history of how they came to be. ***Discussion point 5.20***

It may help, in understanding this, to think of registration first, and normativity second. Remember what I want to say about registration: that it is a mechanism whereby you arrange things so that you can track long distances, put together machinery and external signs and external scaffolding and so on and so forth, so as to stand in relationship to more and more and more—leading, ultimately (this is where consciousness and objectivity merge) to a profound and care-full orientation to the whole world. Do we need evolution to understand that? In a constitutive sense, I think not. In an historical sense, I think we do. It doesn't seem to me that evolution plays a constitutive story in understanding how the strategies of exploiting local effective structure can stand you in relationship toward that with which you are not physically coupled (though I admit: the hardest issue—the nub of the matter, as it were, and maybe for that reason an appropriate subject for drinks, later—is what 'being oriented to' really means, in all its respectful, concernful richness and depth). For now, let me

---

[40] This seems to me a distinction that philosophers, if anyone, should be happy with—reminiscent as it is of the warhorse distinction between syntax and semantics.

just say that I believe the same thing about the norm-side: that an evolutionary account may tell us how we got here, and may tell us in detail what the costs and trade-offs are, in regards to honouring norms, but it won't give us a constitutive account of the structure of normativity itself.

It is time to stop; but I hope that this makes it at least a little bit clearer why I want to accept evolution as the train, but not confuse it for the goods that were transported on that train; to accept it, as I said at the beginning, as a flying buttress, but not the rock on which our registration of the world is founded. *Final discussion*

Discussion

5.1 CUMMINS This is what anti-realists do on purpose.

p. 225 DENNETT Commit this inscription error?

CUMMINS Just, lots of them.

SMITH Here's a simple case, to see what's going on. Suppose you want to know if your cat recognizes you as an individual as opposed to as just more 'Hughness'. And suppose people say, 'Yeah, look, because here's its neurophysiology and *this cell* lights up every time—same cell, so it must be the same person.' But how do you *know* it's the same cell? Maybe it's just reinstantiating some type in there. How do we decide that's a second use of a single token, as opposed to new instantiation of a single type? See, when you say 'one cell, so one individual', you're making one assumption about object identity in the head of the cat, and then assuming that you can use that identity to warrant a claim about object identity in the content of the cat, in what the cat's identifying. But I can redescribe the situation in the brain, and then get the presumptively competing suggestion about the content. All you're really doing, in other words, is piggybacking your analysis of content identity off brain identity. We should worry if our analysis of whether the cat recognizes Hugh as a type or an object depends on empirically equivalent ways of us theorists individuating its brain, especially since the cat itself doesn't individuate its brain at all.

I think these things happen very subtly, even in modest cases. Earlier today we were talking about whether we objectify things on a map. And it depended on how we registered the map in the first place. Take a line: do we call that a *relationship* between two points, where the points are the objects? Or are the *lines* the objects and the points just relationships between two lines—where they cross? Problem is, in one case you end up saying we're objectifying the line, and the other case you don't. It's that kind of thing. How we as theorists register the problem domain affects our analyses in ways that are stunningly consequential.

CLARK So it's a worry about the baggage that comes along with the labels. Like all those worries people have about how you label the nodes of your semantic network.

DENNETT So, good. You can go way, way back to Drew McDermott's old paper 'Artificial Intelligence Meets Natural Stupidity' [1976], and that was a sort of ur-anxiety about inscription errors which Brian has generalized.

SMITH In a way, I think what I might say is: Look, inscription like this, it's something you have to do. It has enormous consequences; so you want to be tremendously modest and humble and cautious. It's not black and white; it's not as if you can say 'Here's an inscription error, here's not.' You always have to inscribe. The issue's just this: don't let the fact that you have to inscribe license you to project all sorts of ontological assumptions all over the subject matter without taking responsibility for them.

CLAPIN OK, so that's Rob's point. That's what anti-realists maybe are doing, is that they are allowing a license for them. They say, well we've got to do this anyway, so there are no constraints.

CUMMINS Yeah, other than internal coherence.

CLAPIN So the way you're describing color, Brian's kind of saying is true for... 5.2 p. 226

DENNETT Objects.

SMITH Everything. To think that taking human relativity seriously implies irrealism is only true on a Cartesian view that we're not part of the world. But if someone were to write a book called *Being There*, or something like that, and actually realize that we are here, then from that (correct!) point of view, human relativity shouldn't be metaphysically scary. It is profoundly consequential, but it's not skepticism or irrealism.

DENNETT I think it's like this. I think we can talk about the colors of things on distant galaxies by helping ourselves, and knowing we're doing that, to human color vision, and using that as our standard. And Brian's saying we can talk about primordial objects by using human object vision and recognizing that's what we're doing, as long as we keep track of the fact that we're using human object and property vision as our standard, as our perspective, we can sort of discount—sort of like discounting the illuminants. That's the idea, and I'm snowed by it, whether I should be or not. I sort of like it, so, we'll see.

HAUGELAND Is this also an example of the same point—I can't remember what I've thought about this in the past—that, before the human race evolved, the moon was 240 thousand miles away, even though there weren't any miles then?

CLAPIN In that kind of an example, is the thought to go sort of *de re*—because miles didn't exist, *de dicto* how many miles is just not a sensible way of talking?

HAUGELAND Well the trouble with that way of putting it is that it supposes that *de re* just is as it always was.

DENNETT But thank you for raising it, Hugh, because that helps with one of the reasons why I'm attracted to this: because it helps me fend off that awful *de re/de dicto* stuff.

SMITH Also, it will have more bite when one realizes that taking the world in terms of objects and properties is underestimating the world. That's when the approach really starts to fight back—not in a way that Rob will swallow, perhaps, but in a way that is at least akin to something Rob would swallow.

5.3
p. 227 HAUGELAND 'If everything were rigidly blocked in the universe, there were no flex and slop and slippage, nothing could be out of touch with anything else'—that seems to me to be completely wrong. What is rather the case is that there couldn't be a distinction between being in touch with and not being in touch with. You couldn't be in touch with anything else specifically if moving this moved everything.

SMITH Well I couldn't be some *thing*. I don't disagree. I think the very language we speak so presumes that there is a certain looseness in the world that our attempts to describe what it would be like if there weren't a certain looseness will all fail. But they don't fail completely. We can have this conversation which we're having, and it makes some sense. I actually think it's impressive that we can agree, 'Yeah, all these things fail, but, we actually do get a sense of what we mean.' We can actually reach a kind of consensus which, if we all said, 'OK, now we've got it; let's try to say it,' we wouldn't do any better than we just did.

CLARK So it's not essential for there being objects that the universe not be connected like that?

SMITH Yeah, it is, because in order for it to be an object it's got to have distance. And it's got to have *shear*.

HAUGELAND It's got to have distance and it's got to have an internal life that is different from what's around it.

CUMMINS This was Cartesian physics. Everything was locked together. It's just that minds were allowed to slop around a good deal—but the physics was all locked.

SMITH Well $\frac{1}{r^2}$ dissipations of forces are tricky. The problem with Cartesian physics is that it isn't theoretically precluded that you can tell everything from just how one little thing is vibrating.

DENNETT That's just what Newton saw. This is right. You're sort of recapitulating a Newtonian revolution here with your point about flex and slop.

SMITH One thing that might help explain it is that I don't think space-time points are *echt* individuals. Other than particularity, I actually think they lack all of the characteristics that individual objects actually have to have to be objects. Think about the field theoretic interpretation of classical physics which is actually doing some work in this story. Imagine a rubbery manifold with forces going up and down, and all that kind of stuff. You can imagine that if everything were just spatio-temporally infinite manifolds, there could be lots of space-time points as it were, but there would be no clumping of them together into reidentifiable individuals that have heft, size, or separateness, and so on. I think that field theory, this rubber manifold stuff, is probably the best imaginative route in. By particularity I just mean roughly spatio-temporally concrete occurrence.

5.4 p. 227

CLARK So it's like saying particularity is not objecthood. They're not objects, are they, space-time points?

CUMMINS Cartesian points don't move around, although they do have properties.

SMITH That's right. They don't move around, because they don't do anything—that's the problem with them.

DENNETT A nice way of thinking about it might be to think about the individual cells in Conway's life world—they are particular but not individuals. But a glider can be individual.[41]

---

[41] [Dennett gives a short description of Conway's Game of Life in 'Real Patterns' (1991*b*: 105–10). See also Poundstone (1985)—ed.]

SMITH I think if I were to write the book over again I might have said either 'occurrent' or 'concrete' instead of 'particular'.

HAUGELAND Well, I think what you want is concreteness. I'm not sure what you mean by occurrent, or do you just mean actual?

DENNETT Concreteness is not individuality.

SMITH Right; that is close to what I mean. Note, for example, that in the book I embrace a 'criterion of ultimate concreteness', so using 'concreteness' as a word would be relatively straightforward. I do believe that everything is concrete. But as a word, 'concrete' is misleading, too...

CLARK And what are space-time points here, they are...?

SMITH They are concrete, but not individuals. You wouldn't treat them as individuals.

CLARK That seems kind of funny if space-time points again come out as concrete. They seem like paradigm cases of something that's not...

HAUGELAND Well, look, what do you understand by concreteness? This is what I understand by concreteness. That in every respect in which it can have a feature, say, in some degree, that degree is fixed. Nothing is left free.

CLARK OK, so it's well-definedness or something.

HAUGELAND Well, no, it's more than that, it is in a way, the difference between kinds and particulars. It's a metaphysical thesis and I can't make up my mind whether it's analytic or not, that particulars are concrete. That is, you can have the picture of the man that doesn't indicate whether or not his fly is open, or whether or not he's got a bald spot on the back of his head, this is left open. A sentence likewise leaves things open. But the man is...everything is settled.

DENNETT That's what I find appealing.

SMITH Another thing that I want to say, which seems to me a simple point, but is hard to phrase using traditional terminology, is that objects—individuals, essentially—are *also abstractions*. And by being abstractions I mean that some of their concreteness has been...

CUMMINS Lost.

SMITH Well, in a way, but it's tricky. Consider a cup. On the one hand, the cup is fully concrete. Taking it *as* a cup, however—gathering and clumping this chunk or region of the concrete flux, and treating it as an individual unity—saying, 'Okay, this is a cup'—to do that is to ignore some of its concreteness.

DENNETT That's the price you pay.

HAUGELAND That's to say that the kind isn't concrete.

CLARK So this is just the price of my kind of data compression.

SMITH It's tricky. It's not just the *kind* that is abstract. I want to agree that the kind is abstract.[42] But the cup is not abstract in the way that the kind is abstract. In taking the particular cup to be a cup, to be an individual; that act of objectification is an act that ignores some of the concreteness.

HAUGELAND That is there in that vicinity.

SMITH Right, it's in that vicinity. Taking it as a cup ignores, it packages the thing together, takes this distributed part of the flux as a unity, a whole lot of things like that. Come at it epistemologically. It's really that *objectifying* is an act of abstraction. At least at first blush, it's not that the thing that's objectified is abstract, really, because it actually is as fully concrete as you think.

HAUGELAND Right, the definition of concreteness is that everything that could be determinate about it, is fully determinate.

CLARK I'm having trouble with the 'it' here.

DENNETT That's where we get the inscription error you can't get out of.

SMITH You are right that 'it' is the problem. You have to realize that there is more to the cup than figured in you're taking the cup as a cup.

HAUGELAND Well, that's really true.

SMITH Perhaps, for now, I should take that platitude that you, John, would agree with, about everything being determinate, and then just locate the individuality of the cup more in the act of taking it as an individual, and less in the concrete patch of the world there might be—

HAUGELAND Here's a motto I would think you would be sympathetic with (even though it isn't actually using the words quite the way you want to), which is to say that the achievement of objectification is achieving an 'it' such that concreteness makes sense. So, to be objective just is to be, and, I think, a thing, an object. Actually, not just a thing, an object. You have to get it into a space of possible determinacies such that for talking about 'this one', full concreteness makes sense.

SMITH Yep, but we still differ, for several reasons. One is that I want things to be concrete that aren't objects—

HAUGELAND That's cool.

CUMMINS That's all right.

---

[42] I myself may *not* ultimately want to say that kinds are purely abstract—but that is a separate issue. It would only confuse things to bring it in here—B.C.S.

SMITH But I want the determinacy—no I'm not sure it's cool with what you just said, is it?

CUMMINS Yeah, sure, that's OK.

HAUGELAND Yeah, I said objectification, is—the mark of success is—that you've gotten the sense of the possible determinacy in place such that it *can* be fully concrete. But that doesn't limit where else might be concrete.

5.5
p. 227

CUMMINS OK and then so from the point of view of the structure, the data structure you do create, a lot of futures don't count as cup futures. So you get this distinction between qualitative and substantial change just built into the finitude of your representation.

CLARK So here's what's getting balanced. In thinking about these things, you have to recognize them as objects. To recognize it as an object is precisely to think that it has all these features and that they are fixed. And on the other hand, what you really want to do is have a sense of what differences don't make a difference. So there can be all sorts of things that can change but you still ought to recognize it as the same object; the cup can get chipped, you still want it to be the cup. Hence even the Y2K thing, you might think that the problem here is that there's a difference that does make a difference that we never thought about.

SMITH It also has to do with *projects*. The commitments that underwrite identity arise in part from one's commitments. It follows that the identity of an object doesn't inhere in the object itself—that is a very important theorem of this view. So that 'being an object is not an intrinsic property' would be a way to say it.

DENNETT And that's why when the hyper-intelligent extra-terrestrials arrive and find that we're still stuck with objects and properties, this is the ultimate Y2K problem for us. Everything stops.

5.6
p. 228

DENNETT What holds constant when you turn the knobs—sort of tuning for the null, as we say, in radio direction finding.

CUMMINS Yeah, or my idea of which invariant you need to track in order to understand the variance in the error signals.

DENNETT Yeah, we're reaching convergence on this way of thinking of the idea.

SMITH This idea is massively more applicable than just in the case of objects.

CLAPIN The non-modularity of the mind as somebody said earlier in the   5.7
p. 230
   week.

DENNETT Well, the main thing is that Brian is saying, the overcoat is really thick, and that's where all the action is, or a great deal of the action is.

SMITH I don't want us to infer wrongly from the fact that we theorists   5.8
p. 234
   don't quite *know* what's going on, that there isn't something quite precise going on—even if what's going on is something that neither we nor anyone else can actually say. The lack of being able to say it doesn't mean that there isn't a fact of the matter.

DENNETT Let me go back to my ur-example of indeterminacy of content. In 'The Ability of Men and Machines' [1978b] I describe a case where the engineers find this device on the beach and they study it and they agree completely about its physical constitution, and every atom of its being. They agree on exactly what trajectories it will follow under all circumstances. They disagree about what it is, what it's for. And it's only when we get to their content level, where they treat certain things as malfunctions—one of them treats certain events as malfunctions, the other one has a different gloss and says those aren't malfunctions, that's signal not noise—and I claim that it is not the case that there must be a fact of the matter about which is the right content gloss on this object.

CUMMINS There's still a scope ambiguity, because the way you put it leaves out the possibility that there is a fact of the matter but they're both right. I get this all the time, because they say—'which isomorphism?' You know? All of them. They don't like that. Somehow something couldn't have two structures at once.

DENNETT Right, but of course you can have them.

CUMMINS And really, there's a real fact of the matter that they have all of them.

DENNETT But there isn't a real fact of the matter about which one is privileged.

CUMMINS That's right.

DENNETT And that's the one point that I've always wanted to insist on.

CUMMINS Privilege is always observer-relative as it were.

DENNETT Thank you.

CUMMINS Right, but it is a bad argument from the observer-relativity of privilege, and some premise that somehow builds in that it isn't there if it isn't unique to just rampant conventionality of all this. And you write sometimes in a way that suggests to me that you think that there's—

DENNETT I issue a tentative *mea culpa*. I think I probably do write as if, I think you may have me there—

CLAPIN But with the multiple isomorphisms in the same thing—usually the case is that only one of those structures is actually doing the effective work.

DENNETT That's perspectival too.

CUMMINS Yeah, that's perspectival too. There's any number. It's simple and clean to think of these couplings one at a time. But the fact of the matter is, this is just another one of these things. In Dan's case, you've got one engineer, as it were, coupled into one structure, and another engineer coupled into another structure. And since those two are different there's a temptation to infer that there's no fact of the matter of which structure is there. They're both there because after all, if they weren't, the two engineers couldn't be coupled to them.

DENNETT I have a Quinian crossword puzzle. It's very simple as a crossword puzzle, but there's two solutions to it. I hand it out to my students and I say this is a simple little crossword puzzle, see if you can solve it. And they come up with the two solutions.

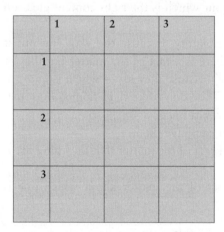

Across
1. Suck the resources out of
2. Epoch
3. Sleep furniture

Down
1. Retentive membrane
2. Earlier
3. For some kids, a best friend

Fig. 5.4 Dennett's Quinian crossword puzzle

CLARK If someone found a third solution, what do you say about that?

DENNETT That's fine, too.

CUMMINS They're all fine.

SMITH Let me just say a bit about these two isomorphisms—two structures in one thing, right? I think what I would want to say is, there is one thing, of which two abstractions hold.

DENNETT Yeah, that's fine.

SMITH But it's not exactly as if there's indeterminacy in the concrete.

DENNETT No, of course not. We agree.

CUMMINS I think there's a metaphor that may be misleading you here, Brian. You tend to think of structures like shape. You say 'Well out in the world there's the cookie, and I've got a whole drawerful of cookie cutters,' right? And, in some sense, if all the cookie cutters are different shapes, then it just seems to follow that they couldn't all fit the cookie. But that's just because you've got a very limited notion of structure.

SMITH No, look, that's not the point. I have no trouble thinking that seventeen different cookie cutters could fit the cookie. All equally well. What's indeterminate in that case is which type this token is an instance of.

CUMMINS Why isn't it an instance of all of them?

SMITH It is an instance of all of them. That's fine. What I'm saying is that one question one might ask is, 'Look, I'm not sure which of these cutters applies,' and the answer is 'All of them.' That's the question you're talking about; it has to do with the cutters. That's not what I am talking about. What I'm saying is determinate is the *cookie*, not the cutters.

CUMMINS But you don't want to understand the determinacy of the cookie as somehow a matter of how many cutters fit.

SMITH You absolutely don't. I agree with that. So I want to say, 'That's right: in the actual concrete thing there's no indeterminacy.'

CUMMINS Why isn't the determinacy just the determinacy of fit? It determinately fits this cutter, it determinately fits that cutter, and it determinately fits that other cutter, and that's all there is to it. You exhaust those facts you're just done.

DENNETT Let me read the passage I stubbed my toe on, all right? On page 68 of OO, Brian says. 'Somehow or other—and this I take to be the most important and difficult task facing the cognitive sciences—*it must be possible to have determinate representational content, i.e., for there to be a fact of the matter as to how the world is represented.*' Brian goes on to say, 'it will have to be an answer that does not depend on how anyone registers or individuates those mechanisms—again, for the simple reason that it happens in people, for example, without anyone doing that.' Right. It doesn't depend on how any observer registers or individuates the mechanisms, but there may still be many different ways of interpreting those mechanisms. And no one of those ways is privileged.

CUMMINS And, moreover, all of them might be either a little or a lot wrong.

SMITH Sure, but the point is, if I'm looking at the rug, registering the rug, and you're a theorist and you're looking at my mechanisms, you've got all kinds of ways of doing it. That's fine. But no amount of slippage or indeterminacy or multiple categorization or simultaneous truth or anything in your interpretation of my content has any consequence as to how I take the rug.

CLARK It doesn't follow from that that you take the rug just one way though, does it? The fact that how you take it isn't determined by how someone, as it were, takes you to be taking it, doesn't imply that you take it just one way.

DENNETT This really is Brian's problem of the indeterminacy of radical translation.

SMITH It may be that the way I take the rug is in fact to take it simultaneously as instantiating three different types or something. I'm not saying that I can't multiply categorize the rug. It's not the plurality there that is worrying me. Nor, given my love of smeariness, do I have any problem with saying that I take it to be an indeterminate category.

CLARK But you do think that there is something about your state that absolutely fixes, as it were, whether it's a plurality of three or four or—

SMITH Think about this fact: that while there may be questions about, as it were, the classification of the cookie, it doesn't make sense that the cookie is indeterminate. I guess what I'm saying is that when I take the rug to be a certain way, there's a concrete situation here and a concrete situation there and a concrete relationship, about which there are then questions of how to categorize. And something that's going on here is that I may be categorizing the rug in some way, or not, or something like that.

CLAPIN Don't you have to *be*, to be taken as an object?

SMITH That's right, but there are lots of ways to have a take on it, but not take it as an object. I guess I'm saying that this situation here that is happening is itself fully concrete.

DENNETT Of course it is. But now look—

HAUGELAND Fully concrete under some descriptions.

SMITH No, no, that's where we go back about an hour.

DENNETT It's fully concrete.

SMITH Concreteness is not a property of characterizations of things.

HAUGELAND I'm not sure that you can just say that.

SMITH Well, I certainly can't just say it in a peremptory sense!

HAUGELAND But the thesis of the indeterminacy of translation, carefully named, is that there are some characterizations of things which cannot be fully determinate. There are just systematically different ways to characterize them which are all equal, there's no choosing among them except sort of randomly or on convenience or something.

DENNETT They all tie for first.

HAUGELAND They all tie for first. And there isn't a right answer, there just isn't a right answer.

SMITH The problem is that I object to something in that thesis.

DENNETT I think you do too. That's where there's a problem.

CUMMINS Now I don't think you need to object to that. I think you can allow that—and still hold on to your concreteness.

CLAPIN I thought concreteness was open to all possibilities—you know, it's kind of, before it's been conceptualized, before it's been categorized, so it's open to all of those categorizations, all of those interpretations. There's a sense in which the concrete things are precisely indeterminate, that all categorizations tie for first because concreteness is before categorization.

SMITH That's right, that concreteness comes before categorization. That's why it is a metaphysical *position*, not an *argument*. That the world, as it were, comes completely concrete. Subsequent to that, there are issues of categorizing.

CUMMINS Yeah, sure. I think I'm with you on this, because I think that when, as it were, the world gets targeted, when it becomes the case that the thing that is the target is fully concrete, nothing in the structure of my intenders will allow me to read off all that concreteness or anything. The intender is a pretty sloppy instrument, but fortunately, in this case, the world is there to saturate, to fill in all the holes in the cheese, in a way. And of course equally my representations will just sort of skim the surface in various kinds of ways. But the—whatever it is—

SMITH The stuff.

CUMMINS Yeah—it is fully concrete. I don't have any problem with that. But I think you [Smith] ought to have a problem with that.

CLARK It seems like what you're appealing to is just the fact that there's something absolutely determinate going on. But of course there is. It's like, OK, so something absolutely determinate is going on when the thing crosses the electric eye, and that event triggers something else. But that doesn't make it, as it were, determinate whether or not the electric eye is taking it as a bee-bee rather than a fly, or whatever.

SMITH I appreciate that. I appreciate that if I'm looking at the rug, there's something absolutely determinate about the rug. And there's something absolutely determinate about my state. And there's something absolutely determinate about the relation I bear to the state I am in. So there's something absolutely determinate going on around here (in the vicinity of my head). And the question is, one of the things that's going on over here is a taking, right?

DENNETT Not one. That's the point.

SMITH OK, there's some taking going on around here. (In the end, of course, what one has to say is that part of what is absolutely determinately going on around here can be taken as a taking—or taken as *some* taking.) The question, though, with respect to that absolutely determinate taking, is whether it has an absolutely determinate content?

DENNETT Yes, that's the question.

CLARK OK, so 'taking' there is irrespective of content. I'm having trouble keeping them apart.

DENNETT Here's the question as I understand it. There's Brian looking at the rug, and three neuroprousts are scoping out the situation. As neuroprousts, they know everything about what's going on in his brain and about the light impinging and so forth. So they agree on the absolute determinate situation *vis-à-vis* Brian and the rug, right down to the finest details. So that's the absolutely determinate thing, and they all go to write their neuroproustian accounts of Brian's taking. And they come out different because it's like my Quinian crossword puzzle. It just turns out—extraordinarily implausibly, but you want to make this just an actuarial point. That they come out with three different contents for Brian's taking, and now the question is whether one of those is privileged.

SMITH OK, so, go on, suppose they come out with three.

DENNETT Now, there is this Cartesian intuition—it has been Quine's job and my job and a number of other people's jobs to beat it up at every opportunity—which is the museum myth of meanings, which insists that at least two of those neuroprousts are wrong, and you, from the inside, know what the truth is. And that is the fundamental intuition that Quine is setting out to destroy, and I think he's right.

SMITH Right, but notice something. My claim that there is an absolutely determinate content—that *my* content is absolutely determinate—doesn't imply that there is any way to settle the question of which of these three others is right. It doesn't imply that there is any way, in this world, to grant one of them priority.

HAUGELAND Does it imply that at most one of them is right?

SMITH No. Nor does it imply that the subject of the taking *knows*, as it were, what is and what isn't right. The reason it implies none of those solutions is because all of these things that the neuroprousts are doing, and what the—what does Descartes call it?—infallible introspection is presumed to do, the transparency of the . . .

HAUGELAND The natural light.

DENNETT The light of reason, yes.

SMITH All of those things are more *registrations* of the taking. They are registrations of my original registration.[43] Both the neuroproust's registration of my original registration, and my own meta-registrations of my original registration will approximate and categorize and lose detail and so on and so forth. That is part of my picture: that absolutely every story massively misses what it registers. So part of what I'm saying is that this picture of registration and the location of ontology is in fact a kind of negotiation between the epistemic act and that to which it's directed. Such a picture makes room for all the Quinian kinds of points, and the sorts of points you're making. Just as you, Rob, were saying a moment ago, it is because our ways of getting at the world are approximate and sloppy; there are all kinds of room for error. But the picture also preserves, I think, a durable intuition, which I think is right: not only are there absolutely determinate phenomena, but also that there may be absolutely determinate *content*, even if that content doesn't totally tie down the part of the world it registers.[44] Note that the fact that the content is absolutely determinate in my story doesn't mean that content captures all of what's absolutely determinate

[43] It's not that I disagree that there is a fundamental, even inexorable, indeterminateness in all these situations. Where I disagree is on the locus of that indeterminateness. According to Dennett, it is indeterminateness in the original registration. What I'm saying is that the indeterminateness is in the (second-order) registration of the first registration's content—B.C.S.

[44] Maybe one way to put it is that, in the indeterminacy of translation, the word 'translation' is really important. Translation always involves a second layer of registration—B.C.S.

about the rug—as usual, it massively misses; that's why this is a story of
loss, as I keep saying in the book. My only point, here, is that I think
that in all of the cases that you are bringing up to show that my
position is wrong, there is an extra layer of reference or registration
or description, between what I am claiming is determinate and what you
are claiming is not determinate. And I'm saying that in one sense you are
right, but that that is why—

DENNETT All right, I see where that's going. As long as you clarify all
these things that don't follow from your position.

CUMMINS Can I just ask one really quick question? Inscription isn't
always error?

SMITH No—or rather: yes, you're right. I actually meant to say that.

CUMMINS So it's open for Dan to say, OK, when I tell my evolutionary
story I'm inscribing like mad, but I'm getting it right.

SMITH In a way I'm trying to be really clear about this in the irreduction
chapter. I say look, what I require is not that you don't inscribe. What I
want you to do is to *take responsibility* for the fact that you are
inscribing (as, of course, you must).

CUMMINS Well if inscriptions are errors there must be some mismatch
between them and something.

DENNETT They must miss their targets.

SMITH It's a better or worse kind of story.

HAUGELAND Dan, why didn't you reply to Brian just now, when he made
the response to you, that he's pointing out that any registration of any
phenomenon is bound to fall short of the full determinacy of the
phenomenon—and so there's obviously various ways in which different registrations can fall short—that the issue isn't the certainly un-
deniable fact that any registration must fall short, but rather that, in
some cases, any registration which is sufficient to capture a certain kind
of richness in what's there, must inevitably overcapture it, and so
there's more than one way to do that? And there's no choice between
those.

DENNETT I like that because it nicely conveys a point which people have
been making in different ways, and that is, there's a real benefit in
carving the world one way or another. The cost is—it's presumptive,
and you always get some leverage that won't work as it will turn out,
that goes beyond what you've been given.

CUMMINS There's no free lunch. Getting A right inevitably means you
compromise B.

SMITH By saying 'overcapture' do we mean not only that it doesn't, as it were, represent things that are the case, but does represent things that aren't the case?

HAUGELAND No, it will render some things in a determinate way. It cannot but render them in a determinate way, to capture as much as it does capture, when there would be other ways of rendering it in a determinate way, distinct determinate ways, which are equally good— I mean, indeed capture exactly the same part of what they capture from the original structure.

SMITH But anyway my answer to that is going to be the same: from the fact that no registration is preferable, maybe even in principle (which is sort of being assumed here) the indeterminacy of the thing registered doesn't follow for me.

CLARK But nor does its determinacy. Isn't that kind of the point?

SMITH No, that is right. That is why the stuff about determinacy is only on page 52, instead of page 252. It is because it is a metaphysical kind of determinacy, not a—

CLARK But what makes you think that's a determinacy of content? The fact that there's more to the content than any story will capture doesn't imply that the content's determinate.

SMITH No it certainly doesn't imply that. However, neither does it imply the falsehood. The fact that there's more to something than a story will capture doesn't imply that the story's content is either determinate or indeterminate.

CLARK No, that's right.

CUMMINS When you're taking scientific laws here, you're thinking of 5.9 dynamical laws? You're not thinking of laws that, for example, just p. 242 tell me what's in the kit? I mean, I think it's a scientific law that there are electrons.

SMITH Right.

CUMMINS Rather than tell me what's going to happen next, or anything like that. It's not dynamical. It doesn't—

SMITH Right. I'm saying that it's not obvious to me that physics is committed to there being electrons as opposed to the (weaker) claim that the electron feature is spatio-temporally instantiated in various ways. That, whether it's one electron or seventeen, and so on and so forth— physics doesn't care: it makes no commitment to reidentifiable individuals.

CUMMINS Well, in my view of things, a lot of science is about mechanisms and how things are built and put together out of stuff, and—it all sounds less plausible as a story about those things than it does—

SMITH It may be less plausible about engineering—

CUMMINS As a story about dynamical physics.

5.10   CUMMINS And you mean this in some very strong sense, I mean Dan
p. 243   believes this too, because if the laws of physics were arbitrarily different then nothing would ever replicate and so, as it were—

SMITH Right. I mean it very strongly.

5.11   CLARK You don't think of them as inscription errors, field theories?
p. 243   SMITH Like all registration, they are somewhat pre-emptive. But since they don't register in terms of objects, they give us a leg up on what it is for subjects to register the world in terms of objects.

5.12   CUMMINS I want to make sure I understand the project. The image I get is
p. 246   sort of, OK, because, for example the way we're built, there's going to be this sort of keyhole effect, that you can't, your actual coupling with the world is pretty limited. So the question is, how can you see so much through such a little hole?

SMITH That's right.

5.13   HAUGELAND Unlike homing in on a magnet if you're an iron filing?
p. 248   SMITH Yes, exactly: unlike homing in on a magnet. There (if you are made of iron) you can be driven by the magnetic field. The problem is, it is hard for me to be driven *directly* by most of the things I care about— such as by Andy's philosophical views.

DENNETT So, in the past I've talked about making something that can detect whether something has once been on my desk. It's extraordinarily hard, unless, of course, my desk was made of uranium or something and it imparted some Geiger-countable property—then, you could use that as a proxy. But in fact we are able to detect all sorts of properties for which there are no natural cheat proxies. How the hell do we do it? We have this elaborate technology for tracking things so that we can, with really very little effort, register, think about, all these weird properties.

CLARK There does seem to be a sense in which it's our practices of timing things that brings 4 o'clock into being. It's not exactly as if it's sort of out there and we just have trouble tracking it.

DENNETT You're not accusing him [Smith] of making an inscription error are you!?

SMITH Andy, you are right; o'clock properties are pure human constructs. You might think that they are so stunningly non-effective in part because they were created, but that can't be quite right. What really matters about the o'clock properties, for the point of the example, is not that they are *constructed*, but that they are *purely formal*, in a certain (not so simple) sense.

CLAPIN So it's kind of like adding to physics. Physics has numbers, has maths, it's just adding a bit of sort of logic and what we now think of as implementation theories as a bit of extra formal apparatus for physics—there's a bit more maths. 5.14 p. 251

DENNETT It's a different maths.

CLAPIN It's a slightly different maths that's being used.

SMITH Yep, it is new math. But what is important about (so-called) computability theory is not the math *per se*, but that it *makes new claims*—claims that get at concrete regularities that seem to hold, in the world, that involve issues of stabilization and digitization and so forth, claims that seem to be *level*-independent, that appear to hold across different substrates and at different scales.

CLAPIN Like numbers do. Like cardinality does.

SMITH Well I'm a little reluctant to cosy up too close to the numbers, because many people think that they are a genuinely abstract phenomenon, whereas what I am talking about here are concrete phenomena, at different levels of abstraction.

DENNETT So it's sort of dependencies that are scale-independent and substrate-independent.

SMITH Right! Or rather, originally it was exactly that—genuinely independent. Increasingly, though, it is morphing into a theory of dependencies understood in relationship to (arbitrary) scale, in relation to different kinds of substrate.

HAUGELAND Well, substrate-independent and scale-independent don't mean substrate-less and scale-less; rather that you can have different and in some sense perhaps arbitrarily different scales and substrates and see the same phenomenon.

SMITH Right. Exactly. All I am saying is that I think the theory of how they relate to different substrates may actually end up being part of the new theory, the direction the theory is taking.

DENNETT Oh, well, certain features, like resistance to decay independently of the process you're considering, or constancies...

SMITH And compensations for stability, you know, and for tunneling, cosmic rays, things like that—what kind of circuits will be stable in a nanometer scale, what kinds of stability will in fact hold over periods of weeks, years, etc.

DENNETT Insulation properties, in fact.

HAUGELAND Well, you can't make a Turing machine tape with frogs either.

SMITH Right! There was a person, I remember, when [Digital Equipment Corporation's] DEC 20 was made, whose responsibility it was to track the radius of curvature of the lines etched into silicon, because the bits tended to fly off the tracks, if they went around sharp corners too fast—like errant Ferraris. The pulses would just radiate, you know; not make it around the corner. I don't know exactly how medium-independent or non-independent that is.

HAUGELAND Well, medium-independence never meant that you could do it in any medium whatever. It never meant that the medium is irrelevant. It just meant that you could have the very same thing in quite different media.

CLAPIN Two media would be enough.

HAUGELAND No, the thing has to be sort of open-ended.

SMITH Suppose I say, 'Look—this table leg is medium-independent because I can take away the wood and put in aluminum...'

DENNETT Try putting in water.

SMITH Right, you can't make a leg out of water.

HAUGELAND You can't make your computer out of water, either.

SMITH Right. It is all a little gray. Absolute medium-independence won't work, as if it didn't make any difference what you build it out of. We all agree with that. And pure medium-*de*pendence doesn't work either, as if it had to be that of this specific set of electrical components, or that specific piece of protein. What we need is an appropriate 'middling' level of dependence and independence.

This gets to a point you've made, John, about the importance of engineering. I think our engineering practices have very refined intuitions about what kinds of properties materials need to have, in order for what we are building to work. Anything that has those properties will serve.[45]

---

[45] The problem I have with the theory of computability, as so far developed, is that it relies on those properties, it applies to things that exemplify those properties, but it doesn't say what those properties are. Ultimately, I think that is something we are going to have to explain. They

If you want to calculate π, then a wide variety of materials will work. If you want something that will run at gigahertz, the range is smaller. If you want something to hold up a table, the range is (perhaps) more constrained yet. My prediction is that this whole terrain will eventually be mapped. And as it is mapped—this is really my claim—the maps will tie together physics as we know it today, which is ultimately concrete, and the (alleged) 'theory of computability' as we know it today, which looks very abstract.

CLAPIN Why isn't that logic? Why isn't that properly logic?

SMITH Because they are merely constraints on physics.

5.15
p. 252

CLAPIN But one way to think of logic is precisely as a description of how to just set up the physics the right way. This was the insight of computation: to turn syntax into something physical. So it seems to me that there is this match between logic and physics and the kind of representational redescription you're talking about, when you use a new representational code—

SMITH What matters about logic is that there are physically-realizable syntactic configurations *that you can interpret*, in such a way that the effective transitions end up being *semantics-preserving*. It was that *honoring of the semantic* that I take to be the fundamental insight of logic. What happened, historically, I believe, is that computer science borrowed all the theoretic apparatus of logic—including terminology that had been developed in order to talk about semantics-honoring transitions, but then, in a deep way, *forgot about the issue of honoring semantics*. They took vocabulary that comes from a tradition that was interested in things like *proof*. But they used that vocabulary to study issues that are really about pure (uninterpreted) mechanism. For example, think of what is called 'denotational semantics' in computer science. Obviously, the word 'semantics' occurs in that label; you might think it would have to do with meaning. But what I believe this phrase really refers to, in computer science, is the relationship, given some machine, between effective arrangements that can be given to that machine as an input (called the 'program'), and *a mathematical model of the behavior that results*, when the machine is started up on that input. That's not semantics! Note, in particular, that you can

aren't going to be simple physical properties, like having a certain mass, or stiffness, or charge; those are too concrete. So they have to be framed more abstractly. But not totally abstractly (as they are today)—B.C.S.

construct such a mathematical model for any piece of machinery whatsoever. I can construct a denotational semantics of a can-opener, for example, or for arbitrary mechanisms built out of Meccano.

DENNETT So it's logic gates...

SMITH Yes, except the 'logic' part is gone! See, I think the theory of effective computability has a wonderful first name. It is a theory of the *effective. C'est tout!* It is the second part of the name that is problematic: the *computing* stuff, which I think *has* to do with issues of interpretation. Real world computing, I firmly believe, is drenched in genuinely semantic issues. But the theory of computability, the body of work we teach in computer science departments, fails to deal with these semantic issues—issues that actually constitute the practice.

HAUGELAND You say that in the history of computer science and the portion that has to do with the 'computability issues' and so on, took over the apparatus that went with the problem of the formalization of logic and issues of proof and so on. But in fact that wasn't really part of their topic, right?

CLAPIN Part of whose topic?

HAUGELAND The computer scientists'. That, actually, semantic issues weren't the real issues that were being solved with the computability theory. You're not dismayed by the fact that the semantics fell away. If you're dismayed by something it's that they didn't realize that the semantics fell away and kept using the words.

SMITH That's right. Because it's hellishly hard to tell them that semantics matters, when they are already using the word for something else! This all gets back to the points made in the 100 billion lines of $C++$ paper. What computer science uses the word 'semantics' for is the relationship between a static program and the dynamic process it engenders.[46]

HAUGELAND As in Scott semantics?

SMITH Yes, as in denotational semantics, more generally, of which Scott semantics is a type.[47] In fact denotational semantics and operational

---

[46] This explains the work of Girard (1987), a brilliant (if idiosyncratic) fellow in France, who has written about logic as 'the geometry of interaction'. It's astounding! At first I was appalled; everything that mattered to me about logic falls away, in his account. But then I realized, just as you say, that the right way to understand his work was *not* as a bad theory of logic, but as a *good* theory of something else. What was unfortunate was that everyone was using the name 'logic' for it—that was what was distracting me—B.C.S.

[47] [For a general introduction to Scott semantics, see Winskell (1993)—ed.]

semantics are two characterizations of the same relation (one abstract, one more concrete—the relation between a program and the behavior it engenders.

DENNETT This is Allan Newell and what I call my Julie Christie problem.[48]

SMITH Yes, absolutely. So you've got to find a use for it, and all this apparatus and stuff. Why are they interested in Martin-Löf [1984] and the intuitionists and so on and so forth? The fact is computer scientists aren't radical hyper-intuitionists like Yessenin-Volpin [1970]. All that's going on is that they are studying an *intrinsically effective subject matter.* The relation between a program and the behavior it produces *must* be effective. Of course, if you want to study *that* relationship, and use mathematics to do so, you will be interested in mathematics that concentrates on what is effective. With just a bit of detachment, in other words, and a bit of historical perspective, you can understand why the mathematics went in the direction it did.[49]

CUMMINS A footnote about pointers. Pointers are, in a way, the kind of parade case of embedded intenders, or nested intenders. Because the example you had, in a sense, the low-level intender got fooled because, as it were, the world switched targets on it. The problem was that there's a higher level intender in which it was nested to get something else.

SMITH It's more complicated than that because it was a copy of the pointer that got fooled.

CUMMINS Oh yeah, it is more complicated, but do you see what I mean about the nesting?

SMITH That's right. The interaction between that and the object identity... and I'm just saying we're assuming object identity. It blows fuses in your brain. It's amazing stuff.

5.16
p. 259

---

[48] [In a couple of places Dennett takes Newell to task over his understanding of 'semantics', using as an example Dennett's ability to refer to the actress Julie Christie despite having no contact with her. See Dennett (1986; 1993)—ed.]

[49] As so often happens, the real clue to what is going on is in the details. For example: if you look to sub-log mathematical complexity results (algorithms that run in sub-log time, or complexity bounds specified to sub-log precision), you have to use *unary* numerals, as opposed to binary ones. Why? Because suddenly the difference in complexity between the number and the numeral that denotes it, if there is one, enters the complexity class, and wipes out your results. This is a smoking gun: it shows that what really matters is the complexity of the *numeral*, the *mark*. The number is just being used as a theoretical model of the mark, to allow the resulting theory to be framed in mathematical terms—B.C.S.

5.17   HAUGELAND The world, or taking the world as mattering, is ultimately
p. 261   what matters?

        SMITH The former: the world is what matters.

        HAUGELAND Either could be an intelligible claim.

        SMITH That's right, but I think the latter is derivative from the former. It is
        the world as a whole that matters. *Understanding* that the world
        matters—taking the world to matter—that stance matters, too. But it
        is a subsidiary normative condition, a condition on what it is to be
        human (or perhaps 'humane'). So taking the world to matter is what
        ultimately matters about *you*. That's the sort of humility built into this
        Brentano-esque form of being oriented. The thing that matters most
        about you is that you recognize that the world matters more than you do.

5.18   CUMMINS One of the disputes between myself and Millikan on functions
p. 261   all along has been that I wanted to say she can't understand how
        evolution works unless she can first identify the functions, and she
        thinks it's the other way around. I think this is a similar kind of thing.

        SMITH Right; I think it's a similar point.

5.19   CLARK Strong enough to be the norms, or to give rise to them?
p. 263   DENNETT Give rise to them, yes.

        SMITH Actually I am just about to talk about that.

5.20   CLARK But in between is the question, what makes sense of them—what
p. 264   makes sense of the norms. And there you really want to say that evolu-
        tion doesn't make sense of the norms. On the other hand it's part of what
        it takes to make sense of them.

        HAUGELAND 'Make sense of them' means 'that in terms of which we can
        understand them'?

        CLARK Yeah. It's part of that in terms of which we can understand them.

Final   CUMMINS I'm with Dan on this, in that I think that just like species, what
discussion   evolution stumbled on, the 'it' that it stumbled on is something that is
p. 265   constituted by the fact that it's the endpoint of that branch on the tree,
        and nothing else. And so you said we want to understand registration
        such that we can figure out why it was a good thing to stumble on, and I
        think actually that's a really kind of misleading way to put it. Evolution
        didn't stumble on registration. It built it out of smaller things, and there
        wasn't any such thing until it got it, because to be a registration is just

to be the endpoint of that branch, developmental branch. I don't really believe this, but I've got to the point where I know how to say it in a way that sounds so plausible that I have a hard time resisting it.

HAUGELAND I'm with Brian.

DENNETT When you described this wonderful growth of registration and all those wonderful things, you presupposed a 'we' that wanted to do this. The we for whom this was the obvious product. And one wants to know, OK, help yourself, there's an agent. There's an agent with goals, there's an agent with purposes, there's an agent that is trying to find out more about the world. Where'd that come from? Now—

SMITH No, look. Let me try to explain. You may be right that I often speak as if I were presupposing the existence of an agent, but you're misinterpreting me. And, remember, I do think that evolution is what did the work—I wish that I had that statement chiseled right here on this table, so that you're not tempted to think that I don't believe it. But given that, here is what I want to say. Suppose your 12-year-old grandchild and I are flying along in our spacecraft, and we notice a planet, which has plants on it. I say, 'Wow! Evolution is happening, all over again!' He says, 'Hey, can we speed it up?' I say, 'Yes, you know, there is something—a Really Neat Trick—that evolution on this planet doesn't seem to have been stumbled on yet. This trick involves organisms playing games with their internal structure so that they can track stuff that they are not physically coupled to. It might take another 100 million years for that to happen. Why don't we just drop down and do a little genetic engineering, give evolution a shove?'

In principle, this is something that could be done. Registration is a way of being that works. I don't think it is just the endpoint of some evolutionary branch. The world is such that registration is a way of being that is powerful. And it would be powerful, whether evolution found it or not.

DENNETT What's fascinating to me about that is that now you're playing the card which I intend to play, usually, and get hammered on by people like Dick Lewontin who says don't, don't, don't think of evolution as these problems that are posed and then are solved by evolution—these sort of Platonic problems that are solved. And I'm very happy to be this sort of minimal Platonist. You know, there really are these problems independent of history that are posed, or could be posed. We can conceive of them being posed again and again and again across the cosmos, and solve them in the same way. That's what a Good Trick is.

And I think that's fine and I think that's quite consistent with evolutionary theory. It is of course an idealization. There's danger of inscription errors. But it's a deep way to think about evolution. And when people like Gould and Lewontin chastise themselves and their fellow theorists for doing it, it is at the cost—and this is sometimes glaring and even to the point of being comic—that they can't even talk about convergent evolution. That's why convergent evolution is a sort of non-topic for Gould—it's bizarre—and for Lewontin. The reason it's a non-topic for them is because they can't let themselves talk about the same solution to the same problem they reinvented. But I think it's a deep part of evolutionary theory to be able to separate—just as you say, to separate the discovery from the process.

CLARK But I think that one thing that you don't want to do—and this kind of fits in with something Joan [Wellman] was saying last night—is to get forced into a discussion about where normativity comes from when all that really matters, for most of John's projects, is what it's like when it gets there. Yet understanding where you are actually isn't, I suggest, independent of understanding how you got there. When you want to understand where you are, you want to understand where you're likely to go. And the kind of processes that got us there are still, one way or another, operative.

SMITH Remember, I didn't banish Dan to the other side of the town; I took him as a flying buttress; that's right. There's something extremely important about understanding how we got here.

WELLMAN Brian, that's the second thing you said in your list of three last night to me. You said it matters—the way that something is implemented matters to the way it can be.

SMITH Yes, I think that's right. I'm all in favor of understanding history and implementation. At the risk of agreeing with you all so much that I sound wimpy, there is even a reading of 'rides on the coat-tails' that I can agree with: that evolution is the train it took—a train made of coat-tails. Our normativity, our registrational prowess; they all came via that route.[50]

One way to understand this is in terms of the design space. That's one thing that being a computer scientist teaches you: to be interested in the entire space, the whole fitness landscape, not just in the structure

---

[50] Again, especially *initially*. With respect to objectivity, for example, which is a very serious and advanced form of registration, I suspect that it took society and culture and socio-technical practices; we presumably don't want to extend the reach of evolutionary metaphors so broadly as to sweep all these things under an evolutionary rug—B.C.S.

of a particular solution. Maybe on the other side of some great canyon in the fitness landscape there lies an enormously powerful and possible way of solving some of the problems you face—but evolution will never find it, because it is too bloody expensive to go in that direction. No creature could survive an attempt to cross that canyon.

So just as I think how you build something is really important, but not necessarily constitutive, I also think that understanding what's constitutive, and what the space of possibilities is and so on, has got to be helpful in terms of how the evolutionary story went. So I'm all in favor of this handshake with evolutionary theorists. I just don't think that norms and mattering rest constitutively on evolution.

DENNETT Then I think we agree.

CLARK I don't see any reason to deny that.

CUMMINS I'm not sure I do.

SMITH I don't believe there's complete agreement, but I do think there's a kind of—

DENNETT I think there's still some tension here . . .

HAUGELAND There's a question which I've been sitting here trying to formulate, and I'm not sure how it bears, but I have this inkling that it does. And that is, we were talking about Good Tricks and having a phrase like, 'it's a Good Trick in one's kit'. But there's some question as to how these are individuated, what makes them a trick and what makes them good. And then how they could be brought about; whether evolution is the only way. For instance, why isn't it a Good Trick to produce planets composed of heavy elements; to get a whole lot of hydrogen to attract itself to the point where it then fuses into helium and then collapses into a dwarf where the helium fuses—then it explodes and those pull together and then you've got a planet. That's a pretty tricky process, right?

DENNETT Read Lee Smolin [1997] and you'll see somebody who says, add it right in there, another Good Trick. That's what evolutionary cosmology is about.

HAUGELAND There's no selection there.

DENNETT Oh, there is for Smolin. I'm agnostic about Smolin's cosmology, but I think it is a not provably incoherent cosmology that simply embraces what you're trying to do as a reductio, and says no, look, we actually do have an evolution with selection of whole universes, that is, whole ways of having the basic so-called constants of physics. And some of them produce—

HAUGELAND Yeah, but you've changed the subject. I'm talking about this universe with our constants of physics—

DENNETT It is a Good Trick and can be seen to be a Good Trick, but, as usual, you never see it against the background of the failed universes that don't happen.

SMITH What about saying 'Look, why don't I just inhale some dioxin and decompose...'

CLAPIN Why is that a bad trick?

SMITH Yeah, what's the 'good'—

CUMMINS Well, you have to have replication in the picture. Replication and selection wasn't in the picture that John told. It is in the story that Smolin told.

DENNETT It is in Smolin's story.

CUMMINS I don't believe it for a minute. I don't disbelieve it, either. I just don't get it.

DENNETT But my point is, you've asked the right question, but don't presume that there isn't an answer to it.

HAUGELAND Well, the question is not to Smolin, whom I've never heard of, but rather to you, who don't believe in the alternative universes, let alone them procreating and competing. Just to you, believing, like we Weinbergians or whatever, that it started back there in big bang and it's been buzzing along ever since. Well there it's been evolution in the sense of the trajectories but not evolution in the sense of selective pressures. And yet there are things which it's not obvious why you wouldn't call them Good Tricks. Unless you build selectiveness into the notion of good thing, and that's a suspicious move.

DENNETT Well, I've got a long answer to it, but I don't have a short answer to it, and it's time for lunch. But you can read the long answer because it's in my book *Darwin's Dangerous Idea*.

PART 6

Tacit Representation in Functional Architecture

HUGH CLAPIN

6.1.1 Introduction and Overview

The thesis I am pursuing is that tacit content is required for explicit content, and thus there will be no full story about mental content without a proper consideration of tacit content. There are two basic intuitions behind the category of tacit representation: that explicit symbolic representational schemes owe some of their semantic features to the inexplicit structural 'background' of that scheme; and that intelligent systems embody information without representing it explicitly.

There are four broad consequences to be drawn:

1. Tacit representation offers a bridge between symbolic representation and embodiment.
2. An adequate account of symbolic computation ought to understand explicit representations as dynamic structures with a fluid existence, quite unlike the well-formed formulae of a formal language.
3. An adequate account of symbolic computation must recognize the content tacit in a running computational process.
4. Cognition ought be understood to include architectural change (cf. classicism).

I want then to draw explicitly some important connections I see between this notion of tacit representation and the work of those here this week.

6.1.2   Tacit Representation

In 'Styles of Mental Representation' (1983), Dennett distinguishes between explicit and tacit styles of representation. Tacit representation is differentiated from explicit representation in two ways. First, the 'know-how' embodied by a system that can manipulate explicit representations is a form of tacit representation; and secondly certain states of the system that reliably co-vary with aspects of the system's relationship to the world tacitly represent those states of the world.

Dennett has two points to make here. First is a Rylean point that the using of systems of representation is a skill that requires certain kinds of knowledge, and even computers must have this know-how in order to operate. The computer's skill at using explicit symbols is embodied in its hardwiring, and it is this that explains the symbols' representational capacities. Dennett's second aim is to explore how explicit, symbolic representation might evolve out of naturally occurring tacit representa-tion. He offers the example of an amphibious creature that operates according to different sets of embodied rules or dispositions according to whether it is in water or on land: 'Simply *getting wet* could be the trigger for changing internal state from one set of rules to the other' (Dennett 1983: 223). Dennett suggests that such situations might be the beginnings of a complex set of transiently tacit know-how from which explicit representation might emerge.

Dennett's distinction between explicit and tacit representation suggests a conceptual priority: explicit presupposes tacit, but not vice versa. It follows that embodied tacit content has a foundational role in cognitive explanation.

The first idea of the explicit presupposing tacit is well illustrated by modern computers. The central processing unit (CPU) of a von Neumann architecture computer is a functional arrangement of electronic components that has the ability to follow instructions in a programming language. These instructions are typically commands to add two binary numerals together, test whether a given numeral represents zero (or a negative, or odd number); move to a new instruction, move a binary numeral in or out of memory, and so on. Dennett's point is that the CPU hardware embodies the know-how to follow these instructions and in this way tacit know-how is used by explicit representations such as program instructions.

6.1.3 Functional Architecture

Zenon Pylyshyn (1980; 1984) argues for the importance of the notion of *functional architecture* to distinguish between cognitive and non-cognitive levels of explanation in understanding the mind. Pylyshyn's project is to set some *prima facie* bounds to the domain of cognitive science.

Computational systems of representation have basic operations and resources that serve to define the system. The lowest level of functional architecture in a computer consists in its ability to understand machine code instructions. The functional architecture of a computational cognitive system—its *cognitive* architecture—is thus understood to be those resources that underpin cognitive representations.

Additionally, the cognitive architecture is understood to be cognitively impenetrable. That is, cognitive operations themselves cannot affect the nature of the cognitive architecture. If one of the basic resources that comprises the cognitive architecture is an implementation of *modus ponens* (that is, if every time there exists two representations of the form $P \supset Q$ and P, a new representation of the form Q will come into being), then the cognitive impenetrability condition demands that no amount of thinking (that is, of manipulating symbols) can change either one's ability at, or the manner in which, one applies *modus ponens*.

The basic metaphor to keep in mind here is that of a lock and key. If a representation is seen as a key, then the lock the key fits is analogous to the functional architecture. Both the key and the lock are required for the successful operation of either element. If the key is faulty, then it won't turn the lock, but conversely if the lock is faulty, then the key won't work. Not only are lock and key jointly necessary and sufficient for the operation of a lock, but each also 'defines' the other in an important sense. Knowledge of the details of the lock is sufficient for knowledge of what key would turn the lock. Similarly, knowledge of the key is sufficient for knowledge of what kind of lock could be operated by that key. At the conceptual level, just as the concepts 'lock' and 'key' come as a 'package deal' (to use Armstrong's 1968: 253 phrase), so do the concepts of 'physical symbol system' and 'functional architecture'. A proper understanding of one concept requires a proper understanding of the other. If you're talking about a physical symbol system you're actually also talking about the functional architecture that underpins and allows it to prosper.

6.1.4 CPUs, Levels, and Virtual Architectures

One of the most straightforward examples of how a physical symbol and its functional architecture interact comes from the CPU of a computer. At the level at which symbolic and electronic descriptions meet, we find the hardwired functional architecture.

A key notion in this analysis is that of the primitive operation. An important component of a system's functional architecture is the set of primitive operations that can be carried out on the symbols by the system. In the case of the CPU, these operations would include addition of two symbols, shifting symbols into and out of registers and onto busses, and the reading of the next program instruction.

Another important feature of the CPU hardware is that to all computational intents and purposes it is unchangeable—it provides the fixed substratum in which all the computer's abilities are founded.

Of course, computers have the flexibility they do because they are programmable, and programming a computer is a means of changing the effective architecture of the computer. Thus while the CPU's physical structure determines a certain programming language (machine code), this language can be used to implement another computing language with different symbols and different primitive operations. This is made possible because the high-level language rests on a *virtual* architecture, implemented in the physical functional architecture defined by the wiring of the CPU.

Thus part of the power of the notion of functional architecture is its ability to distinguish different levels of analysis of symbolic systems. On a computer running a sophisticated program written in a high-level language, we can choose the level of analysis on the basis of which architecture we recognize, for example, C + + or machine language, and so on.

The implementation-independence of the description of the virtual architecture is important to cognitive science. At the level of a virtual architecture specified in an ordinary programming language such as C + +, multiplication is a primitive operation. From the perspective of the physical CPU architecture, it may be a complex operation requiring iterations of the operation of addition (which is a primitive operation). But exactly how multiplication occurs can differ from CPU to CPU because programs written in C + + are blind to this implementation detail. Similarly, Pylyshyn argues that discovering the cognitive architecture of human thought will allow theorists to understand thought without recourse to understanding the details of how primitive cognitive operations are implemented. Thus the cognitive scientist's job is made significantly more tractable because she need not know anything much about how thought is physically realized, just as the computer programmer need not know much about how $C++$ programs are physically realized. This is a central feature of classical cognitive science.

6.1.5 Embodied Syntax

The combination of Dennett's notion of tacit representation and Pylyshyn's descriptions of the CPU gives rise to a powerful conceptual tool for cognitive science: the idea that functional architectures represent. They represent tacitly, and this tacit content is distinct from whatever is represented explicitly by the symbols that are supported by the functional architecture. *Discussion point 6.1*

Terry Winograd's well-known early AI program SHRDLU (1972) uses a system of explicit representation that consists of names, predicates, and action-representations. Thus the explicit representation '(#WHITE :BIN)' says that the color of the thing called ':BIN' is white, while '(#AT :B5 (400 600 200))' says that the block called ':B5' is at the Cartesian coordinates specified. The content tacit in the functional architecture includes that assertions such as '(#AT :B5 (400 600 200))' take a 3–tuple to specify location, thus precluding the possibility of a 4D description of an object's location. Similarly that fact that '#WHITE' is a one-place predicate is also tacit in the functional architecture. Artificial intelligence systems such as SHRDLU typically don't have the ability to change these aspects of their representational schemes, which is why they conform to the classical notion of functional architecture.

We also see from this example that functional architectures can embody syntactic descriptions of formal systems. SHRDLU uses a system of symbolic representation, and the syntactic constraints on that symbol system—what is and isn't a legal symbol, how complex symbols are composed from atomic symbols, what transformations from one symbol to another are allowed—are all determined by the functional architecture. When a program is actually running on a computer, the running of the program brings into existence a virtual architecture, and thus a virtual symbol system, since the symbols are both defined by, and brought into existence by the implementation of a functional architecture through the running of a program.

6.1.6 Logic: Ontological Assumptions

Comparing the propositional and predicate calculi illustrates that representational systems come with ontological assumptions. The predicate calculus demands a model that can make sense of the object/predicate relationship, as this structure is unchangeable within the system, while the propositional calculus is not so choosy.

Of course the constraints on possible models found in the predicate calculus bestow representational power not found in the simpler system. This suggests that greater representational power (of the sort that the predicate calculus has more of than the propositional calculus) requires the system to make more specific ontological commitments. The more the desired model is 'built in' to the system of representation, the better the fit between that representational system and the model. This observation is reflected in the importance in AI of crafting specific sorts of data structures for specific ends.

The ontological assumptions in the case of logics are clearly very broad, and, in most contexts, are not very controversial. Nonetheless, it is the case that symbolic systems make assumptions about the way the represented world is to be carved up. The key point about this observation for the purposes of cognitive science is that the ontological assumptions built into the system's architecture constitute a vitally important aspect of the architecture's semantic significance.

There are, of course, semantic issues that the architecture will not resolve. Thus the particular interpretation of any particular symbol is left open by the architecture. But the point to note is that once the interpretation of some symbols becomes fixed, the system constrains the possible interpretation of other symbols. Take a simple logical system that takes the connectives $\wedge$ and $\neg$ to be primitive, and define the connective $\vee$ in the familiar way:

$$A \vee B \Leftrightarrow \neg(\neg A \wedge \neg B)$$

If we then additionally interpret $\wedge$ as conjunction and $\neg$ as negation, we are constrained in how we interpret the symbol $\vee$. This sort of architectural constraint is widespread.

The thought that cognitive architecture makes a vital contribution to cognitive processing isn't necessarily new. I think Kant can be understood as making such a claim, for example, and reading Kant this way emphasizes the deep significance of this idea for cognitive science.

For example, I take Kant's *Critique of Pure Reason* account of the various kinds of misleading reasoning that have dogged metaphysics—the so-called 'dialectical inferences of pure reason'—to be, in part, based on a recognition that not adhering to the constraints built into a system of representation can lead you astray. Thus Kant's response to Descartes's ontological argument for the existence of God (that existence is not a predicate) is a response that draws attention to the functional architecture of representational systems.

In Kant's terminology, existence is a 'pure concept of the understanding'—a 'category'. As I've argued in 'Kantian Errors in "Classical" Cognitive Science' (1999*a*), Kant's categories and the 'Pure Forms of Intuition' may be understood as an expression of the tacit content of the architecture of cognition. If existence is built into both thought and language in roughly the same way as it is built into the predicate calculus (as a quantifier), then to add a predicate to the system with the same meaning as the quantifier is to flout the semantic constraints set by the functional architecture.

The point I would like to make (whether or not it was actually Kant's) is that adding existence as a predicate to a system where it already exists as a quantifier is asking for trouble. It allows you to state things like:

$$\exists x \, (\neg \, \text{Exists}(x))$$

Which, assuming both the quantifier and the predicate have the same interpretation, is clearly self-contradictory. The form hides the self-contradictory nature of the expression, which is particularly galling in a formal language designed precisely to bring such logical problems to the surface.

The example drives home the semantic, and thus cognitive, importance of architectural content. Once we accept the semantics of the functional architecture, we realize that this tacit content may interact in complex ways with explicit content. Not only does tacit content make possible explicit; it can alter the contribution of explicit content to the overall system.

6.1.7 Perception

Imagine a computational system that uses n-tuples as the vehicles for representing appearances (for example, 'red there now' would be represented by the tuple (C, x, y, z, t), where C represents the content (*red*), and the other components represent spatial and temporal location). If the architecture demands that all fields of this n-tuple be well defined in

order that the n-tuple be well-defined, then all perceptions must carry
spatial and temporal information. This would be a simple case in which
the syntactic *form* (in combination with a certain interpretation of the
symbols) demands that perceptions carry spatio-temporal information.

Notice how this view of form would justify Kant's (1781/1929) claim
that 'We can never represent to ourselves the absence of space, though we
can quite well think it as empty of objects' (A24 = B38). If your system of
representation demands that there be spatial coordinates for every appearance, then all objects of appearance must exist in space.

The Kantian connections are worth drawing because they emphasize
how fundamental are the assumptions tacit in the functional architecture
of systems of explicit representation. Kant's suggestions that causation,
predicate structure, modality, space, and time are contributed by cognitive
structure warn us that tacit architectural content could provide the fundamental structures of a cognitive system's experience.

Note here the similarity of this reading of Kant to Smith's (1996)
description of representation as an achievement that creates subject/
object/predicate divisions out of the mere 'flex and slop'.[1] In these terms,
Smith's suggestion that representation creates the objective world is a
recognition of the ontological significance of the tacit content of representational schemes. In contrast to Kant, however, Smith emphasizes that the
achievement of object stability is equally an achievement of the world.
Similarly the idea that the architectures of logics and other representational systems need to be crafted to suit their domains allows the represented world to be reflected in the representing structures. This Kantianism
is not then committed to an unknowable noumenal world. Until we better
understand the architecture with which we represent the world, however,
we cannot be confident that the world is as we represent it.

The example of the simple perceptual system above shows how difficult
it is clearly to pin down tacit content. To say that three-dimensionality is
built into such a system is in fact too strong. The referents of the individual
elements of the 5–tuple must be fixed as physical dimensions in order for
the whole compound symbol to be said to represent a particular place.
Such a symbolic structure might be used for a quite different representational purpose (for example, velocity, color, and size of an object), which
would mean that the content tacitly represented by the architecture would
be quite different.

[1] See e.g. ch. 9, 'Middle Distance' and Part 5 of this volume.

In this way tacit content depends partly on explicit content. Without knowing how the explicit symbols are to be interpreted we can't pin down the content of the architecture. In this way my use of Dennett's insight is in tension with his aim of grounding explicit content in tacit. Specifying tacit content requires knowing what the symbol represents *explicitly*. This is constrained by tacit content; but not fully specified by tacit content.

From the suggestion that functional architectures tacitly represent important assumptions and skills of a cognitive system follows the first of the four consequences noted above: the very physicality of symbols contributes to their content. The physical shape of symbols is the embodiment of syntax, and syntax carries with it broad semantic significance. Thus the idea that functional architectures carry tacit content is a deeply embodiment-oriented thesis. All sorts of physical constraints can have semantic significance—from resource limits such as storage space to an accidental rewiring that permits the representation of four–dimensional space.

6.1.8 Computational Processes

On this picture we are reminded that computer programs function to create virtual architectures, and thus there is a critical difference between the representations used to program the computer (the programming language) and the data representations used by the computer. Both Smith (1997) and Robert Cummins (1986) have emphasized this, but to different ends. The notion of tacit content has important consequences for how we understand computation.

The program, as written in the programming language, is the blueprint for a virtual architecture that could be replaced by hardwiring. When the program is run, the architecture of the equivalent hardwired computer is present 'virtually' as we say. There are two basic ways in which programs are run: compilation and interpretation. The most straightforward case is compilation.[2]

In compiled languages, the sequence of high-level instructions is transformed into a list of instructions in machine code—the most basic programming language for that computer. Let's take a simple example of a program that allows access to a library catalog. The data structures it

---

[2] The picture is more complicated for interpreted languages; however the basic lesson still holds: the program could be replaced with a hardwired machine where the only explicit representations were data structures.

recognizes are library item records (e.g. a record that holds information about title, author, date of publication, Dewey number, shelf number, etc.). This program will also handle search requests, so it must make use of data structures that hold information about a particular search request. When this compiled code is run, the computer is functionally identical to a computer with a different CPU that is hardwired to follow search instructions and to read and manipulate library records. The shape of a book record in the actual architecture will be reflected in the wiring of the logic gates.

If we take seriously the functional equivalence of the virtual and equivalent hardwired architectures, then the machine code—whose execution constitutes the virtual architecture—effectively evaporates. And it is only in this situation that the data structures have robust causally efficacious existence; the functional architecture that constitutes the system of representation in question—book records and search requests—only exists while the machine code is being executed. All that is relevant about machine code to the architecture of the library catalog is that it give rise to a process that is functionally equivalent to the associated hardwiring. In particular, the representational nature of machine code is irrelevant to the data structures that running the machine code program bring into existence.

The idea of functional architecture suggests that machine code representations and data structure representations exist at different levels. Programming languages, including machine code, have representational significance only inasmuch as they cause the computer to behave in certain ways. Programming languages do not consist of explicit symbols that say anything about the world. In contrast, data structures do consist of explicit symbols that have a more ordinary semantics; they are about the world.

Thus in considering computational examples of representations, the cognitive scientist ought be more interested in the data structures than in programming languages. In 'Inexplicit Information' (1986: 123) Cummins argues that information embedded procedurally in a running computational process, even if explicitly represented in the program, isn't any kind of knowledge or belief because it is 'not available for reasoning or evidential assessment.' While this is some reason to distinguish tacit from explicit information, in special cases it is undermined, as we'll see.

The fact that the actual architecture is virtual rather than real does have some significance: it means that the data structures are ephemeral objects brought into existence by the running of the computer. Like any system of explicit representation, they depend essentially on their associated architecture. These ephemeral objects sometimes supervene on the bit pattern of a hard disk or zip drive, however the information these bit patterns hold is inaccessible unless they are processed in the appropriate manner. That is, unless they are processed according to their subsuming architecture. Data structures only exist *across* time, rather than at an instant. Determining whether a given bit pattern is the numeral 62, or the letter a, requires looking at the history and future of that bit pattern. It is the broad processing environment across time that determines the existence of explicit representations. So we should conclude that the only computational representations that matter are dynamic, ephemeral objects, and are certainly not contained in a printout of the high-level code, for example. *Discussion point 6.2* (They are specified in such a printout, of course, but they don't have causally efficacious existence there.) This is the second significant consequence of acknowledging tacit content.

Let's now combine this picture of classical computation with the insights regarding tacit content in functional architectures. The running program, specified by the written program, constitutes the functional architecture of the data structures it brings into being. As we've noted, all such functional architectures carry tacit content about the structure of the world represented by the explicit data representations. Thus programs do represent, but they don't represent what is captured by their explicit symbols. (However, what they tacitly represent in virtue of being functional architectures may significantly overlap with what their specification—that is, the written program—explicitly declares.)

Programmable computers allow the possibility of run-time changes to the functional architecture of the currently active process by that same process. They present the real possibility of a cognitive system that learns by 'rewiring' itself; by changing its representational scheme.

We can note that in systems where the architectural content is changeable by the system itself, the way is opened for that content to be available for 'reasoning and evidential assessment' (in Cummins' terms), and thus be considered on a representational par with explicit beliefs.

To my knowledge, very few applications take advantage of this flexibility, though genetic algorithms are a step in that direction.[3] In terms of tacit and explicit content, this ability for data structures to re-engineer their own architectures is the ability of explicit content to change tacit content.

---

[3] See Ballard (1997) for a good introduction to genetic algorithms.

So while tacit content is an unavoidable precondition of explicit content, and it determines strong constraints on explicit content; none the less explicit representations can change tacit content, and thus change the nature of the explicit representations. In classical computers, at least, tacit and explicit contents are deeply intertwined.

So we have the third of our consequences (one which closely mirrors Cummins' view): understanding computation requires that we appreciate that the semantic significance of programs is the content they carry tacitly, not explicitly. *Discussion point 6.3*

6.1.9 Changes to Functional Architecture: Classical Cognitive Science

Acknowledging the tacit content of cognitive architectures is in tension with a fundamental feature of the classical picture of cognition. Fodor and Pylyshyn make use of the architecture/symbol distinction to ground the cognitive/non-cognitive distinction, in the following way (Pylyshyn 1984; Fodor and Pylyshyn 1988). Pre-theoretically, cognition is semantic, and the implementation of cognition is not. If we assume that symbols have semantic properties but the architecture doesn't, we can then identify the architecture with the non-cognitive implementation of cognition and symbol systems with the cognitive domain. The picture I'm urging here doesn't allow this neat division, however.

On my picture, some cases of learning—for example, paradigm shifts and other significant conceptual changes—could be explained in part by changes to the representational scheme rather than simply by the addition of new theorems to the existing scheme. In this sort of case we will want to say that the *architecture* has made the semantic difference, in which case we are recognizing that the architecture makes a contribution to the semantics of the system as a whole. It is the architecture that embodies the content.

We can, however, maintain the core classical intuitions that both cognition and computation are importantly characterized by content. Allowing that there is content embodied in the architecture of representational systems, we simply find that we have concomitantly broader notions of computation and of cognition. In particular, changes to functional architecture ought be understood, in certain circumstances, as a kind of cognition.

The classicist assumes that architectures are fixed, and that the way to understand cognition is solely in these terms. It seems clear that children's basic cognitive capacities develop—or mature—as they get older. On the classical account, maturation is an architectural and not a cognitive change. But it seems at least an empirical possibility that some of the thinking that children do while growing up makes a difference to the cognitive architecture they have as adults. Thus it could be that continuous listening to, and thinking about, the proposition 'all elephants are gray' can lead to the tacit knowledge that 'elephants are gray' (that is, to the disposition to infer grayness of elephant) even if the explicit thought 'all elephants are gray' is long forgotten. This is perhaps most plausible in the case of skill acquisition: the skilled expert has little conscious access to the details of her smoothly executed behavior, while the novice plods through the process jerky step by jerky step. The process of becoming skilled looks like a good candidate for a process where explicit information becomes tacit. The term 'compiled' when used in reference to 'compiled skills' reflects this picture very ably.

A significant flaw in the classicist position is thus the assumption that there must be a clear distinction between cognition and maturation. The fourth main consequence is that acknowledging tacit, architectural content clears the way for a graded and complex notion of cognition; one that includes both architectural change and symbol manipulation as cognitive processes.

6.1.10 Explicitness and Redescription: Clark

On Andy Clark's definition (1993: ch. 6), information is explicitly represented in a system when it is easily and multiply deployable in that system. The sort of examples of tacit content I've been discussing fit this definition quite well: the know-how of a CPU is easily deployable, but fails Clark's multiply deployable test, and is thus inexplicit; the ontological and similar assumptions built in to the syntax of a system of representation is similarly easily deployable (indeed, its deployment is mandatory for any use of a token of the representational scheme in question), but once again not multiply deployable. The kind of inexplicit information focused on here thus illustrates the importance of Clark's second condition on explicitness: multiple deployability.

This analysis thus questions the adequacy of Kirsh's (1991) 'easily deployable' condition: not all easily deployable content is intuitively explicit. If Clark intends that ease of use and multiple deployability are *jointly* necessary and sufficient, then there is no tension. But it is clear that ease of use is not sufficient by itself for explicitness.

Our discussion of the various representational significance of a computer program—considered as a written text, a series of binary-encoded instructions, or embodied in a running process—illustrates the relativity of explicitness. The computer program is explicit with respect to the compiler or interpreter, but not with respect to the running process it constitutes (except, perhaps, in special cases of self-modifying programs).

On Clark's picture, Karmiloff-Smith's (1992) suggestion that maturation requires representational redescription is the idea that content moves from less to more explicit representation (since it becomes more multiply deployable when re-represented). Thus the suggestion in the previous section that content might move from being explicitly represented to being tacit in the architecture—as in compiled skills—is the opposite process to re-representation. Both processes demand an account of the relation between tacit and explicit content, and how an item of information might move from one mode to another. The picture I'm urging here offers a glimpse of such an account.

6.1.11 Embodiment

Clark also emphasizes the importance of action-oriented representations: representations that simultaneously encode some aspect of the world, and what to do about it. For example, the coordinates of an object in visual space might be represented in terms of how the head must move—which muscles to move—in order to place that object in the center of the visual field. We may say that part of the tacit content in the architecture of this scheme of representation is information about how the head is moved by the relevant muscles. Thus increasing recognition of idiosyncratic representational schemes (action-oriented and Ballard's (1991) 'personalized representations') is to my mind simply a special case of the increasing recognition of the importance of the content tacit in the functional architecture of representational schemes. It is very important to a cognitive system that relies on inner representations of the world that those representations code information in a manner that is suitable for the purposes of that system.

This is in contrast to natural languages, for example, which are almost perfectly general representational schemes: we expect to be able to represent or communicate just about anything using language. Perhaps the price we pay is a linguistic architecture stripped as much as possible of its tacit content. Formal languages are even more pared down, hence the minimal tacit content in their architectures: roughly, that there are objects and they have properties, in the case of the predicate calculus.

Thus fuller appreciation of the importance of tacit content leads to fuller appreciation of embodiment: the physical structure of explicit representations, given their physical context, is critical to their being able to do their job of standing in for the outside world. We should expect to find more and more representations with very particular structures suited to very particular purposes. As well as action-oriented representations, perhaps we should expect to find memory-oriented representations and food-oriented representations. Language, on this way of seeing things, might be a form of communication-oriented representation.

6.1.12 Representational Genera: Haugeland

In 'Representational Genera' (1991) Haugeland argues that the differences exhibited by logical, iconic, and distributed representations are the result of different kinds of content; not of the different kinds of representational schemes. Haugeland argues for this by showing that it is too easy to recode a logical representation into an iconic one, and so on. For example, digitizing a picture or photographing a sentence is easy; however translation between genera ought be hard, as in *describing* a photograph.

I'm inclined to think Haugeland is right to point to different kinds of content (thought I'd like to understand better the kinds of content he identifies). I don't think, however, that content genus is independent of scheme genus. First, I think Haugeland's worries about intertranslatability can be headed off by treating the problematic cases of translation as cases of re-representation. One reason I think this has to work is that the idea that representational schemes carry with them significant tacit semantic baggage means that every translation or recoding from one scheme to another must add to or change that tacit content. In the simple cases, however—pictures of sentences, for example—there doesn't appear to be much of a change in the explicit or tacit content associated with the sentence. This is explained if we posit two distinct representational schemes operating simultaneously according to a hierarchy: the original linguistic scheme uses the string 'cows are brown' to represent the brownness of cows making use of the tacit content of that scheme (for example, that everything is an object, and can have properties). But the pictorial scheme that codes the sentence with the photograph is not picturing the brownness of cows; it is picturing the visual properties of the sentence. Hence the tacit content inherent in picturing (whatever that is) doesn't affect the content of the sentence. It is only relevant in recovering the sentence, which is then understood according to the linguistic scheme alone.

Secondly, if, as I am urging, all representational schemes are constrained in what they can represent (these differences captured in the idea of tacit content), you'd expect radically different tacit contents in radically different representational schemes. Thus if Haugeland is right about there being content genera, then these genera go along with scheme genera in the way you'd expect: absolute contents are carried only by logical schemes; relational contents are carried only by iconic schemes, and associative contents are carried only by distributed schemes. *Discussion point 6.4*

6.1.13 Targets as Architectural Content: Cummins

Robert Cummins (1996*a*) argues that the key to understanding mental representation is distinguishing between what a representation represents and what it is meant to represent—the former is the content of the representation proper, while the latter he terms the 'target'. There is then a third mode of content produced by applying the representation to its target.

The function of a certain part of the perceptual system might be to represent the color of the currently foveated object, hence the target would be 'color of the currently foveated object'. If the currently foveated object is a ripe lemon, then a representation with the content *yellow* would yield a correct application with the content *the color of the currently foveated object is yellow*. If the representation applied to the lemon meant *blue*, then the application would be a case of erroneous representation.

One aspect of this story that appeals is that targets might be thought of as a form of architectural content. That is, the content of a given application of a given representation is partly constituted by which system used it for which purpose. The target is not itself explicitly represented.

We noted earlier that describing the tacit content of the 5-tuple vision data structure as including the assumption that the visual world has three spatial dimensions is not justified simply by the form of the data structure. Following Cummins we might ascribe a general target to this whole scheme of representation, whenever tokened. Thus the target of *any* token 5-tuple is (in part) the specification of location in three spatial dimensions and one temporal dimension. (A story about how such targets are fixed is still owed, of course.)

Cummins may have in mind more specific targets than the kinds of contents I've used to exemplify tacit architectural content—his examples are 'currently foveated object' or 'chess board position after move M' or individuals; my examples are broad assumptions such as three-dimensionality, subject-property ontology, and the know-how to follow explicit rules.

My hope is, however, that on the one hand the concept of target might be extended to these more generic contents, and on the other that part of the job of specifying targets is done by the architecture of the system of representation.

6.1.14 Conclusion

From Dennett's definition of tacit representation I've developed an account of the relation between tacit and explicit representation. This is one way in which the work of the five authors discussed herein comes together–but it is by no means the only way. *Final discussion*

Discussion

6.1   CLARK   Just a clarification. What would it represent? What kind of thing?

p. 299   CLAPIN   Things like, that this [#WHITE] is a one-place predicate, that this [400 600 200] is a 3-tuple.

CLARK   Does that mean that the know-how represents?

CLAPIN   Know-how is a form of representation, is the idea.

DENNETT   It may be my fault for calling it tacit representation.

6.2   CUMMINS   What makes them dynamic?

p. 305   CLAPIN   Because they only exist over time and they exist because of a dynamic process.

CUMMINS   It doesn't mean that the representation itself is spread out in time? That's part of its syntax.

DENNETT   It doesn't mean that.

CLAPIN   I do mean that. I do mean that that's the case.

HAUGELAND   In this situation?

CLAPIN   Yup.

SMITH   Well, you mean it existentially. You don't mean that it is necessary that it has no interpretation at an instant.

CLAPIN   No, I mean—

CUMMINS   That's what I was worried about.

CLAPIN   The inference is this: representations need architectures. They come with an architecture—just like a lock and key. But the architecture only exists over time, spread out over time. Only by running the program does the architecture actually come into existence and do causal work, thus the representation is in the same boat.

CLARK That just means that it has to persist more than an instant. Just long enough to have a bit of physical push.

CLAPIN Maybe the emphasis on time isn't very deep. If you can show me an architecture that exists at an instant, then I'm happy for the representation to exist at an instant. And maybe at the moment we're still thinking through the example of von Neumann architecture computers. When we're looking to them, as people did for a long time and maybe still do in thinking about cognitive science, then we've got to remember that the representations aren't static entities.

CLARK See, I thought when you used 'dynamic', that you meant that the representation wouldn't have the content it has were it not for its behavior over time.

CLAPIN I'm saying that it wouldn't be a representation at all, and therefore not exist in order to have content.

CUMMINS Just a clarification. I understand this better in a connectionist setting. Learning is flatlining, and I'm not getting any worse, so I grow a bunch of new nodes, and try again. 6.3 p. 306

CLAPIN Why have you grown the new nodes?

CUMMINS I'm monitoring my flatlining and that just causes me to grow new nodes. So that's the kind of thing you have in mind.

CLAPIN Yep. That's the kind of case where it's kind of blind luck; it's very different to a classical case of cognition which is—

CUMMINS I'd argue that the kind you're talking about has to be. But that's OK.

CLAPIN Well, no, it doesn't.

CUMMINS Over a long time it's selection.

CLAPIN I don't know what you mean by 'has to'. I mean, in a classical computer, in an AI system, you could have a reasoning that says, 'I'm assuming a two-dimensional world here. Damn, I'd better add a new dimension to my representational scheme.' You can imagine a system set up able to do that.

HAUGELAND How are you deciding that that's a change to the architecture as opposed to a change to something else?

CLAPIN Because it makes a difference to the structure of the representations, the data structures that represent its knowledge about the world.

SMITH But it's tricky, because if you get it into the program, you get into reflection stuff which I used to work on.[4] But if you do it at the data structure level, if you actually go into a program and actually try to assign semantics to data structures—which no one in computer science ever does—enormous numbers of data structures end up with meta-level representational content.

DENNETT That's what he's saying, isn't it?

SMITH Maybe he's saying that... but if we're on the level of representation, data structures not programs, than I think it's not the least bit rare.

CUMMINS But what's hard is the idea of saying, you have a computer and it's got a robot arm and at some point it says, 'You know, I'm just not doing so hot here, so I've just resoldered this connection.' It just takes its arm out and literally goes in and resolders a circuit board somewhere. Now, I can imagine that being some sort of selection algorithm, or process which makes that a sort of directed process. But it's very hard for me to think of it as a case of reasoning and inference, in the sense of saying, well, it's just this connection I need to do in order to get it right next time.

CLAPIN Well, one of the points I'm about to get to is precisely that you lose the distinction, the strict distinction that Pylyshyn and Fodor use between cognition and implementation. So, they might be kind of different, but I want to say that they're on a continuum.

6.4
p. 310

SMITH Is it your conclusion there that John is right that these different types of representational genera differ in content, but wrong that form isn't implicated in how it is that they differ in content... is that what the disagreement is with John?

CLAPIN Yes.

SMITH Good.

CLAPIN Except that I'm just not sure about the different contents thing. It sounds like a wacky idea—

HAUGELAND That's the best thing about it!

CLAPIN And I don't understand it yet. So I'm not necessarily signing up for the different kinds of content program, but I'm just saying, there's a kind of natural fit...

SMITH But you are signing up for different kinds of tacit content in the two schemes.

---

[4] [See Smith (1984) and Smith (1996): 37–41—ed.]

CLAPIN What I'm committed to is there being big differences in tacit content. I haven't given you any argument that there should be differences in kind, but I'm just saying, John's idea could fit with that idea quite nicely.

CLARK When you talk about schemes there, talking about John, that's a level different than implementation, of course. A lot of what you talked about when you talked about tacit knowledge, seems to me to do with implementation.

CLAPIN Yes, but not everything. The logic example is meant to show that even in an uninterpreted formal system, there's some constraint. If it's uninterpreted the content isn't objects and properties, but there's some constraint.

CLARK This last bit where you're trying to tie it up with Rob's thing about targets . . . the target is what it's supposed to be about. Right?

Final discussion p. 311

CUMMINS What it's aimed at.

CLARK What it's aimed at. That may be different. I was thinking, you could have a library catalog or something, that only has a field of 'author', but it was actually supposed to have, and is indeed aimed at, objects that it can only cope with if it has a field for 'author' and 'title'. So then, in the architecture it looks as if you've got, as it were, a tacit content, which is to say, 'The things that I'm about just have one label.' When you think about what the target actually is, what it's supposed to be doing, then you think, 'OK, then it should have two.'

CUMMINS But 'supposed to be', you're thinking of the designer of the thing. But, I mean, once the field comes up, and you ask, 'Well, what goes in that field?' it's an 'author'. And what in fact gets put in that field is a string of nonsense syllables or a picture of your Aunt Tillie, then you get error.

CLARK What's the architectural content in that case then, when you put the wrong thing in the field?

CLAPIN Well, it stays the same. Because the architectural content doesn't change with different explicit representations.

CUMMINS Exactly. Let's say, instead of putting the title in there, you put a numeral in there. Then the idea is well, OK, the consumer of this information is entitled to think that the author is 525. That the author of the book being searched for is 525, which is indeed exactly what the system will assume. Why? Well, because, what that field is for, is the representation of an author. So, whatever you put in there is going to be taken as a representation of the author by the consumer. Whether it is or not, is not its business.

SMITH Suppose it then says, 'Let's see, what else do I know about 525?' And it comes back with, 'It's divisible by 5.'

CUMMINS Does it then think the author's divisible by 5?

SMITH Yes, now, what's the target of the 'it' in the statement 'it's divisible by 5'? Is it still the author or has it somehow—?

CUMMINS Actually, we are going to talk about this later, so let's postpone it. [See Part 4—ed.] But I think that's an interesting case. But the short answer is, 'Yeah.' It is architecturally determined in just that way, because you've got this format that's sitting there.

CLAPIN This picture is maybe driven by learning computer science when strong typing—strongly typed languages—were in: strong typing enforces strict divisions between different kinds of data.[5] It's more difficult to tell the story about interpreted languages, or indeed any case where a representation is being used according to different representational schemes. I think there's something to say about that though, which is that it is going to be treated very differently according to the representational scheme that's currently active, that's currently using it.

CUMMINS Well, you can get gross mismatches, and Brian gives an example, and, I think those are really interesting kinds of cases, because I think there's a certain kind of learning procedure that can deal with situations where what happens is that you're in the ballpark but your accuracy is off. I don't mean just that you want more, because sometimes you want less. I am not a believer that more accuracy is always better. I think it's often more expensive than it's worth. So sometimes what you need to do to get better is sacrifice some accuracy. But you're not doing something really stupid, like what Ryle would have called a category mistake, for example when what you want is a phrase marker for the current linguistic input, and what you've got is your memory of some childhood experience or something. I think that kind of thing can trigger learning, too, but I think it's a whole different kind of story when that happens. Because it isn't gradient descent. It's more like . . .

DENNETT It's 'tilt'.

CUMMINS Yeah, that's it. It is a certain kind of tilt. The thing is that some of those kinds of cases are important. And some of them are just

---

[5] [For example, forbidding the addition of an integer and a real—ed.]

malfunctions, they're just glitches, they're just blips in the great cosmic mess. And some of them are important things.

CLAPIN I guess I want to say that the blips still carry semantic content.

CUMMINS Oh yes.

CLAPIN Which is why you get good blips and bad blips.

CUMMINS Oh yes, I do too.

DENNETT Well, we'll get to this tomorrow [Part 4] with targets. But the suggestion that targets are what I was calling sort of transient tacit representations, as part of the architecture . . . I think that this is really pretty close . . .

CUMMINS I think they are part of the architecture . . . except for this, that I do think that targets can be created on the fly.

DENNETT Exactly. That's where I was headed. But now the question is, hasn't Hugh given us a reason for treating those as changes in the architecture?

SMITH Well, no, but I think that something needs to be said about the beginning of Hugh's talk to clarify that. Because, one of the things that I think about data structures is that data structures are in a vast territory between what we classically think of as distinct functional architectures. To take Rob's phrase, they're what's assessable and revisable, over which anything resembling thought can happen. And it seems to me many of these cases are in the middle. So I'm not sure architecture . . . I'm not sure we should be using the word 'architecture' because it seems to me that your intuitions about tacit include the architecture, data structures, and the linguistic.

DENNETT So, it just turns out that 'architecture' is not a useful term here.

CUMMINS No, I think a better way to approach this is to ask, when you make the alterations, what sort of process drives it? One of the things about Fodor's position about this is that only a certain kind of inference counts as learning for him. And so, if you don't have the kind of inference that roughly can be cashed in terms of the sort of standard semantic decomposition and truth conditional inclusion and stuff like that—it has the sort of standard set-theoretic semantics, right? That doesn't look like inference, and hence, not like learning to him. So, nothing that isn't like that counts as learning for him. So, from that point of view he will say, 'Look, architectural changes can't be learned.' Well, you don't want to fight over the word. They can be improved. They can be improved in a systematic way that could be given a rationale. And in this respect the hardware, the data structures, the structure of intenders, as I call the targets, and all these things can be altered in different kinds of ways. And so, I think it's more useful to think about these things in terms of what kinds of process, and what drives those processes, can produce changes that aren't just sort of random or something like that. But can, over the long haul, be controlled.

CLAPIN So, the point here is: just remember that there's a kind of semantic significance. Maybe 'representation' is too strong. There's semantic significance to almost anything to do with, and particularly changes that change the structure of, the representations that you're using to represent the world.

CUMMINS You can't learn a new scheme in Fodor's narrow sense.

CLAPIN No, exactly.

CUMMINS And I think that that's right, but that just says something about that narrow sense of learning. That's all I'm saying.

DENNETT We'll have a lot of fun badmouthing the classical view over the next few days. But, one might say this: it was a nice try. It wasn't a bad idea at all, in general.

HAUGELAND It was a terrific idea.

DENNETT Wouldn't it be neat if you could take all the content and hive it off in those predicates of the language of thought, and then everything else would be content-free. You keep all the semantics in one place, and you can just keep it there. Great opportunistic move, it just doesn't work.

SMITH I just want to say one thing, which is that one of the things that Jerry [Fodor] wants is to characterize this stuff in pretty broad terms, right? Like, imagery, like, learning, central thoughts.

HAUGELAND Well he wants to do it on the basis of first principles.

SMITH Well, the thing that really worries me, forget Jerry, is that if we take seriously what you're saying here, and what Rob has a sense of as well, and I think he's right . . . what the hell theoretical terms are we going to use to give a characterization of these various . . .? It seems to me we are committed to a fine-grainedness of how to describe these things.

CLAPIN Which things?

SMITH Well, forms of learning. Forms of belief revision.

DENNETT And you're afraid we're going to end up reinventing Jerry's categories . . .

CUMMINS No, I think what's going to happen is we're going to find out that the sort of normal concept of learning is going to turn out to be about as useful to cognitive science as dirt was to chemistry.

REFERENCES

ALLEN, C., and BEKOFF, M. (1997). *Species of Mind*. Cambridge, Mass.: MIT Press.

ALSTON, W. (1964). *Philosophy of Language*. Englewood Cliffs, NJ: Prentice-Hall.

ARMSTRONG, D. M. (1968). *A Materialist Theory of Mind*. London: Routledge & Kegan Paul.

ARTHUR, W. B. (1994). 'On the Evolution of Complexity', in G. Cowan, D. Pines, and D. Meltzer (eds.), *Complexity: Metaphors, Models and Reality*. Cambridge, Mass.: Perseus Books, 65–83.

BALLARD, D. (1991). 'Animate Vision'. *Artificial Intelligence*, 48: 57–86.

—— (1997). *An Introduction to Natural Computation*. Cambridge, Mass.: MIT Press.

BARWISE, J., and PERRY, J. (1983). *Situations and Attitudes*. Cambridge, Mass.: MIT Press.

BECHTEL, W., and ABRAHAMSEN, A. (1991). *Connectionism and the Mind*. Oxford: Basil Blackwell.

BLOCK, N. (ed.) (1981). *Imagery*. Cambridge, Mass.: MIT Press.

—— (1986). 'Advertisement for a Semantics for Psychology', in P. French, T. Euhling, and H. Wettstein (eds.), *Studies in the Philosophy of Mind*, Midwest Studies in Philosophy, 10. Minneapolis: University of Minnesota Press, 615–78.

BRENTANO, F. (1874/1973). *Psychology from an Empirical Standpoint*. Ed. O. Kraus. English edn. ed. L. L. McAlister. Trans. A. C. Ranurello, D. B. Terrell, and L. L. McAlister. London: Routledge & Kegan Paul.

BROOKS, R. (1991). 'Intelligence Without Representation'. *Artificial Intelligence*, 47: 139–159.

BURGE, T. (1979). 'Individualism and the Mental', in P. French, T. Euhling, and H. Wettstein (eds.), *Studies in the Philosophy of Mind*, Midwest Studies in Philosophy, 4. Minneapolis: University of Minnesota Press, 73–121.

CARRUTHERS, P. (1996). *Language, Thought and Consciousness: An Essay in Philosophical Psychology*. Cambridge: Cambridge University Press.

CHALMERS, J. (1990). 'Syntactic Transformations on Distributed Representations'. *Connection Science*, 2: 53–62.

CHOMSKY, N. (1968). *Language and Mind*. New York: Harcourt, Brace, & World.

CHURCHLAND, P. M. (1981). 'Eliminative Materialism and the Propositional Attitudes'. *Journal of Philosophy*, 78(2): 67–90.

——(1989). *A Neurocomputational Perspective*. Cambridge, Mass.: MIT Press.

——(1995). *The Engine of Reason, the Seat of the Soul*. Cambridge, Mass.: MIT Press.

CHURCHLAND, P. S. (1986). *Neurophilosophy*. Cambridge, Mass.: MIT Press.

CLAPIN, H. (1991). 'Connectionism isn't Magic'. *Minds and Machines*, 1(2): 167–84.

——(1997). 'Problems with Principle P'. *Pacific Philosophical Quarterly*, 78(3): 261–77.

——(1999a). 'Kantian Errors in "Classical" Cognitive Science', in J. Wiles, T. Dartnall, G. Halford, D. Saddy, E. Watson (eds.), *Perspectives in Cognitive Science*. Norwood, NJ: Ablex, 149–67.

——(1999b). 'What, Exactly, is Explicitness?' *Behavioral and Brain Sciences*, 22(1): 150–1.

——(1999c). 'Kantian Metaphysics and Cognitive Science', in D. Aerts, J. van der Veken, and H. van Belle (eds.), *Worldviews and the Problem of Synthesis*. New York: Kluwer, 169–86.

CLAPIN, H., and O'BRIEN, G. (1998). 'A Conversation About Distributed Representation'. *Noetica* (Open Forum), 3(10) (url: http://psy.uq.edu.au/ CogPsych/Noetica/ Last accessed 18 Sept. 2001).

CLARK, A. (1989). *Microcognition*. Cambridge, Mass.: MIT Press.

——(1993). *Associative Engines*. Cambridge, Mass.: MIT Press.

——(1997a). 'The Dynamical Challenge'. *Cognitive Science*, 21(4): 461–81.

——(1997b). *Being There: Putting Brain, Body and World Together Again*. Cambridge, Mass.: MIT Press. [*BT*]

——(1998a). 'Where Brain, Body and World Collide'. *Daedalus*, 127(2, Spring 1998): 257–80.

——(1998b). 'Magic Words: How Language Augments Human Computation', in P. Carruthers and J. Boucher (eds.), *Language And Thought: Interdisciplinary Themes*. Cambridge: Cambridge University Press, 162–83.

——(2001). *Mindware: An Introduction to the Philosophy of Cognitive Science*. Oxford: Oxford University Press.

CLARK, A., and CHALMERS, D. (1998). 'The Extended Mind'. *Analysis*, 58: 7–19.

CLARK, A., and GRUSH, R. (1999). 'Towards a Cognitive Robotics'. *Adaptive Behavior*, 7(1): 5–16.

CLARK, A., and THORNTON, C. (1997). 'Trading Spaces: Connectionism and the Limits of Uninformed Learning'. *Behavioral and Brain Sciences*, 20(1): 57–67.

CRANE, T. (2001). *Elements of Mind: An Introduction to the Philosophy of Mind*. Oxford: Oxford University Press.

CUMMINS, D. D. (1991). 'Children's Interpretations of Arithmetic Word Problems'. *Cognition & Instruction*, 8: 261–89.

——(2000). 'How the Social Environment Shaped the Evolution of Mind'. *Synthese*, 122(1–2): 3–28.

CUMMINS, R. (1975). 'Functional Analysis'. *Journal of Philosophy*, 72: 741–60.

——(1983), *The Nature of Psychological Explanation*. Cambridge, Mass.: MIT Press.

——(1986). 'Inexplicit Information', in M. Brand and R. M. Harnish (eds.), *The Representation of Knowledge and Belief*. Tucson: University of Arizona Press, 116–26.

——(1989). *Meaning and Mental Representation*. Cambridge, Mass.: MIT Press.

——(1991). 'The Role of Representation in Connectionist Explanations of Cognitive Capacities', in W. Ramsey, S. Stich, and D. Rumelhart (eds.), *Philosophy and Connectionist Theory*. Hillsdale, NJ: Erlbaum, 91–114.

——(1996a). *Representations, Targets and Attitudes*. Cambridge, Mass.: MIT Press. A Bradford Book. [*RTA*]

——(1996b). 'Systematicity'. *Journal of Philosophy*, 93(12): 591–614.

——(2000). 'Reply to Millikan'. *Philosophy and Phenomenological Research*, 60: 113–28.

CUMMINS, R., and POIRER, P. (forthcoming). 'Representation and Indication', in H. Clapin, P. Staines, and P. Slezak (eds.), *Representation in Mind: New Approaches to Mental Representation*. Westport, Conn.: Praeger.

CUSSINS, A. (in preparation). *Constructions of Thought*.

DAVIDSON, D. (1967). 'Truth and Meaning'. *Synthese*, 17: 304–23.

DEACON, T. W. (1997). *The Symbolic Species: The Co-evolution of Language and the Brain*, New York: Norton.

DEHAENE, S. (1997). *The Number Sense*. Oxford: Oxford University Press.

DEHAENE, S., SPELKE, E., PINEL, P., STANESCU, R., and TVISKIN, S. (1999). 'Sources of Mathematical Thinking: Behavioral and Brain Imaging Evidence'. *Science*, 284: 970–4.

DENNETT, D. C. (1971). 'Intentional Systems'. *Journal of Philosophy*, 68(4): 87–106. Repr. in *Brainstorms* (Dennett 1978a).

——(1977). 'A Cure for the Common Code'. Originally appeared as 'Critical Notice: *The Language of Thought* by Jerry Fodor', in *Mind*, April 1977. Repr. as ch 6 of *Brainstorms* (Dennett 1978a).

——(1978a). *Brainstorms: Philosophical Essays on Mind and Psychology*. Montgomery, Vt.: Bradford Books (later MIT Press).

——(1978b). 'The Ability of Men and Machines'. Ch. 13 of *Brainstorms* (Dennett 1978a).

DENNETT, D. C. (1981). 'True Believers', in A. F. Heath (ed.), *Scientific Explanation*. Oxford: Oxford University Press. Repr. in *The Intentional Stance* (Dennett 1987).

——(1982), 'Beyond Belief', in A. Woodfield (ed.), *Thought and Object*. Oxford: Clarendon Press, 1–95. Repr. in *The Intentional Stance* (Dennett 1987).

——(1983). 'Styles of Mental Representation'. *Proceedings of the Aristotelian Society* 83: 213–26. Repr. in *The Intentional Stance* (Dennett 1987). [SMR]

——(1986). 'Is There an Autonomous "Knowledge Level"?' (commentary on Newell), in Z. Pylyshyn and W. Demopoulos (eds.), *Meaning and Cognitive Structure: Issues in the Computational Theory of Mind*, Norwood, NJ: Ablex, 51–4.

——(1987). *The Intentional Stance*. Cambridge, Mass.: MIT Press.

——(1991a). *Consciousness Explained*. New York: Little Brown.

——(1991b). 'Real Patterns'. *Journal of Philosophy*, 88(1): 27–51. Repr. in *Brainchildren* (Dennett 1998).

——(1993). 'Review of A. Newell, *Unified Theories of Cognition*'. *Artificial Intelligence*, 59(1–2, Feb.), 285–94.

——(1995a). *Darwin's Dangerous Idea: Evolution and the Meanings of Life*. New York: Simon & Schuster. [*DDI*]

——(1995b). 'Animal Consciousness: What Matters and Why'. *Social Research*, 62(3): 691–710. Repr. in *Brainchildren* (Dennett 1998).

——(1996). *Kinds of Minds*. New York: Basic Books.

——(1997). 'The Path Not Taken', in N. Block, O. Flanagan, and G. Guzeldere (eds.), *The Nature of Consciousness*. Cambridge, Mass.: MIT Press.

——(1998). *Brainchildren: Essays on Designing Minds*. Cambridge, Mass.: MIT Press.

——(1999). 'Review of John Haugeland: Having Thought: Essays in the Metaphysics of Mind', for *The Journal of Philosophy*, 96(8): 430–5.

——(2000). 'Making Tools for Thinking', in D. Sperber (ed.), *Metarepresentations: A Multidisciplinary Perspective*. Oxford: Oxford University Press, 17–29 [MTT].

——(forthcoming). 'Things about Things'. (Draft for Lisbon conference on Cognitive Science, May 1998), available as a preprint at ase.tufts.edu/cogstud/pubpage.htm, last accessed 19 Sept. 2001. [TAT]

DEVITT, M. (1981). *Designation*. New York: Columbia University Press.

DRETSKE, F. (1981). *Knowledge and the Flow of Information*. Cambridge, Mass.: MIT Press.

——(1988). *Explaining Behavior*. Cambridge, Mass.: MIT Press.

DREYFUS, H. (1972/79/92). *What Computers Can't Do*. New York: Harper & Row. (Second edn. slightly revised with a new introduction, 1979 (New York:

Harper & Row); 3rd edn., under the title *What Computers Still Can't Do*, with a third introduction, 1992 (Cambridge, Mass.: MIT Press).

ELMAN, J. (1991). 'Incremental Learning or the Importance of Starting Small (Technical Report 9101)'. Center for Research in Language, University of California, San Diego.

EVANS, G. (1982). *The Varieties of Reference*. Oxford: Oxford University Press.

FODOR, J. A. (1968). 'The Appeal to Tacit Knowledge in Psychological Explanations'. *The Journal of Philosophy*, 65(20): 627–40. Repr. in *Representations* (1981).

—— (1975). *The Language of Thought*. New York: Crowell.

—— (1978). 'Tom Swift and His Procedural Grandmother'. *Cognition*, 6: 229–47. Repr. in *Representations* (1981).

—— (1981). *Representations*. Cambridge, Mass.: MIT Press.

—— (1987). *Psychosemantics: The Problem of Meaning in the Philosophy of Mind*. Cambridge, Mass.: MIT Press.

—— (1990). *A Theory of Content and Other Essays*. Cambridge, Mass.: MIT Press.

—— (1994). *The Elm and the Expert*. Cambridge, Mass.: MIT Press.

FODOR, J. A., and LePORE, E. (1992). *Holism: A Shopper's Guide*. Cambridge, Mass.: MIT Press.

FODOR, J. A., and PYLYSHYN, Z. (1988). 'Connectionism and Cognitive Architecture: A Critical Analysis'. *Cognition* 28: 3–71.

FREGE, G. (1892/1960). 'Sense and Reference', in P. Geach and M. Black (eds.), *Translations from the Philosophical Writings of Gottlob Frege*. Trans. M. Black. Oxford: Basil Blackwell.

GAUKER, C. (1990). 'How to Learn Language Like a Chimpanzee'. *Philosophical Psychology*, 3(1): 31–53.

GIRARD, J. (1987). 'Linear Logic'. *Theoretical Computer Science*, 50: 1–102.

GOODMAN, N. (1976). *Languages of Art* (2nd edn.). Indianapolis: Hackett.

GRUSH, R. (1995). 'Emulation & Cognition'. Ph.D. Dissertation, University of California.

—— (1998). 'Skill And Spatial Content'. *Electronic Journal of Analytic Philosophy*, 6 (http://ejap.louisiana.edu/,last accessed 19 Sept. 2001).

HARE, M., and ELMAN, J. (1995). 'Learning And Morphological Change'. *Cognition*, 56: 61–98.

HARMAN, G. (1987). '(Non-Solpisistic) Conceptual Role Semantics', in E. LePore (ed.), *New Directions in Semantics*, London: Academic Press.

HAUGELAND, J. (1981). 'Analog and Analog'. *Philosophical Topics*, 12: 213–25 Repr. in Haugeland (1998*b*).

—— (1985), *Artificial Intelligence: The Very Idea*. Cambridge, Mass.: MIT Press.

HAUGELAND, J. (1990). 'The Intentionality All-Stars', in J. E. Tomberlin (ed.), *Philosophical Perspectives, 4: Action Theory and the Philosophy of Mind.* Atascadero, Calif.: Ridgeview, 383–427. Repr. in Haugeland (1998*b*). [IAS]

——(1991). 'Representational Genera', in W. Ramsey, S. Stich, D. Rumelhart (ed.), *Philosophy and Connectionist Theory.* Hillsdale, NJ: Lawrence Erlbaum, 61–89. Repr. in Haugeland (1998*b*). [RG]

——(1992). 'Understanding Dennett and Searle'. First published in A. Revonsuo and M. Kamppinen (eds.), *Consciousness in Philosophy and Cognitive Neuroscience.* Hillsdale, NJ: Lawrence Erlbaum, 115–28. Reprinted in Haugeland (1998*b*). [UDS]

——(1995). 'Mind Embodied and Embedded', in L. Haaparanta and S. Heinämaa (eds.), *Mind and Cognition: Philosophical Perspectives on Cognitive Science and Artificial Intelligence*, Acta Philosophica Fennica, 58: 233–67. Repr. in Haugeland (1998*b*).

——(1996). 'Objective Perception', in K. Akins (ed.), *Perception: Vancouver Studies in Cognitive Science.* New York: Oxford University Press, V. 268–89. Repr. in Haugeland (1998*b*). [OP]

——(1998*a*). 'Truth and Rule-Following', in Haugeland (1998*b*), 305–61. [TRF]

——(1998*b*). *Having Thought.* Cambridge, Mass.: Harvard University Press. [*HT*]

HENSER, S. (2000). 'Natural Language Use in Habitual Propositional-Type Thought: Support from Japanese–English and English–Japanese Bilingual Covert Codeswitching Data'. Ph.D. thesis, University of London.

HUME, D. (1739/1978). *A Treatise of Human Nature*, ed. L. A. Selby-Bigge. Second edn. edited by P. H. Nidditch. Oxford: Oxford University Press.

HUTCHINS, E. (1995). *Cognition in the Wild.* Cambridge, Mass.: MIT Press.

JACKENDOFF, R. (1996). 'How Language Helps Us Think'. *Pragmatics and Cognition*, 4(1): 1–34.

KANT, I. (1781/1929). *Critique of Pure Reason.* Trans. N. Kemp-Smith. New York: Macmillan.

KARMILOFF-SMITH, A. (1992). *Beyond Modularity: A Developmental Perspective on Cognitive Science.* Cambridge, Mass.: MIT Press.

KIRSH, D. (1991). 'When is Information Explicitly Represented?', in P. Hanson (ed.), *Information, Thought, and Content.* Vancouver: University of British Columbia Press, 340–65.

KRIPKE, S. (1972). 'Naming and Necessity', in G. Harman and D. Davidson (eds.), *Semantics of Natural Language.* Dordrecht: D. Reidel, 253–355.

KOSSLYN, S. (1980). *Image and Mind.* Cambridge, Mass.: Harvard University Press.

KUHN, T. (1962). *Structure of Scientific Revolutions*. Chicago: University of Chicago Press.

LAMBEK, J. (1999–2000). 'The Foundations of Mathematics', in *Encyclopedia Britannica*: (http://www.britannica.com/, mathematics, foundations of > the quest for rigour > formal foundations > computers and proof (last accessed 13 Aug. 2001).

LAWRENCE, J., and LEE, R. E. (1982). *Inherit the Wind*. New York: Bantam.

LEWIS, D. (1969). *Convention*. Cambridge, Mass.: Harvard University Press.

——(1971). 'Analog and Digital'. *Nous*, 5: 321–7.

LYCAN, W. (1984). *Logical Form in Natural Language*. Cambridge, Mass.: MIT Press.

McDERMOTT, D. (1976). 'Artificial Intelligence Meets Natural Stupidity'. *SIGART Newsletter* (of the Special Interest Group on Artificial Intelligence, of the Association for Computing Machinery), 57 (April). Repr. in J. Haugeland (ed.), *Mind Design* (1st edn. only, 1981). Cambridge, Mass.: MIT Press, 143–60.

McGINN, C. (1989). *Mental Content*. Oxford: Blackwell.

MARTIN-LÖF, P. (1984). *Intuitionistic Type Theory*, Studies in Proof Theory, 1. Naples: Bibliopolis.

MILLER, G. A., GALANTER, E., and PRIBRAM, K. H. (1960). *Plans and the Structure of Behavior*. New York: Holt.

MILLIKAN, R. (1984). *Language, Thought and Other Biological Categories*. Cambridge, Mass.: MIT Press.

——(1993). *White Queen Psychology and Other Essays for Alice*. Cambridge, Mass.: MIT Press.

——(1995). 'Pushmi-pullyu Representations', in J. Tomberlin (ed.), *Philosophical Perspectives*, IX. Atascadero, Calif.: Ridgeview. Repr. in L. May, M. Rediman, and C. Clark (eds.), *Mind and Morals: Essays on Ethics and Cognitive Science*. Cambridge, Mass.: MIT Press.

——(2000*a*). 'Representation, Targets and Attitudes'. *Philosophy and Phenomenological Research*, 60(1): 103–11.

——(2000*b*). *On Clear and Confused Ideas: An Essay About Substance Concepts*. Cambridge: Cambridge University Press.

MINKSY, M. (1985). 'Why Intelligent Aliens Will be Intelligible', in E. Regis (ed.), *Extraterrestrials*. Cambridge: Cambridge University Press, 117–28.

NEURATH, O. (1932/3), 'Protocol Sentences'. *Erkenntnis*, 3. Trans. by George Schick and repr. in A. J. Ayer (ed.), *Logical Positivism*. Glencoe, Ill.: The Free Press, 1959 (repr. in 1978, Westport, Conn.: Greenwood Press).

NEWELL, A. (1980). 'Physical Symbol Systems'. *Cognitive Science*, 4: 135–83.

——(1982). 'The Knowledge Level'. *Artificial Intelligence*, 18(1): 87–127.

NEWELL, A., and SIMON, H. (1958). 'Heuristic Problem Solving: The Next Advance in Operations Research', *Operations Research*, 6: 1–10. Address given to the Operations Research Society of America, 14 November 1957.

—— (1972). *Human Problem Solving*. Englewood Cliffs, NJ: Prentice-Hall.

O'BRIEN, G., and OPIE, J. (1999). 'A Connectionist Theory of Phenomenal Experience'. *Behavioral and Brain Sciences*, 22: 127–96.

PERLMAN, M. (2000). *Conceptual Flux: Mental Representation, Misrepresentation and Concept Change*. Dordrecht: Kluwer.

PINKER, S. (1994). *The Language Instinct*. New York: William Morrow.

PLACE, U. T. (1956). 'Is Consciousness a Brain Process?' *British Journal of Psychology*, 47: 44–50.

PORT, R., and VAN GELDER, T. (1995). *Mind as Motion*. Cambridge, Mass.: MIT Press.

POUNDSTONE, W. (1985). *The Recursive Universe: Cosmic Complexity and the Limits of Scientific Knowledge*. New York: William Morrow.

PRESTON, B. (1998). 'Cognition and Tool Use.' *Mind and Language*, 13(4): 513–47.

PUTNAM, H. (1975). 'The Meaning of "Meaning"', in K. Gunderson (ed.), *Language, Mind and Knowledge*, Minnesota Studies in the Philosophy of Science, 7. Minneapolis: University of Minnesota Press.

—— (1988), 'Much Ado About Not Very Much'. *Daedalus*, 117: 269–82.

PYLYSHYN, Z. (1980). 'Computation and Cognition: Issues in the Foundations of Cognitive Science'. *Behavioral and Brain Sciences*, 3: 111–69.

—— (1984). *Computation and Cognition*. Cambridge, Mass.: MIT Press.

QUINE, W. V. O. (1951). 'Two Dogmas of Empiricism', *Philosophical Review* (January). Repr. in W. V. O. Quine, *From a Logical Point of View* (2nd edn.). Cambridge, Mass.: Harvard University Press, 1961.

QUINE, W. V. O., and ULLIAN, J. S. (1978). *The Web of Belief* (2nd edn.). New York: Random House.

RUMELHART, D. E., and McCLELLAND, J. L. (1986). 'On Learning the Past Tenses of English Verbs', in J. L. McClelland and D. E. Rumelhart (eds.), *Parallel Distributed Processing*. Cambridge, Mass.: MIT Press, II.: 216–71.

RYLE, G. (1949). *The Concept of Mind*. London: Hutchinson.

SEARLE, J. (1980). 'Minds Brains Programs'. *Behavioral and Brain Sciences*, 1: 417–24.

—— (1983). *Intentionality*. Cambridge: Cambridge University Press.

SEJNOWSKI, T. and ROSENBERG, C. (1987a). 'Parallel Networks that Learn to Pronounce English Text'. *Complex Systems*, 1: 145–68.

—— (1987b). 'Connectionist Models of Learning', in M. S. Gazzaniga (ed.), *Perspectives in Memory Research and Training*. Cambridge, Mass.: MIT Press.

SHEPARD, R. N., and COOPER, L. A. (1982). *Mental Images and Their Transformations*. Cambridge, Mass.: MIT Press.

SIMON, H. (1996). *The Sciences of the Artificial* (3rd edn.). Cambridge, Mass.: MIT Press.

SLOMAN, A. (1984). 'The Structure of the Space of Possible Minds', in S. Torrance (ed.), *The Mind and the Machine*. Sussex: Ellis Horwood, 35–42.

SMART, J. C. C. (1959). 'Sensations and Brain Processes'. *Philosophical Review*, 68: 141–56.

SMITH, B. C. (1982). 'Procedural Reflection in Programming Languages'. Ph.D. thesis, Massachusetts Institute of Technology, Cambridge, Mass.

—— (1984). 'Reflection and Semantics in Lisp'. Salt Lake City: *Proceedings of the 11th Annual Principles of Programming Languages Conference* (POPL), 22–35.

—— (1987). 'The Correspondence Continuum'. *CSLI Technical Report*, CSLI—87—71, Center for the Study of Language and Information, Stanford University, January 1987.

—— (1996). *On the Origin of Objects*. Cambridge, Mass.: MIT Press. [OO]

—— (1997). 'One Hundred Billion Lines of C+ +', *CogSci News*, 10(1), also available at http://www.ageofsig.org/people/bcsmith/papers/index.html, last accessed 18 Sept. 2001.

—— (forthcoming *a*). 'Who's on Third?'

—— (forthcoming *b*). *The Age of Significance: An Essay on the Foundations of Computation and Intentionality*, vol. iii. Cambridge, Mass.: MIT Press.

—— (forthcoming *c*). 'Rehabilitating Representation'. [RR]

SMOLENSKY, P. (1988). 'On the Proper Treatment of Connectionism', *Behavioral and Brain Sciences*, 11: 1–23.

SMOLIN, L. (1997). *The Life of the Cosmos*. Oxford: Oxford University Press.

SPERBER, D. (1982). 'Apparently Irrational Beliefs', in M. Hollis and S. Lukes (eds.), *Rationality and Relativism*. Oxford: Blackwell.

STICH, S. (1983). *From Folk Psychology to Cognitive Science*. Cambridge, Mass.: MIT Press.

STRAWSON, P. (1959). *Individuals*. London: Methuen.

TARSKI, A. (1944). 'The Semantic Conception of Truth', *Philosophy and Phenomenological Research*, 4.

THOMPSON, A. (1997). 'Temperature in Natural and Artificial Systems', in P. Husbands and I. Harvey (eds.), *Fourth European Conference on Artificial Life*. Cambridge, Mass.: MIT Press, 388–97.

THOMPSON, A., HARVEY, I., HUSBANDS, P. (1996). 'Unconstrained Evolution and Hard Consequences', *Cognitive Sciences Research Report*, 397. University of Sussex. (Available at http://www.cogs.susx.ac.uk/, last accessed 18 Sept. 2001.)

THOMPSON, R., ODEN, D., and BOYSON, S. (1997). 'Language-Naive Chimpanzees (Pan Troglodytes) Judge Relations between Relations in a Conceptual

Matching-to-Sample Task', *Journal of Experimental Psychology: Animal Behavior Processes*, 23: 31–43.

TYE, M. (1991). *The Imagery Debate*. Cambridge, Mass.: MIT Press.

VAN GELDER, T. (1991). 'What is the "D" in "PDP"? A Survey of the Concept of Distribution', in W. Ramsey, S. Stich and D. Rumelhart (eds.), *Philosophy and Connectionist Theory*. Hillsdale, NJ: Lawrence Erlbaum, 33–59.

WELLMAN, C. (1999). *The Proliferation of Rights*. Boulder, Col.: Westview Press.

WINOGRAD, T. (1972). *Understanding Natural Language*. New York: Academic Press.

WINOGRAD, T., and FLORES, F. (1986). *Understanding Computers and Cognition*. Reading, Mass.: Addison-Wesley.

WINSKELL, G. (1993). *The Formal Semantics of Programming Languages: An Introduction*. Cambridge, Mass.: MIT Press.

WITTGENSTEIN, L. (1958). *Philosophical Investigations* (2nd edn.). Trans. G. E. M. Anscombe. Oxford: Basil Blackwell.

YESSENIN-VOLPIN, A. S. (1970). 'The Ultra-Intuitionistic Criticism and the Antitraditional Program for Foundations of Mathematics', in A. Kino, J. Myhill, and R. E. Vesley (eds.), *Intuitionism and Proof Theory*. Amsterdam: North-Holland, 1–45.